Reporting the Road to Brexit

Anthony Ridge-Newman
Fernando León-Solís · Hugh O'Donnell
Editors

Reporting the Road to Brexit

International Media and the EU Referendum 2016

Editors
Anthony Ridge-Newman
Liverpool Hope University
Liverpool, UK

Hugh O'Donnell
Glasgow Caledonian University
Glasgow, UK

Fernando León-Solís
University of the West of Scotland
Paisley, UK

ISBN 978-3-319-73681-5   ISBN 978-3-319-73682-2   (eBook)
https://doi.org/10.1007/978-3-319-73682-2

Library of Congress Control Number: 2018934652

Cover illustration: Credit by WINS86
Cover design by Fatima Jamadar

Printed on acid-free paper

This Palgrave Macmillan imprint is published by the registered company Springer International Publishing AG part of Springer Nature
The registered company address is: Gewerbestrasse 11, 6330 Cham, Switzerland

Preface and Acknowledgements

Preface

The decade since the global financial crisis has seen a number of major international events that could be argued to demonstrate a disruption to a period of relative continuity, which some consider to have been characterized by a growing globalized trajectory towards progressive 'liberalism' prior to 2008. From the global proliferation of new digital technologies to the election of President Trump in the USA, the public spheres of international media and politics seem somewhat transformed and indicative of, what some might call, a new age. Concerns have been voiced about regressive 'populist' political trends becoming more prevalent. Diversions from the status quo have given way to rapid change, uncertainty and, to some extent, episodes of social and economic volatility. The United Kingdom of Great Britain and Northern Ireland (UK), as a member state of the European Union (EU), contributed significantly to this changing global picture in its own unique way.

Britain's democratic decision to leave the EU via the 2016 EU referendum has been framed as a wide number of things, including a rejection of globalization, and a lurch towards populism. Frequently denoted by the popular neologism 'Brexit' (Britain's exit from the EU), the outcome of the referendum, which questioned Britain's membership within the EU, sent shockwaves throughout British society, Europe and beyond. It would be no overstatement to claim that, since the referendum, British news and political agendas have been dominated by Brexit debates, Brexit negotiations and Brexit impacts. Academics, activists, business leaders, civil servants, governments, journalists, lawyers, politicians, think tanks and, indeed, swathes of wider society have been frantically scrambling to piece together implications and make sense of the decision of the British people to leave the EU.

While this edited collection aims to examine media responses to the 2016 EU referendum in a range of national and international contexts, given the rate of change and often frenetic developments amid a multitude of perpetually unfolding events, it would not be possible to represent all of the complex dynamics associated with the referendum and the Brexit result. This book largely focuses on media coverage in the run-up to and shortly after the referendum. Therefore, this preface seems the most appropriate place to acknowledge briefly other key developments in the Brexit narrative up to the point of this book's final submission in early 2018. Interestingly, but unsurprisingly, the Brexit narrative has been most notably entwined with, at times, turbulent events within the British Conservative Party; the party whose Governments led the 2016 EU referendum and Brexit processes.

Brexit: A Tory Saga

The Conservative Party has had a long-standing internal debate between two informal wings comprising Eurosceptics and Europhiles within its organization, the saga of which has continued well into the 'post-Brexit' context. However, in the run-up to 2016, for some, the party was not Eurosceptic enough and the Conservatives leaked support and members to the United Kingdom Independence Party (UKIP), most famously led by the staunchly Eurosceptic Member of the European Parliament (MEP) Nigel Farage. UKIP's campaign agenda and growing popularity among the British electorate partly placed pressure on the Conservative Prime Minister David Cameron to grant a referendum on Britain's EU membership. On 17 December 2015, the European Union Referendum Act received Royal Assent permitting a referendum on EU membership in the UK and Gibraltar. Either side of this event, Cameron attempted to negotiate a better deal for Britain within the EU. On 23 June 2016, overall, the United Kingdom and Gibraltar voted 52% in favour of the UK leaving the EU. Cameron's resignation on 24 June 2016 was both a reaction to the Brexit outcome, symbolizing his failure to lead a victory for the Remain campaign, and a catalyst for further 'post-Brexit' events.

Filling the void left by Cameron's resignation, the leader of the Scottish National Party (SNP), Nicola Sturgeon, soon took the opportunity to capitalize on the stark difference in the EU referendum result between England and Scotland and use it as a rhetorical tool in order to argue for a second Scottish independence referendum. Media attention soon turned to the Conservative Party's contest for a new leader, which was punctuated by some internal party turbulence and alleged backbiting between the prominent Leave campaign colleagues and leadership candidates Boris Johnson and Michael Gove. Further events amid the selection process resulted in Theresa May becoming Leader of the Conservative Party and Prime Minister of the UK on 13 July 2016. On 16 March 2017, the European Union (Notification of Withdrawal) Bill received Royal Assent. It was followed shortly after by the Prime Minister pushing the proverbial 'red button' by writing a letter to Donald Tusk, European Council President, with notification of the UK's intent to withdraw from the EU. This triggered Article 50 of the Treaty on European Union—Lisbon Treaty, which permits the withdrawal of a member state on constitutional grounds.

Enjoying relatively significant popularity, on 18 April 2017, Theresa May called a General Election that was held on 8 June 2017. Underestimating her main opponent, Labour's Jeremy Corby, Leader of the Opposition, and overestimating her own ability to win votes where they counted most for the Conservatives, the election turned out to be a grave miscalculation by May. Her campaign slogan 'strong and stable' was reduced to pejorative 'weak and wobbly' antonyms within hours of a poor Conservative electoral performance (in terms of numbers of seats in the Commons) becoming apparent and resulting in a hung parliament. May gambled, and ultimately exchanged, a comfortable majority for the Conservatives in the House of Commons for a minority government propped up by a controversial parliamentary deal with Northern Ireland's Democratic Unionist Party (DUP), led by Arlene Foster.

On 19 June 2017, led by David Davis, Secretary of State for Exiting the European Union, on behalf of a significantly weaker Conservative Government, the first round of Brexit negotiations began with the EU. With Brexit negotiations reaching a number of sticking points, like the cost of the 'divorce' for the UK and sensitive border issues between the UK and the Republic of Ireland, the Prime Minister put forward the UK's stance in Florence with a key speech on Brexit on 22 September, and met with Donald Tusk shortly after on 26 September 2017. These events took place against the backdrop of consistent turbulence in the Conservative Party, in which tensions between Leave and Remain supporters continued to intensify.

Following May's lacklustre performance in the 2017 General Election and criticism about her engagement with those affected by the Grenfell Tower fire disaster, which occurred shortly after the election in June 2017, the Prime Minister had been plagued by negative headlines in the UK. Her Leader's speech at the Conservative Party Conference on 4 October 2017 was meant to bring renewal to her position as Leader. However, with a range of challenges during her speech and certain controversies related to comments made by Boris Johnson, her Foreign Secretary, news headlines continued to paint the Conservatives and May in an unfavourable light. Scrutiny of May, the Government, and turbulence in the Conservative Party intensified as the UK approached an impending deadline in December 2017, by which point the first stage of Brexit negotiations were required to be completed.

On 4 December 2017, the Prime Minister met European Commission President Jean-Claude Juncker. The two were thought to be close to agreeing a way forward, particularly in relation to the Northern Ireland and Republic of Ireland border issue. However, a call from the DUP's Leader, Arlene Foster, not only interrupted May's and Junker's lunch together, but resulted in May entering into urgent negotiations with the DUP. Interestingly, the crescendo in the Tories' Brexit saga was yet to come. And, when it came, on 13 December 2017, it came in the form of a rebellion by key members of the Conservative Parliamentary Party, which led to a government defeat in the Commons and paved the way to a parliamentary a vote on any final Brexit deal. Some hailed the Government's defeat as Parliament claiming back its sovereignty.

After months of Tory embarrassment, including repeated allegations about the conduct of Conservative ministers of state and a number of Cabinet resignations, the media continued to question May's ability to carry on as Prime Minister. However, within 48 h of the Government defeat in the House of Commons, the Prime Minister successfully negotiated a way forward supported by the other 27 EU member state leaders, thus permitting Brexit negotiations to progress to the next, and more complex, stage of trade deal negotiations. The last-minute success of the first-phase negotiations was accompanied by a tweet of relief by Donald Tusk, who congratulated the Prime Minister. It marked another extension to May's weak and wobbly tenure in 10 Downing Street. At the time of writing, the Prime Minister's future and that of the Brexit process remains in flux and in question.

ACKNOWLEDGEMENTS

In researching this Brexit saga, as other scholars can testify, preparing a book project can feel like a saga in itself. An edited collection of this scale would not be possible without committed and extensive teamwork. Therefore, on behalf of my fellow editors, I should like to acknowledge the contributions made to this book by the many dedicated and patient contributors. We cannot thank them enough for their hard work and contributions; without them this project would not be possible. We would also like to thank Palgrave Macmillan, especially the excellent editorial team for all their support throughout this project. Finally, thanks to our family, friends and colleagues for bearing with us and for their ceaseless encouragement.

Childwall, Liverpool, UK   Anthony Ridge-Newman

CONTENTS

EDITORS AND CONTRIBUTORS

About the Editors

Anthony Ridge-Newman is a lecturer in the Department of Media and Communication, Liverpool Hope University. He is the Convenor and Vice-Chair of two specialist groups at the Political Studies Association (PSA). Previously, Ridge-Newman's research and teaching were based at the Universities of Glasgow, London and Oxford. His earlier book publications include: *Cameron's Conservatives and the Internet: Change, Culture and Cyber Toryism* (Palgrave Macmillan, 2014); and *The Tories and Television, 1951–1964: Broadcasting an Elite* (Palgrave Macmillan, 2016).

Fernando León-Solís is Senior Lecturer in Spanish and Head of Languages at the University of the West of Scotland. His academic interest and publications concern media representations of national identity and politics in Spain. His latest research output is a co-authored chapter for the *Scotland's Referendum and the Media: National and International Perspectives* (Edinburgh University Press, 2016).

Hugh O'Donnell is a Professor of language and popular culture at Glasgow Caledonian University. He has published widely on national and international news, sport and national identity, television drama and more recently cultural aspects of tourism.

Contributors

Ángela Alameda Hernández is Assistant Lecturer at the Department of English Studies, University of Granada, Spain. She lectures on English grammar and English culture. In 2006, she was awarded a Ph.D. for her work on the discursive construction of national identity in the community of Gibraltar. Since then, her research has focused on discourse analysis, media discourse and terminology. She has extensively published academic articles, book chapters and a textbook on these topics.

Stephen Baker is a Lecturer in film and television studies at Ulster University. With his colleague Greg McLaughlin he is the co-author of *The Propaganda of Peace: The Role of the Media and Culture in the Northern Ireland Peace Process* (2010); and *The British Media and Bloody Sunday* (2016), both with Intellect Books.

Helena Bassil-Morozow is a Lecturer at Glasgow Caledonian University. She is a cultural philosopher, media and film scholar, and academic writer, whose publications include: *Tim Burton: The Monster and the Crowd* (Routledge, 2010); *The Trickster in Contemporary Film* (Routledge, 2011); *The Trickster and the System: Identity and Agency in Contemporary Society* (Routledge, 2014); *Jungian Film Studies: the Essential Guide* (Routledge, 2016; co-authored with Luke Hockley); and the forthcoming *Jungian Theory for Storytelling* (Routledge).

Laurent Binet is the French Programme Director in the School of Modern Languages, Cardiff University. Originally a graduate from Sciences-Po Paris and Celsa-Sorbonne, he also worked as a PR consultant and head of press relations for Deloitte in Paris. His main areas of research are contemporary French politics and, in particular, French Eurosceptic discourses. He also conducts research in food studies.

Enric Castelló is Senior Lecturer at the Department of Communication Studies of the Universitat Rovira i Virgili, Catalonia, Spain, specializing in media and cultural analysis. He was a guest researcher at Glasgow Caledonian University and Loughborough University. Among his books and articles, he co-edited (with Alexander Dhoest and Hugh O'Donnell) *The Nation on Screen. Discourses of the National on Global Television* (CSP, 2009).

Rinella Cere is a Reader in media and cultural studies at Sheffield Hallam University. Her publications include books, chapters and articles on news media and popular culture in Italy and Britain. Recent publications include: chapters for the edited collection *Postcolonial Studies Meets Media Studies: A Critical Encounter* (Transcript Verlag, 2016); and *Representing Communities, Discourse and Contexts* (Palgrave 2017).

Marina Dekavalla is Senior Lecturer in journalism at the University of Sussex. Her research interests are the relationship between media, politics and identity. She was Principal Investigator on television framing of the 2014 Scottish independence referendum, a research project funded by the ESRC (2015–2016), and has published on media coverage of the Scottish referendum, as well as post-devolution elections, in academic journals and edited collections. She is author of *Framing Referendum Campaigns in the News* (MUP, 2018).

Birgitte Kjos Fonn is an Associate Professor of journalism and media studies at Oslo Metropolitan University. She holds a Ph.D. in history and is editor of the *Norwegian Journal of Media History*. Economic journalism is another of her research interests. Fonn is a former foreign news journalist, and currently Co-ordinator of HiOA's non-fiction prose programme.

Yair Galily is founder and Head of the Sport, Media and Society (SMS) Research Lab at the Sammy Ofer School of Communications Interdisciplinary Center (IDC), Herzliya. He was a co-founder and Head of the Olympic Studies Centre, a joint venture of the Israeli Olympic committee and Zinman College, Wingate Institute (2011–2013).

Michael Higgins is a Senior Lecturer and Director of Media and Communications at the University of Strathclyde. His numerous publications span media discourse, politics and identity, and his latest book is the co-authored *Belligerent Broadcasting: Synthetic Argument in Broadcast Talk* (Routledge, 2017).

Giorgos Katsambekis is a Lecturer in European and international politics at Loughborough University. He has previously worked at the Aristotle University of Thessaloniki and remains a member of the POPULISMUS research team. He is the co-editor of the volumes *Radical Democracy and Collective Movements Today* (Ashgate, 2014) and *The Populist Radical Left in Europe* (Routledge, forthcoming), while his recent work has appeared in the *Political Quarterly*, *Constellations* and the *Journal of Political Ideologies*.

Thomas Martin teaches in the French Department at King's College London. Following the completion of his Ph.D. focusing on the anti-racist movement in France, conducted at Leeds under the supervision of James House and Sarah Waters, he has also taught at the Universities of Leeds, Southampton and Lancaster. His primary research interests are questions of language and power in contemporary French politics and society.

Fiona M. McKay is completing a Ph.D. in journalism studies at the University of Strathclyde. Her thesis explores the media representations of gender in the Scottish public sphere during the independence referendum of 2014 and has been funded by the Carnegie Trust for the Universities of Scotland. Her work has also appeared in the journal *British Politics.*

Klaus Peter Müller retired as a Chair of English at Johannes Gutenberg-University Mainz in October 2017. In teaching, research, and publishing, his main focus has been on cultural, literary, media and translation studies, especially the connections between culture and epistemology, narration and cognition; in other words, the ways in which the world is understood.

Simon Gwyn Roberts is Senior Lecturer at the University of Chester. His current research interests include: the role of online media in the communication strategies of minority language groups, regionalism and the representation of place; and the relationship between the news media and political devolution. He has published widely in both academe and journalism.

Tal Samuel-Azran is the Head of the International Program at the Sammy Ofer School of Communications. His main fields of research are political communication, new media and media globalization. He has lectured at New York University, University of Melbourne, Victoria University at Melbourne, Australia, the Hebrew University and Tel Aviv University. In 2014, he was selected by Google to deliver a series of lectures on inspirational teaching to Israeli school principals.

Oisín Share is a graphic designer specializing in visual communication management. He has an M.A. in media and communication studies from Malmö University, Sweden. He has research interests in European identity and its socio-economic influence on the creative industries.

His chapter is based on his thesis that examines the representation of migrants in the UK press prior to the EU referendum.

Isabel Simões-Ferreira is Head Co-ordinator Professor at Escola Superior de Comunicação Social—Instituto Politécnico de Lisboa. She teaches media discourse analysis, and culture and media. She has published on post-colonial studies and the media coverage of world events, ranging from the colonial discourse on British India and the British discourse on Portuguese seafaring voyages to the mediatization of the British monarchy.

George Souvlis is currently a Research Assistant at the European University Institute of Florence (EUI), where he is completing his Ph.D. on the Greek Metaxas regime, its organic intellectuals and the role of women within the 'New State' in the Department of History and Civilization.

Andrew Tolson is Honorary Visiting Fellow in the Department of Media and Communication, University of Leicester. Until 2014, he was Professor of Media and Communication at De Montfort University, Leicester. His research interests revolve around the analysis of broadcast talk; he has been a member of the Ross Priory Broadcast Talk Seminar since it started in 1992. His publications, such as *Media Talk* (Edinburgh University Press, 2006), analyse different genres of broadcast communication, particularly those that foreground talk such as 'chat' shows, news and current affairs and some types of documentary.

Christopher Waddell is a Professor at the School of Journalism and Communication, Carleton University, Ottawa, where he holds the Carty Chair in Business and Financial Journalism. He is a former senior journalist for the Canadian Broadcasting Corporation (where he oversaw election coverage between 1993 and 2001) and at the *Globe and Mail* newspaper. He is completing a book on public broadcasting in a post-broadcast world, forthcoming in 2018.

Lyndon C. S. Way is a Lecturer in media and communications at Liverpool Hope University. He is interested in critically examining the multimodal nature of popular culture, publishing in the areas of both popular music as discourse and news representations. He has recently co-edited a book on music as multimodal discourse and published a monograph on music and politics in Turkey.

Abbreviations and Contractions

BBC	British Broadcasting Corporation
Brexit	Britain's exit from the European Union
CBC	Canadian Broadcasting Corporation
CDA	Critical Discourse Analysis
CETA	Comprehensive Economic and Trade Agreement
DUP	Democratic Unionist Party
EEA	European Economic Area
EEC	European Economic Community
EFTA	European Free Trade Association
EU	European Union
GB	Great Britain
GLP	Gibraltar Liberal Party
Grexit	Greece's exit from the European Union
GSLP	Gibraltar Socialist Labour Party
Italexit	Italy's exit from the European Union
M5S	MoVimento 5 Stelle
UK	United Kingdom of Great Britain and Northern Ireland
UKIP	United Kingdom Independence Party
UN	United Nations

LIST OF TABLES

PART I

Introduction

CHAPTER 1

Reporting the Road to Brexit: The EU Referendum and the Media

Anthony Ridge-Newman

INTRODUCTION

On 24 June 2016, BBC (British Broadcasting Corporation) News published a story exploring the reactions of newspapers from around the world, following the internationally prominent referendum held the previous day in which voters of the United Kingdom of Great Britain and Northern Ireland (UK) and Gibraltar (a British Overseas Territory, bordering Spain) voted overall to leave the European Union (EU). The BBC claimed that:

> Britain's vote to leave the European Union has caused widespread dismay in the European media and beyond. Many commentators see the future of the entire EU at risk from further Eurosceptic challenges. (*BBC News* 2016)

The BBC story presented front pages of select newspapers from around the world, which played into a narrative that the outcome of the referendum was an international crisis akin to a natural disaster, with an emphasis on language like 'widespread dismay'; 'Earthquake in Europe';

A. Ridge-Newman (✉)
Liverpool Hope University, Liverpool, UK
e-mail: ridgena@hope.ac.uk

© The Author(s) 2018
A. Ridge-Newman et al. (eds.), *Reporting the Road to Brexit*,
https://doi.org/10.1007/978-3-319-73682-2_1

'Goodbye to Europe'; and 'Domino effect'. Crisis frames and periods of significant political change have a long-standing relationship (Hay 1999). The discursive activities centred on the 2016 EU referendum are thought to be no exception (Higgins 2016), which is indicated by a number of chapters in this book.

Caiani and Guerra (2017) suggest that Euroscepticism is a growing crisis across Europe and that the media are central to the relationship between citizens and the democratic functions of the EU. While scholars argue that news media, like broadcast news and the press, play a crucial role in referendum campaigns (for example, Jenssen et al. 1998; de Vreese and Semetko 2002; Dekavalla 2016), academic analysis of the dynamics between referendums and news media is relatively thin when compared to related areas of political communication, like, for example, the more developed understanding of media and general elections (for example, Strömbäck and Dimitrova 2006; Strömbäck and van Aelst 2010; Negrine 2017; Cushion and Thomas 2018). Blain et al. (2016) is a notable contribution to our understanding of the relationship between referendums and the media. With a focus on Scotland's 2014 independence referendum, the collection of scholarly works explores issues of media 'representation' versus media 'construction' in national and international contexts. It sheds light on how a referendum in one locale can generate public discourse and catalyse introspective debate related to the internal dialogues of another.

This EU referendum project takes a similar approach. It aims to contribute to the growing literature on referendums and the media, with interests related to the representation versus construction question in the context of the 2016 EU referendum and 'Brexit' (Britain's exit from the EU). It aims to do this through presenting and comparing a range of analyses of British and international news media contexts. This introductory chapter aims to offer insights into the project's: major themes; key contexts and definitions; the scope of the book; and a brief outline of the chapters.

EU Referendum and the Media Project

Recent developments and global media interest in events such as Spain's Catalonia independence debate and Brexit suggest the mounting importance for scholarly analyses of the relationships between media discourse, the '"global" public sphere' (Volkmer 2003) and these increasingly common democratic phenomena. Such analyses fit the study of international political communication in which two key debates around the 'globalization (homogenization) and "domestication" (diversification) of news content' (Clausen 2004: 25) inform observations in international news contexts. The globalist paradigm posits that international political communication flows outside of traditional media systems in their domestic contexts, thus creating a transformed transglobal media environment in which news media construct a global public sphere characterized by discourses with broader transitional, transregional and transcontinental relevance (Volkmer 1999, 2003). However, this is in contrast to the notion that international news undergoes a 'domestication' process in which global news items are constructed around the 'dominant ideologies' of their locale, thus resulting in news outlets 'domesticating the foreign' and constructing more 'culturally specific' discourses (Gurevitch et al. 1991: 205–206). Clausen (2004) argues that both factors contribute to news production in the global news environment.

Examples like the BBC article above have stimulated research interests in the examination of ideology, bias and framing impacts in media discourses (Cotterrell 1999; Entman 2007, 2010). The chapters of this book engage with such topics and debates using a range of methodological approaches (for example, discourse analysis; and content analysis) in order to examine whether and how news media in different locales constructed events in the run-up to and shortly after the 2016 EU referendum. Therefore, the book focuses on media reaction to the referendum campaign and the result, rather than the lengthy and ongoing aftermath of 'post-Brexit' events (see the Preface for context). The study of media and politics offers interdisciplinary opportunities. Therefore, the project aims to take a pluralistic approach in order to engage perspectives from diverse geographical locales. The chapters offer a range of cases for comparison, from empirical analyses to essays, all of which offer perspectives that contribute to the exploration of the book's overarching questions.

The Questions

Since the 2016 EU referendum, the Europhile ideal in which the European public sphere would embody a transnational citizenry with equal access and ability to understand and interpret communications in relation to EU policies and initiatives (Schlesinger 1999) seems a distant prospect. Research suggests that European news media are yet to foster a dedicated agenda that engages publics in EU issues and promotes collective support of Europeanization (de Vreese 2007; Valentini and Nesti 2010; Papathanassopoulos and Negrine 2011; Lloyd and Marconi 2014). So, then, how did international news media react to Britain's EU referendum?

As indicated above, a consistent curiosity throughout this book centres on themes related to how news media construct narratives around Brexit debates in different contexts that are specific to certain geographical locales. News outputs in reaction to significant global events are thought to embody ingredients that are selected in order to offer a particular flavour for media consumption (Neureiter 2017; Venkataraman 2018). It is, therefore, pertinent for academic analysis to explore how media frames and constructed narratives in one context compare to others. As the following section suggests, understanding how international media responded to the UK's 2016 EU referendum, and Brexit, is ripe for analysis. This edited collection aims to go some way in developing an early elucidation of this question with 18 scholarly contributions that represent media output from diverse geographical locales across the UK, the European Single Market, and beyond.

The Importance

Adler-Nissen et al. (2017) suggest that analysing perceptions of Brexit beyond the UK has significant value because: (1) it informs an understanding of British identities and the basis on which Brexit is used to shape new international debates around the European integration project; (2) the way in which Brexit narratives are constructed internationally are likely to impact on EU-UK trade negotiations; and (3) Brexit is not necessarily an isolated case—as chapters in this book will suggest, there are Eurosceptic movements gaining momentum across the EU. Therefore, analysing media representations of the referendum and Brexit provides important international insights for comparison with cross-cultural importance and value.

Democracy, Referendums and the News Media

Both referendums and the news media are manifestations of democratic activity in which publics place trust to perform roles and functions in a variety of political contexts. Referendums offer forms of direct democracy to the citizenry at local, regional and national levels (Held 2006; Caiani and Guerra 2017). Prominent recent examples include same-sex marriage referendums in Ireland (2015) and Australia (2017); and the independence referendums in Scotland (2014) and Catalonia (2017). These cases all received notable national and international media attention, respective to their locales. Collectively, various forms of media, some newer, some more traditional, play increasingly complex roles in political discourse and the communication of political messages across democratic states (McNair 2017).

Therefore, it is important to recognize that traditional forms of news media tend to be the focus of this book, with limited reference to the role of social and digital media. Subsequently, this project represents a more focused perspective within a broader and rapidly developing media landscape. Pioneers like Howard and Kollanyi (2016) have begun interesting early work examining the role of automated bots in cyberspace. They found that automated social media output from a small number of Twitter accounts played a strategic role in EU referendum discourse, which was dominated by the Leave stance. Further comparative research examining international digital media responses to Brexit would make a significant contribution to the literature and add further context to the findings of this book.

In the recent UK context, referendums, including the alternative vote referendum (2011), have acted as democratic tools employed by governments in order to consult electorates on significant potential policy developments (Held 2006). The process exhibits unique characteristics when compared to votes in elections. For example, the campaigns associated with referendums can cut across typical political party identities, boundaries and ideologies (Dekavalla 2016). In the 2016 EU referendum, key figures, like former prime ministers Tony Blair (Labour) and John Major (Conservative) of the Remain campaign, shared prominent campaign platforms (see Chapter 6). Campaign moments such as these can become media events in themselves that in turn catalyse public discourse. Moreover, the campaign discourse associated with referendums can be volatile (LeDuc 2002; Schuck and de Vreese 2009). The Scottish and EU referendums in Britain were no exception and left behind deep divides (Ford and Goodwin 2017). Analogous with the Yes/No choice in the 2016 Scottish independence referendum (Dekavalla 2016), general media discourse suggests the Leave/Remain binary outcome of the EU referendum contributed to a polarization of the British electorate.

Chalmers (2017) argues that Brexit has the potential to undermine the British tradition of representative democracy and, following the EU referendum game-changer, democracy in the UK would benefit from being re-imagined.

Contextualizing and Defining the Study of Brexit

Three academics based in UK universities edited this project. For the editors, and for a number of the contributors, the weight and enormity of Brexit have been felt first-hand and largely from an 'insider' perspective. In other words, a number of the contributors to this book were resident in the UK at the time of the 2016 EU referendum. It is important to recognize the significance of this because, naturally, it has influenced, in some way, the orientation of the book and the subsequent chapter selections. It is also important to recognize that many of the contributors examine the topic from an 'outsider' perspective insofar as they were generally resident in international contexts, beyond the UK, where exposure to the referendum and its day-to-day campaign discourse would have been less encountered compared to UK-based colleagues. However, some international colleagues contributed chapters with a focus on UK contexts; and some UK-based colleagues authored contributions focusing on international contexts. Therefore, for clarity, references to the 'international' perspective generally refer to chapters focusing on media in locales beyond the UK and its overseas territories. The 'national' perspective tends to refer to studies of media based in the UK and its constituent parts.

United Kingdom of Great Britain and Northern Ireland

The overall result of the EU referendum vote includes the UK overseas territory of Gibraltar; and the UK's four constituent parts, often referred to as countries and, particularly in sporting contexts, as the 'home nations' of England, Northern Ireland, Scotland and Wales. Notwithstanding its historical relationship with the EU, constitutionally, the UK Parliament's sovereignty is supreme. It holds ultimate legislative power in the UK, with certain powers devolved to the assemblies of Northern Ireland and Wales, the Scottish Parliament, and local governments in England. Pressures related to these complex constitutional and political relationships have been recognized as a challenge to the sovereignty of the UK Parliament (Elliott 2004; Chalmers 2017). Moreover, recent Brexit events have brought questions about parliamentary sovereignty to the fore in public discourse (for example, Douglas-Scott 2017; Hammond 2017; Watts 2017).

Given the frequent confusion around the formal usage of the names associated with the UK, in the interest of clarity, it seems pertinent in the context of this project to offer brief clarification. When using the term 'the UK' (the United Kingdom of Great Britain and Northern Ireland), the four collective parts that form the sovereign country of the United Kingdom are generally in focus. Moreover, 'Britain' is a term that can refer to the UK and, therefore, usually includes Northern Ireland. However, Britain is sometimes confused with 'Great Britain', which tends to refer to the island that encompasses the mainland parts of England, Scotland and Wales, thus excluding Northern Ireland. The demonym for the UK is British or Briton, with some citizens identifying as English, Irish, Scottish, Welsh, among others, and, more recently, European.

2016 EU Referendum and Brexit

On 23 June 2016, the British Conservative Government, under Prime Minister David Cameron, held a referendum that questioned whether the UK should 'leave' the EU or 'remain' as a member state. The vote included the UK overseas territory of Gibraltar, which has a land border with Spain, another EU member state. At the publication of this book, the EU included 28 member states, including the UK. The referendum resulted in a Brexit outcome in which a 52% majority voted to leave the EU. However, as the second part of this book will examine, the vote revealed the UK as a divided country. Not only was the vote close in percentage terms, but the Leave vote was strongest in England and Wales. Gibraltar, Northern Ireland and Scotland voted to remain in the EU. England's significantly larger population dominated the overall outcome. Subsequently, the Brexit result triggered a chain of events. Firstly, Cameron resigned as prime minister. His successor, Conservative Prime Minister Theresa May, became famous for her mantra 'Brexit means Brexit'—a phrase that came to symbolize her ardent approach to setting Britain's course towards an exit from the EU, expected on 29 March 2019, following complex withdrawal negotiations (Walker 2017). (See the Preface for a more detailed timeline.)

EUROPEAN UNION

The EU is a political and economic union of 28 European countries, which developed from the European Economic Community (EEC). The Treaty of Rome (1957) established the EEC and the principle of a common market in Europe. In 1993, this project was fully realized as a single, or internal, market offering 'four freedoms' related to the movement of goods, people, services and capital across the EU. The European Economic Area (EEA) includes countries like Norway and Iceland, which are non-EU countries with negotiated access to the Single Market. Switzerland is not a member of the EU or EEA, but does have negotiated access to elements of the Single Market. Canada is a non-European country that negotiated a Comprehensive Economic and Trade Agreement (CETA) with the EU. Canada is also a former British colony and part of the Commonwealth of Nations, with strong links to the UK. The editors considered these sorts of historical, political and economic factors when contributions to this project were initially sought; and when the five parts of this edited collection were subsequently organized. (See the outline of the book below.)

EUROPEAN INTEGRATION AND THE UK

The EU is a supranational union of intergovernmental states directed by the Institutions of the EU, which include seven decision-making bodies; for example, the European Parliament, European Council, European Commission, and Court of Justice of the EU. The UK has had an inconsistent history and, at points, a sceptical relationship with the EU, its institutions and European integration projects (McLean 2003). The aftermath of the Second World War, imperial decline of the British Empire, and complexities around Britain's relationship with Europe, are key themes related to a delay in the UK joining the EEC, which eventually came to fruition in 1973. Unlike 2016, the UK's referendum on the EEC in 1975 resulted in two-thirds of voters supporting a continuance of Britain's membership. However, in the 1990s, British Euroscepticism became apparent when the UK did not join: (1) the Euro: a currency union between a majority of EU states, known as the Eurozone; and (2) the Schengen Area: a borderless area across much of the continent of Europe. Maintaining the British Pound and controlling UK borders and immigration have been two central EU-related issues capturing media interest and the public mood in recent decades (Goodwin and Milazzo 2017; Thompson 2017).

The British public mood is thought to hold potential to drive political events and outcomes (Rahn et al. 1996). Correlations between media reporting and public mood have been demonstrated, including impact outcomes linked to both negative and positive frames in media output (Leshner and Thorson 2000; Schuck and de Vreese 2009). The progressive transition from the EEC to the EU through new treaties, like the Maastricht Treaty (1992), historically captured the attention of the British media. Furthermore, this transition created contention for many Britons and is argued to have contributed to growing UK Euroscepticism (Startin 2015). Following the democratically evident Europhilia of 1975, campaigns for a referendum on the UK's membership of the EU intensified over a 40-year period, which contributed to the labelling of Britain as the 'awkward partner' of Europe (George 1990).

Decisively summing up the role of the media in the public mood of Britons and their attitudes towards the EU is challenging. Trust in the news media as a source of information has changed significantly over the last four decades. That said, Daddow suggests that there has been a 'collapse in media support for the EU project' (2012: 1219), which correlates with trends in British attitudes. However, it is important to remain cautious. The impact of new forms of information and technology are still only beginning to be understood in contemporary contexts (Williams and Carpini 2011). Furthermore, in the run-up to the EU referendum, British political dynamics shifted considerably, resulting in a fragmentation of the two-party system and political identification in Britain (Green and Prosser 2016). Political pressures on the governing Conservative Party and its indirect relationship with developments in the greatly Eurosceptic UK Independence Party (UKIP) ultimately culminated in Cameron's decision to placate his party and the Eurosceptics in granting a long-campaigned-for referendum on Britain's EU membership (Startin 2015). (See the Preface for richer context.)

Brexit, Trump and Right-Wing Populism?

Brexit was one of two momentous international news events in 2016 that represented political seismic shifts on both sides of the Atlantic. The other being the election of Donald Trump, a conservative 'anti-establishment' Republican, to the office of President of the United States. Both cases have been the centre of scholarly analyses that suggest a shift towards right-wing populism across a number of advanced democracies (Inglehart and Norris 2016; Wilson 2017). Therefore, in reference to this project, it seems timely to develop further our understanding of how national and international media compare in their responses to the referendum, and Brexit.

SCOPE OF THE BOOK

The book is organized into five parts, with Part I offering this introduction and Part V a conclusion to the project. In Parts II–IV, the project offers 18 chapters that overall represent 18 geographical locales in the UK and globally. The organization of these is based on the nature of the geographical, political and historical relationships between the individual locales, the UK and the EU. Part II includes the UK and its overseas territories, with seven chapters featuring the locales of Britain, England, Northern Ireland, Scotland, Wales and Gibraltar. Part III has a further seven chapters that analyse nine European Single Market countries, excluding the UK, seven of which are the EU member states of France, Germany, Austria, Spain, Italy, Portugal and Greece; and two non-EU countries, Norway and Switzerland. Part IV offers four locales from outside the Single Market, including Turkey, Israel, Canada and Russia. It seems that few other contemporary events could inspire such an eclectic array of geographical contributions on a single academic topic. It certainly adds weight to the assertion that Brexit is a global game-changer with impacts reaching far beyond the UK (Adler-Nissen et al. 2017).

As with any research project, there are limitations. As globally comprehensive as this project had aimed to be, it falls short in terms of representing some key locales. The locales included in this book were selected based on the expectation that they would provide interesting and pertinent perspectives rooted in the nature of their relations with the EU and the UK. Given the post-Brexit events surrounding border negotiations between the EU, UK, Northern Ireland and Republic of Ireland, the book's lack of a detailed analysis from the Irish media perspective is a significant omission. Other interesting contributions would include media perspectives from Australia, the USA, the conservative Middle East and, indeed, representation from Asia, like China and/or India, and South America, like Argentina and/or Brazil. That said, contributing 18 diverse case studies to the wider literature on referendums and the media, and the emerging literatures on the advent of Brexit, seems a worthy endeavour. It also leaves space for reflection and opportunities for further research.

OUTLINE OF THE BOOK

In the concluding chapter of this book (Chapter 20), key theoretical, conceptual and contextual themes introduced above are returned to in order to analyse the book's main themes across the following 18 contributor chapters. Key findings representing each of the three groups are compared in order to offer conclusions related to the central puzzle about whether and how the media across a variety of international locales represented and/or constructed narratives related to the 2016 EU referendum. The following sections offer an outline of the rest of the book.

PART II

Following this introductory chapter, Part II opens its analysis of the UK and its territories with Oisín Share's contribution in Chapter 2. Through a discourse analysis, utilizing post-Marxist analysis of hegemony, Share argues that coverage in the British press constructed discourses of conflict framed around the 'symbolic migrant' debates leading up to the 2016 EU referendum. Similarly, in Chapter 3, Higgins, Ridge-Newman and McKay's discourse analysis of Scottish and Welsh press provides evidence of narrative constructions that centred on discourses of danger and fear in relation to the prospect of Brexit. The authors liken it to the construction of 'Project Fear' during Scotland's independence referendum.

Continuing the Scottish theme, Marina Dekavalla's examination of Scottish television, in Chapter 4, employs strategy and policy frames to analyse comparisons between coverage of the 2014 independence and 2016 EU referendums. Whereas in 2014 there were clashes between Scottish political elites, the discourse in 2016 was rather more consensual and, thus, reflective of Scotland's strong remain vote in the EU referendum. Interestingly, Chapter 3 suggests that themes constructed across the Welsh and Scottish press were similar in both cases, whereas Chapter 4 indicates a divergence between television output from

Scotland and London, England. Dekavalla suggests that in Scotland there was less emphasis on the political game and more on policy implications compared to London-generated content. Following this theme and returning to Wales in Chapter 5, Simon Gwyn Roberts offers a rich contextual analysis that argues how, unlike Scottish voters, Welsh voters are largely informed by London newspapers. Roberts suggests that similarities between EU referendum voting results in England and Wales are related to a democratic deficit in Welsh media—a theme that is also touched upon in Chapter 3, when comparing the quality of Scottish and Welsh media.

In Chapter 6, Stephen Baker, assesses newspaper coverage of the referendum in Northern Ireland and suggests that output was framed in a manner that played to specific readerships that are divided along distinct historical and political lines of unionism and nationalism. Glancing back at Chapter 4, and its depiction of Scottish TV output being framed around policy in contrast to London's emphasis on the elite campaign dynamics, Baker's findings suggest that press content in Northern Ireland was more akin to that of television news in England. Like Chapters 1–3 and 6, it provides evidence of narratives constructed around fears, crises and threats.

Andrew Tolson, in Chapter 7, analyses content from three of the main British television news networks (BBC, ITV and Channel 4), and identifies cases in which 'phoney balance' (Gaber 2016) is evident. Tolson identifies a problem embedded within news rituals involving television events in which the interactions of politicians and journalists blur lines between participation and reporting, resulting in the co-construction of referendum narratives. In keeping with Chapter 4, London-based television, which is often referred to as 'British', but is often thought to serve English audiences rather than wider UK-interest, appears somewhat frivolous and glib when compared to more geographically specific coverage in locales like Scotland. In Chapter 8, Ángela Alameda Hernández offers a key example of this through her critical discourse analysis (CDA) of opinion articles in newspapers that serve the British overseas territory Gibraltar. Hernández found evidence of discourses around 'duty', in relation to voting, and 'unity' and 'Britishness', in relation to protecting Gibraltar against the spectre of Spain. Again, like Chapters 1–3 and 6, it appears that Gibraltarian narratives were constructed around fear and framed around threats from Madrid, Spain, following a Brexit outcome.

PART III

Part III brings together a collection of perspectives under the broad grouping of countries with access to elements of the European Single Market, most of which are EU member states, with the exceptions of Norway and Switzerland. Chapter 9 marks the departure from the UK, through a symbolic hop across the English Channel with Martin and Binet's analysis of French newspapers' reactions to Brexit. The authors assess French media discourse from a political perspective and suggest that the Brexit narrative is constructed around ideological dialogues that largely criticize the UK and, more specifically, the English. A similar critique in the media is evident in Chapter 10. Klaus Peter Müller takes a storytelling approach that analyses media texts in the quality press across Austria, Germany and Switzerland. Müller suggests that key media frames include a dis-United Kingdom and a dis-United Europe that plays into the construction of a narrative around Brexit being a failure of democracy.

Chapter 11, by Birgitte Kjos Fonn, examines reaction to the EU referendum in three Norwegian daily newspapers, through which four competing frames are identified as constructing a narrative that centres on the negative impact of a Brexit outcome. The commonly recurring themes (also identified in Chapters 1–3, 6, and 8) of fear, catastrophe, threats and panic again relate back to the links between significant political change and crisis frames (Hay 1999) and the *BBC News* (2016) example presented at the beginning of this chapter. León-Solís, Castelló, and O'Donnell also demonstrate this consistent theme within the Spanish context in Chapter 12. They suggest that Madrid's media constructed Brexit as an existential crisis for the EU with the use of frames like danger and disaster; and language related to natural disasters. Again, like Chapter 11, this is in keeping with the BBC's initial post-Brexit portrayal of global media coverage (*BBC News* 2016). Chapter 13, by Isabel Simões-Ferreira, examines three Portuguese newspapers using a CDA and political concepts. Simões-Ferreira argues that the media plays a role in both constructing and deconstructing Europe and, therefore, has a responsibility as a discursive agent. In keeping with Chapters 1–3, 6, 8, and 11–12, crisis frames are identified and the author suggests the Portuguese media liken Brexit to a Shakespearean tragedy.

In Chapter 14, Rinella Cere's analyses the Italian press and a television talk show, and suggests that there was a clear split along political lines within Italian media in which the left supported Remain and the right favoured the Leave stance in the UK's EU referendum. It adds further weight to the suggestion that there is healthy Euroscepticism in other EU countries (Caiani and Guerra 2017). Another EU member that has exhibited Eurosceptic tendencies is Greece, the locale in focus in Chapter 15. The authors, Katsambekis and Souvlis, engage in an Essex School discourse analysis in order to examine media constructs in four Greek national newspapers. In sharp contrast to Chapter 10, in which the Austrian, German and Swiss media are suggested to have framed Brexit as a failure of democracy, key themes in the Greek case include: (1) referendums being constructed as the ultimate expression of democracy; and (2) critiques of German hegemony in Europe.

In Chapter 12, the authors make a distinct reference to the Spanish media case being an example of the 'domestication' of news (Gurevitch et al. 1991) in that the news media interpreted Brexit as a global event within domestic/Spain-specific frames, which sits in contrast to Volkmer's (1999) globalization theory presented above. Although less evident in the Norwegian, Austrian, German and Swiss cases, the domestication concept also seems highly applicable to the French, Portuguese, Italian and Greek cases (in Chapters 9 and 13–15 respectively), all of which are EU countries exhibiting elements of Euroscepticism. In Part II, domestication or rather localization, given that the cases are locales within an already domestic context, is a theme also significantly evident in the Gibraltar case (Chapter 8); to some extent in the Scotland case (Chapter 4); and to a lesser extent in the Northern Ireland case (Chapter 6). Evidence of the domestication theme continues in further international cases in Part IV.

Part IV

Turkey is often considered to be a bridge between Europe and Asia. Therefore, it seems a good place to bridge the transition between Parts III and IV. Part IV of the book groups together the chapters representing locales beyond the UK and other European Single Market countries. In Chapter 16, Lyndon C. S. Way uses CDA to examine opinion pieces in Turkish English-language online news. In keeping with the domestication theme evident across a range of cases in Part III, and to a lesser extent in Part II, the chapter argues that Brexit is used as a vehicle to criticize the Turkish government. Samuel-Azran and Galily also examine online discussions in the Israeli context in Chapter 17; however, in contrast to the previous chapter, they employ trend tracing software to analyse digital data. The authors find that mentions of Brexit occurred most frequently in the financial press; and on Twitter more than on Facebook. They argue that Brexit was viewed to have limited impact on interests in Israel; and findings from the Israeli financial press data indicate another case of domestication. Similar to other cases in Parts II and III, the term 'disaster' was found to be highly frequent in the financial press.

In Chapter 18, Christopher Waddell's essay offers a perspective on how the Canadian media constructed narratives of Brexit. The author argues that Canadians view EU relations through a prism of trade; and the media framed the coverage around questions related to Canadian interests. Again, the Canadian case, a locale with close economic interest in the EU, demonstrates the domestication trend evident in the Turkish, Israeli and other cases in Parts II and III. Finally, Helena Bassil-Morozow, in Chapter 19, takes a similar essay-style approach to argue how the government-controlled media in Russia exhibit inward-looking tendencies that resulted in an apparent lack of interest in events associated with Brexit. The author suggests this is because Russia is distracted by its own significant internal problems, and events like Brexit seem too distant to impact on Russian interests. In this sense, the Russian case is the exception in terms of the media agenda being focused away from wider international affairs, but highlights another case with a tendency towards the domestication of a significant international news story.

CONCLUSIONS

The UK's 2016 EU referendum and its Brexit outcome were major international events that fuelled significant coverage in both national and international contexts. News media serving locales with closer cultural, political and economic proximities (Straubhaar 1991) to the UK and EU appear to exhibit higher discursive tendencies in reporting the road to Brexit, and the outcome of the referendum, as a crisis. Moreover, the use of crisis frames (Hay 1999) that construct narratives around 'fear' and 'disaster' are most evident in the British and European cases. This trend represents a degree of European homogeneity and thus supports the globalist paradigm (Volkmer 1999) in the Single Market context, but less so in the wider international context. Daddow's portrayal (2012) of a Eurosceptic British news media does not appear to be limited to the UK. The French, Italian, Portuguese and Greek cases also point to what Caiani and Guerra (2017) describe as a growing crisis for the EU.

Gurevitch et al.'s (1991) 'domestication' concept is evident as a distinct theme across a majority of chapters. It suggests international political communication around Brexit issues leans towards a heterogeneous construction of more localized narratives. Domestication is most prominent in the international cases, but, interestingly, some UK locales, like Scotland and Gibraltar, also demonstrate features of a localization trend. It suggests a homogenous UK-wide construction of Brexit in the British media cannot be assumed. In EU countries where there is the potential for deeper self-reflection on the question of Europe, a domestication of Brexit in the media is evident, thus constructing an internal analysis of the locale's own place in Europe. In countries like Norway and Switzerland, which are outside the EU, and countries like Germany and Austria, which are more Europhilic in nature, the use of Brexit in the media, as discursive tool for self-reflection, seems less evident.

BIBLIOGRAPHY

PRIMARY SOURCES

BBC News. 2016. Brexit: What the World's Papers Say. *BBC News,* June 24. http://www.bbc.co.uk/news/world-europe-36619254 (Accessed 22 January 2018).

Douglas-Scott, S. 2017. Amendment Seven: Has Parliament Finally Taken Back Control on Brexit? *Prospect,* December 15. https://www.prospectmagazine.co.uk/ (Accessed 25 January 2018).

Hammond, S. 2017. I'm Proud to Be a Conservative Brexit 'Traitor'. We Had to Take Back Control, Brexit Opinion. *The Guardian,* December 15. https://www.theguardian.com (Accessed 25 January 2018).

Walker. 2017. Brexit Timeline: Events Leading to the UK's Exit from the European Union. Briefing Paper, House of Commons Library, No. 07960, 18 October.

Watts, J. 2017. Tory Rebels Explain Why They Defied the Government: "We Had to Make Clear Hard Brexiteers Are Not Running the Country". *Independent,* December 14. http://www.independent.co.uk/ (Accessed 25 January 2018).

ACADEMIC LITERATURE

Adler-Nissen, R., C. Galpin, and B. Rosamond. 2017. Performing Brexit: How a Post-Brexit World Is Imagined Outside the United Kingdom. *The British Journal of Politics and International Relations* 19 (3): 573–591.

Blain, N., D. Hutchison, and G. Hassan (eds.). 2016. *Scotland's Referendum and the Media: National and International Perspectives.* Edinburgh: Edinburgh University Press.

Caiani, M., and S. Guerra. 2017. *Euroscepticism, Democracy and the Media: Communicating Europe, Contesting Europe.* London: Palgrave Macmillan.

Chalmers, D. 2017. Brexit and the Renaissance of Parliamentary Authority. *The British Journal of Politics and International Relations* 19 (4): 663–679.

Clausen, L. 2004. Localizing the Global: "Domestication" Processes in International News Production. *Media, Culture and Society* 26 (1): 25–44.

Colin, H. 1999. Crisis and the Structural Transformation of the State: Interrogating the Process of Change. *British Journal of Politics and International Relations* 1 (3): 317–344.

Cotterrell, R. 1999. Transparency, Mass Media, Ideology and Community. *Journal for Cultural Research* 3 (4): 414–426.

Cushion, S., and R. Thomas. 2018. *Reporting Elections: Rethinking the Logic of Campaign Coverage (Contemporary Political Communication).* Cambridge: Polity Press.

Daddow, O. 2012. The UK Media and 'Europe': From Permissive Consensus to Destructive Dissent. *International Affairs* 88 (6): 1219–1236.

de Vreese, C. 2007. A Spiral of Euroscepticism: The Media's Fault? *Acta Politica* 42 (2/3): 271–286.

de Vreese, C., and H. Semetko. 2002. Cynical and Engaged: Strategic Campaign Coverage, Public Opinion and Mobilization in a Referendum. *Communication Research* 29 (6): 615–641.

Dekavalla, M. 2016. Framing Referendum Campaigns: The 2014 Scottish Independence Referendum in the Press. *Media, Culture and Society* 38 (6): 793–810.

Elliott, M. 2004. United Kingdom: Parliamentary Sovereignty Under Pressure. *International Journal of Constitutional Law* 2 (3): 545–627.

Entman, R.M. 2007. Framing Bias: Media in the Distribution of Power. *Journal of Communication* 57 (1): 163–173.

Entman, R.M. 2010. Media Framing Biases and Political Power: Explaining Slant in News of Campaign 2008. *Journalism* 11 (4): 389–408.

Ford, R., and M. Goodwin. 2017. Britain After Brexit: A Nation Divided. *Journal of Democracy* 28 (1): 17–30.

Gaber, I. 2016. Bending Over Backwards: The BBC and the Brexit Campaign. In *EU Referendum Analysis 2016: Media, Voters and the Campaign*, ed. D. Jackson, E. Thorsen, and D. Wring, 54. Bournemouth: CSJCC.

George, S. 1990. *An Awkward Partner: Britain in the European Community.* Oxford: Oxford University Press.

Goodwin, M., and C. Milazzo. 2017. Taking Back Control? Investigating the Role of Immigration in the 2016 Vote for Brexit. *The British Journal of Politics and International Relations* 19 (3): 450–464.

Green, J., and C. Prosser. 2016. Party System Fragmentation and Single-Party Government: The British General Election of 2015. *West European Politics* 39 (6): 1299–1310.

Gurevitch, M., M.R. Levy, and I. Roeh. 1991. The Global Newsroom: Convergences and Diversities in the Globalization of Television News. In *Communication and Citizenship: Journalism and the Public Sphere in the New Media Age*, ed. P. Dahlgren, and C. Sparks, 195–216. London: Routledge.

Hay, C. 1999. Crisis and the Structural Transformation of the State: Interrogating the Process of Change. *British Journal of Politics and International Relations* 1 (3): 317–344.

Held, D. 2006. *Models of Democracy*. Cambridge: Polity Press.

Higgins, M. 2016. Remembrance of Referendums Past: Scotland in the Campaign. In *EU Referendum Analysis 2016: Media, Voters and the Campaign*, ed. D. Jackson, E. Thorsen, and D. Wring, 24–25. Bournemouth: CSJCC.

Howard, P.N., and B. Kollanyi. 2016. Bots, #strongerin, and #brexit: Computational Propaganda During the UK-EU Referendum. COMPROP Research Note, Working Paper No. 1 (available at SSRN).

Inglehart, R., and P. Norris. 2016. Trump, Brexit, and the Rise of Populism: Economic Have-Nots and Cultural Backlash. HKS Working Paper No. RWP16-026 (available at SSRN).

Jenssen, A., P. Pesonen, and M. Gilljam (eds.). 1998. *To Join or Not to Join: Three Nordic Referendums on Membership in the European Union*. Oslo: Scandinavian University Press.

LeDuc, L. 2002. Referendums and Elections: How Do Campaigns Differ? In *Do Political Campaigns Matter? Campaign Effects in Elections and Referendums*, ed. D. Farrell, and R. Schmitt-Beck, 145–162. London: Routledge.

Leshner, G., and E. Thorson. 2000. Overreporting Voting: Campaign Media, Public Mood, and the Vote. *Political Communication* 17 (3): 263–278.

Lloyd, J., and C. Marconi. 2014. *Reporting the EU*. London: IB Tauris.

McLean, I. 2003. Two Analytical Narratives About the History of the EU. *European Union Politics* 4 (4): 499–506.

McNair, B. 2017. *An Introduction to Political Communication*. Abingdon: Taylor & Francis.

Negrine, R. 2017. How Did the British Media Represent European Political Parties During the European Parliament Elections, 2014: A Europeanized Media Agenda? *International Communication Gazette* 79 (1): 64–82.

Neureiter, M. 2017. Sources of Media Bias in Coverage of the Israeli-Palestinian Conflict: The 2010 Gaza flotilla Raid in German, British, and US Newspapers. *Israel Affairs* 23 (1): 66–86.

Papathanassopoulos, S., and R. Negrine. 2011. *European Media*. Cambridge: Polity Press.

Rahn, W.M., B. Kroeger, and C.M. Kite. 1996. A Framework for the Study of Public Mood. *Political Psychology* 1: 29–58.

Schlesinger, P. 1999. Changing Spaces of Political Communication. *Political Communication* 16 (3): 263–279.

Schuck, A.R., and C.H. de Vreese. 2009. Reversed Mobilization in Referendum Campaigns: How Positive News Framing Can Mobilize the Skeptics. *The International Journal of Press/Politics* 14 (1): 40–66.

Startin, N. 2015. Have We Reached a Tipping Point? The Mainstreaming of Euroscepticism in the UK. *International Political Science Review* 36 (3): 311–323.

Straubhaar, J.D. 1991. Beyond Media Imperialism: Asymmetrical Interdependence and Cultural Proximity. *Critical Studies in Media Communication* 8 (1): 39–59.

Strömbäck, J., and D. Dimitrova. 2006. Political and Media Systems Matter. A Comparison of Election News Coverage in Sweden and the United States. *International Journal of Press/Politics* 11 (4): 131–147.

Strömbäck, J., and P. Van Aelst. 2010. Exploring Some Antecedents of the Media's Framing of Election News: A Comparison of Swedish and Belgian Election News. *International Journal of Press/Politics* 15 (1): 41–59.

Thompson, H. 2017. Inevitability and Contingency: The Political Economy of Brexit. *The British Journal of Politics and International Relations* 19 (3): 434–449.

Valentini, C., and G. Nesti. 2010. *Public Communication in the European Union.* Newcastle upon Tyne: Cambridge Scholars Publishing.

Venkataraman, N. 2018. What's Not in a Frame? Analysis of Media Representations of the Environmental Refugee. In *Exploring Silence and Absence in Discourse*, ed. M. Schröter, and C. Taylor, 241–279. Cham: Palgrave Macmillan.

Volkmer, I. 1999. *News in the Global Sphere: A Study of CNN and Its Impact on Global Communication.* Luton: University of Luton Press.

Volkmer, I. 2003. The Global Network Society and the Global Public Sphere. *Development* 46 (1): 9–16.

Williams, B.A., and M.X.D. Carpini. 2011. *After Broadcast News: Media Regimes, Democracy, and the New Information Environment.* New York: Cambridge University Press.

Wilson, G.K. 2017. Brexit, Trump and the Special Relationship. *The British Journal of Politics and International Relations* 19 (3): 543–557.

PART II

The UK and UK Territories

CHAPTER 2

Mobilizing Migration: Analysing the Role of the 'Migrant' in the British Press During the EU Referendum 2016 Debate

Oisín Share

INTRODUCTION

This chapter examines the role the British press played in the mobilization of migrants in public discourses prior to the United Kingdom's (UK's) referendum on European Union (EU) membership in June 2016. This discourse crystallized around several topics, few of them as contentious as public opinion surrounding immigration; indeed, in the weeks prior to the vote, polls showed that immigration was the leading concern for voters (Anon, *The Economist*, 2 April 2016c), and the British press responded to this with regular coverage on migration, emphasizing its own role as a primary source of information about political developments occurring outside our everyday experiences.

The heightened nature of public unease regarding immigration runs in parallel with increased levels of displacement of refugees throughout Europe, coverage of which has remained widespread in the British

O. Share (✉)
Malmö University, Malmö, Sweden
e-mail: oisin@worksofoisin.eu

© The Author(s) 2018
A. Ridge-Newman et al. (eds.), *Reporting the Road to Brexit*,
https://doi.org/10.1007/978-3-319-73682-2_2

media following an intense period of reporting in 2015 (see Berry et al. 2015). With refugee arrivals in 2016 eight times higher than during the same period in 2015 (Dearden, *The Independent*, 23 February 2016), migrants and refugees received increased media attention during the referendum debate.

This study seeks to shed light on the mechanisms used by the British press to shape the discourse in the referendum debate, central to which was the politically charged and highly mediated figure of the 'migrant'. Assessing the means by which the British press aimed to capitalize on such polarized political rhetoric during the referendum can provide us with a precursory lens; a valuable perspective into the mechanics of media campaigns and their influence.

To do this, I examine how concepts in discourse emerge as hegemonic, whereby journalistic tendencies of the British press accumulate to 'reshape the broad interests and values evident within society' (Nyberg et al. 2013: 8). This analysis of hegemony is primarily informed by Laclau and Mouffe's (1985) post-Marxist discourse theory, a relatively underused yet valuable framework for 'investigating the relationship between migration and media' (Moore 2012: 66) and thus a beneficial tool for developing an insight into how the EU referendum 2016 presents a valid test case for such an approach.

This reading relates to the *contingency* of discursive structures, a characteristic central to Laclau and Mouffe's theory which asserts that change can occur in an area (in my case, the meaning of migration in the media) no matter how sedimented the concept is with negative assumptions provided by press coverage. I will be identifying signs and objects, known as floating signifiers, which are overflowing with possibility for *meaning*. These are of course the symbolic figure of the 'migrant', but also 'threat', 'Britishness', or 'European'. When these signs (known as nodal points) stabilize in discourse, they obtain meaning. It is these meanings that amass and sediment, asserting power, establishing a 'common sense' social reality, or hegemony. It is this process, and the resulting hegemonic projects, that I aim to analyse so as to assess the role of the 'migrant' as mobilized in the debate.

Such an analysis determines the conduct and practices that the migrants inhabit in discourses, such as language, power, politics and reflection of social 'truths'. In this way, a broad interpretation of the common identities and social relations articulated can be obtained. We can identify ideas and practices that are deemed appropriate to use in association with migrants, and additionally how the readers of these publications were also socially reproduced, persuaded to think of themselves, their wider society and their prospective participation in the upcoming referendum (see Moore 2012; Korkut et al. 2013).

These interpretations are examined using a qualitative discourse analysis of a corpus of articles collected from five British newspapers. Three key milestones in the timeline of the referendum debate have been identified, and articles rich in floating signifiers concerning these events have been selected for analysis.

Analysing the Migrant Discourse

Threadgold (2012: 270) affirms that 'theory matters in this kind of research', as 'the issues are complex and have for too long been insufficiently theorized, often relying on relatively decontextualized content analysis of media texts alone'.

The discourse theory of Laclau and Mouffe used in this study is a complex though highly rewarding framework for analysis of structures of power and conflict, subjects that are of course at the forefront of the referendum debate. For this study, I have selected a reading of the theory that focuses on antagonism and hegemony, lending focus to the relationship of the social constructs in the migration discourses, and how they obtain meaning. Sedimentation of these meanings leads to the establishment of a 'common sense' reality, or hegemony, an established dominance in society which can persuade, or dissuade, political motivations.

The starting point of the theory proposes that all social phenomena and objects in society obtain meaning through discourse. Prior to this, objects and other social agents are *contingent* in meaning, free to be defined. It is this contingency that 'creates the space for subjectivity and the particularity of human behaviour' (Carpentier 2010: 253), so crucial to media content. Discourse itself emerges from a process known as *articulation*: 'any practice establishing a relation among elements such that their identity is modified as a result of the articulatory practice' (Laclau and Mouffe 1985: 105). The process of articulation of discursive elements plays a vital role in how objects and social agents obtain their identities, whether this is via a welding of ideas, or through the positioning of subjects in discursive structures. Is the 'migrant' a social agent formed through a union of its own elements, or does its identity become affixed as a result of its position within a semantic system? It is this fixation of meaning that needs to be assessed, as 'regularities merely consist of the relative and precarious forms of fixation which accompany the establishment of a certain order' (Laclau and Mouffe 1985: 98). To change the identity of the 'migrant', a subject at the centre of voters' concerns in the lead-up to the referendum, may well be to change the widely expected outcome.

To assess how this meaning is fixated for the symbolic 'migrant' in the debate discourses, I will be looking in the texts for floating signifiers, signs that are almost *swelling* with meaning. Acting almost as warehouses of identity, these floating signifiers go on to assume different meanings in different discourses.

With so many different meanings available, these signifiers do have to be partially fixed, rather than completely contingent, as to be otherwise would be to render any meaning impossible, such is their number. The points at which the discourse is partially fixed are known as the nodal points. Nodal points are privileged within discourse, and can fix their meaning to chains of other moments, such as smaller objects or notions. As a result, the addition of a floating signifier to discourse may be to change its meaning altogether. By identifying the key nodal points in the migrant discourse, I can gain insight into the role of the key players in the debate, assess how their meanings are affixed, changed, or used to mirror. These meanings attributed to signifiers are not exclusive to one particular discourse, and several discourses can articulate the same signifier; indeed, these nodal points can take on different meanings in the different discourses that articulate them, a point very evident when analysing 'migrants' in the referendum debate.

At the stage where these nodal points establish the ability to define or exhibit power in the discourse, the theory of Laclau and Mouffe refers to the concept of hegemony, originally developed by Gramsci. Hegemony is a useful concept for this study, as Gramsci (2000: 261) related this theory to the notion of consent ('the combination of force and consent variously balancing one another') rather than simply dominance over the other, though without barriers, pressure or repression (Carpentier 2010: 254). Referendums are politicized projects of democratic mass consent, with media coverage offering balance (or not) as it establishes hegemonic projects. Projects such as these 'aim to construct and stabilize nodal points that are the basis of a social order, the main aim of which is to become a social imaginary' (Carpentier 2010: 254) or what Moore (2012: 66) terms 'common sense'. It is these realities that form the active platforms of the referendum debate, in which the symbolic 'migrant' can be found at the centre of multiple attempts to construct and reconstruct its social identity.

Research Design: Contexts and Analysis

To reveal these hegemonic projects, three key events during the debate were analysed to produce a corpus of articles reflective of some of the most salient issues that occurred in the lead up to the referendum.

Event 1: British Prime Minister David Cameron's 'Key Speech': 10 November 2015

On 10 November 2015, British Prime Minister David Cameron outlined his 'wish list' of demands for European leaders which would form the basis of his negotiation for the UK's continued EU membership. Among the demands were measures to curtail the number of EU migrants arriving in Britain. The following day, Cameron joined EU leaders at a summit with other European and African leaders to discuss solutions to the escalating levels of displacements of refugees throughout Europe. The summit provided the environment for the converging issues of EU membership and immigration to be jointly debated by the media.

Event 2: Official Calling of the Referendum: 20 February 2016

Following several months of negotiations with EU heads of state regarding his reform 'wish list', on 20 February 2016 Cameron announced that he was confident that his demands had been recognized and as a result set a referendum date. Restrictions on EU migrants, referred to throughout the corpus by the somewhat 'disaster-like' signifier of an 'emergency brake', were discussed as part of the current state of Europe, its ongoing 'crises' and the potential for 'real change' post-referendum.

Event 3: EU Deal with Turkey to Deport Migrants: 4 April 2016

An occasion when the 'refugee crisis' and EU political policy were in dual focus, the announcement of the deportation of primarily North African and Middle Eastern migrants to Turkey was used by the media as an opportunity to offer interpretations of how the EU was (mis)handling the crisis, and, as a result, provided further commentary on what continued British membership could mean with regard to migrant numbers. The deportation of asylum seekers from the EU formed the backbone of a deal whereby one 'official' refugee would be taken for every 'failed' refugee returned to Turkey. This was done on the premise of finance for Turkey, and assurances of progression in its aim of eventual EU membership, despite such an eventuality remaining unlikely due to the promise of vetoes from France, Germany and the UK (Tisdall, *Guardian*, 22 May 2016). This event presented media titles prone to anti-migrant discourse with an opportunity to articulate criticism of refugees and Turkey, whilst at the same time criticizing the EU's handling of the situation.

The news sources selected represented differing political stances regarding the EU referendum and migration (Berry et al. 2015), as well as a mix of quality (*Telegraph, Guardian*) and tabloid outlets (*Daily Express, Daily Mail, Mirror*). Using the date ranges of the above events, a corpus was collated for discourse analysis. This data was collected by accessing the online archive of articles from each title, using a date range of one day prior and after the day under focus, which allowed for precursory and reactive analysis. Data was collected using the following variables identified on the basis of their relevance to the debate: im/migrants OR im/migration OR refugee/s OR referendum OR Brexit OR Europe OR EU. The results were manually scanned and only articles that explicitly focused on the selected referendum issues were specifically compiled. Overall, 262 articles were identified, leading to a relevant corpus of 148 articles.

In these articles, I identified key nodal points present in the discourses in the texts. Following this, to ascertain their resulting meaning, the next step was to examine the *chains of equivalence*, nodal points that sediment in the discourses to constitute and organize social relations, which aided in highlighting signification strategies. For example, 'refugee', a nodal point present in the texts, operates as a floating signifier through which a possible function is articulated, welding together demands for recognition, shelter, security and safety. But it is also a signifier in relation to which other political demands, such as combating war and poverty, are expressed: each demand signifies an opposition to insecurity for people. It is thus that a chain of equivalence between demands that have no necessary link can be jointly constructed with 'refugee', mobilizing a persuasive mechanism in a media debate.

Analysis of this helps to determine degree of hegemonic closure; in other words, the extent to which one of the discursive articulations is able to provide (more or less) fixed meaning to the nodal point and thus, however provisionally, establish a hegemonic project or 'common-sense' social reality. The results of this analysis are discussed in relation to three questions: (1) What is the overall role the figure of the 'migrant' fulfils during this referendum debate? (2) How do the media mobilize migrants in the debate to establish a 'common-sense' reality? (3) What are these hegemonic projects, and what can they reveal about the role the British press had in influencing the referendum outcome?

The Role of the Migrant in the Referendum Debate

Whilst immigration was not the only topic under discussion during the debate, its prominence in the articles as a subject in the negotiations was aided by the long-established precedents in the media of actively constructing negative social reproductions of migrants in discourses. Migrants in or from Europe remained a 'go-to hot-topic', present in the data on each event analysed in each title. As a result, the symbolic 'migrant' fulfilled an expansive role in the debate.

In the conservative and tabloid titles, articles responded to the already highly mediated public concerns about immigration by positioning successful curbs on inward migration as the most visible 'win' that Cameron could hope for. Discourse constructed Europe and migrants as mired in 'threat' and 'crises', with both competing to be the enduring focus of the campaign. In a particular response to Cameron's speech, the *Daily Mail* constructed on each side of the political divide concepts of 'misery' ('gruel') and 'battle' ('retreats', 'showdown', 'attacking', 'blood') (Slack, *Daily Mail*, 11 November 2015) which together bolstered a discourse that established a conflict-heavy framework for the debate:

> *Cameron's EU wish list dismissed by Tory MPs as 'thin gruel' as he retreats on banning benefits for migrants four years*
> But faces showdown with EU leaders over attacking freedom of movement London Mayor Boris Johnson warned there will be 'blood on the carpet' in Brussels as Mr Cameron pushes for change. (Chorley, *Daily Mail*, 10 November 2015)

'Threat' was mobilized as a dominant nodal point regarding refugees and Europe. The Continent, and the EU itself, emerged as a failing entity, permeable, yet still a powerful construction of what was certainly a symbolic 'crisis' situation. Attention was frequently drawn to the ongoing prominence of immigration as a European social 'crisis' and the EU's perceived mishandling of the worsening issue. As a nodal point, 'crisis' in particular resonates in both migration and political spheres. EU migrants, refugees and asylum seekers converged as one unified immigrant entity, becoming the frequent human face of the debate, in which their voiceless presence was reported alongside regular images of politicians and politicized rhetoric.

The *Daily Express* in particular presented Cameron's speech as an opportunity to signal the risk of societal catastrophe, with natural disaster metaphors applied to migrants such as 'explosion', 'gigantic waves', 'hordes of foreigners' and 'colossal flood', suggesting the unavoidable and 'alien values' which would be among the after-effects:

> In a wilfully deluded report published last week the European Commission laughably claimed that the migrant explosion will have 'an additional positive impact on growth' through 'the increase in the labour supply'. Such assertions could hardly be more absurd. As we have already experienced, the millions of new migrants will impose a phenomenal burden on welfare systems and public services. JUST as importantly, social cohesion will be further eroded by the import of alien values that are antithetical to the European liberal traditions of pluralism, democracy, free speech and individual rights. (McKinstry, *Daily Express*, 9 November 2015)

Such constructions of migrants as a source of crisis were not so much countered as simply discounted in the *Guardian*, which often chose an example of how the referendum itself was misinformed and distracting from more serious societal issues, going as far as to discredit the need for this level of attention directed against immigrants, using migrants as a persuasive tool to provide calm, yet directed critique. Regarding Cameron's speech and resulting 'wish list' of demands, the 'threat' posed by migrants was mobilized as 'the toughest nut to crack' and a 'phoney war'. The notion of a symbolic 'migrant crisis' emerged as simply a 'crisis of facts'; and an article titled 'EU migrants on benefits: separating the statistics from the spin' called for clarification as:

> Britain's referendum on EU membership may be decided in large part by the issue, but the information available is scant at best [...] The debate over restricting migrants' benefits is likely to dominate the campaign. It may even decide the outcome of the vote. (Nardelli, *Guardian*, 10 November 2015a)

Suggesting that migration levels caused by EU membership constituted a threat to 'Britishness' and British society, the referendum was promoted as providing an exit route from harmful conditions. Articles in the *Daily Mail*, the *Daily Express* and the *Telegraph* particularly sought to dismantle the notion of the EU itself, with suggestions that one of its key principles, freedom of movement, may be what causes its eventual demise:

> *The migrant crisis is a mere gust of the hurricane that will soon engulf Europe*
> Both the Schengen border-free zone and the eurozone are central projects of EU unity which are now driving disunity, and which need a new approach if they are to survive the future strains which we do not need an expert to predict. The European Union now needs to show it can change in order to survive. (Hague, *Telegraph*, 11 November 2015)

> *Europe's REAL crisis: Terror warning as 6,000 refugees arrive on Lesbos in just three days with no end to the human tide of misery.* (Slack et al., *Daily Mail*, 19 February 2016)

> *EU migrants claiming benefits: questions the government must answer*
> The government says nearly half of EU migrants receive benefits during their first years in Britain, but how is it arriving at these figures? Based on these figures, the proportion of claimants that are new arrivals seems improbably high. (Nardelli, *Guardian*, 10 November 2015b)

A Europe struggling to cope with economic migrants was regularly contrasted with concepts of nationalism, emphasizing a role for the 'migrant' whereby nodal points in the sample formed chains of equivalence in which 'Britain' and contingent concepts of 'border' were sedimented under 'threat' from Europe experiencing 'crisis':

> *Romanian and Bulgarian workers top 200,000 for first time, say official figures*
> The figures give further evidence of how the EU's free movement rules affect Britain's ability to control its borders. (Barrett, *Telegraph*, 11 November 2015)

For the *Guardian*, in contrast, mobilizing migrants through discourse served the purpose of expressing what were seen as shared 'European' values worthy of consideration in the debate. As a result of this, anti-Europe rhetoric was almost absent. Similarly the *Mirror*, whilst advocating a symbolic migrant 'voice', took offence on behalf of the voting public at Cameron's demands:

> *David Cameron should be ashamed of this 'dodgy, deceitful and dishonest' speech*
> Unable to produce stats to prove lazy foreigners are coming over here to go on the dole because they don't, he conjured figures to claim 43% of new arrivals receive in-work benefits. That suggests they're striving not skiving, to throw back at Cameron the prejudiced language Tories love, but watch the calculation unravel during the day. (Maguire, *Mirror*, 10 November 2015)

These supportive discourses were in the minority in the press sample but also wholly aware of their own importance in offering an alternative view, aware of what was at stake regarding voter concerns. Writing for the *Guardian*, Labour leader Jeremy Corbyn aired frustration at a nationwide misunderstanding, or crisis of facts, describing the debate ahead as follows: 'Cameron's deal is the wrong one: but Britain must stay in Europe' (Corbyn, *Guardian*, 20 February 2016); or from Conservative MP Philip Hammond, 'Better to stay in Europe with a deal that will answer voters' frustrations' (Hammond, *Guardian*, 20 February 2016), and:

> The risk for Cameron is that the terms he has negotiated do not address public concerns [...] The more immediate question, of course, is whether it is enough to convince the large numbers of British people who are yet to make up their minds. (Editorial, *Guardian*, 21 February 2016b)

Mechanisms of Mobilization

Whilst It was common across the sample for the nodal points of symbolic 'threat', 'Europe' and 'crisis' to be present across the discourses, it is the mechanics of mobilization of migrants in these news stories that reveal the perspectives of the press titles in the sample. Throughout the corpus, these titles sought to establish chains of equivalence in an increasingly common set of discourses whereby migrants represented the 'other', an 'unknown entity' composed of vast numbers to be avoided:

> *Britain's future: migrant split reveals growing EU divide*
> Britain is thinking of leaving. Greece feels isolated. Austria and Denmark are pushing controversial measures for coping with asylum-seekers despite

what their neighbors think [...] Rarely has the EU seemed as fragmented and impotent as on Friday, when leaders grappled with a possible British exit and tried to find a united response to the refugee emergency. (Anon, *Daily Mail*, 19 February 2016a)

24 hours after EU leaders pledge to deal with the refugee crisis harrowing pictures show the tide of human suffering is far from waning. (Calderwood, *Daily Mail*, 20 February 2016)

EU summit: Cameron's deal is weak, weak, weak. The only real alternative is Brexit
Proof? The flimsiness of this deal. Consider the issue of immigration. The Prime Minister is overly excited about the fact that he has won the promise of a break [sic] on the ability of migrants to collect some benefits. Who cares? The real issue when it comes to migration isn't welfare, it's numbers. (Stanley, *Telegraph*, 20 February 2016)

'Othered' migrants were systemically mobilized to reflect a 'common-sense' social reality whereby restrictive British immigration policies were politically justified with government and public support, and EU measures to control the crisis outside of this legal perimeter were presented as an example of a political bloc unable to conform to British expectations to control inward migrant numbers. Migrants who were already present, or entering Europe, became assuredly positioned as bargaining chips on both sides of the debate:

The Guardian view on the Brussels summit deal: Cameron delivers a practical package
The section on benefits for migrant workers is the most problematic part of the package. It was good that several EU member states made clear that they would not accept second-class treatment for their nationals. Nor should the UK have sought such a status for migrants who have come here to work and who are net contributors to the UK. Nevertheless, there need to be rules on benefits for migrant workers and the rules agreed should logically reassure British taxpayers while not mistreating migrants who are here already or rightly entitled to come here in future. (Editorial, *Guardian*, 19 February 2016a)

Nigel Farage slams 'Cam-Sham' as he sounds 'clarion call' for Brexit
Clarion call signal that says to the British people: vote to leave the EU, vote to get back control of our borders. Because all these people who have gone to Germany and elsewhere will have EU passports within a few years – we need to protect our country. (Anon, *Daily Mail*, 20 February 2016b)

Several titles presented graphical analysis suggesting that 'uncontrollable' numbers of migrant workers had much in common with the refugee crisis. This frequent collocation of EU migrants with the refugee developments, particularly through the means of photography of both UK-based migrants and refugees sharing the same article (as visible in the *Daily Mail* and the *Daily Express* in particular) created a reality where EU economic migrants were affixed similar if not identical media identities to refugees and asylum seekers. Regularly, articles hundreds of words in length discussing EU migrant numbers would be interspersed with images of boats of refugees at sea or attempted border crossings. Whilst these issues both concern immigration, Cameron's negotiations on migrant benefits were only linked to the refugee crisis in that they were said to aim to reduce the pull factor of the UK. Discourse populated with iterations, both literal and visual, of Bulgarians, Romanians and Poles did not belong in these reports if one is to expect factual representations from mainstream quality press titles, especially at a time when democratic principles are soon to be exercised:

> If you think it's madness that we cut child benefit to middle-class, single-earner families in this country to save money, but still have to pay that benefit to children in Romania and Poland, who have never set foot here, then you have no option but to vote Leave. If you think we should be able to let in the people we want and need from all parts of the globe and kick out those who hate us, you have to vote Leave. If you think our NHS and our schools can't support another million migrants, then you must pluck up courage and vote Leave.
>
> Anything can happen between now and June, particularly as the milder weather beckons yet more migrants across the Aegean and the EU itself threatens to implode. All it will take to blow apart the PM's 'best of both worlds' argument is a single terrorist bomb. (Pearson, *Telegraph*, 20 February 2016)

The notion of 'Europe' and its meanings underwent notable transformation in the corpus, with a highly visible shift in its prominence in articles, particularly in the tabloid sample. Over the date range, mentions of the EU itself were present to a degree that seemed to suggest over-mobilization. Articles and headlines presented notable increases in *literal* mentions of the EU, Europe, European cities, citizens, leaders and individual nations, which were mobilized with the nodal point of 'migrant crisis' and asserted a continent that was no stranger to bad news. When concepts of Europe were active in discourses alongside the symbolic 'refugee crisis' or 'job seeking EU migrant', this sedimented an anti-Europe rhetoric 'common sense', clouding facts, ensuring that 'Europe' was synonymous with concepts of strife, conflict and political mismanagement. This tactic presented the EU as worthy of a Leave vote, stubbornly unmoved by Cameron's demands, unable to control its borders and therefore to avoid symbolic 'chaos'. This tendency towards literal mentions of Europe is most evident below from headlines of articles sourced in one day from the *Daily Express*:

> *Fortress Europe: Slovenia rolls out the barbed wire fencing amid migrant chaos* (Batchelor, *Daily Express*, 11 November 2015)
>
> *Europe's migrant crisis is the CATALYST for collapse of EU, warns Luxembourg minister* (Hall, *Daily Express*, 11 November 2015)
>
> *Europe in CRISIS? Portugal rejects austerity measures and ousts government* (Virtue, *Daily Express*, 11 November 2015)

Although headline analysis alone provides insight into the mechanics of the discourse, it is notable that articles concerned with topics such as setting limits on EU migrant benefits were presented alongside photo galleries of the European refugee 'crisis'. This media tug-of-war created a space for a debate about *all* migrants in Europe, one that was highlighting doubts, highlighting risk, questioning their status and the reality of personal traumas.

> *Thousands of migrants to be housed on luxury CRUISE SHIP with SWIMMING POOL onboard* (Wood, *Daily Express*, 19 February 2016)
>
> *Cologne rapists WERE refugees: Prosecutor slams reports exonerating migrants as 'nonsense'* (Gutteridge, *Daily Express*, 19 February 2016a)
>
> *UKIP's Nigel Farage brands EU a BURNING BUILDING and urges public to RUN for the exit door* (Bucks, *Daily Express*, 21 February 2016)
>
> *Europe facing biggest terror threat in DECADE as THOUSANDS of ISIS militants at large* (Culbertson, *Daily Express*, 21 February 2016)

The mechanics of mobilization continued to differ throughout the corpus. The *Guardian* mobilized consistent sympathy towards the EU with its coverage of migrant deportations, ready to trade off perceived political progress in favour of refugee advocacy, utilizing the symbolic 'migrant' to promote a wider ideal. In a stand-alone journalism act from the analysis, the *Mirror* went to some lengths to suggest Europe represented positive labour rights, a position that aligned with their political ties to the Labour Party. In both cases the symbolic 'migrant' formed a figure shaped by media mechanics in order for the key players in those groups to be placed in and therefore inhabit the same 'common sense' as the audience. These mechanics may result in a positive spin; however, they mirror the same tactics of influencing readers as is evident in more Eurosceptic titles:

> *Jeremy Corbyn warns David Cameron's migrant benefit cuts could drive down pay for Brits*
> Instead of welcoming this week's record employment figures of 31.5 million, Nigel Farage focused on the two million EU migrants among them, and claimed they were ruining the prospects of 'ordinary British workers'. (Blanchard, *Mirror*, 21 February 2016)

> *5,000 jihadists 'have returned to Europe after training with ISIS in Iraq and Syria'*
> [...] but there was no proof the migrant crisis was making us less safe. (Relph, *Mirror*, 20 February 2016)

> *Iain Duncan Smith blasted for 'scaremongering' as he claims being in EU risks a Paris-style terror attack.* (Blanchard and Bloom, *Mirror*, 21 February 2016)

HEGEMONIC PROJECTS

The selected press titles conformed to previous studies concerning migration and the British press (see Buchanan and Grillo 2004; Berry et al. 2015) with the *Daily Mail*, the *Daily Express* and the *Telegraph* representing the conservative, Eurosceptic titles in the sample, establishing social visions and 'common-sense' realities where migrants of all backgrounds were a force that should be prevented or, indeed, legally restricted. What separated this study was the prospect of an audience being able to obtain this legal restriction and assert change through democratic process in a forthcoming referendum on EU membership, presented by several titles as being the first opportunity to regain popular control since British accession to the EU in 1973.

BRITAIN DIVIDED: Moment protesters burnt EU flag as migration anger spirals out of control
BRITAIN was tonight perilously divided as simmering anger about mass migration boiled over into ugly violence on the streets of Dover.
The impact of mass migration is expected to play a key role in the upcoming referendum on Britain's membership of the EU, with Brexit campaigners saying severing ties with Brussels is the only way to secure our borders. (Gutteridge, *Daily Express*, 3 April 2016b)

When Cameron emerged from his key speech with questionable results, Eurosceptic titles attempted to establish themselves as the authoritative sources of migration and EU-related knowledge. At no point in the analysis did these titles form a hegemonic project largely in favour of Europe, its principles or its political organizations; this was relegated to the culture, sport and travel sections that also appeared in the initial search results. Overall, the issues for the referendum shifted in focus from being journalism-led coverage to being a fully fledged and politicized media campaign.

On the pro-Europe liberal side of the debate, there was perceptibly less interest in being the leading source of referendum information, perhaps due to lack of precedent for the British press to prioritize EU matters over home-grown news, and a leading impression that a vote to leave was unexpected. Thus, the hegemonic projects apparent in the sample were less vocal, and decidedly less visible. The *Mirror* struggled with its Labour Party associations when faced with low support for the EU and acceptance of the refugee 'crisis' discourse among its readership, as was evident in online polls sourced from the sample that were heavily in favour of a 'Leave' vote. Pro-Remain articles were the lowest in the sample, opting instead for pro-migrant content highlighting topics such as workers' rights, rights of Britons abroad in Europe and criticism of a 'cowardly' Leave campaign that threatened workers already with 'lousy prospects':

What the cowardly Brexit brigade REALLY want is to axe are your rights at work
Workers on low pay with lousy prospects deserve a better deal. But don't blame migrants when the guilty men and women are the greedy bosses slashing wages and exploiting toilers. (Maguire, *Mirror*, 3 April 2016)

EU campaigners at war over Brits' healthcare abroad
Britain Stronger in Europe spokesman James McGrory said: 'To leave Brits to face a massive bill on their sickbed miles away from home would be damaging and inhumane.' (Glaze, *Mirror*, 5 April 2016)

The *Guardian*'s argumentation revealed a dependence on the same signifiers found throughout the study, though with frequent dismissal of the contexts surrounding what was causing these issues to become 'common sense' and enter the debate.

> *Calm as EU migrant deal takes symbolic first step but true test is to come*
> For politicians watching in Europe, this was one small step for an anonymous man, but one giant leap for the continent. Finally, they had created a means of curbing the Aegean smuggling route, which brought more than 850,000 people to Europe via the Greek islands in 2015. It was, said an approving EU spokesman, 'very well organised'. (Smith and Kingsley, *Guardian*, 4 April 2016)

Connection of the EU with such dismissals of political events allowed the EU to escape much critique: indeed, the *Guardian* was the only title clearly advocating a social, 'Europeanized' social reality ahead for the UK.

Emerging from the analysis of these titles was a polarized media referendum debate. Widespread focus on the refugee 'crisis' led to an intensification of negative portrayals of migrants due to those on the 'Leave' side fostering antagonistic hegemonic projects. The effects of this were no doubt extensive: migrants had already formed an unwarranted fulcrum for right-wing discourse following their 2004 accession to the British labour market. The presence of the voice of refugees in the media continued to be hampered by regular and systematic connection of the crisis with tumultuous European politics and self-serving nationalist interests. It presented a challenging task for voters to be able to separate immigration from the referendum campaign and the 'common sense' as presented by the media in the upcoming poll.

Conclusion

I set out to explore how the British press mobilized migrants in its response to public perceptions on immigration and EU membership during a time of heightened displacement of refugees throughout Europe. This media landscape, where focus on purported migration 'crises' was reported in parallel to debate on British membership of the EU, presented a unique opportunity to analyse how the 'migrant' is constructed for persuasive politicized means.

My findings confirmed the long-established and problematic position migration has in the UK press, a position that became further intensified during this debate. This study was economical in its scope; however, it was able to assess in a narrow date range what was a near saturation of articles concerning both immigration and the upcoming vote. With immigration as a leading concern for voters in the EU referendum, not only was the refugee 'crisis' frequently mobilized as a means to further political agendas on both sides of the debate, but the press sought to go further and actively shape a 'common sense' in which an audience of prospective voters would be determining their views on Europe as they in turn contemplated immigration.

Migration was of course not the only concern held by voters; however, the figure of the 'migrant', mediated and no stranger to coverage, became a powerful persuasive tool in the discourses. On both sides of the debate, the mechanisms of mobilizing migrants were the same, but to different effects: in some cases the 'migrant' was used to affix an identity of a struggling political body to the EU, or simply to highlight flaws in the wider media coverage. The overarching ideology was apparent, namely that to change the meaning of 'migrants' was to change the nature of the debate itself. Identities of several migrant communities, from EU economic to asylum seeker, were placed under one umbrella for popular consideration. The EU referendum 2016 was promoted as a democratic opportunity to control immigration, whether as a means to retain the status quo of EU-wide free movement of citizens, or, as suggested by many in the 'Leave' campaign, to regain 'control' of UK borders. Such hegemonic projects formed evolved and problematic landscapes in the media debate. To vote was to disenfranchise or empower, to block or to allow.

This approach, established as a means to furnish a debate with topical subjects, continued the dominant media tendency to represent immigration as separate from a community, especially in this case, the community of the UK electorate. Migrants were suspended in the debate, objectified for politicized outcome, voiceless and characterized by quantification or metaphorical forces. Migrants were central in the debate, yet altogether separate from participation. The study confirmed what Threadgold (2012: 267) describes as 'the narrow range of migration which is actually seen to have "news value"'. The nodal points analysed in this study point to established practices for mobilizing migration, such as highlighting the 'crises' or threat; opportunity or positive outcome were rarely considered newsworthy in the corpus.

The referendum debate revealed an intensification of these practices and highlighted how anti-immigration rhetoric can dominate a ' common-sense' reality, prevent further public knowledge about the root causes of events such as refugee displacement, or the role of EU economic migrants in communities. To counter this, liberal broadsheets needed to go further in their efforts to draw attention to factual crises by highlighting how negative representations of migrants continue to be so commonplace. More space and direct citation needed to be given to those individuals and groups present in the discourses, to allow the subjects to articulate personal experience and lessen the effect of particular press ideologies, giving explanatory capacity to those who were directly affected. A valuable further development of this study would be to extend the analysis to post-2017 referendum discourse to ascertain the contributing factor of the June 2016 vote to leave the EU in the active construction of negative social reproductions of the 'migrant' in the British press and any alteration in the hegemonic projects. The capacity for the 'migrant' to have its identity shaped by the media may now have altered, taking into account perceived campaign success in the conservative titles, or failings in advocacy by the liberals. Assessment of such mechanisms of mobilizations can aid in identifying opportunities to ensure migrant voices reach media platforms in both social and politicized spheres.

BIBLIOGRAPHY

ACADEMIC SOURCES

Berry, M., I. Garcia-Blanco, and K. Moore. 2015. *Press Coverage of the Refugee and Migrant Crisis in the EU*. UNHCR, Cardiff School of Journalism.

Buchanan, S., and B. Grillo. 2004. What's the Story? Reporting on Asylum in the British Media. *Forced Migration Review* 19: 41–43.

Carpentier, N. 2010. Deploying Discourse Theory. An Introduction to Discourse Theory and Discourse Theoretical Analysis. In *Media and Communication Studies Intersections and Interventions*, ed. B. Cammaerts, N. Carpentier, R. Kilborn, T. Olsson, P. Pruulmann-Vengerfeldt, H. Nieminen, E. Sundin, and I. Tomanić Trivundža, 251–265. Tartu: Tartu University Press.

Gramsci, A. 2000. *The Gramsci Reader: Selected Writings, 1916–1935.* New York: New York University Press.

Korkut, U., G. Bucken-Knapp, A. McGarry, J. Hinnfors, and H. Drake. 2013. *Immigration and Integration Policies: Assumptions and Explanations: The Discourses and Politics of Migration in Europe.* New York: Palgrave Macmillan.

Laclau, M., and C. Mouffe. 1985. *Hegemony and Socialist Strategy: Towards a Radical Democratic Politics.* New York: Verso books.

Moore, K. 2012. "Asylum Crisis", National Security and the Re-articulation of Human Rights. In *Migrations and the Media*, ed. K. Moore, B. Gross, and T. Threadgold. New York: Peter Lang.

Nyberg, D., A. Spicer, and C. Wright. 2013. Incorporating Citizens: Corporate Political Engagement with Climate Change in Australia. *Organization* 20 (3): 433–453.

Threadgold, T. 2012. Conclusion. In *Migrations and the Media*, ed. K. Moore, B. Gross, and T. Threadgold. New York: Peter Lang.

NEWS MEDIA SOURCES

Anon. 2016a. Britain's Future, Migrant Split Reveal Growing EU Divide. *Daily Mail*, February 19. http://www.dailymail.co.uk/wires/ap/article-3455198/Britains-future-migrant-splitreveal-growing-EU-divide.html.

Anon. 2016b. Nigel Farage Slams 'Cam-Sham' as he Sounds 'Clarion Call' for Brexit. *Daily Mail*, February 20. http://www.dailymail.co.uk/wires/pa/article-3456420/Nigel-Farage-slams-Cam-Shamsounds-clarion-call-Brexit.html.

Anon. 2016c. Let Them Not Come. *The Economist*, April 2. http://www.economist.com/node/21695958.

Barrett, D. 2015. Romanian and Bulgarian Workers Top 200,000 for First Time, say Official Figures. *Telegraph*, November 11. http://www.telegraph.co.uk/news/uknews/immigration/11987954/Romanian-and-Bulgarian-workers-top-200000-for-first-time-say-official-figures.html.

Batchelor, T. 2015. Fortress Europe: Slovenia Rolls out the Barbed Wire Fencing Amid Migrant Chaos. *Daily Express*, November 11. http://www.express.co.uk/news/world/618719/Europe-migrant-crisis-Slovenia-building-wire-fence-refugees.

Blanchard, J. 2016. Jeremy Corbyn Warns David Cameron's Migrant Benefit Cuts Could Drive down Pay for Brits. *Mirror*, February 21. http://www.mirror.co.uk/news/uk-news/jeremy-corbyn-warns-david-camerons-7414504.

Blanchard, J. and Bloom, D. 2016. Iain Duncan Smith Blasted for "Scaremongering" as He Claims Being in EU Risks a Paris-style Terror Attack. *Mirror*, February 21. http://www.mirror.co.uk/news/uk-news/iain-duncan-smith-blasted-scaremongering-7411216.

Bucks, J. 2016. UKIP's Nigel Farage Brands EU a BURNING BUILDING and Urges Public to RUN for the Exit Door. *Daily Express*, February 21. http://www.express.co.uk/news/uk/646058/UKIP-Nigel-Farage-burning-building-voteleave-EU-referendum.

Calderwood, I. 2016. 24 hours After EU Leaders Pledge to Deal with the Refugee Crisis Pictures Show the Human Suffering Continues. *Daily Mail*, February 20. http://www.dailymail.co.uk/news/article-3456324/Merkel-presses-ahead-EU-solutionrefugee-crisis-photographs-tide-human-suffering-far-waning.html.

Chorley, M. 2015. David Cameron EU Wishlist Dismissed by Tory MPs as 'Thin Gruel'. *Daily Mail*, November 10. http://www.dailymail.co.uk/news/article-3311261/My-EU-mission-possible-vows-Cameron-four-page-negotiating-letter-lambasted-short-detail.html.

Corbyn, J. 2016. Cameron's Deal is the Wrong One: But Britain Must Stay in. *The Guardian*, February 20. http://www.theguardian.com/commentisfree/2016/feb/20/jeremy-corbyn-commentbritain-eu-reform.

Culbertson, A. 2016. Europe Facing Biggest Terror Threat in Decade as Thousands of ISIS Militants at Large. *Daily Express*, February 21. http://www.express.co.uk/news/world/645822/Europe-terror-threat-decade-thousands-ISIS-militants.

Dearden, L. 2016. Refugee Crisis: Concern over "Unprecedented" Arrivals in Greece and Italy After 2016 Total Passes 100,000. *Independent*, February 23. http://www.independent.co.uk/news/world/europe/refugee-migrant-crisisconcern-unprecedented-numbers-greece-italy-2016-passes-100000-a6891101.html.

Editorial. 2016a. The Guardian View on David Cameron's Speech on Europe: Time to End the Phoney War. *The Guardian*, February 19. http://www.the-guardian.com/commentisfree/2015/nov/10/the-guardian-view-on-david-cameron-speech-on-europe-time-to-end-the-phoney-war.

Editorial. 2016b. The Observer View on David Cameron's EU Deal. *The Observer*, February 21. https://www.theguardian.com/commentisfree/2016/feb/21/observer-view-eu-deal.

Glaze, B. 2016. EU Campaigners at War over Brits' Healthcare Abroad. *Mirror*, April 5. http://www.mirror.co.uk/news/uk-news/eu-campaigners-war-over-brits-7691228.

Gutteridge, N. 2016a. Cologne Rapists WERE Refugees: Prosecutor Slams Reports Exonerating Migrants as 'Nonsense'. *Daily Express*, February 19. http://www.express.co.uk/news/world/644379/Cologne-attacks-German-prosector-New-Years-Eve-rapists-migrants-refugees.

Gutteridge, N. 2016b. Dover Riots: Protesters Burnt EU Flag as Migration Anger Spirals Out of Control. *Daily Express*, April 3. http://www.express.

co.uk/news/uk/657708/Dover-riots-protesters-burn-EU-flag-migration-anger-video-refugees.

Hague, W. 2015. The Migrant Crisis is a Mere Gust of the Hurricane that Will Soon Engulf Europe. *Telegraph*, November 11. http://www.telegraph.co.uk/news/newstopics/eureferendum/11986994/The-migrantcrisis-is-a-mere-gust-of-the-hurricane-that-will-soon-engulf-Europe.html.

Hall, M. 2015. Europe's Migrant Crisis is the CATALYST for Collapse of EU, Warns Luxembourg Minister. *Daily Express*, November 11. http://www.express.co.uk/news/politics/618739/Europe-s-migrant-crisis-is-the-CATALYST-for-collapse-of-EU-warns-Luxembourg-minister.

Hammond, P. 2016. Better to Stay in Europe with a Deal that Will Answer Voters' Frustrations. *The Guardian*, February 20. http://www.theguardian.com/commentisfree/2016/feb/20/philip-hammond-commenteurope-deal-cameron.

Maguire, K. 2015. David Cameron Should be Ashamed of this 'Dodgy, Deceitful and Dishonest' Speech. *Mirror*, November 10. http://www.mirror.co.uk/news/uk-news/david-cameron-should-ashamed-dodgy-6803849.

Maguire, K. 2016. What the Cowardly Brexit Brigade REALLY Want Is to Axe Your Rights at Work. *Mirror*, April 3. http://www.mirror.co.uk/news/uk-news/what-cowardly-brexit-brigade-really-7683707.

McKinstry, L. 2015. Leo McKinstry Comment on Britain Leaving EU. *Daily Express*, November 9. http://www.express.co.uk/comment/columnists/leomckinstry/618003/Leo-McKinstryon-leaving-EU.

Nardelli, A. 2015a. EU Migrants on Benefits: Separating the Statistics from the Spin. *The Guardian*, November 10. http://www.theguardian.com/uk-news/datablog/2015/nov/10/eu-migrants-on-benefitsseparating-the-statistics-from-the-spin.

Nardelli, A. 2015b. EU Migrants on Benefits: Questions the Government Must Answer. *The Guardian*, November 10. http://www.theguardian.com/uk-news/datablog/2015/nov/10/eu-migrants-claimingbenefits-questions-the-government-must-answer.

Pearson, A. 2016. EU Referendum: Britons Must Summon the Courage to Leave the European Union. *Telegraph*, February 20. http://www.telegraph.co.uk/news/newstopics/eureferendum/12166422/EU-Referendum-Britons-must-summon-the-courage-to-leave-the-European-Union.html.

Relph, S. 2016. 5000 Jihadists Have Returned to Europe After Training with ISIS in Iraq and Syria. *Mirror*, February 20. http://www.mirror.co.uk/news/uk-news/5000-jihadists-have-returned-europe-7405815.

Slack, J. 2015. Is that It, Mr. Cameron? Tories Mock David Cameron's EU Wishlist as 'Thin Gruel'. *Daily Mail*, November 11. http://www.dailymail.co.uk/news/article-3312978/Is-Mr-Cameron-Tories-mock-EUwishlist-gruel-Brussels-fight-migrant-benefit-curbs.html.

Slack, J., J. Doyle, J. Stevens, K. Strick, and S. Tomlinson. 2016. Europe's REAL Crisis: Terror Warning as 6000 Refugees Arrive on Lesbos in Just Three days with No End to the Human Tide of Misery. *Daily Mail*, February 19. http://www.dailymail.co.uk/news/article-3454726/More-2-000-migrants-arrive-Lesbos-just-ONE-DAY.html.

Smith, H., and P. Kingsley. 2016. Calm as EU Migrant Deal Takes Symbolic First Step but True Test is to Come. *The Guardian*, April 4. http://www.theguardian.com/world/2016/apr/04/symbolic-first-step-eudeportation-deal-greece-turkey-dikili.

Stanley, T. 2016. EU Summit: Cameron's Deal is Weak, Weak, Weak. The only Real Alternative is Brexit. *Telegraph*, February 20. http://www.telegraph.co.uk/news/newstopics/eureferendum/12165318/EU-summit-Camerons-deal-is-weak-weak-weak.-The-only-real-alternative-is-Brexit.html.

Tisdall, S. 2016. Could Turkey Really Join the EU by 2020? *The Guardian*, May 22. http://www.theguardian.com/politics/2016/may/22/vote-leave-turkey-warningignorance-european-realities.

Virtue, R. 2015. Portugal in Crisis as Government Ousted Just TWO WEEKS After Being Elected. *Daily Express*, November 11. http://www.express.co.uk/news/world/618480/Portugal-government-ousted-just-TWOWEEKS-after-being-elected.

Wood, V. 2016. Thousands of Migrants to be Housed on Luxury CRUISE SHIP. *Daily Express*, February 19. http://www.express.co.uk/news/world/645534/Thousands-migrants-housed-luxurycruise-ship-swimming-pool-onboard.

CHAPTER 3

Scotland, Wales and Press Discourses Amid the 2016 EU Referendum

Michael Higgins, Anthony Ridge-Newman and Fiona M. McKay

INTRODUCTION

This chapter analyses press coverage of the 23 June 2016 EU referendum in the Scottish and Welsh contexts. A range of newspapers from these two devolved nations in Great Britain are sampled, from the three months prior to the referendum. In the United Kingdom (UK), the Scotland vote demonstrated the highest support for remaining in the European Union (EU). The Wales result matched almost identically the overall UK vote in favour of leaving the EU. In contrast to Wales, the EU referendum in Scotland had a precursory context of the

M. Higgins (✉) · F. M. McKay
University of Strathclyde, Glasgow, Scotland
e-mail: michael.higgins@strath.ac.uk

F. M. McKay
e-mail: fiona.mckay@strath.ac.uk

A. Ridge-Newman
Liverpool Hope University, Liverpool, UK
e-mail: ridgena@hope.ac.uk

© The Author(s) 2018
A. Ridge-Newman et al. (eds.), *Reporting the Road to Brexit*,
https://doi.org/10.1007/978-3-319-73682-2_3

independence referendum of 2014 and a future possibility of a second independence referendum in the event of a UK wide vote in favour of Britain exiting the EU, also known as 'Brexit'.

Taking a critical discourse analysis (CDA) approach, this chapter analyses key lexical themes in the Scottish press and Welsh press. Looking at how key tropes of public discourse are developed in the press, particularly through accusations of 'Project Fear', the chapter explores discourses of danger and imperilment that predominate in the newspaper coverage. The chapter suggests that this campaign exemplifies the association between 'fear' as a discursive weapon in contemporary politics (Wodak 2015) and constitutional change. However, we also suggest that these discourses are used knowingly and tactically for a variety of political ends.

SCOTLAND, WALES AND THE 2016 EU REFERENDUM

The place of Scotland in discussions about the EU referendum was assured as soon as the results became apparent. A UK-wide vote of 52% to leave against 48% to remain contrasted with a Scottish vote of 62% in favour of remaining against 38% wanting to leave (BBC 2016). As Higgins (2017) argues, the 2016 referendum on Scottish independence occasioned sustained public and political discourse around the possible alienation of the Scottish electorate. Even though a comparatively close and uneven result seems likely to revitalize talk of a second referendum on Scottish independence, known as 'indyref2', the difference in outcome hints at a quite different campaign in Scotland from that in other parts of the UK.

The situation in Wales provides a number of contrasts with that of Scotland. In Wales, with a result of 52.5% Leave and 47.5% Remain, the vote closely mirrored that of England's 53.5% Leave and 46.5% Remain (BBC 2016). Since the rebirth of the Scottish Parliament in 2003, there has been a surge in support for the independence-supporting Scottish National Party (SNP) in Scotland, whereas the inauguration of the Senedd (National Assembly for Wales) in 2006 has failed to bring similar political gains for their Welsh counterpart Plaid Cymru (The Party of Wales).

Jeffery and Hough (2009) offer one potential explanation for this disparity by suggesting that differences in 'state-wide' elections can occur when there are differences in the balances of power at 'sub-state' levels, as we see in the cases of Scotland and Wales in the devolved UK context. Even so, historic rhetoric depicting shared mutual affections, by some political leaders, has laid claim to a Celtic pact between these two devolved nations of the UK. However, the Brexit vote in Wales seems to contradict the two commonly held assumptions that the Welsh are pro-EU and that they occupy a similar political point on the political spectrum to the Scots, and suggests there may be more substantial differences between the Scottish and Welsh contexts.

THE ANALYSIS

The analysis will focus on Scottish and Welsh middle-market to quality press, representing a sample from the two devolved nations in Great Britain. There are a number of Scottish papers nationally distributed in Scotland and it is possible to reflect the opposing sides of the campaign on the UK's place within the EU. In keeping with the greater number of Scottish papers, and in order to represent newspapers against and in favour of exiting the EU, the Scottish papers examined are the *Scottish Daily Express* and *Scottish Daily Mail* in favour of leaving the EU; and the quality broadsheet the *Herald* and middle-market tabloid the *Daily Record* in support of Remain. Scottish coverage of the referendum followed similar contours to that of the previous independence referendum in making the most of the uncertainty inherent in a significant change in the arrangements of state: previously, in respect of the potential break-up of the UK and now in the UK's proposed departure from the EU.

In contrast, the *Western Mail/Wales on Sunday* is the only Welsh national paper and it supported the remain campaign. Two other newspapers in Wales with some national prominence in the run-up to the referendum were the North Wales regional paper the *Daily Post*; and the South Wales regional the *Evening Post*. (The *Evening Post*'s online presence merged with *WalesOnline* [part of the *Western Mail*] in March 2017 [*WalesOnline* 2017].) Both Welsh regional papers claimed to have taken a neutral position on the 2016 EU referendum; however, a senior representative for the *Evening Post* acknowledges that the paper was criticized for 'leaning toward the Remain vote'. The Welsh component of the analysis, therefore, features the *Western Mail/Wales on Sunday*, the *Daily Post* and the *Evening Post*.

Across both case samples, the analysis focuses on the various lexical options used to define the terms of the debate. In this regard, we will follow the principles of CDA in seeing the choices and arrangements of language as concerned in the expression and the maintenance of relations of power (Fairclough 1995; Fairclough and Wodak 1997). Particularly, we are interested in how sustained lexical frames produced help shape media's contribution to the public sphere (Higgins 2017). CDA maintains a significant degree of flexibility in order to keep pace with the flexibility and dynamism associated with the political use of language. This adaptability in CDA is also necessary to understand the variety of contexts in which political discourse of the referendum unfolds, and the various contexts of interpretation these invite.

DISCOURSES OF DANGER

One of the frames of discussion in the run-up to the referendum concerned the 'dangers' that an exit from the EU posed. Discursive frames associated with crisis and imperilments have a long-standing association with significant political change (Hay 1999), and occupied a prominent place in public discourse around this referendum (Higgins 2016). Indeed, this continued after the result with President Obama engaging in such a frame to warn of a 'dangerous' nationalism in a post-EU setting (quoted in Squires 2016). A search on Lexis Nexis for appearances of 'referendum' and 'danger' during the three months up to the referendum yields a total of 190 articles in the Scottish newspapers and 36 articles in the Welsh newspapers, albeit that there is one more Scottish paper in the sample than Welsh. While not all instances in which the terms appeared in the same article offer a straightforward relationship between danger and the referendum outcome, the following extract from a Scottish *Herald* opinion article engages with this link in a vivid manner:

Extract: *Herald*, 18 June 2016 (Scotland)

1	[...]
2	WHATEVER the outcome of the referendum, politicians will have had
3	confirmed their obvious belief that they can obfuscate without fear of
4	retribution. Our democracy is in great danger, not only as a result of the
5	totally unacceptable behaviour of our elected representatives but also as a
6	consequence of the longstanding disengagement of the public from the
7	democratic processes, an eager acceptance of easy solutions and an
8	alarming willingness to indulge in scapegoating.
9	Nevertheless, the answer lies in the hands of the community of citizens, or at
10	least sufficient numbers thereof, assisted perhaps by those politicians who
11	recognise the danger our society is in. I would go so far as to suggest that
12	the public's reaction to the tactics adopted by both campaigns could be as
13	important as the outcome of the referendum. Disempowering cynicism and
14	despair, while welcomed by those who hold the reins of power, would be an
15	absolute disaster.
	[...]

A lexicon of menace dominates this extract, anchored with items such as 'retribution' and 'great danger'. Within this overarching discourse, the irresponsibility of politicians, anchored in their designation as 'elected representatives' (line 5), is amplified as 'totally unacceptable', and pursued in a sequence of negative constructions: 'easy solutions' (line 7), 'alarming willingness' (line 8) and 'absolute disaster' (line 15). Importantly, 'danger' itself is not offered as part of an assertion or political claim on the part of the writer, but instead provides the grounds for an account of the politicians' own understanding (as 'those [...] who recognise the danger our society is in' (lines 10–11).

However, the next extract, from the opposing *Scottish Daily Mail*, presents the notion of danger as an article of dispute. Indeed, the use of the word itself is outsourced to senior Bank of England official Mark Carney:

Extract: *Scottish Daily Mail*, 17 June 2016b (Scotland)

1	GIVEN his past as a banker with Goldman Sachs— arguably one of the
2	world's most amoral financial institutions—Mark Carney's conduct during
3	the referendum campaign will come as no surprise.
4	Both the Governor of the Bank of England and Goldman—a bank which was
5	inextricably linked to the greed and hubris that sparked the 2008 economic
6	crash—have issued dire warnings about what fate awaits post-Brexit.
7	But while the bank, which has considerable financial links to the EU, has
8	made its own position clear with a £500,000 donation to Remain, Mr Carney
9	implausibly insists that he is neutral.
10	The Mail disagrees with him. We find it difficult to reconcile his lurid public
11	statements about the dangers of leaving with his claim yesterday that he has
12	limited himself to fulfilling the Bank's 'statutory responsibilities'.

A parallel rhetoric of amplification is in evidence here, but rather than lending negative weight to any danger in leaving the EU this intensifies the negative portrayal of Carney and the Bank of England ('inextricably linked' line 5; 'considerable financial links', line 7). This lends an ironic tone to the modification of their warnings as 'dire' (line 6); and building on this mood of contempt, Carney's 'public statements about the dangers' are pre-defined as 'lurid' and juxtaposed with the formal register of the 'statutory responsibilities' of the Bank (line 12), rendered using the disassociating tactics of scare quotes. A similar use of 'danger' to characterize and then dismiss officially sanctioned warnings can be found in the framing of an expert voice in a *Scottish Daily Mail* report published three days earlier on 14 June 2016a: 'David Blake, professor of pension economics at Cass, which is based at City University London, accused the Treasury of churning out "grossly exaggerated" warnings on the dangers of Brexit' (*Scottish Daily Mail*, 14 June 2016a).

In the Wales case, the following *Western Mail* news article continues the theme of economic danger through highlighting an attack on the Leave campaign's 'dangerous fantasies' (line 1) by a group of leading economists in support of Remain:

Extract: *Western Mail*, 23 June 2016 (Wales)

1	LEAVE campaigners are misleading voters and using 'dangerous fantasies'
2	to support their economic case, according to several Nobel prize-winning
3	economists.
4	The group of 12, including 2015 victor Sir Angus Deaton, were joined by
5	more than 150 other economists to reiterate their support for Remain in the
6	final hours of the referendum campaign.
7	Their intervention came after Michael Gove compared economic experts
8	warning about the fall-out of Brexit to the Nazis smearing Albert Einstein in
9	the 1930s. The Economists for Remain statement said a recession is
10	'significantly more likely' due to the 'shock and uncertainty' should Brexit
11	occur, adding the cost of goods would increase due to a drop in the pound
12	and increased tariffs on imports.
13	[...]

A tone of trepidation and the ferocity of debate are further demonstrated in the rhetoric of the Leave campaign through reference to Nazi history (lines 7–9). This is immediately countered with an emphasis on economic 'shock and uncertainty' (line 10) and impacts on the pound (lines 11–12) in the event of Brexit.

Like the Scottish extracts, a discourse of peril pervades both sides and seems to be used as a rhetorical tool in order to amplify the tone of the debate. Linking these fears with an economic context serves to intensify this further. Dekavalla (2016) argues that the press frame referendums, like the one on Scottish independence, as they would General Election campaigns, and therefore focus on pragmatic outcomes like impacts on the economy. Although nationalism in Wales has not seen the same intensity of support as was demonstrated in Scotland during the 2014 independence referendum, there is initial evidence for a similar crisis frame (Higgins 2017) in which messages of economic dangers are embedded in Welsh press coverage of the EU referendum.

The Re-appropriation of Project Fear

Another prominent item of political coinage related to the perceived tone of the campaign is 'Project Fear'. In a manner related to the discourses of danger outlined above, this appeared as a disobliging sobriquet applied by supporters of the 2014 campaign for Scottish independence in order to condemn the tactics of those supporting Scotland's place in the UK. The basis of the project is that those in government, and keen to support the constitutional status quo, are well positioned to produce scare stories around the implications of change, with the apparatus of government and much of the media at their disposal.

Chaput (2010: 10) calls attention to the discursive power of 'fear', likening its use value to that of a 'commodity', able to lend an 'affective value or energy' to a 'given rhetorical situation'. The motif Project Fear was revitalized and used to frame many of the warnings of opponents of Brexit. In his debate clash with Nicola Sturgeon, Boris Johnson deployed this now-established trope as a means of diminishing the veracity of the Remain position. Ironically ventriloquizing Sturgeon's description of the anti-independence campaign from 2014 as 'miserable, negative and fear-based—and fear-based campaigning of this kind starts to insult people's intelligence' (quoted in Phipps 2016), Johnson thereby deployed dominant discourses from the previous Scottish referendum, bearing the implication that Sturgeon had previously opposed and now engaged in such tactics.

A search for the phrase 'Project Fear' through Lexis Nexis in the three months prior to the EU referendum reveals 233 examples of its use across UK newspapers. While at first glance it appears that 'Project Fear' presents what Pecheux (1988) describes as a 'preconstructed' item for the political lexicon (a rapidly established and loaded rhetorical weapon, based upon a more long-standing normative concern about the mood of political discourse), in Scotland in particular there is evidence of contestation and adaptability in its use. These extracts from popular tabloid the *Daily Record* and quality newspaper the *Herald*, a month apart, draw attention to the shift of Project Fear from its context in one referendum to its place in the next:

Extract: Crichton, *Daily Record*, 3 June 2016 (Scotland)

1	The big 'i' word (not independence). The flip side of economic uncertainty is
2	the Brexiteers' own Project Fear on immigration and the effect it will have on
3	the UK. People fear immigration and think their communities are changing
4	with no one asking them.

The re-appropriation of the description 'Project Fear' (line 2) is emphasized in the *Daily Record* extract by its designation as 'the Brexiteers' own' (line 2). To the initiated reader, a reference is offered to the former version of the Project in the mock assurance that the 'big "I" word' (line 1) does not refer to independence. The possible persuasiveness of the Project (contrary to the editorial agenda of the paper) is expressed in a third-person reference to the electorate as 'People' (line 2).

Extract: MacWhirter, *The Herald*, 3 May 2016 (Scotland)

1	You can see this in the EU referendum, where the self-same Project Fear
2	that defeated independence only 18 months ago has been rolled out to
3	oppose Brexit. It has almost been a comic parody. Day by day the press has
4	been filled with stories about currency instability, firms leaving, black holes in
5	the financial accounts. Even President Obama has stepped in, as he did
6	before the independence referendum.
7	Becoming a new country, like leaving the EU, involves a leap of faith and
8	modern electorates don't like taking chances. Why should they? Most of the
9	middle classes in Scotland are comfortably off and don't want to lose their
10	security and privileges. Setting up a new independent nation is not as difficult
11	as the Project Fear propagandists claim, but it would inevitably involve
12	disruption, uncertainty and difficult choices.

In the *Herald* extract, having already been named in the headline, Project Fear is presented as an established political strategy, stressed in the popular alliterative modifier 'self-same' (line 1). Popular language, a register ordinarily alien to the formal expression associated with the *Herald*, is also apparent in the active metaphors 'rolled out' (line 2), 'stepped in' (line 5) and popular idiom 'leap of faith' (line 7). The exposure of the *Herald* readership to the implications of any outcome is emphasized in their presentation in the third person, this time with greater socio-specificity as 'the middle classes in Scotland', with a three-part list deployed in rehearsing the dangers they face in 'disruption, uncertainty and difficult choices' (line 12). Even though the *Herald* then supported the aims of the previous version of Project Fear, the agents responsible for the current iteration are described in the heavily stigmatized terms of 'Project Fear propagandists' (line 11).

In North Wales, the following *Daily Post* extract conveys a more muted tone with a positive narrative of economic prosperity proposed as a result of a potential Brexit:

Extract: *Daily Post*, 16 April 2016 (Wales)

1	[...]
2	Vote Leave coordinator Matthew McKinnon will claim that Wales' steel
3	industry could have a better chance of survival if the country votes to quit the
4	EU on June 23.
5	Making the case for Brexit, [Liam] Fox urged Welsh voters to turn down 'EU
6	plans for a United States of Europe'.
7	He said: 'Leaving the EU and taking back control of our own affairs would be
8	a huge boost to public services in Wales, with more money available for
9	hospitals, schools, and local services. Proponents of 'project fear' claim that
10	Wales will be worse off financially if we leave the EU, but there is no such
11	thing as EU money—it's already yours.'
12	[...]

'Project fear' is used by the prominent Leave spokesperson Liam Fox (line 9) in its characteristically pejorative form, providing a loaded and substituted term of reference to the Remain campaign. There is a subtle, but evident, distinction between the positive messages of hope mooted in the event of a Brexit outcome (lines 2–4) and the framing of the Remain side's excessive circumspection. The use of the term 'United States of Europe' (line 6), which likens the trajectory of the EU to the type of union observed among the United States of America, is itself a cynical rhetorical tactic designed to inject fear into the minds of voters; a fear rooted in the perceived progressive loss of British sovereignty.

This rhetorical commoditization of 'fear' (Chaput 2010) that we see included in the quote attributed to Liam Fox is packaged together with messages that carry powerful political capital, particularly when embedded amid key political components (lines 3 and 9) that speak to the lives of ordinary voters in Wales. In doing so, the Leave campaign successfully capitalized on combining the versatile power of a fear-based discourse hidden amid a tone of hope, while strategically labelling their opposition (the status quo) as the propagators of Project Fear.

Two months later, the following feature article from the South Wales *Evening Post* turned Project Fear on its head and framed the fear-based narrative as a positive position taken by the Remain campaign:

Extract (feature): *Evening Post*, 14 June 2016 (Wales)

1	[...]
2	I've never met anyone in the Swansea Bay region who can give me an
3	example of how they've been disadvantaged first-hand by Britain's
4	membership of the EU.
5	The leave camp label the arguments to stay as 'Project Fear'. They're damn
6	right.
7	I'm fearful about taking a leap in the dark for no more than vague and
8	contradictory promises of jam tomorrow from people who I implicitly distrust.
9	It's like standing in front of an electrified fence with someone nudging you in
10	the back telling you to ignore the warning sign.
11	Sorry and all that, but when the Bank of England, Sir Terry Matthews and a
12	small cast of Nobel prize-winning scientists collectively talk about exercising
13	caution then my instinct is to listen up.
14	I have no idea what will happen if Britain leaves the European Union and
15	that's the problem.

The writer introduces Project Fear as Leave campaign rhetoric (line 5) and promptly claims it (lines 5–6) to support the argument for a Remain vote in the rest of the article. Such usage further demonstrates the versatility of Project Fear and its appropriateness as a 'preconstructed' rhetorical weapon. The explicit outpouring of fear (line 7) is symbolic of the tangible anxieties of the British electorate in the run-up to the EU referendum campaign; déjà vu for voters in Scotland. In contrast to the *Daily Post* article, the tone of this piece is characterized by an openness and blatant honesty, which piggybacks the credibility of leading economists (lines 11–13) (also featured in earlier extracts) in order to support the stance of the article, which in places conveys a tone of desperation.

So how was Project Fear dealt with in those newspapers that approved of exiting the EU and were therefore in accord with its overall purpose? What follow are references to Project Fear in the Leave-supporting *Scottish Daily Mail* and *Scottish Daily Express*:

Extract: Slack, *Scottish Daily Mail*, 17 June 2016b (Scotland)

1	Yesterday, the Bank issued a fresh warning that the pound would be hit if
2	Britain leaves the EU. But, speaking before the suspension of campaigning
3	yesterday, Mr Johnson hit back, saying: 'We're obviously going to be hearing
4	Project Fear moving into its final fusillade.
5	'It has failed to make much of an impact because everyone can remember
6	what the PM said only a few months ago when he said Britain would do very
7	well outside of the EU. The pound is roughly where it has been. It is no lower
8	today than it has been in the last few months.

Extract: *Scottish Daily Express*, 15 June 2016 (Scotland)

---

1   I would like to think we have now reached peak Project Fear. Forget David
2   Cameron's warning that we would cause World War Three if we leave the
3   EU, bonkers as that scare tactic was. Forget the idea that we would suddenly
4   be plunged into a recession from which there will be no escape. In fact,
5   forget all the nonsense the Remain camp have spouted as they desperately
6   try to stop the British people voting to leave.

The first extract pursues the same story as a *Mail* extract above on the 'warnings' of a senior official from the Bank of England. On this occasion, the article refers to Project Fear, outsourced as a direct quotation from Brexit-supporting MP Boris Johnson. The statement and response arrangement in which Johnson's words appear are presented in timely and vivid terms, with the bank's contribution described as a 'fresh warning' and Johnson's response expressed using the violent metaphor 'hit back', before Johnson develops this theme in his dismissal of Project Fear as a volley of shots ('final fusillade', line 4).

This dismissive reference to Project Fear is still more explicit in the next extract from the *Scottish Daily Express*. In dealing with the term itself, the prefix 'peak', denoting a fashion that has traversed its apex, is applied to Project Fear. An informal lexicon of dismissal is then scattered through the remainder of the extract, with the Project Fear-associated 'scare tactics' described using the mildly taboo term of 'bonkers', and the mockingly exaggerated past participle 'plunged' in referring to the prospect of recession.

In summary, while there is ample evidence of newspapers' willingness to entertain perspectives on the referendum that are not necessarily supportive of their editorial line, Project Fear offers a particular kind of discursive tool: one that enables the portrayal of the opposing arguments as marshalled and co-ordinated with particular political ends in mind, and therefore able to be dismissed on the basis of motive. The negative weight of 'fear' is consistent with Project Fear's motivated status as an exercise in political cynicism. However, its overtly contested status in public discourse also enables it to be used to highlight such positive interpretations as the virtue of caution.

TONE OF THE DEBATE

We have attempted to show that, for all their potency, discourses of fear and danger can be deployed flexibly and correspond with strategic uses of language. Indeed, contrary to the aims of 'Project Fear', earlier research by Huysmans (2000) shows how notions of imperilment can be mobilized against the EU in dispute over policy. Across the European press, too, Trenz (2007) shows how the relationship between the EU and its mediation can be characterized by 'struggle'. This chimes with the analysis of Stråth and Wodak (2009: 32), who describe any European public sphere as a maelstrom of competing narratives of national identity and interest, producing a mediated vision of the EU that produces, in their words, 'an emphasis on crisis and value contention'.

Picking up in particular on Huysmans's theme of migration, Wodak (2015) discusses the political use of fear within discourses around right-wing populism. For Wodak, fear is directed towards establishing threats to national and cultural identity and producing grounds for 'othering' a politics of exclusion. Our own analysis develops Wodak's (2015: 72) argument that fear is mobilized in defence of a cultural and national ideal: a set of inherently-national norms that are under threat from outsiders and the imposition of diversity. In our analysis, discourses of fear extend across a variety of threats to the political settlement, including democratic challenges to constitutional state arrangements and established interstate relationships. As Chaput (2010) describes it, fear offers a means of generating an 'affective energy' in favour of commitment to the political status quo.

At the UK-wide level, this formed part of a more broadly expressed set of concerns about the aggressiveness of the debate. Reflecting on the death of Labour MP Jo Cox, London Mayor Sadiq Khan characterized the referendum campaign until that point as producing a 'climate of hatred, of poison, of negativity, of cynicism' (quoted in Mason 2016). While undoubtedly warranted by some of the public discourse, this drew upon and contributed to wider concerns around the poisoning of the well of public discourse.

CONCLUSION

It remains to be seen whether this campaign signals the shift from what Mouffe (2005) describes as an 'agonistic' clash of ideas to an 'antagonistic' trade of insult and spite. It may be that the bipolar character of a referendum, and the comparative loosening of the bonds of party, encourages a more rancorous mode of engagement. However, the Scottish experience of the two campaigns suggests that the tone of the campaign is as much determined by such conditions as the political personas involved and the stakes of their involvement. In Wales, perhaps driven by the nation's historic battle to maintain and develop industrial continuity, and questions about how EU membership has benefited that battle, the tone of the debate on both sides seems to have centred on concerns related to employment and economic prosperity.

REFERENCES

ACADEMIC SOURCES

Chaput, Catherine. 2010. Introduction: Fear, Affective Energy, and the Political Economy of Global Capitalism. In *Entertaining Fear: Rhetoric and the Political Economy of Social Control*, ed. Catherine Chaput, M. J. Braun, and Danika M. Brown, 1–22. New York: Peter Lang.

Dekavalla, Marina. 2016. Framing Referendum Campaigns: The 2014 Scottish Independence Referendum in the Press. *Media, Culture and Society* 38 (6): 793–810.

Fairclough, Norman. 1995. *Media Discourse*. London: Arnold.

Fairclough, Norman, and Ruth Wodak. 1997. Critical Discourse Analysis. In *Discourse as Social Interaction*, ed. Teun A. van Dijk, 258–284. London: Sage.

Hay, Colin. 1999. Crisis and the Structural Transformation of the State: Interrogating the Process of Change. *British Journal of Politics and International Relations* 1 (3): 317–344.

Higgins, Michael. 2016. Remembrance of Referendums Past: Scotland in the Campaign. In *EU Referendum Analysis 2016: Media, Voters and the Campaign*, ed. Dan Jackson, Einar Thorsen, and Dominic Wring. Bournemouth: CSJCC.

Higgins, Michael. 2017. Impending Crisis in Scotland: Political Discourse in Interesting Times. In *Crisis and the Media*, ed. Marianna Patrona. Amsterdam: John Benjamins.

Huysmans, Jef. 2000. The European Union and the Securitization of Migration. *Journal of Common Market Studies* 38 (5): 751–777.

Jeffery, C., and D. Hough. 2009. Understanding Post-devolution Elections in Scotland and Wales in Comparative Perspective. *Party Politics* 15 (2): 219–240.

Mouffe, Chantal. 2005. *On the Political*. Abingdon: Routledge.

Pecheux, Michel. 1988. Discourse: Structure or Event? In *Marxism and the Interpretation of Culture*, ed. Cary Nelson et al., 633–650. Basingstoke: Macmillan.

Stråth, Bo, and Ruth Wodak. 2009. Europe—Discourse—Politics—Media—History: Constructing "Crises"? In *The European Public Sphere and the Media: Europe in Crisis*, ed. Anna Triandafyllidou, Ruth Wodak, and Michal Kryzyzanowski, 15–33. Palgrave: Basingstoke.

Trenz, Hans-Jörg. 2007. *Quo vadis* Europe? Quality Newspapers Struggling for European Unity. In *The European Union and the Public Sphere*, ed. Fossum John Erick and Philip Schlesinger, 89–109. London: Routledge.

Wodak, Ruth. 2015. *The Politics of Fear*. London: Sage.

NEWSPAPER ARTICLES

BBC. 2016. EU Referendum Results. *BBC News*. www.bbc.co.uk/news/politics/eu_referendum/results (Accessed 20 March 2017).

Crichton, Torcuil. 2016. Turning Project Fear to the Remain Agenda. *Daily Record*, June 3.

Daily Post. 2016. 'Fox and Hain Clash on 'Brexit to Make Wales Better-Off' Claim; EU Referendum Campaign Takes off; "Leave" Puts Focus on Steel Crisis at Launch', *Daily Post*, April 16.

Evening Post. 2016. A Choice Between the Frying Pan and the Fire. *Evening Post*, June 14.

MacWhirter, Ian. 2016. SNP Would be Wise to Continue to Pursue Independence by Stealth. *The Herald*, May 3.

Mason, Rowena. 2016. Sadiq Khan Calls for More Respectful Tone in EU Referendum Debate. *The Guardian*, June 17.

Phipps, Clair. 2016. EU Referendum Morning Briefing: What We Learned from Sturgeon v Johnson. *The Guardian*, June 10.

Scottish Daily Express. 2015. Scare Tactics from Project Fear Are Ever More Absurd. *Scottish Daily Express*, June 15.

Scottish Daily Mail. 2016a. Treasury an EU Propaganda Machine, Warn Academics. *Scottish Daily Mail*, June 14.

Scottish Daily Mail. 2016b. Bank Chief Who Can't Stop Scaremongering. *Scottish Daily Mail*, June 17.

Slack, James. 2016. 'Scaremonger' Carney Angers Senior Tories. *Scottish Daily Mail*, June 17.

Squires, Nick. 2016. Obama Warns of Dangers of Crude Nationalism in Wake of Brexit and Election of Trump. *The Guardian*, November 15.

The Herald. 2016. We Should Look at Past Before Deciding Which Way to Vote. *The Herald*, June 18.

WalesOnline. 2017. WalesOnline and the South Wales Evening Post Have Merged. *WalesOnline*. http://www.walesonline.co.uk/news/wales-news/walesonline-south-wales-evening-post-12703451 (Accessed 21 March 2017).

Western Mail. 2016. Leave Campaign's Danger Fantasies. *Western Mail*, June 23.

CHAPTER 4

The EU Referendum 2016 on Scottish Television

Marina Dekavalla

INTRODUCTION

The 2016 EU referendum was arguably a critical point not only in the relationship of the United Kingdom (UK) with the European Union (EU) but also in that of Scotland with the rest of the UK. It came two years after Scotland held its own referendum on becoming an independent country, where Scotland's continued EU membership was one of the issues in the debate (Kenealy 2014). In the months that followed the EU referendum, its outcome was linked with the possibility of a second referendum on Scottish independence, with the Scottish National Party (SNP) proposing in early 2017 to give the electorate another say on this issue before the finalization of the process that would take the UK out of the EU.

Although the UK has long been considered one of the most sceptical members of the EU (Haesley 2001), Scotland tends to be generally perceived as less Eurosceptic than Britain overall (Curtice 2016). Attitudes towards the EU in Scotland became gradually more positive between the two devolution referendums in the 1970s and the 1990s, and some even

M. Dekavalla (✉)
University of Sussex, Brighton, UK
e-mail: M.Dekavalla@sussex.ac.uk

© The Author(s) 2018　　　　　　　　　　　　　　　　　　　　61
A. Ridge-Newman et al. (eds.), *Reporting the Road to Brexit*,
https://doi.org/10.1007/978-3-319-73682-2_4

claim that the prospect of Scotland becoming an independent country within the EU at some future time had an impact on the vote in favour of Scottish devolution in 1997 (Dardanelli 2005). More recently, the number of those in Scotland who would like to see a reduction of the EU's powers increased (Curtice 2016), but this did not translate into outright support for leaving the EU, as the result of the referendum demonstrated.

In 2016, Scotland voted to stay in the EU with 62% of the overall vote, the highest among the four UK nations. In every constituency the majority of voters opted to remain, although there were differences between individual areas; in Edinburgh, for instance, the Remain vote reached almost 75%, whereas in Moray it was just 50.1% (*BBC News* 2016). In most regions, though, the Remain vote was nearer the Scottish average of about 60%.

This chapter analyses the coverage of the 2016 EU referendum on British and Scottish television, comparing the BBC's Scottish early evening news bulletin, *Reporting Scotland*, with its UK-wide equivalent, BBC *News at Six*. It applies frame analysis to address the question of how the referendum was constructed in the two news programmes. It also compares findings from this analysis with previous research on how the 2014 Scottish referendum was framed in Scottish media (Dekavalla 2016a, b, 2018) and finds that the strategic game frame and the policy frame were the most dominant ways of defining both referendums, especially in the final month, although in 2016 there were differences in their prominence between the Scottish and the British bulletin.

MEDIA FRAMING

Frames are cognitive schemata which help us make sense of issues and events by defining 'what is going on' in a specific context (Goffman 1974). They are central in how we understand a situation and how we communicate about it to others; therefore they are key structuring components of news reports. To frame is 'to select some aspects of a perceived reality and make them more salient in a communicating text, in such a way as to promote a particular problem definition, causal interpretation, moral evaluation, and/or treatment recommendation' (Entman 1993: 52).

Frames are promoted by interest groups involved in an event or issue, and different frames compete with each other for prominence in the media and in public discourse. In the case of referendums on European integration, political coalitions and actors promote different understandings of what is at stake, and these frames encourage voters to think about their decision along specific lines. The frames promoted by political campaigns have been said to play an important role in public perceptions, especially when they are 'vivid, concrete, image-provoking, emotionally compelling frames that contain negative information'; such messages, it is argued, have been successful in altering people's positive views of the EU in past referendums in France, the Netherlands, Luxembourg and Ireland (Atickan 2015: 7–8).

Although it is well established that public opinion is more volatile in referendums than in elections (LeDuc 2002) and voting intentions often change during the campaign period, the proposal that voters can be swayed by media frames in a straightforward and consistent manner is highly questionable and is challenged by a number of factors, including voters' pre-existing knowledge and opinions, experience, influences from their direct environment and how credible they perceive different media or political sources to be (Druckman 2001). Particularly in relation to media coverage of the EU, the media have been found to play an important role in opinion formation, but only when citizens are exposed to a considerable amount of coverage containing the same evaluative tone; when they are exposed to mixed messages, as is often the case in referendum campaigns, the influence is less easy to prove (de Vreese and Boomgaarden 2006).

In any case, the frames that the media put forward remain significant in shaping public debate, if not necessarily private opinions, and in providing audiences with the available range of definitions from which to choose how they understand what is going on and based on which factors they are meant to reach a decision on how to vote in the referendum.

This chapter will thus explore which frames were put forward in the coverage of the EU referendum on the BBC's most watched news bulletins in Scotland and in the rest of the UK, in order to establish similarities and differences in how the campaign was defined publicly. Considering the perceived distinctiveness of Scottish public opinion on the EU as discussed at the start of the chapter, one would expect the debate to be framed differently between the two news programmes, which are produced to address different national demographics.

METHOD

The game (or strategy) frame and the policy (or issue) frame are two key ways of representing political issues, across many different national contexts. The game frame constructs politics as a contest between political actors, focusing on who is winning and who is losing, what strategies they employ to win, and how they perform in the competition. Cappella and Jamieson identify its indicators in media texts as consisting in a prominence of: '(1) winning and losing as the central concern; (2) the language of wars, games, and competition; (3) a story with performers, critics, and audience (voters); (4) centrality of performance, style, and perception of the candidate; (5) heavy weighing of polls and the candidates' standing in them' (1997: 33). This frame is often contrasted with the issue (or policy) frame, which focuses on matters of public policy, politicians' proposals on how they should be dealt with and the implications these may have for the public (Lawrence 2000).

These two frames have been found to dominate the coverage of election campaigns (Strömbäck and Dimitrova 2006; Strömbäck and van Aelst 2010) but also that of referendums in different countries (Robinson 1998; de Vreese and Semetko 2004), including the coverage of the 2014 Scottish independence referendum (Dekavalla 2016a, b). In fact the coverage of the 2014 referendum in both Scottish television and newspapers was consistently framed as being about the game of the campaign and as a decision on different policy areas, with the game frame becoming most prominent across mainstream media towards the end of the campaign (Dekavalla 2016a, b, 2018). Other frames, which were present in that coverage but were not as prominent, included the identity frame (proposing that the referendum was a decision about national identity), self-determination (the decision was about Scotland taking control of its own affairs and making its own democratic decisions), divorce (the referendum was the potential dissolution of an interpersonal relationship between partners), national division (the referendum was a cause of division in society) and democratic achievement (the referendum was a major achievement of democratic processes) (Dekavalla 2016a, b, 2018). All these frames could potentially also apply in the case of the 2016 EU referendum which, like the 2014 independence referendum, dealt with the severing of a political and economic union.

The present study adopts an inductive approach (Semetko and Valkenburg 2000), and measures the prominence of the above, previously established frames in the BBC's UK-wide and Scottish early evening news bulletins. The sample includes all news items about the 2016 EU referendum that were broadcast on the BBC's *News at Six* and *Reporting Scotland* between 23 May and 23 June 2016. These programmes are the most watched news bulletins produced by the broadcaster for a UK-wide and a Scottish audience respectively (BBC Scotland 2016). Both are shown in Scotland, with the Scottish bulletin following the UK-wide one. Therefore, as Scottish viewers have access to both, *Reporting Scotland* tends not to repeat the same coverage presented on the *News at Six*, unless an item shown in the UK-wide programme specifically takes place in Scotland. The indicators set out above were used to identify whether each frame was present or absent in the news items (the coding was done on a presence-absence basis, not on the basis of the frames' relative weighting inside the story), while the date and duration of each item were also recorded.

What Was the EU Referendum About?

In this section, I will suggest that three features distinguished the coverage on BBC *Reporting Scotland* from that on the *News at Six*: the Scottish bulletin had considerably less coverage of the EU referendum overall, it focused less on the political game of the campaign and the performance of politicians, and it gave less attention to debates on immigration.

A key characteristic of the Scottish coverage was that there was rather little of it. There were just 29 news items about the EU referendum in the Scottish bulletin, with a total duration of 2 hours 13 minutes. Of this time, 47 minutes were taken up by a debate between Scottish politicians representing the two options of the referendum question, which was staged inside the BBC building in Glasgow on 20 June, and was shown as part of that day's news bulletin. Without this lengthy debate item, the purely news-based coverage of the Scottish programme amounted to 1 hour and 26 minutes. By contrast, the UK-wide bulletin consisted exclusively of news updates (any political debates were shown as separate programmes outside the bulletin at other times) and included 48 news items with a total duration of 3 hours and 40 minutes. If one excludes the Scottish studio debate, the news coverage of the UK-wide bulletin in the final month of the campaign was more than double in length.

This difference suggests that the EU referendum was a more newsworthy topic for the UK-wide than for the Scottish bulletin. As discussed at the start of this chapter, public opinion about EU membership in Scotland was seen as less divided than in other parts of the UK and it was widely expected in opinion polls before the referendum that Scots would vote to remain in the EU. At the same time, all the major Scottish political parties officially supported the Remain camp and there was little disagreement among politicians in relation to the issue. Therefore, news values like elite conflict or controversy (Harcup and O'Neil 2001) were absent in the Scottish case, making the referendum a less newsworthy topic for journalists.

The key battleground of elite conflict was in London. The most prominent figures of both the Leave and Remain campaigns were senior figures of (primarily) the Conservatives and the opposition parties at Westminster, and their daily activities were covered extensively on BBC *News at Six*. It would therefore have been superfluous for the Scottish bulletin to repeat the same coverage, without any noteworthy controversy between Scottish political actors to add to the debate.

Apart from the difference in the overall amount of coverage, this factor seems to also partly explain the relative prominence of different frames in the coverage of the two bulletins. As can be seen in Fig. 4.1, the strategic game frame (which emphasizes the process of the campaign, the strategies of the two sides, the performance of politicians and the

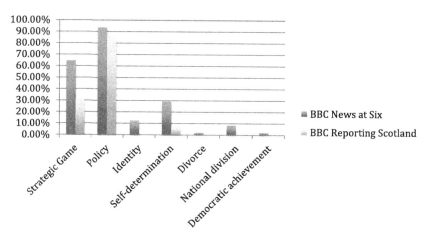

Fig. 4.1 Prominence of frames per news programme (Percentage of programme's overall coverage)

competition between them in opinion polls) was present in 65% of the *News at Six*'s coverage and in only 31% of the *Reporting Scotland* stories.

It is thus clear that for the UK-wide coverage, the game of the campaign determined to a great extent what the referendum was about. Political coalitions advocating each of the two outcomes were considerably more active in promoting their messages on the UK-wide programme in an attempt to win over public opinion, and the political game became a more central organizing concept in the UK-wide than in the Scottish bulletin. In the latter, politicians did not appear as often, probably because the official position of most Scottish parties was supportive of remaining in the EU (with the exception of UKIP and individual politicians within the other parties), and this was also in line with public opinion before the vote. Westminster politicians were not prominent in the Scottish coverage, as their views and statements were primarily dealt with in the UK-wide bulletin.

The policy frame, on the other hand, received similar degrees of attention across the two news programmes. It was present in 94% of the *News at Six* coverage and 86.2% of the *Reporting Scotland* equivalent (Fig. 4.1). It was the most prominent of all frames in both programmes, which suggests that in both cases the emphasis was on the impact staying in or leaving the EU would have on different policy areas. The decision therefore was framed as a pragmatic one, to be based on which outcome would deliver better conditions for practical aspects affecting citizens' lives.

There was however some disparity regarding the types of policy that received attention under this frame. Immigration (together with economic policy) dominated the debate on the *News at Six*, but it had a rather marginal role in the Scottish coverage. The centrality of the impact of the referendum on immigration policy and the economy on the *News at Six* is consistent with the overall focus on these issues across the print and broadcast coverage of the EU referendum in England (Cushion and Lewis 2016; Deacon et al. 2016).

Economic policy received considerable attention in both bulletins, but in Scotland the focus was not on macro-economics or the overall economy of the UK, but on the local economy in different Scottish regions. Moreover, several news items in the Scottish programme looked at the impact of the vote on agriculture, fisheries and transport in different parts of Scotland, interviewing local actors and voters. The debate on *Reporting Scotland* was thus not only or primarily about the common market and

Britain's access to it, but also about the impact of the outcome on various sectors of the Scottish industries. This gave it a diversity of focus, touching on issues that were not central in the UK-wide coverage.

Considerations about the perceived benefits of EU membership on a country's economy are a key factor in shaping attitudes about the EU in all European countries (Curtice 2016). Another important influence involves national identity. According to Curtice:

> [...] voters who have a strong sense of national identity together with little in the way of European identity are inclined to question the right of EU institutions to 'meddle' in their country's affairs, may well have concerns that their country's distinctive culture is threatened by the EU's activities, and are more likely to be concerned about the impact of EU migration. (2016: 9)

However, the national identity and self-determination frames were not particularly prominent in any of the news coverage. The national identity frame in the present analysis consisted in explicit references to British (or Scottish) people belonging to a distinctive national community defined by common values, traditions, its own 'way of life' and a common history. The indicators of the self-determination frame included references to the UK managing its own affairs, determining its own future, or making its own decisions without the EU 'meddling' in its affairs. Both frames were relatively marginal in the coverage compared to the policy and game frames (Fig. 4.1).

Although issues of identity were not discussed explicitly in symbolic and abstract terms, in the UK bulletin they did translate into questions around the pragmatic issue of the impact of EU immigration to Britain. Concerns about immigration account for a significant part of the debate under the policy frame on the *News at Six, as explained earlier.* These debates were much less present on *Reporting Scotland,* an absence that might potentially be connected to perceptions of the public's attitudes on immigration, and/or the discourses promoted by political actors in Scotland, as will be discussed directly below.

Overall, public opinion on immigration in Scotland is less negative compared to any other part of the UK except London (McCollum et al. 2014). Although a majority of Scots may wish to see immigration reduced (WhatScotlandThinks.org 2014; The Migration Observatory 2014), this proportion is not as large as in other parts of the UK.

The difference has been attributed to mainstream political discourse in Scotland portraying immigration as being useful for the nation, to the fact that Scotland has long experienced population loss through emigration and therefore it relies on immigration for stability, and also to the fact that it has traditionally had a relatively small number of immigrants (McCollum et al. 2014).

Perhaps the first of the above factors, relating to the predominant political discourse on this issue, may also explain why the immigration debate did not become as prominent in the Scottish coverage. Scottish nationalism, as expressed by the SNP over the last decades, has emphasized an inclusive, civic definition of Scottishness (Johns and Mitchell 2016) which views immigration positively. Other mainstream Scottish parties which do not support independence have not challenged this inclusive and civic perception of Scottish identity, and there is a general political consensus in Holyrood in favour of immigration and diversity, as opposed to the more cautious approach of Westminster politicians (Bond 2017: 23). Therefore, during the EU referendum there were few Scottish political sources (at least among the key political players) who might promote a debate on immigration along the lines of the discussion that took place South of the border, and this was likely reflected in the television news coverage analysed here.

As has been seen so far, although the EU referendum was an important topic in the agenda of the Scottish news bulletin, it did not occupy as much space as in the London-produced programme and focused less on what the political campaigns had to say in the competition against each other and more on the impact of the decision for different aspects of policy. This treatment contrasts with the coverage of the independence referendum a couple of years earlier.

In the final month of the 2014 Scottish independence referendum, *Reporting Scotland* had broadcast 8 hours and 32 minutes of news about that referendum. In addition to this, BBC Scotland also had considerable current affairs coverage throughout that month, including the daily programme *Scotland 2014* and a range of one-off debates and special productions. The quantity of Scottish news coverage dedicated to the 2014 referendum in the final month was therefore considerably higher than both *Reporting Scotland's* and the *News at Six's* equivalent coverage during the last month of the 2016 EU referendum campaign.

Moreover, in 2014 there was considerably more focus on the process and contest of the campaign in Scotland. Some 70% of BBC Scotland's overall referendum coverage in 2014 focused on the strategic game of the campaign and 68% contained the policy frame (Dekavalla 2016b, 2018). By contrast to the 2016 EU referendum, in the Scottish referendum Scottish parties took opposing positions in the debate, and senior politicians were the key sources used by journalists in that coverage (Dekavalla and Jelen-Sanchez 2016). The game frame was thus employed to establish journalistic distance from political opponents and to provide an exciting narrative structure to what was a highly contested, binary decision on which public opinion was split (Dekavalla 2016b). In comparison, the 2016 EU membership debate in Scotland was not as highly contested, did not involve the major political players, and took place with a sense of distance from the main stage of the political contest in London. This allowed television to explore a wider range of issues outside the formal political agenda.

CONCLUSION

The 2016 EU referendum in Scotland was very different from the experience of the independence referendum a couple of years earlier. The Scottish independence debate in 2014 was contentious, dominated by political elites, and there was a perception among the public that the coverage of the two sides of the argument in the mainstream media could have been fairer. In 2016, by contrast, the EU membership debate in Scotland was broadly consensual, there were no major clashes or any controversy about the content of media coverage, and the television coverage focused on the 'issues' and not on the process of the campaign.

The controversy in 2016 was rather about the coverage of the referendum outside Scotland, where the UK-wide media were criticized for failing to scrutinize claims made by the two campaigns; question the statistical evidence presented by the two sides to back their claims; challenge the truthfulness and credibility of politicians' competing claims; and allow independent non-partisan actors much space in the debate (Cushion and Lewis 2016). The consensual nature of the debate in Scotland is likely to have meant less pressure for journalists covering it, and more freedom for them to cover it in a way that was diverse and inclusive of different issues and actors.

The outcome of the referendum in Scotland was in line with opinion polls and predictions long before the vote, as discussed earlier in this chapter. Thus, this case study does not provide fertile ground to analyse media or campaign effects on voters, as there appeared to be little shift in Scottish opinion during the campaign. It may rather be a more promising case to explore the processes through which the political climate and mainstream perceptions of public opinion influence the way in which the media deal with a potentially controversial issue.

The EU referendum in Scotland was arguably positioned nearer the outer borders rather than the centre of the sphere of legitimate controversy: although different points of view existed and were covered in the news, there was also a perceived agreement in political and public opinion. This is likely to have had an impact on the nature of the coverage North of the border.

In the aftermath of the 2016 referendum, the debate in Scotland shifted onto the potential impact the difference in voting between the UK nations might have for the future of the British Union. Although all the key political actors agreed in their support for staying in the EU, they did not equally support the Scottish Government's proposal to hold a second independence referendum in a bid to keep Scotland in the common market. Future debates on the issue in the media are likely to be more contested than the EU referendum campaign, as national independence is likely to remain part of future conversations on Brexit (the UK's exit from the EU) within the Scottish context.

REFERENCES

Atickan, E. 2015. *Framing the European Union. The Power of Political Arguments in Shaping European Integration.* Cambridge: Cambridge University Press.

BBC Scotland. 2016. Annual Review 2015/16. http://downloads.bbc.co.uk/scotland/aboutus/management_review_2015_2016.pdf (Accessed 27 March 2017).

BBC News. 2016. EU Referendum Results. http://www.bbc.co.uk/news/politics/eu_referendum/results (Accessed 27 March 2017).

Bond, R. 2017. Minorities and Diversity in Scotland: Evidence from the 2011 Census. *Scottish Affairs* 26 (1): 23–47.

Cappella, J., and K. Jamieson. 1997. *Spiral of Cynicism: The Press and the Public Good.* New York: Oxford University Press.

Curtice, J. 2016. How Deeply Does Britain's Euroscepticism Run? NatCen Report. http://whatukthinks.org/eu/wp-content/uploads/2016/02/Analysis-paper-5-How-deeply-does-Britains-Euroscepticism-run.pdf (Accessed 27 March 2017).

Cushion, S., and J. Lewis. 2016. Scrutinising Statistical Claims and Constructing Balance: Television News Coverage of the 2016 EU Referendum. In *EU Referendum Analysis 2016: Media, Voters and the Campaign*, ed. D. Jackson, E. Thorsen, and D. Wring, 40. Poole: CSJCC Bournemouth University.

Dardanelli, P. 2005. Democratic Deficit or the Europeanisation of Secession? Explaining the Devolution Referendums in Scotland. *Political Studies* 53: 320–342.

de Vreese, C., and H. Boomgaarden. 2006. Media Effects on Public Opinion About the Enlargement of the European Union. *Journal of Common Market Studies* 44 (2): 419–436.

de Vreese, C., and H. Semetko. 2004. *Political Campaigning in Referendums: Framing the Referendum Issue*. Abingdon: Routledge.

Deacon, D., J. Downey, E. Harmer, J. Stanyer, and D. Wring. 2016. The Narrow Agenda: How the News Media Covered the Referendum. In *EU Referendum Analysis 2016: Media, Voters and the Campaign*, ed. D. Jackson, E. Thorsen, and D. Wring, 34. Poole: CSJCC Bournemouth University.

Dekavalla, M. 2016a. Framing Referendum Campaigns: The 2014 Scottish Independence Referendum in the Press. *Media, Culture and Society* 38 (6): 793–810.

Dekavalla, M. 2016b. Issue and Game Frames in the News: Frame-Building Factors in Television Coverage of the 2014 Scottish Independence Referendum. *Journalism*, Online First, https://doi.org/10.1177/1464884916674231.

Dekavalla, M. 2018. *Framing Referendum Campaigns in the News*. Manchester: Manchester University Press.

Dekavalla, M., and A. Jelen-Sanchez. 2016. Whose Voices Are Heard in the News? A Study of Sources in Television Coverage of the Scottish Independence Referendum. *British Politics*, Online First, https://doi.org/10.1057/s41293-016-0026-4.

Druckman, J.N. 2001. The Implications of Framing Effects for Citizen Competence. *Political Behaviour* 23 (3): 225–256.

Entman, R. 1993. Framing: Toward Clarification of a Fractured Paradigm. *Journal of Communication* 43 (4): 51–58.

Goffman, E. 1974. *Frame Analysis: An Essay on the Organisation of Experience*. New York: Harper Colophon.

Haesley, R. 2001. Euroskeptics, Europhiles and Instrumental Europeans. European Attachment in Scotland and Wales. *European Union Politics* 2 (1): 81–102.

Harcup, T., and D. O'Neil. 2001. What Is News? Galtung and Ruge Revisited. *Journalism Studies* 2 (2): 261–280.

Johns, R., and J. Mitchell. 2016. *Takeover: Explaining the Extraordinary Rise of the SNP*. London: Biteback.

Kenealy, D. 2014. Much Ado About (Scotland in) Europe. *Scottish Affairs* 23 (3): 369–380.

Lawrence, R. 2000. Game-Framing the Issues: Tracking the Strategy Frame in Public Policy News. *Political Communication* 17 (2): 93–114.

LeDuc, L. 2002. Referendums and Elections: How Do Campaigns Differ? In *Do Political Campaigns Matter? Campaign Effects in Elections and Referendums*, ed. D. Farrell and R. Schmitt-Beck, 145–162. London: Routledge.

McCollum, D., B. Nowok, and S. Tindal. 2014. Public Attitudes Towards Migration in Scotland: Exceptionality and Possible Policy Implications. *Scottish Affairs* 23 (1): 79–102.

Robinson, G. 1998. *Constructing the Quebec Referendum: French and English Media Voices*. Toronto: University of Toronto Press.

Semetko, H., and P. Valkenburg. 2000. Framing European Politics: A Content Analysis of Press and Television News. *Journal of Communication* 50 (2): 93–109.

Strömbäck, J. and D. Dimitrova. 2006. Political and Media Systems Matter. A Comparison of Election News Coverage in Sweden and the United States. *International Journal of Press/Politics*, 11 (4): 131–147.

Strömbäck, J., and P. Van Aelst. 2010. Exploring Some Antecedents of the Media's Framing of Election News: A Comparison of Swedish and Belgian Election News. *International Journal of Press/Politics* 15 (1): 41–59.

The Migration Observatory. 2014. Immigration and Independence: Public Opinion on Immigration in Scotland in the Context of the Referendum Debate, February 10. http://www.migrationobservatory.ox.ac.uk/wp-content/uploads/2016/04/Report-Immigration_Independence.pdf (Accessed 27 March 2017).

What Scotland Thinks. 2014. Do You Think the Number of Immigrants to Britain Should Be Increased, Remain the Same as It Is, or Reduced? Survey Results. http://whatscotlandthinks.org/questions/do-you-think-the-number-of-immigrants-to-britain-should-be-increased-remain-the (Accessed 27 March 2017).

CHAPTER 5

'A Pit We Have Dug Ourselves': The EU Referendum and the Welsh Democratic Deficit

Simon Gwyn Roberts

Introduction

The apparently self-destructive paradox whereby those areas that have benefited most from EU investment recorded particularly high 'leave' votes was widely covered in the news media after the 2016 EU referendum. Post-industrial areas were among the most likely to vote leave, although the focus on them was arguably unhelpfully reductive, with Wales a particularly frequent target for journalistic inquiry. Newspaper features tended to focus on forensic dissections of the socio-economic circumstances of the South Wales valleys. The *Guardian*'s Adittya Chakrabortty (2016), for example, filed a 1500-word feature from South Wales on 7 June, using it as an exemplar for the wider themes on several additional occasions both before and after the vote. The clear subtext behind such pieces was that 20 years of devolution, a disproportionate amount of EU structural funding, and an oft-stressed, new, national

S. G. Roberts (✉)
University of Chester, Chester, UK
e-mail: Simon.roberts@chester.ac.uk

© The Author(s) 2018
A. Ridge-Newman et al. (eds.), *Reporting the Road to Brexit*,
https://doi.org/10.1007/978-3-319-73682-2_5

self-confidence should have seen Wales vote firmly for remain in a deliberate Scottish-style attempt to separate itself from England. The Welsh 'leave' vote appeared to be a bid for political and national oblivion: final confirmation of the *Economist's* old mocking description of the country of 'And Wales', forever dependent on England and now inextricably entwined in its post-Brexit (Britain's exit from the EU) future.

The contrast with Scotland was painful for many Welsh politicians, particularly those from Plaid Cymru (the Welsh nationalist party) which has spent recent years pushing a civic nationalist, strongly pro-EU agenda echoing that of the SNP and specifically designed to broaden its appeal to encompass post-industrial regions of South Wales. Prior to the referendum. Plaid Cymru MEP Jill Evans voiced her fears that 'the simple mathematics of a referendum may see Wales dragged out of the EU against our wishes' (Evans 2016). For Plaid, however, even this 'worst case scenario' proved to be wishful thinking, with Welsh voting effectively mirroring that of England. In the immediate aftermath of the vote, the BBC's Nick Servini (2016) tweeted: 'Plaid clearly devastated. Rhun ap Iorwerth [former BBC journalist and Plaid Assembly Member] says the poorest will pay the price and we have woken up into a pit we have dug ourselves.' The immediate diagnosis seemed clear. The dissatisfaction with Labour, exploited so successfully by the SNP in Scotland, expressed itself in Wales not in support for the civic nationalism and pro-European sentiments of Plaid Cymru, but rather the populist British nationalism of UKIP.

Contained within the overarching theme of the sharp and seemingly baffling contrast with Scotland also lies a more nuanced and coherent explanation for the Welsh vote that this chapter proposes to explore. It will argue that two related factors, both revolving around the wider media, provide some explanation for the Welsh decision: first, the fragmented cultural and political geography of Wales, with the Welsh language a key contextual factor, central as it has naturally been to processes of post-devolution 'nation building' and, historically, to the concept of Welsh nationalism itself; second, the relative lack of pan-Welsh institutions beyond the National Assembly, in particular the lack of independent English-language news media, meaning Welsh voters were almost entirely dependent on a combination of the BBC and the message from the London tabloids, which retain immense cultural and political traction over the border despite declining circulations. The lack of independent English-language Welsh media has long been identified as an issue in Welsh public life, the resultant 'democratic deficit' cited by politicians and journalists for many years. The referendum result, viewed in that historical media-driven context was, if not a foregone conclusion, then considerably less surprising than many political journalists suggested.

As with all interpretations of Brexit, any rationale or explanation can only be partial. Just as the blunt tool of the referendum lends itself to endless definition, so the vote to leave itself can be (and is being) explained in myriad different ways. A caveat, then, for the following chapter, which locates the Welsh vote within the nation's fragmented cultural landscape alongside the wider media environment, and the associated democratic deficit that has deepened over several decades despite the ongoing process of devolution.

Brexit and Welsh Internal Diversity

The political and cultural fragmentation of Wales was a defining factor in the vote. Apart from the metropolitan centres of Cardiff and neighbouring Vale of Glamorgan, and the prosperous (and somewhat atypical) border country of Monmouthshire, the Welsh-speaking areas of Ceredigion and Gwynedd were the only authorities to vote to remain (by 58.1% in the case of Gwynedd). All countries are fragmented at some level (indeed, the Brexit vote exposed significant divisions in England), but the degree of cultural fragmentation in Wales, driven by language and wider markers of identity politics, is often not fully appreciated outside the nation. Writing about the origins of this fragmentation, Williams cites the inexorable nineteenth-century merging of Wales into the overarching culture of the world language of English, which 'threatened to create two, and more, "nations" out of a Welsh people' (Williams 1985: 181).

As early as the 1920s, Zimmern observed (from his US perspective) 'three different traditions' in Welsh culture, adding that 'they are moving in different directions, and if they all survive, they are not likely to re-unite' (Zimmern 1921: 29). But the best-known attempt to provide a theoretical framework for the cultural and political fragmentation of the Welsh nation remains Denis Balsom's 'Three Wales Model' (1985). Building on Zimmern's observations, Balsom argued that Welsh voting patterns, as well as what might usefully be described as a broader historical pattern of 'identity politics' can best be encapsulated by dividing the country into three units: the 'Welsh Wales' of the South Wales valleys (traditionally Labour-voting, Welsh-identifying but largely English-speaking), the 'Fro Cymraeg' of the North-West and West (Welsh-speaking, with significant levels of support for Plaid Cymru, the Welsh nationalist party) and 'British Wales' (parts of Pembrokeshire and the North Wales coast, along with most areas adjacent to the English border, with allegiance to the UK prioritised over 'Welshness' and significant levels of support for the Conservative Party). Although rather dated and reductive, Balsom's simple summary retains considerable relevance.

Post-devolution, the two strongest and most stereotypical national narratives of 'Welshness' (Balsom's Welsh Wales and Fro Cymraeg) were pushed by an Assembly Government keen to engage in a version of nation building. Both have long been the dominant national images of Wales, for both internal and external consumption, and devolution naturally heightened a tendency for the media and politicians to accentuate them. Nairn and James (2005: 138) argued that the 'post-imperial return' of Wales has, in contrast to Scotland, resembled much more closely the typical ethno-linguistic trajectory of repressed nationhood, where cultural mobilization is directed towards nation building. There is a good reason for this, as this chapter will go on to explore: not least the historical lack of real political and legal institutions combined with the remarkable resilience of the Welsh language.

Those two distinct cultures (Welsh Wales and Y Fro Cymraeg) were already in place, and identified as somewhat divergent, by the end of the nineteenth century. Indeed, a high-profile TV series written and presented by historian Gwyn Alf Williams in 1985, entitled 'The dragon has two tongues', was intended to emphasize the importance of English-language Welsh culture (Balsom's 'Welsh Wales'), suggesting it was sometimes lost or marginalized amidst the politics of the language, and its concomitant defining role in Welsh political identity. Plaid Cymru's recent strategy has been to attempt to bridge the two cultures by, for example, appointing English-speaking Leanne Wood (from the Rhondda Valley, archetypal 'Welsh Wales') as leader. However, this (and arguably all subsequent attempts at nation building) perhaps understandably ignored the lurking presence of 'British Wales', which remained firmly in the background as the process of building coherent, and strong, national narratives intensified after devolution in 1997.

In the Remain-voting 'Fro Gymraeg' (Ceredigion and Gwynedd), Welsh-language news media remains strong, although it is dominated by S4C, the Welsh language channel established in 1982 after years of protests including the threat of a hunger strike by Plaid Cymru's first MP, Gwynfor Evans (incidentally the first nationalist from either Wales or Scotland to enter Westminster, winning the Carmarthen by-election in 1966). Welsh-language newspaper *Y Cymro* is supported by a grant from the Welsh Books Council, sales are small but stable, and the paper is profitable with a vibrant online edition (Hughes 2011: 47). In addition, the tradition of the *Papurau Bro* (neighbourhood newspapers) continues, with 59 titles across Wales. Although these are rarely overtly partisan, they are independent with diverse ownership, reaching almost two-thirds of the half-million strong Welsh-speaking population. For Hughes (2011: 48) they are a 'major success story' despite their shortcomings. Further, although frequently dismissed as trivial and non-political in tone, this is not entirely accurate and there are often differences between titles. Indeed, some of these papers carried partisan features in the run-up to the 2016 EU referendum. For example, *Yr Odyn* (from the Conwy Valley) carries miniature political comment pieces which are distributed throughout each edition of the newspaper (headed *Pytiau Crafog*, literally 'itchy bits' or 'contentious points'). The February 2017 edition contained five such pieces, including the following (translated) piece: 'Empty talk yet again. The Prime Minister met leaders of the devolved nations in Cardiff [to discuss Brexit]. She did not promise to accept or consider any of their suggestions. So why call the meeting?' (*Yr Odyn*, February 2017). In short, the message Welsh-speakers get from their media is more balanced, notwithstanding the obvious caveat that almost all Welsh speakers also access English-language media on a regular basis.

From a broadly cultural perspective, however, perhaps the single most remarkable fact about the leave vote in Wales is that it reverses what had seemed to be an inexorable trend away from 'British Wales' and its cultural traction. British Wales appeared to be becoming less relevant as a predictor of voting patterns as devolution took root. To take Flintshire (in the North-East of Wales, bordering urban areas of North-West England and archetypal 'British Wales') as an example, it voted 62.8% against the establishment of a Welsh Assembly in 1997, which seemed conclusive evidence of its cultural and political leanings (turnout was also the lowest in Wales, at 41%). But support for devolved government then increased markedly: Flintshire voted 62.1% to 37.9% in favour of increased assembly powers in the subsequent devolution referendum of 2011. It seemed reasonable to assume that the cultural and emotional appeal of 'British Wales' was in retreat, just as its equivalent was in Scotland.

But none of this carried through to the 2016 EU referendum, which instead reversed years of academic and political assumptions about the direction of travel in post-devolution Wales. Balsom's model, for example, appeared to be an anachronism post-1997, its crude characterisation of Welsh divisions swept aside by the new dawn of devolution. In the immediate aftermath of Welsh devolution, Snicker (1998: 153) argued that 'the evidence suggests that the "Three Wales Model" may not have a long-term future, because the future political dynamic of Wales lies less in regional differences than in generational ones', and that 'key individuals within the Conservative and Unionist administration have presided over, and in some cases colluded in, the widening and deepening of Welsh identity particularly among younger people'. Further, the work of Jones and Scully (2004) found that the percentage of people describing themselves as 'Welsh, not British' rose from 17.2% at the time of the referendum in 1997 to 22.7% in 2003, adding that an exclusive sense of Welsh identity is strongest among younger voters.

In the context of Brexit, more remarkable than the mere persistence of 'British Wales' is the fact that the leave vote was even stronger in areas that typify Balsom's 'Welsh Wales': the stereotypical Wales of coalfields, male voice choirs and rugby union. Places like Ebbw Vale and Blaenavon voted overwhelmingly to leave.

In other words, it is not just that 'British Wales' persists as a cultural and political force in those areas identified as 'British' by Balsom, but also that the attitudes, emotional appeal and allegiances encompassed by the descriptor have arguably spread (or just strengthened) in areas most closely associated with 'Welsh Wales'. Indeed, the areas most likely to vote leave typify Balsom's 'Welsh Wales'. These were also, as was widely reported at the time, the areas that have received the highest levels of EU funding, benefiting from Objective 1 status for many years and disproportionately dependent on the EU for its exports.

An indirect parallel might be drawn here between the SNP's largely successful neutering of religious sectarianism and, by association, unionism (at least as a high-profile political force) in some urban parts of western Scotland and Plaid's failure to do the same to the values of 'British Wales'. As this chapter's evidential section will outline, much political and media rhetoric in Wales suggested that many of the more idealistic and positive EU principles, such as co-operation, compromise and pooled resources, should, in theory, be more appealing to the traditional values of the Celtic fringe where socialism and communitarianism have long held sway. Again, however, as with the more tangible economic case, the result of the referendum suggests that such notions had no traction whatsoever in Wales. Identity politics, far from finding a natural new home in the civic, socialist-tinged nationalism of Plaid, had (as in England) warped into an expression of Britishness, whatever, in this context, that meant.

Welsh Media Landscape and Democratic Deficit

In the rush to interpret and rationalize the Welsh Leave vote, the state of the media found itself relegated, as poverty and the resentment it breeds were focused on by numerous observers. Yet the wider media played a pivotal role in the vote. Indeed, the particular deficiencies of the Welsh media have been highlighted by politicians, journalists and academics for many years.

The process of devolution merely highlighted a pre-existing problem whereby the decisions of the devolved government were neither scrutinized nor, on occasion, even reported by a news media subject to the pressures of the market and wider commercial forces. A 2014 BBC poll, for example, found that fewer than half of Welsh respondents knew the NHS was devolved, which Thomas (2014) suggests results from a Welsh media landscape in which 'huge numbers of people' get their news from London-based newspapers. Around 1,760,000 people from a total population of 3 million read newspapers with 'virtually no Welsh content' (Davies 2008). The emergent 'democratic deficit' became such a well-known feature of the Welsh political landscape that it is surprising that more was not done to link it to the referendum debate in Wales.

If the dominance of London-based newspapers in Wales has long been apparent in terms of both circulation and cultural import, then the recent studies (for example, Swales 2016) suggesting that anti-EU newspapers, notably the *Sun* and the *Daily Mail*, had a profound impact on the vote take on an extra Welsh dimension. 'When it came to the EU referendum vote, people were more likely to follow the position of the newspaper they read than the political party they identify with,' one such study claimed (Swales 2016). According to the research, 70% of *Sun* readers and 66% of *Daily Mail* readers backed leave, while just 9% of *Guardian* readers did so.

The findings are hardly surprising: indeed, the virulent anti-EU agenda pursued by the majority of the British tabloid press has a decades-old history, long predating the referendum. In the 1990s, Anderson and Weymouth focused on the coverage of EU structural funds (of particular relevance to Wales, which is scheduled to receive £1.9 billion between 2014–2020 [Welsh Government 2016]) in their study of the misinformation and bias surrounding EU coverage in the British media, concluding: 'This structural initiative amounts precisely to the pragmatic, tangible, hands on version of the EU demanded in the Demos Report. But where is it represented in the media? What is striking about the European discourse in the immediate pre-election [1997] period, is that [...] the benefits that may accrue to the British regions from EU structural funding are not mentioned.' Anderson and Weymouth (1999: 175) also argued that:

> In addition to the limited range of European topics represented in the British press, and to the dominant Eurosceptic readings proposed by the majority of titles, there is also the exclusion for commercial, political or other reasons, of information relating to practical policies which touch the lives of large numbers of British people in beneficial ways.

There is again a marked contrast with Scotland here, in this case concerning the communicative and information-providing responsibilities of the news media, although the extent to which those responsibilities are practical or realistic is questionable. Franklin (1997: 231) talked of the irreconcilability of two perceptions of the public character of journalism that it is: (1) a public service; and (2) a market activity. Scottish devolution certainly provided a pretext for London-based national newspapers to reduce news content from all three devolved nations, subject as they are to market forces. But this in itself provided a catalyst for the further development of the long-established independent news media in Scotland itself, and a boost to Scottish media policy. Indeed, in post-devolution interviews, London journalists argued that Scotland now had its 'own news' and its own newspapers to carry it (Denver 2002). Even the 'editionized' Scottish versions of London-based titles are largely independent in their editorial agendas (Hutchison and O'Donnell 2011: 3).

By contrast, there is no real tradition of a Welsh national press, or indeed 'editionized' versions of UK titles. The Welsh *Mirror* was launched as a stand-alone title in 1999, intending to reflect and exploit devolution, but its brief and unsuccessful run ended in 2003 and since then no other UK newspaper has attempted to launch a Welsh edition (Thomas 2004: 162). There have been attempts to launch pan-Wales news websites, but these have also struggled to remain commercially viable (Roberts 2011). With the collapse of the Welsh *Mirror*, the immediate optimism of media coverage of post-devolution Wales faded, to the point that few would dispute the assertion that the dominance of the UK press in Wales hinders the development of an informed political culture in a country which suffers from a 'structurally weak' media (Thomas 2004).

As a result, the BBC essentially has a monopoly over Welsh politics, yet surveys have found even this coverage to be deficient. A review of BBC content from the UK's four nations found that although the BBC was more sensitive to devolved politics in Wales, Scotland and Northern Ireland than other broadcasters, there remains a tendency to present stories concerning England as if they applied to the UK as a whole and there continues to be a focus on England as a source of information (Cushion et al. 2010): 'Some BBC news items still do not make it clear which part of the UK they are referring to, and hence are reported as if they apply to the whole of the UK when it fact stories apply to England.'

More recently, the BBC Wales trustee conceded that the BBC has shown 'slower progress' in the amount of stories from Wales featured on its network news programmes compared to those from other UK nations. In a 2016 survey, Cardiff University found that 1.4% of stories on network TV news bulletins were specifically about Wales, compared to 10.2% about Scotland. In a 2016 updated 'snapshot', with the EU referendum looming, research found the gap had narrowed, with 3.6% of TV news stories about Wales, while 5.9% were about Scotland. This is arguably a fair reflection of respective populations and it should also be noted that the study found that the BBC communicated news about the four nations with 'greater regularity and clarity' than other broadcasters and was 'significantly more accurate' in communicating the geographical relevance of news items than its competitors (BBC 2016a).

This is a particularly relevant issue, because broadcast media in Wales have always been disproportionately influential. In Wales, assumptions about the relationship between TV, linguistic decline and nation building were 'the bedrock on which debates about TV in Wales rested in the 1960s and 1970s [...] shared by critics of the BBC and ITV as well as their defenders' (Barlow et al. 2005: 147). These assumptions became and remain an 'unshakeable dogma' (Barlow et al. 2005) in Welsh cultural life with TV occupying an unusually central position in Welsh politics and culture as a result. Any reading of Welsh media representation must therefore take TV as its point of departure. In this context, the much vaunted (and much criticized) 'neutrality' of the BBC during the 2016 EU referendum debate was again unusually damaging in Wales, so dependent was it on the BBC's virtual monopoly of devolved politics.

THE WELSH REGIONAL PRESS:
THE *WESTERN MAIL* AND THE *DAILY POST*

Although the lack of a national newspaper has often been cited as a fundamental reason for the 'democratic deficit' in Wales, a lesser version of a national conversation still limps on in the form of the two major regional Welsh newspapers, which have traditionally tended to see themselves as surrogate national papers. In reality, the *Western Mail* is sold and read almost exclusively in South Wales, with the *Daily Post* (based in Liverpool for most of its history) its northern equivalent. Both are Trinity Mirror titles. Unlike the London-based press, both were generally pro-EU during the campaign, particularly the *Western Mail*, which carried a relentless series of pro-Remain stories in the crucial weeks before the referendum.

The *Western Mail* took a marked, almost activist, stance throughout: exemplified by the headlines (summarized below) from what was arguably the most active week of campaigning, 14–21 June. It draws on a long history, established in 1869, with its target audience drawn from archetypal examples of Balsom's 'Welsh Wales'. Despite this, the message, backed by key figures from the Welsh establishment, clearly had little traction in what might be thought of as its heartland, for reasons this article will attempt to interpret.

Under the headline 'EU a source of pride, peace and prosperity', the *Western Mail* issued an idealistic and powerful plea for South Wales to vote Remain on 20 June:

> Thursday could be a day that will stand out in the history books. We hope it will be remembered as a moment when Wales chose to reject isolationism and instead resolved to play a full role in Europe's future. Young people in Wales, like their counterparts in France and Italy, have grown up in

the knowledge they can live, study and work anywhere in the EU. If we vote to leave we will deny them this freedom. Successive post-war British prime ministers championed European integration and today's union of half a billion people bears the stamp 'made in the UK'. Britain devised the single market which supports so many thousands of Welsh jobs; we also secured the expansion of the EU to include former Communist states and helped facilitate the most successful transition to democracy in human history.

This editorial was arguably the most emotional and cogent defence of the EU contained in any British newspaper in the run-up to the vote. Indeed, the idealism and passion exhibited by the *Western Mail* was notable only by its absence in much of the London-based press. Although this was the most direct editorial intervention on its part, an analysis of stories carried by the newspaper between 14 and 21 June demonstrates its wider agenda and overt pro-EU tone.

On 21 June, for example, the newspaper carried six stories, all broadly pro-Remain, including the following two headlines which make use of establishment figures, in this case drawn from religion and politics:

'Anger over immigration has prevailed over reason': Recent Brexit adverts have taken the EU referendum campaign beyond what is acceptable, argues Rev Aled Edwards OBE', and '"Brexit could crash economy and kill off investment in Wales" – Darling.'

On 20 June, the newspaper carried eight referendum stories, all but one broadly pro-Remain, along with the previously mentioned editorial. Headlines included: 'Our world is deeply influenced by our common European heritage: Lord Dafydd Wigley lays out the positive case for Wales in Europe'; 'ICT skills shortage could get worse with Brexit'; and 'Language groups warn vote to leave would be "disaster"'.

Key figures from the Welsh establishment were frequently mobilized by the paper, including former diplomat Sir Emyr Jones Parry on 18 June: 'Strength and safety for UK lie in EU', an article in which Jones Parry lays out his arguments for staying in the EU. Similarly, on 17 June, former Labour Minister Peter Hain outlined his case for Remain under the headline: 'Vote remain to help people out of poverty and give hope to our valleys.' The reliance on Welsh establishment figures may have proved counter-productive, another parallel with England, as it merely fed the wider 'anti-elite' meme pushed by UKIP and Conservative 'leavers'. Indeed, this was directly suggested by critics of the Remain campaign in Wales ('Wales Stronger in Europe') after the vote.

Further headlines on 17 June included: 'EU enriches the student experience and encourages tomorrow's leaders'; 'Stay in to protect the steel industry and avoid a crippling recession says ex ambassador'; 'Brexit would spark takeover by Tory right, Salmond warns', alongside the more widely covered 'Please don't go' appeal incorporating the views of other EU countries.

The five pro-EU stories from 16 June provide a good example of the variety of the coverage. Multiple angles were pursued by the *Western Mail* in this key week of campaigning, from specific warnings to the South Wales steelworkers through to the perceived damaging atavism of the Leave campaign, for example: 'Tata warns steelworkers of Brexit vote dangers'; 'Is Wales safer from crime, terrorism and war in the EU?'; '"Brexit is less about wanting the country back than taking it back to a bygone age"—Guto Harri on why a remain vote is so important for Wales'; 'Stronger together—that's the view of most business experts'; and 'Let's not decide on ill-informed whim' (another editorial).

The overarching theme was variety: in the sense that the newspaper's attempt to point out the full implications of what it saw as the potential damage from Brexit was combined with the kind of positive vision lacking from the London press, alongside at least one (daily) opinion piece written by a leading member of the Welsh political establishment. This pattern continued unchanged throughout the week. On 15 June, First Minister of Wales Carwyn Jones was cited: '"Brexit backers can't guarantee Wales' funding", Carwyn warns.' This headline was carried alongside the kind of positive pro-EU feature often missing from the mainstream national press in the wider UK, albeit with a rather clumsy and preachy headline: 'Clean beaches, workers rights and more: How the EU has benefited us; 20 ways in which EU membership has shaped life in Wales for the better and given us superior expectations at work and in our leisure time.' Anderson and Weymouth's (1999) point about the seemingly deliberate exclusion [from UK media news agendas] 'of information relating to practical policies which touch the lives of large numbers of British people in beneficial ways' is thrown into sharp post-Brexit focus here, as such pieces have tended, for several decades, to be exceptions that prove an underlying rule.

A further three stories that day continued the theme: 'Academics warn about effects "misinformation" could have on referendum results'; 'Banks see red as Brexit alarm hits stock market'; and 'Fear of Brexit is stunting my Bebe's growth' (a story about the implications of Brexit for the JoJo Madam Bebe maternity and baby wear company, based in Newport, South Wales).

The *Western Mail*'s equivalent in North Wales, the *Daily Post*, was also broadly pro-EU in its editorial stance and choice of news items immediately before the referendum, albeit a little more equivocal than its South Wales counterpart. The *Daily Post* was founded in 1855 and even by the standards of British regional newspapers has enjoyed a rather chequered history. The Welsh version gained 'independence' from the Liverpool parent edition after devolution in 2003, and is now the only remaining edition (the Liverpool paper folded in 2013).

An analysis of the *Daily Post* over the same week of campaigning points to a more balanced (although marginally pro-Remain) approach, but also (and perhaps related) with far less emphasis placed on the referendum as a story per se. The newspaper carried an average of four referendum stories each day, peaking with eight stories on 16 June. Perhaps unsurprisingly, given their respective geographical areas, the *Daily Post* focused on the impact of the vote on agriculture alongside the broader themes focused on by the *Western Mail*.

For example, on 16 June, it carried the following headline: 'Brexit will send farming back to Depression years' alongside a linked piece: 'All we want is clarity on EU vote—Welsh farmers.'. In the same edition, another prescient agricultural piece: 'New dawn or fool's gold? Brexit should be a turn-off for farmers, yet the leave campaign is gaining ground.'

As with the *Western Mail*, leading figures from the Welsh political establishment were frequently mobilized: '"Who imagined voting blindfold on Wales and Britain's future?"—Dafydd Wigley' (former leader of Plaid Cymru and a particularly articulate advocate of the EU); and, echoing the *Western Mail*'s use of former ambassadors with Welsh links: 'Diplomat warns of Brexit effect on (Welsh) steel industry: Ex-ambassador says creation of single market was "triumph"'.

The overall impression is startling: both key regional newspapers in Wales were pro-Remain during this critical week of campaigning. Indeed, many of the pieces carried, particularly in the *Western Mail*, are remarkable for the stridency with which they defended the EU, accompanied with a positive vision and even that sense of idealism that was notable by its absence in the wider political and public sphere.

However, none of this had any impact on the electorate in South Wales, which voted overwhelmingly for Leave outside Cardiff and its immediate surroundings. The obvious explanation for this disjuncture is the stark commercial reality that both these newspapers, despite their historic significance and perceived importance, have been in decline for decades and now sell very few copies in Wales (and local Welsh newspapers have suffered an even worse plight than these two big regionals, with dozens folding across Wales over the past two decades). The *Western Mail*'s circulation stood at 19,910 in January 2015 (down from well over 100,000 in the 1960s), with the *Daily Post* on 25,426, dropping to 22,251 in 2016, when it incidentally became Wales' best-selling regional newspaper, albeit in a context of terminal decline across the country (ABC Statistics 2016; Evans 2000). In other words, the lack of any correlation between these newspapers' editorial stances and Welsh voting patterns is merely a further indication of regional papers' lack of real influence in contemporary Britain. The fundamental problem, that of the debilitating absence of a Welsh public sphere, is not made any less relevant or serious by either of these near-moribund regional newspapers.

In this context, it is also worth noting that the *Western Mail* carries a certain amount of historical baggage in South Wales, and remains (in some quarters) identified as an establishment mouthpiece: the establishment in this case being local industrialists, the newspaper's original owners. Both newspapers are equally strongly associated with devolution and the Welsh political establishment, particularly the *Western Mail*. Many have observed that the advent of devolution and the Welsh Assembly have resulted in a concentration of jobs, power and infrastructure in the Cardiff Bay area. This has caused an unsurprising level of resentment across the rest of Wales, although there has been some attempt to spread smaller Welsh government offices across the nation.

This resentment, whether grounded in perception or reality, was frequently linked to the referendum result in the immediate aftermath of the vote, with some high-profile observers particularly critical of the 'establishment' make-up of the Welsh Government's Remain campaign. Former Labour advisor David Taylor called the Wales Stronger in Europe campaign 'insufferably smug', arguing that it was dominated by a 'self-serving ineffective "Taffia" of old Welsh establishment figures' (BBC 2016b).

CONCLUSION

A commonplace and rather obvious observation gained traction in the referendum's aftermath: it was clear that very few voters in Wales had viewed their decision from a specifically Welsh perspective. Again, the explanation can be located within the wider news media. BBC Wales, for example, had only one Welsh leaders debate about the EU referendum 2016, just days before the poll. The distinctiveness of Welsh post-devolution politics, and the EU's critical role, was simply not conveyed as there were few means of reframing the debate in Welsh terms. The attempts by the two leading Welsh regional newspapers to do so merely confirmed the declining relevance and impact of the British regional press and the continuing cultural hegemony of the UK tabloid press.

Although the positive aspects of Remain were cited by the Welsh regional press, with the fundamental notion of co-operation and compromise given far more coverage than in the London-based press, any idealistic or positive message proved almost impossible to mobilize. Voting patterns were almost identical to England, with the Welsh-speaking heartlands of Gwynedd and Ceredigion the only exceptions, which this article contends confirms the continuing relevance of aspects of Balsom's 'Three Wales' framework, as well as the relative diversity of media output accessible to Welsh-speakers.

In this context it is perhaps not surprising that the internal complexities of Welsh culture and identity, those identified long ago by Balsom, have been inadequately treated and represented by the wider English-language media. Indeed, the media within Wales (such as it is) have arguably failed to accurately represent areas historically marginalized by the dominant national narrative of the newly devolved entity (Roberts 2011). Such areas proved ripe for exploitation by Brexit campaigners, creating a 'perfect storm' of resentment aimed at a confusing blend of political targets from the devolved Assembly up to the EU itself.

The roots of this marginalization run deep. Barlow et al. (2005: 148) point to the fear of TV among Welsh-language campaigners in the 1960s, 'seeing beneath its dominant Englishness a real threat to identity'. In this context, with broadcast media central to nation building and the preservation of the language, for understandable and valid reasons, it is perhaps not surprising that the wider public sphere continued to be neglected post-devolution. McElroy (2008: 247) outlined the ways in which Welsh language TV developed its conversation with the Welsh-speaking community, 'in the process sometimes closing down the routes of belonging among others in Wales'. The associated fraught question of protecting and promoting a fragile culture whilst simultaneously remaining properly inclusive has sometimes been debated in Wales, without a meaningful conclusion; perhaps because the conundrum has no easy answers.

Some movement is detectable, however, even in the aftermath of Welsh Brexit. In early 2017, Assembly Members (AMs) called for an extra £30 m to be spent on English-language broadcasting in Wales: suggesting that Welsh listeners to BBC radio should hear 'opt-out' news bulletins about Wales and Welsh politics. The BBC had previously conceded that aspects of Welsh life have not been 'sufficiently captured' by TV services (BBC 2017).

In a widely quoted speech, Plaid AM Adam Price (2009) called Wales 'a post-colonial country still waiting to be decolonized [...] a hybrid state living in the cracks between a dependent past and an independent future'. That vision of the future has been comprehensively shattered by the Welsh vote for Brexit. It remains to be seen whether it, and a viable, news media-driven, public sphere that resonates with the whole of Wales, might re-emerge.

BIBLIOGRAPHY

ABC Statistics. 2016. https://www.abc.org.uk/.

Anderson, P., and A. Weymouth. 1999. *Insulting the Public? The British Press and the European Union*. London: Longman.

Balsom, D. 1985. The Three Wales Model. In *The National Question Again: Welsh Political Identity in the 1980s*, ed. J. Osmond. Llandysul: Gomer.

Barlow, D., P. Michell, and T. O'Malley. 2005. *The Media in Wales: Voices of a Small Nation*. Cardiff: University of Wales Press.

BBC. 2016a. 'Slower Progress' on BBC Network News From Wales. www.bbc.com (Accessed 24 November 16).

BBC. 2016b. Brexit: Remain Camp 'Insufferably Smug', Ex-Labour Advisor Says. www.bbc.com (Accessed 29 July 2016).

BBC. 2017. AM Bethan Jenkins Urges BBC Wales to Reflect Welsh Life. www.bbc.com (Accessed 1 Febraury 2017).

Chakrabortty, A. 2016. Burning Anger in the Land of Nye Bevan. *The Guardian*, June 7.

Cushion, S., J. Lewis, and C. Groves. 2009. Reflecting the Four Nations? *Journalism Studies* 10 (5): 655–671.

Cushion, S., J. Lewis, and G. Ramsay. 2010. Four Nations Impartiality Review Follow-Up. http://www.bbc.co.uk/bbctrust/assets/files/pdf/review_report_research/impartiality/2010/nations_impartiality_analysis.pdf.

Davies, G. 2008. *Media in Wales: Serving Public Values?* Institute of Welsh Affairs: Cardiff, UK.

Denver, D. 2002. Voting in the 1997 Scottish and Welsh Devolution Referendums: Information, Interests and Opinion. *European Journal of Political Research* 41: 827–843.

Evans, D.G. 2000. *History of Wales 1906–2000.* Cardiff: University of Wales Press.

Evans, J. 2016. An Alternative to Scaremongering: Progressive EU reform. *Planet: The Welsh Internationalist,* 221.

Franklin, B. 1997. *Newszak and News Media.* London: Bloomsbury Academic.

Hughes, G.M. 2011. What's News in Wales? Welsh Language Journalism Today and in Historical Context. In *Centres and Peripheries: Metropolitan and Non-Metropolitan Journalism in the 21st Century,* ed. D. Hutchison and H. O'Donnell. Newcastle upon Tyne: Cambridge Scholars Publishing.

Hutchison, D., and H. O'Donnell. 2011. Introduction. In *Centres and Peripheries: Metropolitan and Non-Metropolitan Journalism in the 21st Century,* ed. D. Hutchison and H. O'Donnell. Newcastle upon Tyne: Cambridge Scholars Publishing.

Jones, R., and R. Scully. 2004. Devolution in Wales: What Does the Public Think? Economic and Social Research Council Research Programme on Devolution and Constitutional Change. Briefing no. 7.

McElroy, R. 2008. Indigenous Minority-Language Media: S4C, Cultural Identity, and the Welsh-Language Televisual Community. In *Global Indigenous Media: Cultures, Poetics and Politics,* ed. P. Wilson and M. Stewart. Durham, NC: Duke University Press.

Nairn, T., and P. James. 2005. *Global Matrix: Nationalism, Globalism and State-Terrorism.* London, UK: Pluto Press.

Price, A. 2009. Institute of Welsh Politics speech Nov 16 2009. http://www.walesonline.co.uk/news/wales-news/wales-first-final-colony—2070487 (Accessed November 2016).

Roberts, S.G. 2011. Transcending a Dysfunctional Mainstream? An Update on the Status of Welsh Online Journalism. *Cyfrwng: Media Wales Journal* 8: 55–72.

Servini, N. 2016. Twitter, June 23. https://twitter.com/nickservini/status/.

Snicker, J. 1998. Strategies of Autonomist Agents in Wales. In *Remaking the Union: Devolution and British Politics in the 1990s,* ed. H. Elcock and M. Keating. London: Routledge.

Swales, K. 2016. Understanding the Leave Vote. http://natcen.ac.uk/our-research/research/understanding-the-leave-vote (Accessed January 2017).

Thomas, H. 2014. Measuring Devolution: How Have the Media Covered Wales? *BBC News*, June 13. www.bbc.co.uk/news/uk-wales-27804380 (Accessed June 2016).

Thomas, J. 2004. Buried Without Tears, May This Never Rise Again. The Welsh Mirror 1999–2003. *Planet: The Welsh Internationalist*, 162, pp. 23–27.

Welsh Government. 2016. http://gov.wales/funding/eu-funds/2014-2020 (Accessed January 2017).

Williams, G.A. 1985. *When Was Wales?* London: Pelican.

Zimmern, A.E. 1921. *My Impressions of Wales.* London: Mills and Boon.

CHAPTER 6

Whither the 'Hand of History'?: Northern Ireland Newspaper Coverage of the 2016 EU Referendum Campaign

Stephen Baker

INTRODUCTION

The United Kingdom (UK) referendum on European Union (EU) membership in 2016 produced a narrow victory for those who campaigned to leave: 51.89 to 48.11% on a 72.21% turnout. This less than emphatic result, on such a huge constitutional question, concealed the 62% of voters in Scotland and 55.8% in Northern Ireland who expressed a preference to remain within the EU. Nevertheless, English votes were decisive in the outcome. England is the UK's dominant partner, with a population that is considerably larger than that of Scotland, Northern Ireland and Wales combined. It voted 53.4–46.6% in favour of Brexit. Wales also voted in favour of leaving, by 52.5–47.5%. Many interpreted the victory for the pro-Brexit campaign as England dragging Scotland and Northern Ireland out of the EU against their wills, a feeling perhaps heightened by the disputed position of both within the UK. In Northern

S. Baker (✉)
Ulster University, Coleraine, Northern Ireland, UK
e-mail: sj.baker@ulster.ac.uk

© The Author(s) 2018
A. Ridge-Newman et al. (eds.), *Reporting the Road to Brexit*,
https://doi.org/10.1007/978-3-319-73682-2_6

93

Ireland's case, we might also refer to its precarious position within the UK. As this chapter argues, the EU referendum emphasized the marginality of Northern Ireland to British politics, as seen in local newspaper coverage of high-ranking British politicians who canvassed the region in the run-up to the poll.

There was a time when a visit by a senior British official to Northern Ireland, especially in the midst of political turmoil and constitutional crisis, would have excited a great deal of public comment. Not so during the EU referendum campaign of 2016, when no less that one British Prime Minister, two ex-Prime Ministers, a Chancellor of the Exchequer; the Mayor of London and Nigel Farage visited the region to little acclaim and less fuss. Only the Chancellor, George Osborne, merited a front-page headline in any of Northern Ireland's indigenous newspapers, and then only in the Belfast *News Letter*. Its headline read, 'Osborne: Brexit will harden Irish border', an assertion that might have delighted the mainly unionist readership of the paper. Boris Johnson was the only other leader whose visit to the region made a front page. Once again, it was the *News Letter*, this time carrying a picture of the London Mayor at the Wrightbus factory in Ballymena, but even then his inclusion on the front page had more to do with his apparent acrobatic prowess (he was pictured swinging from the chassis of a Routemaster bus) than any contribution to the ongoing EU debate.[1] Local interest in British dignitaries peaked briefly when two previous Prime Ministers, John Major and Tony Blair, suggested while on a visit to Derry that leaving the EU might endanger the peace in Northern Ireland. Northern Ireland's First Minister, Arlene Foster, leader of the pro-Brexit Democratic Unionist Party (DUP), rebuked them. She told journalists, 'I do find it rather disgraceful for two prime ministers who know full well the importance of the peace process here in Northern Ireland to come over here and suggest that a vote in a particular direction is going to undermine that.' Her party colleague, Nigel Dodds MP, joined her in criticizing the two ex-premiers, as did the Secretary for State for Northern Ireland, Theresa Villiers. The *News Letter* alone, again, carried the story on its front page under the headline: 'Foster leads outrage against former PMs.'[2]

[1] *News Letter*, 1 March 2016.
[2] *News Letter*, 10 June 2016.

What are we to make of this rather muted coverage of and reaction to high-profile political figures (David Cameron, George Osborne, Boris Johnson, Tony Blair, John Major, and Nigel Farage) as they canvassed Northern Ireland during the referendum campaign? This chapter examines the coverage of their visits in the three indigenous daily newspapers in Northern Ireland: the unionist *News Letter*, the nationalist *Irish News*, and the *Belfast Telegraph*, once considered a moderate unionist paper, now its political, editorial position apparently more and more determined by commercial self-interest. These papers are interesting for the insight they give into a variety of partisan opinions in Northern Ireland. Within them, the chapter pays particular attention to: the reported pronouncements of the political leaders during their visits to Northern Ireland; the stage-management of these occasions; and the response of local politicians and commentators (where there was any). To this end, we look at reports on the day of the visit and the two following days, to allow for editorial reaction and commentary.

The reason for focusing on these often carefully choreographed high-profile visits to Northern Ireland is the anticipation that such occasions would, if only briefly, move the region to the centre of the debate about the UK and EU, the two larger unions of which Northern Ireland is a peripheral member. The feeling of being marginal to big decisions was perhaps implicit in a *Belfast Telegraph* editorial that felt it necessary to point out that what the voters of Northern Ireland thought about the referendum was of some consequence: 'Our views on Brexit as important as any others in the UK', read the headline on 1 March, in the wake of visits from Prime Minister David Cameron and the Mayor of London, Boris Johnson MP. However, Northern Ireland is not only peripheral. It also exists in a precarious relation to the modern civic values that the UK and EU see themselves as representing. Northern Ireland has long been associated with sectarian violence, which made it a byword for atavism and archaic political passions. Only recently has it developed a reputation as an exemplar of a post-conflict society, but the threat of Brexit aroused again the fear that the region might fall into political and civil discord. This was implicit in Blair's and Major's foreboding comments in Derry. However, these were misplaced concerns, certainly in the short term. For it was in England that the EU debate was at its most intemperate and often toxic, taking a tragic turn on 16 June with the murder of Labour MP Jo Cox, in her Batley and Spen constituency, at the hands of a British nationalist extremist. If the EU referendum has brought nothing else into focus, it has shown us that Ireland is not alone in suffering constitutional turmoil and belligerent forms of nationalism.

HISTORY AND CONTEXT

The partition of Ireland under an Act of the UK Parliament in 1920 saw the formation of Northern Ireland. The historic antagonism between Ulster unionists and Irish nationalists has dominated the region's politics. The former, who are predominantly Protestants, want to preserve Northern Ireland's constitutional position within the UK: nationalists are overwhelming Catholic and seek a united Ireland and end to British jurisdiction in the region. From Northern Ireland's inception in 1921, unionists enacted one-party government until the prorogation of the parliament at Stormont in 1972 amid scenes of violent confrontation on the region's streets. The lack of democratic consensus for the unionist regime was its undoing. It had come to depend too heavily on forms of coercion, discrimination and exclusion, directed against a Catholic nationalist minority, too significant in number to be ignored. A peaceful civil rights movement championed reform but when it was meet with loyalist hostility, the British Army was drafted in, ostensibly to protect the Catholic minority. Relations between the two disintegrated, however, hastened by actions like Bloody Sunday in Derry on 30 January 1972 when British Paratroopers shot dead 13 unarmed protesters and injured as many more. Various political initiatives aimed at stopping the violence and achieving political stability failed, and the region endured three decades of sectarian and civil strife which left over 3000 people dead. In 1994, after a period of back-channel communications, political manoeuvring and negations, republican and loyalist paramilitaries declared ceasefires that created the conditions for the peace process that eventually led to the signing of the Good Friday Agreement in 1998.

As to why peace and a political settlement were possible is a question as contested as the conflict and its history. However, a number of regional, national and international events and relationships paved the way for the peace initiative, and these are crucial to understanding the significance of the 2016 EU referendum and its result for Northern Ireland. First among these was the improved relationship between the Republic of Ireland and the UK; indeed they became partners within Europe, both joining the European Economic Community (EEC) in

1973. Ireland's membership of the EU and advancing globalization facilitated the rise of the so-called Celtic Tiger economy, fuelled by foreign direct investment. Unionists in the North had once enjoyed the largesse of the British Empire and access to its markets, and so looked condescendingly at their relatively poorer neighbours to the south. However, by the 1990s, the Empire was long gone and Britain itself was disintegrating, its archaic state increasingly unrepresentative of the national, regional and cultural identities over which it claimed jurisdiction. Globalization, continental partnership and multiculturalism provided the political and intellectual terrain for peace and political accord in Northern Ireland.

That accord is consociational, balancing power between two distinct national allegiances and identities. Initially it was underscored by the assumption of a 'peace dividend'. This would be Northern Ireland's integration, proper, into the global free market and all its perceived benefits, after years of dependency on a subvention from the British Exchequer. But the 'peace dividend' never materialized. The financial crash of 2008 put paid to that, and instead it provided the pretext for more straitened economic circumstances. The crash is also implicated in growing and crystallizing a disaffection among sections of the public across what is euphemistically referred to as the developed world. The Brexit outcome of the referendum; the increasing electoral strength of the far right across Europe; and the election of Donald Trump to the US presidency are consequences of this voter discontent. Ironically, then, Northern Ireland has achieved a post-national accord and entry into the global free market just in time to see the re-emergence of nationalistic politics and protectionist economics throughout Europe and the USA. As such, then, Northern Ireland's new political dispensation and economic expectations fly in the face of these modern political trends.

Fear and Fortune: David Cameron, Boris Johnson and George Osborne

On 20 February 2016, Prime Minister David Cameron announced the date of the EU referendum: 23 June. A week after that announcement he canvassed Northern Ireland. Just two days later, the Mayor of London, Boris Johnson arrived in the region. The two men were not only on opposite sides of the EU debate but seen as rivals for the leadership of the Conservative Party, which might have brought a certain frisson to their Northern Irish engagements, coming as they did so close together. Cameron's visit was explicitly to campaign on the question of the EU referendum, and he took in the famous Bushmills whiskey distillery, as well as a County Antrim farm, where he met members of the farming community. As traditional emblems of Ireland and producers of key Northern Irish exports, a whiskey distillery and farm provided the perfect backdrop to Cameron's message about the economic consequences of Brexit. On the other hand, Johnson's visit was ostensibly to visit the Wrightbus factory in Ballymena and confirm an order of 95 Routemaster buses for London worth £62 m. In the evening, he would address the Northern Ireland Chamber of Commerce, but whatever Johnson's motivations for these engagements, it was inevitable that the question of Brexit and his support for it would loom large.

Cameron arrived with a core message that EU membership was vital for Northern Ireland, allowing the region access to the European market, but he also stated that leaving would result in a 'hard' border between the North and South, and could put the future of the UK at risk. The *Irish News* reported on 27 February that Cameron, speaking ahead of his visit, had emphasized that Northern Ireland's 'economy and farming industry are too closely linked to the EU to risk leaving it'.[3] The *News Letter* in its headline was more inclined to stress a key issue for its unionist readership concerning the fate of the UK if there was a vote to leave the EU: 'Cameron: Vote for Brexit could pose risk to the future of the UK.'[4] The paper described the Prime Minister's visit as a 'whirlwind' 'flying visit', as if to imply that his attention to the region was fleeting. This continued the sceptical tone of its coverage the day before when it described how Cameron planned to 'target' farmers in a 'charm offensive'.[5] The paper's correspondent Ben Lowry, in an analysis piece, said Cameron's tactics were clearly to concentrate on voters' fears about leaving the EU: 'He is hammering on the anxiety point and will do so until the 23 June.'[6]

The *Belfast Telegraph*'s coverage was personalizing, playing up the rivalry of two Conservative colleagues. Its headline, with an allusion to

---

[3] 'North's economy needs EU links says Cameron', *Irish News*, 27 February 2016, p. 11.

[4] *News Letter*, 29 February 2016, p. 4.

[5] 'PM to target farmers in EU charm offensive', *News Letter*, 27 February 2016, p. 8.

[6] 'Leader certain about his main message', *News Letter*, 27 February 2016, p. 4.

fisticuffs ('Cameron beats Boris to the punch as he urges us to vote for Europe'),[7] was a reference to Cameron's visit preceding Johnson's by two days. In the same edition, the *Belfast Telegraph* played further on the men's enmity, carrying a feature by John Meagher considering Cameron and Johnson's relationship since their schooldays. 'The 40 year rivalry that could determine the EU poll', read the headline, accompanied by a picture of the two men holding hands aloft in victory, torn in two to signify their severed alliance.[8] The personalized tone was carried to extraordinary lengths when, on 29 February, the *Belfast Telegraph* produced a feature entitled, 'Betrayal [...] when your friends let you down.'[9] The subheading read: 'No sooner had Prime Minister David Cameron announced that Britain should stay in the EU than two of his closest confidants turned against him.' The article recounted the 'betrayal' of Cameron by Michael Gove and Boris Johnson, before inviting three writers to reflect upon the moment they realized they had been 'stabbed in the back' by friends or colleagues.

As the *Irish News* reported that Boris Johnson had arrived in Northern Ireland with the message that the region's exports had 'nothing to fear' from Brexit and could only gain,[10] the *Belfast Telegraph*'s headline also carried Johnson's assertion of economic good fortune: 'Brexit a chance for NI farms and fisheries to get a better deal insists Boris.'[11] The *Belfast Telegraph* accompanied the report with some trademark images of Johnson acting the buffoon at the Wrightbus factory. Nevertheless, his message had a potential potency given its delivery in the company of Northern Ireland's First and Deputy First Ministers, Arlene Foster and Martin McGuinness, as well as the local MP for the area, Ian Paisley Jnr, and Jonathan Bell, at that time Northern Ireland's Minister for Enterprise, Trade and Investment. Also in attendance was Johnson's pro-Brexit ally Theresa Villiers. With the exception of McGuinness, everyone in the entourage was in favour of leaving the EU.

[7] *Belfast Telegraph*, 27 February 2016, p. 2.

[8] *Belfast Telegraph*, 27 February 2016, p. 25.

[9] Ibid., p. 23.

[10] 'Firms, farmers and fishermen can only gain from Brexit says Boris', *Irish News*, 1 March 2016, p. 12.

[11] 'Brexit a chance for NI farms and fisheries to get a better deal insists Boris', *Belfast Telegraph*, 1 March 2016, p. 6.

Johnson's visit earned an editorial in the *News Letter*, not so much for anything he had to say about the forthcoming referendum, but for his endorsement of Wrightbus Routemaster buses.[12] However, the editorial did remark upon how 'Mr Johnson struck a confident note when he said the future was bright regardless of the coming referendum. If the quality of manufacturing that is apparent in the Routemasters could be widely replicated elsewhere in Northern Ireland and the UK that would assuredly be true.' Where the London Mayor, surrounded by allies, brought good news for the Northern Ireland economy, Cameron brought word of dire consequences. He was, in any case, associated with punishing cuts and austerity. In addition and in contrast to Johnson, the Prime Minister cut an isolated figure. While attired in the sort of outdoor clothing that harmonized with the countryside, photographs showed him confronted by an audience of farmers and their families before whom, as the BBC reported, he 'faced some skeptical questioning' about milk prices and fears that subsidised budgets might be increasingly directed to Eastern Europe.[13]

The visits by the Prime Minister and London Mayor were followed quickly on 1 March with one by Nigel Farage, the leader of the United Kingdom Independence Party (UKIP). However, Farage's high public profile in Britain earned him few column inches in Northern Ireland when he participated in a debate with Labour's Vernon Coaker, hosted by Ulster University in Belfast. The event passed with little coverage, notable only for the predictable 'clash'[14] of views and a £20 bet on the outcome of the referendum.[15] By contrast, the two-day visit (5–6 June) to the region by the UK's Chancellor George Osborne attracted considerably more interest. If the *News Letter*'s Ben Lowry had accused Osborne's colleague David Cameron of trading in fear, the Chancellor's message was similar, albeit this time delivered in bright sunshine and

[12]'The manufacturing success story behind London's red buses', *News Letter*, 1 March 2016, p. 14.

[13]'EU referendum campaign: David Cameron visits Northern Ireland', BBC NI News online, 27 February 2016. http://www.bbc.co.uk/news/uk-northern-ireland-35673442.

[14]'Coaker and UKIP leader in Brexit debate at Belfast campus', *Irish News*, 2 March 2016, p. 6; and 'Farage and Coaker clash during EU debate', *News Letter*, 2 March 2016, p. 8.

[15]'Farage and Coaker argue the bit out in Belfast over Brexit (and have a bet on the side)', *Belfast Telegraph*, 2 March 2016, p. 12.

surrounded by young Remain campaigners, with the Belfast Titanic Quarter (a symbol of Northern Ireland's regeneration) as a backdrop. However, he delivered the substance of his message at Warrenpoint Harbour, within sight of the Republic of Ireland across Carlingford Lough. If Cameron had tried to arouse anxieties about the fate of Northern Irish exports if the UK left the EU, Osborne spoke to the dangers of a hardening Irish border in the event of Brexit.

Beneath its front-page headline 'Osborne: Brexit will harden Irish border', the *News Letter* reported that, according to the Chancellor, 'Brexit would trigger a "profound economic shock"' in Northern Ireland. The *Belfast Telegraph*[16] and *Irish News*[17] relayed the same message, with the *Telegraph* carrying a short article, purportedly written by the Chancellor, emphasizing the dangers of leaving the EU.[18] In it, he reiterated his message that Brexit would mean a loss of 14,000 jobs in Northern Ireland and a 'hit' to the local economy of £1.3bn. Yet despite such alarming figures coming from the UK Treasury, and as with the Prime Minister's dismal forecast for a Brexit result, they provoked no editorials in any of the local newspapers and no headline-grabbing comment from Northern Ireland's elected representatives. It took two former Prime Ministers suggesting that the outcome of the EU referendum could have unwanted consequences for peace in the region to incite a serious response.

'YESTERDAY'S MEN': JOHN MAJOR AND TONY BLAIR

Tony Blair and John Major arrived in Derry on 9 June to warn that leaving the EU would be detrimental to the peace and would risk breaking up the UK. It was a carefully choreographed event at Ulster University's Magee campus in the city, and the two ex-premiers delivered their message before an audience mostly comprising schoolchildren and students, symbolic of the future and therefore of what was at stake in the EU referendum. The symbolism went deeper than that for Northern Ireland. Major had been a key figure at the start of the Northern Irish peace

[16]'Leaving Europe would trigger economic shock for vulnerable NI, warns Osborne', *Belfast Telegraph*, 6 June 2016.

[17]'Profound economic shock for north warns Osborne', *Irish News*, 6 June 2016, p. 14.

[18]'NI would take £1.3bn hit and lose 14,000 jobs if we pull out', by George Osborne, *Belfast Telegraph*, 7 June 2016, p. 14.

process: a signatory, with the then Irish Taoiseach, Albert Reynolds, to the Downing Street Declaration (15 December 1993) which was an attempt to set out the terms of future peace negotiations. Blair was the Prime Minister who saw the process to a successful conclusion, when unionists and nationalists in Northern Ireland signed the Good Friday Agreement on 10 April 1998. If their respective premierships bookended a crucial period in the search for peace, Derry is often thought of as the place where the 'troubles' in Northern Ireland began, and its situation on the border with Donegal in the Republic of Ireland offered a reminder of a potential frontier with Europe should the UK leave. The sight of the two ex-Prime Ministers, from opposing parties, united in their advocacy of the EU and walking onto the city's Peace Bridge in bright sunshine offered a poignant image to complement their key message on this occasion: that leaving the EU was a threat to Northern Ireland's future stability and the peace that both men had worked to achieve.

'Brexit a risk to peace—say ex PMs'[19] ran the *Irish News* headline on 10 June; the *Belfast Telegraph*'s on the same day read 'Brexit risks peace process and UK itself, former rivals Blair and Major say.'[20] However, on this occasion political reaction from local politicians, in particular those in the pro-Brexit DUP, came swiftly. The *News Letter* headlined the Northern Ireland First Minister's response on its front page: 'Foster leads outrage against former PMs.' Beneath this, Arlene Foster, striving to emphasize the former leaders' temporal and spatial separation from Northern Ireland, was quoted as saying it was 'rather sad that people from the past should come over here and try to destabilize Northern Ireland'. In a letter published in the *News Letter*, Northern Ireland-born Labour MP Kate Hoe, echoed Foster's message, accusing Blair and Major of being 'yesterday's men' and assuring its unionist readership that the ex-Prime Ministers were wrong about the threat to the UK's unity.[21]

Prominent also in the coverage of Blair and Major's visit was the angry response of the DUP's Nigel Dodds. He was quoted in the *Irish News* as saying that the ex-Prime Ministers' comments were 'irresponsible nonsense'; in the *Belfast Telegraph* that their remarks were 'dangerous and

---

[19] Ibid., pp. 8–9.

[20] Ibid., pp. 4–5.

[21] 'Yesterday's men: Major and Blair', *News Letter*, 10 June 2016, p. 16.

destabilising',[22] and in the *News Letter*, that Blair and Major had 'devalued their own legacy' and that 'the peace process in Northern Ireland had never been more stable'.[23] The Secretary of State for Northern Ireland, Theresa Villiers, repeated these sentiments in the *Irish News*, which described support for the peace process as 'rock solid'.[24] Despite the confidence of pro-Brexit unionism in the durability of the peace process, it is worth mentioning that on 16 January 2017 the Northern Ireland executive collapsed amid accusations of corruption, incompetence and bad-faith, but in the midst of these controversies was also the question of the UK's exit from the EU and the repercussions for Northern Ireland.

BETWEEN HOPE AND UNCERTAINTY: THE 2016 EU REFERENDUM RESULT

As voters went to the polls on 23 June 2016, only the *Irish News* offered its readers any advice in its daily editorial. Beneath the straightforward instruction 'Vote Remain', the paper argued that the EU was flawed but it was to 'Northern Ireland's financial advantage to stay'.[25] The reaction to the vote was more marked. The *News Letter* greeted the Brexit campaign victory on 25 June 2016 with a front-page headline ('A new Britain') against a pal-blue sky above the Houses of Parliament. 'Momentous vote to leave EU returns power to Westminster and topples Cameron', its strapline read approvingly. Its editorial strove for some semblance of balance: 'The vote for Brexit is a time of joy and hope but also anxiety', read the title. This was a 'new dawn' for the UK:

> [...] one of the most vibrant and successful nations in human history. It has now chosen a new path at a time of great economic opportunity but also great turmoil, danger and tragedy. The wounds from the campaign will take years to heal, but with time they will do, as even nations that went through civil war have done.[26]

---

[22] 'Brexit risks peace and the UK itself, former rivals Blair and Major say', *Belfast Telegraph*, 10 June 2016, pp. 8–9.

[23] 'Foster, Dodds and Hoey all fiercely dismiss the ex-PMs', *News Letter*, 10 June 2016, p. 4.

[24] 'Brexit a risk to peace—Say ex PMs', *Irish News*, 10 June 2016, pp. 14–15.

[25] *Irish News*, 23 June 2016, p. 18.

[26] *News Letter*, 25 June 2016, p. 26.

'A step into the unknown' was how the *Belfast Telegraph* described the decision to leave the EU in its front-page headline, in white letters set ominously against a black background. The headline referred not only to the referendum vote but also to David Cameron, who had announced his resignation from the position of Prime Minister shortly after the vote, pictured on the *Belfast Telegraph*'s front-page stepping out of 10 Downing Street with his wife Samantha Cameron. The uncertainty carried over into the paper's editorial that described these as 'bewildering and truly sensational times'.[27] Like the *News Letter*, the *Belfast Telegraph* was concerned that political divisions should heal; that unionists and nationalists should not turn on one another, but work together to find a way of making Northern Ireland's 'voice louder in the corridors of power', especially given the region's economic vulnerability and peripheral position.

Uncertainty was a key theme of the *Irish News* coverage on 25 June. Its front-page headline perhaps carried a note of exasperation with the First Minster who had campaigned for Brexit. It stated: 'Your move, Arlene: Brexit vote leaves Northern Ireland with litany of fears', accompanied by a peculiarly composed picture of a microphone in the foreground, standing as if awaiting Arlene Foster, who was pictured in the background. The paper's editorial called for stability and leadership.[28] The implications were far-reaching, leaving the island of Ireland with the possibility of a hard border and the North with a loss of European funding. 'We are in a time of deep uncertainty', the *Irish News* concluded, 'and it is up to political leaders to provide a clear sense of direction on the way ahead.'

DISCUSSION

Given the magnitude of the UK's EU referendum, the generally low-key coverage afforded visiting senior British politicians might come as a surprise. Equally startling might be the lack of editorial comment on the day of polling, when only the *Irish News* provide one, urging its readers to vote Remain. Meanwhile, on the front pages of all the local newspapers, the opening of the polls on the 23 June competed for space with

[27] Viewpoint 'Politicians must stop finger-pointing, accept the electorate's decision and heal divisions', *Belfast Telegraph*, 25 June 2016, p. 19.

[28] 'Now executive must provide leadership', *Irish News*, 25 June 2016.

stories about the progress of both Irish football teams in the 2016 UEFA European Championship. The *Irish News* squeezed a column down the left-hand side of its front page, and gave the rest over to coverage of the Republic of Ireland team's progress.[29] The referendum did not feature at all on the *Belfast Telegraph*'s front page; while the *News Letter* at least dignified it with a headline ('Voters face momentous decision in referendum'), but even here it shared the cover with a large photo of Northern Ireland football fans in France.

This is not to say that coverage was uniformly paltry. During the research for this chapter there was no shortage of reports, comment and analysis, but visiting political dignitaries inspired little of it. In terms of prominence and urgency, the coverage of the EU referendum appears in sharp contrast to the last time that Northern Ireland went to the polls on a momentous constitutional question. That was on 22 May 1998, when voters in Northern Ireland and the Republic participated in the referendum to ratify the Good Friday Agreement. Newspaper coverage of the peace process that led to the Agreement often employed epic language to convey the historic significance of what was taking place. Prime Minister Tony Blair set the standard for this, when on 7 April 1998, he and his Irish counterpart Bertie Ahern flew into Belfast to bring some impetus to the flagging talks process. In the entrance portico of Hillsborough Castle, a stately home used as an overnight residence by successive Secretaries of State for Northern Ireland, Blair made an impromptu statement before the waiting press. He told them: 'A day like today is not a day for sound bites, we can leave those at home, but I feel the hand of history upon our shoulder with respect to this, I really do.' Jonathan Powell, Blair's Chief of Staff and key negotiator during that period, recalled how he and Alastair Campbell, the PM's press secretary, giggled at what they regarded as the awkwardness of Blair's comment (2008: 2). Nevertheless, whatever Blair's stated reservations about sound bites on that occasion, and the immediate misgivings of his closest aides, it became one of the most referred-to statements made by any of the participants in the peace talks.

Indeed, press coverage of the peace process matched Blair's grand tone, and on the day of the referendum the *News Letter*, *Belfast Telegraph* and *Irish News* were emphatic and united in their

---

[29] 'North's future in EU on a knife edge', *Irish News*, 23 June 2016, p. 1.

recommendation of a Yes vote.[30] They were at one also in expressing a sense that the future lay in the hands of Northern Ireland's voters. On the day of the referendum, the cover of the *Irish News* proclaimed, 'Let the people decide.' Similarly, the *Belfast Telegraph* editorial emphasized the democratic agency of the local electorate: 'The future lies in our own hands …', while the *News Letter* assured its readers that they were 'the architects and the artisans of a New Model Ulster'.[31] By contrast, during the EU referendum campaign, the *Belfast Telegraph* felt it necessary to remind its readers that their opinions on the UK's membership of the EU was of any consequence at all. In the end, voter turnout in Northern Ireland was 62.7%, down from 81.1% for the Good Friday Agreement referendum, and the lowest of the four constituent parts of the UK. Maybe this relatively low turn-out suggests that there was no great demand for a vote on the EU membership in Northern Ireland, although 44.2%, when given the opportunity, voted to leave. However, there is perhaps a more widespread feeling or appreciation within the region of the role that British and Irish EU membership has played in facilitating a revised conception of sovereignty. Within this, Northern Ireland's consociational arrangements and a relatively open set of socio-economic cross-border relations are capable of accommodating potentially antagonist national allegiances.

If most voters in Northern Ireland wished the UK to stay in the EU, and Scotland was even less inclined to leave, then it is hard not to conclude that the engine driving demands for UK independence is England, and English nationalism in particular. There is a growing literature on contemporary English nationalism (Aughey 2007) and disputes as to its significance and form (English 2011), but as Ben Wellings (2010) has pointed out, English nationalism's ideological foundations lie in a resistance to European integration. It may speak the language of Britishness, he argues, but it is English nationalism in all but name. It also bears the characteristics of a post-imperial melancholia: failing to acknowledge its oppressive imperial past or come to terms with its loss of status and

---

[30] An analysis of the coverage of the referendum on the Good Friday Agreement is available in Greg McLaughlin and Stephen Baker (2010) *The Propaganda of Peace: The Role of the Media and Culture in the Northern Ireland Peace Process.* Bristol: Intellect.

[31] Quoted in Greg McLaughlin and Stephen Baker (2010) *The Propaganda of Peace: The Role of the Media and Culture in the Northern Ireland Peace Process.* Bristol: Intellect, p. 24.

reduced role in the world, while struggling to accommodate perceived others within its imaginary (Gilroy 2004). Post-Brexit Britain, as envisaged by the Conservative Government led by Theresa May, will be a 'great, global trading nation', a reprise of the of what Tom Nairn referred to as the 'imperium of commerce' (Nairn 2002: 33) upon which Britain's past mythological greatness rested.

To some extent, it is the peculiarly English character of this debate that might account for the understated coverage of visiting senior British (we might say, English) politicians during the referendum campaign, confined in large part to the inside pages of Northern Ireland's three daily papers, with scant editorial reaction and political comment. Perhaps when combined with the devolution of limited powers to the Assembly in Stormont, the anxieties and desires of English politics are increasingly remote to voters in Northern Ireland. Only when John Major and Tony Blair brought the future of the peace process into question was there any serious reaction recorded in the local press, and then only from unionists opposed to EU membership. In any case, it was England's peace that was perhaps most obviously and immediately shattered during the EU referendum by the murder of Jo Cox MP. Indeed, the tone of the debate before her death moved veteran journalist Jon Snow to remark: 'In my reporting life I cannot remember a worse-tempered or more abusive, more boring UK campaign than that which is under way right now.'[32]

It is therefore interesting to consider England from the perspective of Northern Ireland at this time. For Ireland, and in particular the North, has always borne the reputation of suffering from an excess of nationalism. As Tom Nairn put it in his prophetic *The Break-up of Britain*, the Irish war appears as a 'marginal aberration in European politics' that 'we modern people can do nothing about' (1977: 223). For Nairn, writing in 1977, this myth of Irish atavism concealed the persisting general political backwardness of Europe (ibid: 224). More specifically, in this contemporary instance, I would argue that Major and Blair's suggestion that Northern Ireland risked a return to the bad old days in the event of Brexit, was a reprise of the myth of atavism. It also wilfully overlooked what they had left behind over the Irish Sea: a growing, nostalgic and socially narrow English nationalism, now stripped of the

---

[32] Jon Snow, 'Why is the EU referendum campaign so boring?', *Radio Times*, 7 June 2016.   http://www.radiotimes.com/news/2016-06-07/why-is-the-eu-referendum-campaign-so-boring.

'banal' façade of Britishness. As Michael Billig argues, established nations ('those at the centre of things') assume that nationalism is a fever afflicting exotic others on the periphery (1995: 5). For England, this notion that it is somehow too modern and civilized to be afflicted with nationalism, is no longer sustainable. In this respect, perhaps Northern Ireland could teach it something about managing constitutional crisis, questions of sovereignty and divided allegiances.

CONCLUSION

The press coverage examined here suggests that the EU referendum accentuated Northern Ireland's peripheral position within the UK and EU. The newspapers that once vigorously and unanimously campaigned on behalf of the peace process, that trumpeted the region's democratic agency after the signing of the Good Friday Agreement, and that acclaimed its ratification in 1998, met the EU referendum in a rather different frame of mind. There was little campaigning zeal and the *Irish News* and *Belfast Telegraph* met the result with uncertainty and apprehension. Even the unionist *News Letter*'s joy was tempered with anxiety, and all seemed acutely aware of the divisive potential of the referendum's fall-out. As Northern Ireland contemplates life outside the EU, dependent upon an increasingly parsimonious Westminster, and faced with a potentially hard border with the rest of the island, it seems that, these days, the hand of history is elsewhere.

REFERENCES

Aughey, Arthur. 2007. *The Politics of Englishness*. Manchester: Manchester University Press.

Billig, Michael. 1995. *Banal Nationalism*. London: Sage.

English, Richard. 2011. *Is There an English Nationalism?* Institute for Public Policy Research. http://www.ippr.org/files/images/media/files/publication/2011/06/Is%20there%20an%20English%20Nationalism%20Apr2011_1838.pdf?noredirect=1.

Gilroy, Paul. 2004. *After Empire: Melancholia or Convivial Culture*. London: Routledge.

McLaughlin, Greg, and Stephen Baker. 2010. *The Propaganda of Peace: The Role of the Media and Culture in the Northern Ireland Peace Process*. Bristol: Intellect.

Nairn, Tom. 1977. *The Break-Up of Britain: Crisis and Neo-Nationalism*. London: Verso.

Nairn, Tom. 2002. *Pariah: Misfortunes of the British Kingdom*. London: Verso.

Powell, Jonathan. 2008. *Great Hatred, Little Room: Making Peace in Northern Ireland*. London: The Bodley Head.

Wellings, Ben. 2010. Losing the Peace: Euroscepticism and the Foundations of Contemporary English Nationalism. *Nations and Nationalism* 16 (3).

CHAPTER 7

Polarized Politics and Personalization: British TV News Coverage of the EU Referendum 2016

Andrew Tolson

INTRODUCTION: A 'BREXIT WHIRLWIND'

In the conclusion to my contribution to the book *Scotland's Referendum and the Media* (Tolson 2016) I quoted some statements made by Jon Snow at the end of a report for *Channel 4 News*. Concluding a visit to Shettleston in the east end of Glasgow he commented that this had been a 'remarkable experience' of an 'exceptional moment' characterized by 'intelligent discourse' and 'coherent arguments'. I suggested that this might have sounded a little patronizing coming from a prominent representative of the London-based media, but that was clearly not the intention. However, for all its best efforts to raise the quality of the debate, not even the highly principled, *Channel 4 News* could arrive at a similar verdict on the 2016 EU referendum campaign. 'Brexit whirlwind' was its headline in the week after the vote as, following the resignation of the

A. Tolson (✉)
University of Leicester, Leicester, UK
e-mail: at382@le.ac.uk

© The Author(s) 2018
A. Ridge-Newman et al. (eds.), *Reporting the Road to Brexit*,
https://doi.org/10.1007/978-3-319-73682-2_7

Prime Minister and leadership challenges in both the main parties, the political establishment seemed to be in meltdown.

In fact, even before the vote, as far as 'intelligent discourse' was concerned, a highly critical metacommentary had developed, principally voiced by politicians themselves. Four weeks earlier, on 27 May, the Treasury Select Committee of Members of Parliament was warning about misleading claims and counterclaims, with clips of its Chair, Andrew Tyrie, on BBC and ITV news talking about 'misleading and impoverishing debate'. However, this kind of commentary was taken to a new level three weeks later in response to the near simultaneous occurrence, on 16 June, of two events: the publication of the United Kingdom Independence Party's (UKIP) 'Breaking Point' poster, widely condemned as racist; and the tragic murder of Jo Cox, Labour MP and Remain supporter. The reaction was immediate, with clips of several MPs on ITV news denouncing the 'aggressive tone' of the campaign with its 'vitriolic' politics, and the former Labour leader Ed Miliband talking about 'too much hatred in politics' (ITV News, 17 June). The campaign was suspended on 18 June out of respect for Cox, but the next day the Conservative Chancellor George Osborne was on ITV's *Peston on Sunday* denouncing the UKIP poster and this was followed on 20 June by a panel interview on *Channel 4 News* (involving former Labour Director of Communications Alastair Campbell, Conservative MP Bernard Jenkin and Labour MP Jess Phillips) discussing the consequences of unacceptable (racist) rhetoric, the 'lies on both sides' and the '[problematic] forces [that] have been unleashed'.

Arguably however, the most insightful comments were made by Cox's fellow Remain campaigner, the Liberal Democrat Baroness Kath Pinnock, on Channel 4 and *BBC news* (also on 17 June). Pinnock's soundbite on *BBC news* was a personal tribute, but on Channel 4 she developed this into a critical judgement about the whole referendum debate, contrasting its 'extraordinarily divisive' and emotive nature with the need to properly engage with 'complex issues'. This is worth quoting in full:

> It has been extraordinarily divisive. It's been a very important public debate which I think has plunged depths which we should not plunge because it's not—we've not been able to focus on the complex issues about Europe so people have narrowed it down to issues which are emotive.

Here, the crisis in British politics that followed the Brexit outcome of the referendum vote was prefigured, in some TV news reports, by critical reflection on the conduct and quality of the public sphere. But of course, mass media are central to the construction of modern public spheres, as spaces for the formation and circulation of public opinion. So the question that follows, to be addressed in this chapter, is how television news played its part in what was perceived, in some quarters, to be a problematic process. Clearly TV news programmes did report and provide space for the critical comments of some politicians; but there are other dimensions to journalistic discourse with possible unintended consequences, as we saw with the Scottish referendum. For journalists not only report, but they also comment and speculate; and they act as participants in the campaigns they follow. How did the journalists in the three main (terrestrial) British TV news programmes (in terms of viewing figures) fulfil these roles, and with what effect(s)? Were they in any way, however unintentionally, complicit in some of the critical issues?

Some Initial Reaction: The Problem of 'Balance'

Quite soon after the Brexit outcome of the vote, criticisms of broadcast news began to emerge, authored by academic commentators and fellow journalists. Unsurprisingly, the latter group tended to be columnists in the Remain-supporting press, such as Catherine Bennett writing in *The Observer* (4 September 2016). Her article referred to research carried out by the Electoral Reform Society (ERS), which had some echoes of Baroness Pinnock in its conclusion that the overall quality of the referendum debate was 'dire'. The ERS also identified the BBC as the main source of public (non-)information, which Bennett linked to its mechanistic 'obsession with balance' whereby 'any carefully argued observation [was ...] promptly followed by its formal opponent's unsubstantiated bluster'. This prompted a response by the BBC's Director of News (James Harding, *The Observer*, 25 September 2016) claiming that the Corporation makes a distinction between 'false balance' and 'due impartiality' which leaves space for journalists to 'make judgements' and 'challenge facts and figures'. Interestingly, Harding went on to argue that the BBC's job 'is to report, to host the argument and to interrogate participants'. This would seem to provide a useful template against which to judge the activities of its journalists.

Early academic commentaries also focused on the issue of balance. A booklet co-produced by the Political Studies Association (PSA) and research centres at Loughborough and Bournemouth (June 2016) contained 79 short (one or two-page) essays written by affiliates to the PSA (Media and Politics Group). Here, some statistical research showed that both sides were indeed given equal airtime, but only a minority of their claims were subjected to critical scrutiny by journalists. Hence 'objectivity in this sense was trumped by impartiality' (Cushion and Lewis 2016). Another polemical contribution to this booklet offered three examples of 'phoney balance' in a 'format of "balanced" news that was stupefyingly predictable' (Gaber 2016); and the BBC's failure to correct Vote Leave's 'big fat lie' about Britain's contribution to the EU was singled out as a particular example of this (Hughes 2016). A further twist to the argument about balance criticized its reduction to 'personality politics of the worst kind' as the TV coverage revolved around letting 'the big guns on both sides slug it out' (Temple 2016). This was confirmed by further statistical analysis which showed that TV news was 'highly presidential', with only five individuals (three Leave, two Remain) accounting for one in four of all media appearances (Deacon et al. 2016).

Thus, an academic consensus was suggesting that TV news, and the BBC in particular, failed in its duty to interrogate the claims made in the referendum campaign. This negative judgement was perhaps inevitable in the immediate aftermath of the Brexit vote, and clearly there are critical questions to be asked about what Gaber called its 'predictable format'. However, in the longer term, it may be useful to adopt a more nuanced approach to these questions; to recognize, for instance, that there were examples of analytic news, even if these was inconsistent. For example, *BBC news* routinely referred viewers seeking further information to its website; but as this was clearly intended as a secondary source, it does not feature in the analysis presented here. In conventional TV news programmes, participants in the campaign were sometimes interrogated in interviews, particularly on *Channel 4 News* (we will return to the use of interviews on the other channels) and 'experts' were routinely recruited to provide counterarguments. Even the 'obsession with balance' is open to some reconsideration. It certainly was a pervasive feature of TV news, but the critical question can be turned around: from one point of view it was a limitation; but from another, perhaps it had a different kind of journalistic intelligibility.

From 'Fact-Checking' to Editorial Commentary

On 27 May, as part of its report on the intervention of the Treasury Select Committee, ITV news illustrated Carl Dinnen's report with onscreen data refuting the 'misleading' claims of Vote Leave. On the BBC (1 June), presenter Reeta Chakrabarti included in a report on Vote Leave's immigration policy figures which showed that only a minority of migrants were from the EU, though this was contradicted by statistics in a later report by Gavin Hewitt (*BBC News* Editor) on claims made by the campaign group Migration Watch. All three news channels offered occasional items on 'fact checking': for example, by Allegra Stratton (ITV's National Editor) on claims made by Cameron and Farage in their ITV debate (ITV, 7 June); Victoria Macdonald (Channel 4's Health Correspondent) in a piece about the National Health Service (NHS) on claims made about 'health tourism' (*Channel 4 News*, 14 June); and by John Pienaar (the BBC's Deputy Political Editor) on the claims made by both sides about payments to the EU, though in this case the critical perspective came in a follow-up clip of an economist from the Institute of Fiscal Studies (IFS) and not Pienaar himself (BBC, 14 June).

Which introduces a further dimension to the critical interrogation of claims: where they were not interrogated by journalists, outside experts were often used, such as economists and financial analysts. For example, the *BBC news* of 23 June had an interview with Jamie Dimon of JP Morgan ('the most famous Banker on Wall Street') describing Brexit as a 'terrible deal for the UK economy', and a similar warning was reported on the BBC (6 June) from Janet Yellen, Head of the American Central Bank. A report from Berlin on *Channel 4 News* (21 June) included a German industrialist warning about Brexit. There were numerous clips of warnings from Mark Carney, Governor of the Bank of England, and the IFS was represented by Paul Johnson (*BBC News*, 23 May) contradicting claims made by Vote Leave. There were some interviews with Leave-supporting business people but generally the 'expert' contributions favoured Remain. Arguably, taken together, the 'fact checking' by journalists coupled with these external contributions did constitute a thread of informed commentary.

However, this had little overall effect. If, indeed, 'objectivity was trumped by impartiality', perhaps we need to know how exactly and why. And here a useful starting point might be to deconstruct the 'impartiality' principle, by recognizing the different forms (at least three) that it takes. The first, (Gaber's 'phoney balance') comprises rebuttals, whereby arguments made on one side are immediately refuted by the other. Typical of these were the appearances by Conservative Remain supporter Amber Rudd on *Channel 4 News* (31 May) dismissing a Vote Leave claim about lower fuel bills as 'fantasy economics'; and clips of Conservative MP Iain Duncan Smith on all the main news programmes on 15 June denouncing George Osborne's 'Brexit budget'. However, perhaps the most notorious rebuttal, because it buttressed a repeated Vote Leave claim, was the appearance of former Conservative Chancellor Nigel Lawson on both the BBC and ITV (23 May) to characterize a Treasury report on the negative consequences of Brexit as part of a 'scare campaign'. Perhaps the reason why such rebuttals are so problematic for some commentators, although Gaber does not say this, is that they almost seem automatic. Campaign managers know journalists are looking for contrasting soundbites, so they promptly field prominent politicians to provide them.

But this is not the only way TV news journalism can seem manipulated. Because it clearly requires visual footage, modern campaigning provides this in the form of stage-managed campaign events, photo opportunities and press conferences. There is little need here to expand on the now well-established argument about 'celebrity' politics (see Washbourne 2010), other than to note that in the UK, because of its size, each 'campaign trail' is led by a 'battlebus', out of which steps, at any particular venue, a cast of central characters. Crucially, however, this cast includes the political editors who themselves contribute to these rituals. They are part of the audience for speeches, they are shown asking questions at press conferences, and in this campaign they were even occasionally filmed aboard a battlebus; for example, Laura Kuenssberg, the BBC's Political Editor, with the Leave campaign (6 June) and Chris Ship, ITV's Deputy Political Editor, who conducted a short interview with Cameron (22 June). It can be argued, then, that this type of campaigning amounts to the co-construction of television events by politicians and by journalists, in which the latter not only report, but also participate.

Three critical points can be made about this form of journalism. First, it was apparent that on any particular day all the TV news organizations were covering the same events (such as the visit by Boris Johnson on 6 June to a cleaning products factory in Stratford-upon-Avon). This meant that the same clips were shown on all three channels and it explains why the same cast of characters (Cameron and Osborne for Remain; Johnson and Gove for Leave) dominated the coverage. This was another reason why the format was so 'predictable'. Second, another form of 'impartiality' was achieved here simply by deploying journalists to cover both 'campaign trails' with film footage of each 'balanced' by the other. Third in this type of journalism any critical interrogation of participants was minimal. The political editors were filmed by their respective organizations asking questions at press conferences, but these were single questions, not the sustained exchanges possible in an extended interview.

What took the place of critical interrogation, for the most part, was editorial commentary. This is a subgenre of news discourse prominent in daily news bulletins (but not in news magazine programmes featuring longer interviews and studio discussions) where political editors contextualize events through voice-over and presentations to camera, sometimes in live '2-ways' (though ITV news now locates its key commentators, such as Political Editor Robert Peston, in studio exchanges with the main presenter, Tom Bradby). These exchanges have been described as 'affiliative interviews' designed to co-produce consensual interpretations of news events (Montgomery 2007). So what kinds of interpretation of the EU referendum campaign were produced in this way? Here is John Pienaar at Westminster on *BBC News* (8 June) following a report on the extension of the deadline to register to vote:

[To camera] The race could be tight. Every vote will count and that's why the campaign has become so frantic with the Leavers warning of more migration if we stay in the EU and the Stronger Inside talking about a meltdown in the markets if we choose to leave. Now there are fresh warnings that if Britain chooses to leave the EU more Scots will want to leave Britain. No-one's holding back.

[...]

Thousands more will be able to vote. Will more young voters swing it for Remain or more voters angry about EU meddling win it for the Leavers?

[voice-over shots of Palace of Westminster, in the rain] There's not much cheer from either side so far. It's been more about competing visions of gloom. But on June 23rd voters will decide once and for all how the country's run and the skies are already darkening on the political fall-out.

No doubt the BBC could defend this as an example of public service broadcasting. Promoting voter registration and emphasizing the significance of the vote (even if its constitutional status was in fact unclear) could perhaps justify Pienaar's use of hyperbole. However, his commentary is also an example of a third form of 'impartiality', with its reference to key arguments on both sides and the open question about who will win. There are two critical observations to make about this discourse, which is a typical example of this type of commentary. The first is that the arguments on both sides are characterized in negative terms, and attributed to the parties concerned, who are cast in mutual opposition. What might have been a debate about Britain's future is thus reduced to 'competing visions of gloom'. The second point is that this competition is also framed (with help from the film footage) in the context of an apocalyptic narrative. Here the referendum vote may be important, but the campaign itself is an unfolding, polarized, dramatic conflict.

A Polarized Narrative

This narrative of the referendum campaign passed through several phases, leading up to the vote and beyond. Initially the focus was on divisions in the Conservative Party, so-called 'blue on blue' splits, probably because both campaigns were dominated by Tory politicians. But this was also a consequence of the way TV news chose to report the campaigns. As we have seen, journalists actively participated on 'campaign trails'. They also showed clips in news bulletins of leading politicians being interviewed in Sunday morning news magazines (The BBC's *Andrew Marr Show* and ITV's *Peston on Sunday*). This allowed, for example, James Mates on ITV News (5 June) to introduce interview clips of Cameron and Gove as a 'civil war', subsequently glossed by reporter Romilly Weeks, in a studio exchange with Mates, as a 'war at the heart of the Tory party'. Up to this point, as noted by Jon Snow on *Channel 4 News* (9 June), 'amid all the blue on blue action' Labour had been 'most notable by its relevant absence', though its former Deputy Leader Harriet Harman did start to appear with the Remain side from 6 June.

One theme of the 'blue on blue action' was a suggestion that the Leave campaign was looking like an alternative government. This became a significant feature of the news agenda on all channels following Leave's announcement of its policies on immigration and fuel bills which, according to Laura Kuenssberg, was 'mashed up with Tory leadership ambition' (*BBC News*, 31 May). The following day on ITV News, presenter Rageh Omaar introduced this as a 'manifesto launch' and Robert Peston talked about Leave being 'on the front foot' as 'a government in waiting'. By 15 June on *BBC news* this agenda had escalated, according to Kuenssberg, from an 'alternative mini-manifesto' to a 'coup in waiting', and this was followed by Ben Wright, a BBC political correspondent, talking about a battle that would be 'hard fought down to the wire' (18 June). In these commentaries, the polarized campaign was not just produced by the politicians themselves, it was also created by a narrative discourse imposed on events by journalists.

To some extent, this was put into context by the murder of Jo Cox. The day after that event, as Baroness Pinnock made her intervention, Kuenssberg commented on the difference between the consensual reaction to the murder and the 'very confrontational' campaign. Later, on the day MPs paid tribute to Cox in the House of Commons (20 June), she speculated about whether the event would cause some voters to reconsider, or whether the 'vibrant and visceral' campaign with the 'strong beliefs that have been expressed' could be contained. That it could not seemed evident almost immediately as, on 21 June, the BBC held its 'great debate' at Wembley Arena. Again, its news used opposing soundbites with Kuenssberg talking about 'big ideas, big characters, big rows'; all of which was distinctly at odds with interviews that same day with Brendan Cox, Jo's husband, on *Channel 4 News* and on the BBC (and the BBC interview was conducted by Kuenssberg) where he spoke about her worries about the tone of the debate and the 'hatred' surrounding politics. But following its debate, it was the BBC's own journalism that apparently could not be contained.

However, the polarized narrative reached a further level of intensity following the referendum vote. Now it was no longer about two sides engaged in rhetorical battles, but rather the apparent implosion of leadership in both the main political parties. Speculation about Cameron's future and Boris Johnson's personal ambition actually predated the poll, with a particular focus on personal divisions between leaders of the Leave campaign (ITV News, 20 and 22 June). Rageh Omaar introduced the ITV News of 22 June by stressing the 'bitter' and divisive nature of the campaign; but this focus went on to dominate news agendas for much of the following two weeks. As Cameron resigned on 24 June, Channel 4 and ITV news both had a clip of Stanley Johnson, Boris's father, supporting his leadership credentials. News of a challenge to

Jeremy Corbyn coupled with multiple shadow cabinet resignations had Laura Kuenssberg on the *BBC News* (26 June) talking about 'Labour Party leadership chaos'. By 27 June this had escalated to a 'fourth day of chaos in government' and 'open war in the Labour Party' according to ITV news; but this narrative reached its climax on 29/30 June as Johnson was forced to resign from the Conservative leadership contest following Michael Gove's withdrawal of support. Now the 'Brexit whirlwind' became explicitly dramatic, being compared to the TV shows *Game of Thrones* (Channel 4) and *House of Cards* (ITV) as Gove 'got up this morning and knifed his friend in the back' (Chris Ship, ITV News, 30 June).

Personalized Interviews and TV Debates

By now it should be apparent that TV news coverage of the EU referendum took the form of an interplay between two levels of activity. At one level there were the campaign events (photo opportunities [often in workplaces], press conferences, soundbites and interviews), which were co-produced by politicians and journalists. At a second level these then fed into a journalistic metadiscourse, where commentary was largely focused on polarization, given some poignancy but not displaced by the murder of Jo Cox. However, I now want to examine briefly two journalistic practices that took the polarized narrative into further interesting, but problematic territory. These were: first, how some interviews were conducted with leading protagonists in both 'teams'; and second, how the TV debates were subsequently covered in news programmes (the BBC's 'great debate' was the third out of four on the channels covered by this chapter).

News interviews are of course a very well-established form of TV ritual, particularly during election campaigns. They have also been extensively studied and there is not the space in this chapter to fully engage with all this work (for a recent summary, see Ekstrom and Tolson 2017). Very briefly then, discourse analysis has made a distinction between two subtypes of news interview (alongside interviews with experts and affiliative exchanges between fellow journalists). These are the classic 'accountability' interview and the so-called 'hybrid' interview, where in the former interviewers adopt a 'neutralistic' stance and in the latter they sometimes engage in combative, even argumentative exchanges with interviewees. In the news programmes covered by this chapter, both of these types of interview were a fairly common feature of *Channel 4 News*, probably because of its greater length and because on the BBC and ITV longer news interviews were largely the preserve of the Sunday morning programmes and the BBC's *Daily Politics*.

What could be found in some BBC and ITV news programmes was a somewhat different kind of approach where the focus was on human interest as much as political argument (This was not without precedent: the BBC's then Political Editor Nick Robinson conducted similar interviews with Cameron and Clegg during the 2015 General Election). One feature of such interviews is that they sometimes cross the boundary between formal and informal spaces: moving out of studios to encounters in private spaces, or where politicians, out campaigning, are in transit. For example, on ITV News (20 June) Allegra Stratton interviewed Boris Johnson on a train; and the following day Peston's interview with Cameron involved joining him in his car 'for a short day out'. What then ensued was what might be termed a 'personalized' form of news interview. Following the contentious Farage poster, Stratton repeatedly asked Johnson whether he liked Nigel Farage's view of Britain; and Cameron was asked by Peston whether he was upset about former friends (like Gove) who had 'turned into seemingly bitter enemies [...] how hard has that been'?

But the apotheosis of this type of personalized interview has to be the encounter between Kuenssberg and Gove on *BBC News* (12 June). This took place in Gove's parental home in Aberdeen, where his father used to be a fish merchant. In a voice-over (as Gove looks at old photographs), Kuenssberg explains that the family continued to blame the EU for the collapse of that business, and Gove remembers 'feeling that some of the debates [about Europe] weren't rooted in real people's experience'. The interview then continued as follows:

LK: But votes are about the future [MG: mm] and as we talk this afternoon ten days away from the vote you can't tell voters how our economy would work. You can't tell voters how we would continue to trade with the rest of the EU. You can't guarantee anything.

MG: I'm not suggesting er that Britain boldly goes where no man has gone before. I'm suggesting erm that Britain becomes an independent self-governing country.

LK: [voice-over] That lack of detail has been roundly and repeatedly attacked by the Prime Minister and the Chancellor, even accusing

him and fellow outers of wilfully misleading the public. [Gove comments on a photograph he is holding.]
The Prime Minister started off giving you the [yeh] space to campaign against him. He said he wanted everything to be respectful. Now he and others are going round saying you're a fantasist. Saying you and Boris Johnson aren't telling the truth. I mean it's got a bit out of hand hasn't it?

MG: I don't mind that. [I-
LK: [] You don't mind the Prime Minister calling you a liar?
MG: Erm I'm not a commentator. I'm a participant in this. So I can't offer and I won't offer a running commentary on er what any individual has said. I'm just here to put my argument and I admire the Prime Minister hugely [...]

What is very clear here is the way political argument gives way to personalization. Actually, in her first intervention (which follows Gove's lament about his father's business), Kuenssberg comes close to the 'hybrid' interview style where she herself appears to be the author of her three accusations. But then she shifts the agenda to interpersonal divisions between the Conservative politicians leading the campaign, firstly with a tag question (which prefers a 'yes' answer) and secondly with a follow-up prompt (which escalates Cameron's alleged accusation). This is clearly an example of polarized politics shading into personal territory; and we can also observe that the TV viewer watching this news item would learn absolutely nothing from it about EU fisheries policy and its more general impact on the UK fishing industry. All that has been reduced to a human-interest story based on one individual's personal experience.

A second problematic journalistic practice occurred in the reporting of TV debates. Unlike news interviews, televised political debates were still something of a novelty in the UK, having been introduced as party leader debates in the 2010 General Election (Coleman 2011). During the referendum campaign there were two main TV debates on ITV (one head-to-head between Cameron and Farage; one panel debate between three representatives of each side) followed by the 'great debate' (also a panel debate) on the BBC and a final debate on Channel 4 featuring rotating panels with celebrities as well as politicians. As far as the news coverage was concerned, ITV in particular both previewed its debates and followed them up with live two-ways between its presenter (Tom Bradby) and political editor (Robert Peston), who was located in a so-called 'spin room', or space at the venue set aside for journalists (the BBC only did this for its own debate, with its Deputy Editor John Pienaar in the 'spin room'). Again, the job of political editors was to produce commentaries which invariably took the form of 'balanced' judgements on how the parties had performed, where 'both sides have claimed victory' (Kuenssberg, 9 June) and we had the spectacle of 'members of the same government at each other's throats' (Peston, 9 June). Once more then, a polarized narrative was very much in evidence.

However, what was also evident was that a 'performance frame' dominated both how the debates were promoted, and how they were received by viewers—at least by the viewers subsequently interviewed. For instance, in his preview of the ITV debate, Peston referred to Nicola Sturgeon as a 'star performer' in the previous year's General Election. ITV followed up both its debates with some 'fact checking', but also with vox pops with voters (students after the Cameron/Farage debate; family groups around the country on 9 June). In the second piece, voters were filmed watching and commenting on the debates to which they reacted and made comments on some of the arguments. But in their final assessments the agenda shifted from substantive arguments to more general performative judgements, seemingly prompted by an (unheard) question that had been asked:

> I was impressed with Nicola Sturgeon again. She knows how to talk. But I was also impressed with Boris Johnson. He was a cool calm collected character.

> I think obviously Nicola Sturgeon she's always a polished performer. Er but she was good tonight erm and I thought Andrea Leadsom was quite good as well.

> People who impressed me most were Andrea and Gisela on the out campaign. They were very calm got their point across very well.

> I'm very much on the fence where I don't want to be and I'm waiting for somebody to guide me one way or the other. And I'm probably like millions of other voters in this country.

Here again, in such commentaries, whether produced by journalists in their spin rooms or by voters in vox pops, the focus is as much, if not more, on 'personality' as it is on the substance of the debate. And in responses to the debates, it wasn't so much that either side won the argument as that their personal credibility was at stake. This then is second example of a polarized narrative producing 'personalized politics'; and as this displaced engagement with substantive argument, it was perhaps not surprising that some voters confessed to being confused.

Vox Pops as Provincial Encounters

Vox pops were singled out by Ivor Gaber in his critique of the 'predictable' format of TV news. He complained about a 'tedious over-reliance' on vox pops, particularly when they involved the denunciation of politicians to the exclusion of more nuanced comments. In fact, this criticism does not reflect the majority of vox pops recorded in my sample, but in one respect Gaber was right: they were ubiquitous, particularly on Channel 4. In total, 76% of Channel 4 news programmes with some referendum content included vox pops, whereas the figure for *BBC news* was 47% and for ITV news 33%. Across the board, discounting the undecided, 36% of vox pops were from Remain supporters with 64% for Leave. Arguably, however, this was not a problem of bias or, as was alleged by some commentators, that the TV news agenda was influenced by the Eurosceptic press. Rather, vox pops were used to illustrate particular issues in the unfolding narrative of the campaign.

With two weeks to go before the vote, one focus was on voter registration and in particular whether young people would vote. This was illustrated in all the news programmes on 7 June by vox pops with students; but it was preceded by a *Channel 4 News* the previous day located in Norwich. Here Jon Snow led a youth debate in Norwich Castle whilst Fatima Manji conducted vox pops with older and younger voters to illustrate the generational divide in voter intentions. By the end of that week, however, the agenda had shifted to the Labour Party and the possibility of a Leave vote in its 'heartlands'. This involved roving reports to such locations: for example, by John Pienaar to West Bromwich (BBC, 10 June), by Carl Dinnen to Worksop (ITV, 10 June) and by Gary Gibbon to Walsall (Channel 4, 13 June). There was also a set of vox pops in Leicester market with ethnic-minority voters being asked 'quiz questions' about Labour's position by Robert Peston (ITV News, 13 June). Their confusion about this, even ignorance, was foregrounded by Peston's approach.

In the wake of the vote itself, all the news programmes seemed preoccupied with visiting areas where the Leave vote was strongest (but, also,

Scotland and Northern Ireland where Brexit would have constitutional ramifications). There is not space here to provide a detailed analysis of this material, other than to say that a highly predictable process took journalists to the working-class heartlands of Essex (Romford, Canvey Island), the Midlands (Birmingham, Mansfield) and the North-East (Hartlepool, South Shields). Starting on 24 June, Penny Marshall (ITV Social Affairs Editor) embarked on a tour of Leave constituencies in the Midlands, visiting not only industrial, but also agricultural (Boston, Lincolnshire) and rural areas (Blaby, Leicestershire). However, following seven vox pops in a clothing factory in Mansfield (six for Leave, one Remain) it was the owner, when interviewed by Marshall, who seemed to put his finger on a crucial point:

> It's a total different world north and south. The north and south divide is true it is true and that's why you got a different reaction [to the vote]. 'Cos in London where all the media spin happens it's a bubble it's a real real bubble. Here in the Midlands, Mansfield Nottingham and as you go further north I mean it's nothing like. We've had it all.

Following the referendum result, some commentators also began to suggest that the TV news coverage had reflected a London-centric 'media bubble'. For instance, the Conservative MP Anna Soubry on the BBC (24 June) mentioned this in her criticism of the focus on 'personalities' rather than 'critical issues'; and the TV presenter Kirstie Allsopp talked on *Channel 4 News* (1 July) about a London-based media elite who did not understand Leave voters. In this chapter we have seen that polarized politics and personal animosities (particularly between prominent Conservatives) were a primary focus of the coverage; but an overview of the vox pops also reveals something of another side to the journalistic coin. For it was not that vox pops were used indiscriminately, though they were certainly subordinated to dominant news agendas. Rather, the key issue here was the encounters between London-based journalists and dispersed, provincial, populations. It is too simple to reduce this to a North-South divide, but it certainly did reflect an imbalance of cultural power between core and periphery. Arguably this distance, even alienation, was a major factor in the Brexit vote, and here the journalistic elite were just as much implicated as the politicians themselves.

REFERENCES

ACADEMIC SOURCES

Coleman, S. (ed.). 2011. *Leaders in the Living Room: The Prime Ministerial Debates of 2010.* Reuters Institute for the Study of Journalism: University of Oxford.

Cushion, S., and J. Lewis. 2016. Scrutinising Statistical Claims and Constructing Balance: Television News Coverage of the 2016 EU Referendum. In *EU Referendum Analysis 2016: Media Voters and the Campaign*, ed. D. Jackson, E. Thorsen, and D. Wring, 40–41. Poole, UK: The Centre for the Study of Journalism, Culture and Community, Bournemouth University.

Deacon, D., J. Downey, E. Harmer, J. Stanyer, and D. Wring. 2016. The Narrow Agenda: How the News Media Covered the Referendum. In op. cit, ed. D. Jackson, E. Thorsen, and D. Wring, 34–35.

Ekstrom, M., and A. Tolson. 2017. Political Interviews: Pushing the Boundaries of Neutralism. In *The Mediated Politics of Europe: A Comparative Study of Discourse*, ed. M. Ekstrom and J. Firmstone. Basingstoke: Palgrave Macmillan.

Gaber, I. 2016. Bending Over Backwards: The BBC and the Brexit Campaign. In op. cit, ed. D. Jackson, E. Thorsen, and D. Wring, 54.

Hughes, K. 2016. Neither Tackling Lies nor Making the Case: The Remain Side. In op. cit, ed. D. Jackson, E. Thorsen, and D. Wring, 65.

Montgomery, M. 2007. *The Discourse of Broadcast News.* London: Routledge.

Temple, M. 2016. A (Very) Brief Period of Habermasian Bliss. In op. cit, ed. D. Jackson, E. Thorsen, and D. Wring, 62.

Tolson, A. 2016. English Television News Coverage of the Scottish Referendum. In *Scotland's Referendum and the Media: National and International Perspectives*, ed. N. Blain and D. Hutchison. Edinburgh: Edinburgh University Press.

Washbourne, N. 2010. *Mediating Politics.* Maidenhead: Open University Press.

MEDIA SOURCES

Bennett, C. 2016. The BBC's Fixation on 'Balance' Badly Skews the Truth. *The Observer*, September 4, p. 35.

Harding, J. 2016. A Truly Balanced View from the BBC: Don't Blame Us for Brexit. *The Observer*, September 25, p. 42.

CHAPTER 8

The 2016 EU Referendum in Gibraltar: Opinion Articles in Gibraltarian News

Ángela Alameda Hernández

INTRODUCTION

The EU referendum that took place in the United Kingdom (UK) on 23 June 2016 had an unquestionable and impressive impact not only on the British Isles and the meaning of the European Union (EU) itself, but also on other parts of the world. This chapter focuses on Gibraltar, one of the British peripheral territories that, although physically separated from the UK, remains politically linked to it. Gibraltar is a narrow rocky peninsula linked to the southern Mediterranean coast of Spain, and its location is privileged for being at a strategic crossroads between the two continents of Europe and Africa and two important masses of water, the Mediterranean Sea and Atlantic Ocean. With a population of around 30,000, it is Europe's only non self-governing territory and its administering power is the UK. Indeed, despite its small size, Gibraltar is principally known for being a piece of British territory on the European mainland.

Á. Alameda Hernández (✉)
University of Granada, Granada, Spain
e-mail: aalameda@ugr.es

© The Author(s) 2018
A. Ridge-Newman et al. (eds.), *Reporting the Road to Brexit*,
https://doi.org/10.1007/978-3-319-73682-2_8

127

This chapter offers a somewhat outsider perspective into the 2016 EU referendum as it focuses on this overseas territory. In the current context, the Gibraltar perspective deserves scholarly attention because of the international political consequences that may arise, affecting the decisions and policies of two European powers, the UK and Spain. The main objective of this chapter is to analyse media coverage of the referendum in Gibraltar. Specifically, the textual corpus consists of editorial and opinion articles drawn from the Gibraltarian press on the dates surrounding the referendum. More precisely, this research adheres to the theoretical paradigm known as critical discourse analysis (CDA), which analyses language in relation to the social context in which it appears, aiming at providing social critique based on linguistic evidence. Since social meanings and values are coded in words, linguistic analysis in this chapter focuses on lexical choices and semantic fields as predicational strategies (Reisigl and Wodak 2001: 45) through which the Gibraltarian press constructs its own representations and evaluation of the EU referendum. Such an analysis becomes paramount in the present research as the evaluation and emotional impact of a text are constructed through these lexical choices (Fairclough 2003). Moreover, my analysis is approached from an interdisciplinary perspective, since, although mainly based on discursive evidence, it necessarily connects with social, political and historical aspects to build up a complete and coherent picture of the situation. In the light of the EU referendum and its consequences, CDA seems particularly suitable since, as described by one of its leading practitioners and founding fathers, CDA is 'primarily interested and motivated by pressing social issues, which it hopes to better understand through discourse analysis' (Van Dijk 1993: 252). Consequently, together with a pure linguistic analysis, social, geographical and historical aspects of the Gibraltarian community will be succinctly presented, because any critical interpretation requires knowledge about the history and the 'social and political fields in which discursive "events" are embedded' (Wodak 2001: 65). Hence, this broad CDA paradigm is used in this chapter responding to the geopolitical specificities of Gibraltar. Indeed, the community that lives on 'the Rock' is the result of complex geographical, historical and social factors that have brought about an interesting and distinctive human grouping, whose individualities and status have been shaken to the core by the recent British referendum on EU membership.

Gibraltar

Gibraltar's physical shape and geographical location have no doubt contributed to its unique evolution. The best-known historical event in this evolution, and the one with the greatest consequences for the present, was the British invasion of the Rock in 1704 in support of one of the candidates in the Spanish War of Succession (Kent 2004: 23) . In 1713, by the Treaty of Utrecht which put an end to the conflict, the Fortress of Gibraltar was officially yielded to Britain. As a result, Gibraltar has been British for over 300 years. Spain, however, has never surrendered its claim to the Rock and attempts to recover it (sometimes violent, more recently diplomatic) have not ceased since the so-called Great Siege which lasted for about four years (1779–1783); through the painful closing of the border from 1969 to 1982, which meant more than a decade of isolation for a tiny territory that depends on the neighbouring mainland for fresh supplies and basic needs; to the more recent, intermittent and unsuccessful negotiations between the foreign affairs ministers of Britain and Spain. Hence, the Gibraltarian community has been exposed to particularly strong challenges in its most recent history.

The last decades have witnessed attempts on the part of the political powers involved (the UK, Spain and the United Nations) to modify the political status of Gibraltar, putting an end to the colonial situation and possibly implying a change of sovereignty, which Gibraltarians themselves felt as a threat to their own social and national identity. Twice in their history Gibraltarians have held referendums on their status (in 1967 and 2002) and on both occasions the outcome was overwhelmingly in favour of retaining their link with Britain and against any form of co-sovereignty, particularly involving Spanish co-sovereignty. Over this period, Britain has also granted Gibraltar greater self-government (Stockey and Grocott 2012: 113). It was granted a Constitution in 1969 and a new Constitution in 2006, which provides a modern relationship between Gibraltar and the Government of the UK, as a British Overseas Territory. The new Parliament of Gibraltar has full self-government in internal affairs, while the UK is responsible for matters of defence and international affairs. These include relations with and representation in the EU. As a result, the outcome of the EU referendum held in the UK in June 2016 leaves Gibraltar in the quicksands of an uncertain future. Indeed, even shortly after the referendum was called, the Spanish government confirmed its intention to raise the issue of the sovereignty of Gibraltar should the UK leave the EU.

The Impact of the EU Referendum in Gibraltar

With such a recent tumultuous history, as well as their familiarity with holding crucial referendums, it is no surprise that the 2016 British referendum on EU membership received extensive coverage in the Gibraltarian press. The interest in and consequences of the result of the referendum were particularly relevant since, on the one hand, Gibraltarians had the right to vote; and, on the other hand, because losing EU citizenship could have significant consequences for the Gibraltarian people. Although, as a British Overseas Territory, Gibraltar had joined the EU along with the UK in 1973, it had not participated in other UK-wide referendums. However, the implementation of the European Union Referendum Act 2015 in Gibraltar enabled the territory's full participation in the 2016 referendum. In addition, it was indeed an issue of paramount importance for Gibraltar considering the omnipresent (even if sometimes dormant) Spanish claims of sovereignty over the Rock.

In the present study, the two main newspapers of Gibraltar have been selected. They are both quality press, with wide distribution and recognized prestige in Gibraltar. First, *The Gibraltar Chronicle* (henceforth *The Chronicle*) is Gibraltar's oldest newspaper and, although it is written entirely in English, it is generally referred to using the Spanish term *La Crónica*. Being the newspaper of a small area, *The Chronicle* necessarily has a small circulation (about 3000), but it covers a necessary intermediary role between a national newspaper and a community newspaper. Indeed, today, *The Chronicle* has become an institution on the Rock. It is the most widely read newspaper and was Gibraltar's only daily newspaper until April 2002. For its part, *Panorama* has become the second-most popular print medium in Gibraltar. It started as a weekly in December 1975 with the desire to offer a different view of local and international news from that presented by the more institutionalized *Chronicle*, eventually becoming the most popular news weekly in Gibraltar (Kellermann 2001: 232) before becoming a daily at the beginning of 2002. Both newspapers are also available on the Internet. Thus, while the print version helps to influence and reinforce the views of each newspaper in the local community, the online version helps to spread their peculiar Gibraltarian view on the Brexit (Britain's exit from the EU) issue beyond its borders. Furthermore, these newspapers reflect the different political slants of the community. On the one hand, *The Chronicle* has always been the vehicle for the publication of official notices, and there is a close relationship between the editorship of the newspaper and the democrat-ically elected government of Gibraltar, currently the Gibraltar Socialist Labour Party (GSLP). Hence, it represents the official governmental voice of the dependency, while *Panorama* has traditionally been associ-ated with the GLP (Gibraltar Liberal Party) and thus reflects liberal ideas, even though in the current term the GLP is in alliance with the GSLP of the Chief Minister, and thus is part of the Government of Gibraltar.

Analysis of these two newspapers focuses on the opinion columns and editorial articles that dealt with the EU referendum and which were published 20 days before and 10 days after. The main motivation for the selection of opinion and editorial articles is that this genre reflects the reactions, attitudes and feelings of people towards current events, situations, individuals and conflicts. In Fowler's (1991) words, newspaper language 'reflects, and in return shapes, the prevailing values of a society in a particular historical moment' (1991: 223). This is true of newspaper language in general, and particularly of this kind of genre within news-papers. Hence, because of the great influence of mass media on the pub-lic, no doubt the two newspapers' representation of the Brexit issue must have influenced Gibraltarian society's perception of it whilst, at the same time, constituting a valuable barometer of the perceptions and attitudes of this community towards the referendum. Being newspapers in a small community, *The Chronicle* and *Panorama* do not include opinion articles, nor even editorials, on a daily basis but only when local or international events are relevant enough to deserve editorial comment. Leaders in *The Chronicle* are more frequent, while in *Panorama* op-eds by the editor appear more sporadically, which explains the smaller number of editorials from this newspaper in the corpus gathered for the present study.

In quantitative terms, coverage of the EU referendum in the opin-ion section of the two main newspapers was extensive. The referendum had caught the attention of the editorial boards of both newspapers as soon as it was called. We can find editorials and opinion articles as early as February 2016, just a few days after the referendum date was officially announced by the then British Prime Minister David Cameron. An edito-rial on 23 February and an opinion article on 22 February in *Panorama*, together with an editorial on 17 March and a lengthy article by a guest contributor on 15 March in *The Chronicle*, are instances in point. In addi-tion, this newspaper even included an article by Chief Minister Fabian Picardo as a guest contributor, in which he expressed his desire to address the people of Gibraltar on 15 April, the date when the official campaign period kicked off, as he would not be allowed to do so in the following months in accordance with the broadcasting rules regulating the EU referendum (Picardo, *The Chronicle*, 15 April). These early articles show the relevance of this event for the Gibraltarian community, and attention grew as the referendum date approached. In the weeks surrounding the referendum, *The Chronicle* dedicated nine articles before the referendum and five in the days after it. Even if the figures may seem small, they constitute the totality of the opinion articles in the newspaper in that time span. The EU referendum completely overshadowed any other topic, issue or problem for the community. Similarly, *Panorama* devoted five of its total of eight opinion articles to the referendum, three before and two after it took place. The other topics that caught the attention of editors and columnists in *Panorama* mainly included the situation in neighbouring Spain with its financial crisis and numerous cases of fraud, and the then forthcoming Spanish General Election (26 June 2016). The shadow of Spain is, then, the other central topic for this community. Therefore, the majority of the articles analysed dealt with the EU referendum directly, that is, as the central topic of the article, while a few of them made indirect comments in connection with these other topics.

Thus, even if an article dealt with other topics, comments or connections were made to the referendum and its aftermath, showing that this issue was always latent in their minds. For example, the opinion section of *Panorama* includes a very popular satirical piece called *Calentita* which re-creates conversations between two Gibraltarian housewives talking about local matters. Even here, sharp comments in their characteristic English-Spanish code switching are included in connection with the referendum. An example would be '*Es que como voten los* English for Brexit *nos vamos* down the drain' (but if the English vote for Brexit we will all go down the drain) or '*Eso* (that's it). See you in the voting booth, ta, ta' (*Panorama*, 20 June 2016a). And after the referendum, we can read 'Never a dull moment, Cloti dear, what a night that was with the Brexit *tangai* (spree/binge). You are telling me, *como que no pude dormir* (I couldn't sleep), my darling husband wanting to hear what was going on' (*Panorama*, 27 June 2016). In their funny and nonchalant manner, they also reflect the fact that the referendum was not just a political issue at the highest level, but of as much significance for ordinary people and grass roots of society.

Thus, the overwhelmingly high proportion of opinion articles that deal with the EU referendum in the Gibraltarian press shows how relevant the issue became for this community, even more so if we bear in mind that there are many issues that appear in the news section of newspapers or even on their front pages, but only important events or crucial questions deserve editorial comment and make their way to the leader pages of newspapers every day. Hence, it is no surprise that the number of articles grew as the date of the referendum drew closer. In fact, on 22 and 23 June it was not only the editorials that dealt with the referendum, but also the rest of the articles written by their regular columnists as well. Interestingly enough, in the time span analysed and in both newspapers, opinion articles were not only signed by well-known intellectuals and other prominent figures from Gibraltar, but also by politicians and the leaders of the main political parties, who did not miss the opportunity to address Gibraltarians and instruct them on the significance of the moment. These included among others Daniel Feetham, leader of the Gibraltar Social Democrats, Joe García, founder and editor of *Panorama* and father of the current Deputy Chief Minister of Gibraltar, of the GLP, and Peter Caruana, former Chief Minister of Gibraltar, holding office from 1996 to 2011, of the GSDP. The latter's statement in his article on 22 June, published in both in *The Chronicle* and *Panorama*, stated that:

> Since standing down from active politics I have avoided getting involved in political debates. But the very serious threats posed to the fundamental interests of Gibraltar and our children and grandchildren by Brexit requires that I do so. (Caruana, *The Chronicle* and *Panorama*, 22 June 2016b)

Being published in the two main newspapers of Gibraltar, he purposefully intended to reach the whole spectrum of Gibraltarian society, emphasizing how relevant it was for everybody in Gibraltar to form their opinion on the matter. Furthermore, *The Chronicle* also included an article by the current Chief Minister Fabian Picardo himself in which, in a fatherly tone, he addressed the people of Gibraltar on the day before polling, as a final call to them to do their duty and vote (Remain).

Except for one opinion column in *The Chronicle* (El-Yabani, 22 June 2016), all of the articles analysed are in favour of the Remain vote. Especially as the referendum day came closer, the voice of the newspapers on the Rock became one: no matter the ideological tendency of the newspaper or the personal creed of the columnist, the referendum was unanimously presented as a crucial moment for this community, and going to the polling stations to ensure Gibraltar's permanence in the EU was presented as an unavoidable 'duty'. This term became a recurrent lexical choice in the Gibraltarian press. Some illustrative examples are: 'It is your duty as a Gibraltarian' (Picardo, *The Chronicle*, 22 June 2016b), 'I urge you all to vote at the referendum, and to vote remain' (Caruana, *Panorama*, 21 June 2016a), and 'Gibraltar expects every man to do his duty and vote in Thursday's referendum' (Barker, *The Chronicle*, 22 June 2016). This last example is purposely loaded with a clear reference to Nelson's inspirational quote before British victory against the French and Spanish navies at the Battle of Trafalgar. Finally, on referendum day itself, we could read 'I urge you, that if you have not done so yet, please go and exercise your democratic right to vote and vote for security and stability for Gibraltar. Vote in' (Pozo, *The Chronicle*, 23 June 2016). If the 2002 referendum held in Gibraltar on the future of the colony was described as the greatest challenge for the community so far (Alameda Hernández 2008: 227), this new 2016 referendum definitely overshadowed the previous one through the use of a range of intensifying qualifiers such as 'an *existential* question for Gibraltar' and 'this *historic* poll' (Barker, *The Chronicle*, 22 June 2016), an '*existential* issue' (Feetham, *The Chronicle*, 22 June 2016), 'a *big* concern' (Daryanani, *The Chronicle*, 22 June 2016), 'an *important* date' (García, *Panorama*, 6 June 2016), 'a *defining* moment in our history (and) a *pivotal* event' (Vasquez, *The Chronicle*, 22 June), and a '*seminal* moment' (Feetham, *The Chronicle*, 25 June 2016b) among others. Indeed, the 1967 and 2002 referendums were mentioned in several articles and were compared to the current one, as done by Reyes (17 June 2016a) and Vasquez (22 June), both in *The Chronicle*. However, as Reyes put it later, echoing the words of a senior official, 'The joint sovereignty challenge in 2002 was simple compared to this one […] It was black and white. This is far more complex' (*The Chronicle*, 1 July 2016c). It was in fact so crucial that the referendum campaign brought together all Chief Ministers in Gibraltar who, coming from different political positions, generally and logically diverge on many other issues. Chief Minister Fabian Picardo expressed the unusualness of such a situation when he stated that by the end of the campaign 'you are no longer surprised to see me and Sir Peter Caruana QC standing shoulder to shoulder on an issue' and:

> You may even have got used to my telling you that it is unprecedented for a current and all surviving Chief Ministers to agree on anything, but we agree on this. (Picardo, *The Chronicle*, 22 June 2016b)

Furthermore, Gibraltar's turnout on referendum day was also presented as utterly essential to tip the scales of the final overall result, which the opinion polls tended to show in roughly equal proportions in favour of remaining and leaving the EU. As repeatedly put by columnists in their opinion articles, 'in those circumstances a massive show of support for REMAIN in Gibraltar by us all together could make all the difference!' (Feetham, *The Chronicle*, 22 June 2016a) or 'our vote could make a difference' (Daryanani, *The Chronicle*, 22 June 2016). Similarly, Joe García considered that 'the comparatively minuscule Gibraltar vote might end up meaning something after all in the wider UK context' (*Panorama*, 6 June 2016). Nevertheless, as the two local women of the comic column Calentita echoed in *Panorama*, after all, the Gibraltar Remain vote could not make a difference: 'Yes, *una noche de votos* (a voting night). *Pero* (but) in the end the millions *mandan* (have the last word), and our 96% *sirvió de poco* (was of little use)' (*Panorama*, 27 June 2016b). With the unexpected result of the referendum, coverage of and articles on the issue did not reduce in the weeks and months that followed, but indeed continued and will presumably continue to appear in the Gibraltarian press as Brexit and particularly its consequences for the Rock continue to be a hot topic for this community.

THE PAST-FUTURE DIVIDE

The body of opinion articles analysed is abundant in temporal references that mark the contrast between the past and the future. In the weeks leading up to the referendum, these references highlighted the opposition between Gibraltar's glorious and heroic past and the disastrous future that lay ahead should the UK leave the EU.

The choice of the present perfect tense was especially significant as it helped connect that glorious past with the remarkable endurance Gibraltarians have achieved as strategies of continuation to discursively construct a sense of stability and security, as in 'Forty years of bitter experiences have taught us', 'Our standard of living has continuously increased decade after decade' (Feetham, *The Chronicle*, 22 June 2016a), 'What we have built over four decades' (Vasquez, *The Chronicle*, 22 June 2016), 'we have faced and overcome many challenges in the past' (Feetham, *The Chronicle*, 25 June 2016b). In the same vein, time adverbials pointed towards the present, as in 'Today in Gibraltar we enjoy a fantastic standard of living […] today's successful and prosperous society'

(Caruana, *Panorama*, 21 June 2016a) in an attempt to emphasize the benefits of being part of the EU. This contrasts with the uncertainty that Brexit meant, which was discursively expressed through the recurrent use of modal verbs such as 'may', 'would' or 'could'. Some illustrative examples are 'with Brexit we would have to re-negotiate our links with the EU' (García, *Panorama*, 6 June 2016) and 'companies [...] may look for alternative jurisdictions. Inward investment would also suffer for much the same reason. That would lead to less jobs' (Feetham, *The Chronicle*, 22 June 2016a).

Other lexical choices that are significant in this respect are those which refer to the future. In the weeks before the referendum, opinion articles were rich in words that highlighted Gibraltarians' doubts and worries about their future. Hence, the possibility of leaving the EU represented 'a leap into the unknown' (Reyes, *The Chronicle*, 17 June 2016a), 'a state of uncomfortable suspense' (Daryanani, *The Chronicle*, 22 June 2016), 'the spectre of not knowing where we are going' (García, *Panorama*, 6 June 2016), 'the potential instability and volatility triggered by a Brexit' (Daryanani, *The Chronicle*, 22 June 2016), and 'there are too many uncertainties' (Pozo, *The Chronicle*, 23 June 2016). Later, the result of 23 June confirmed Gibraltarians' worst fears and, as the title of Brian Reyes's article put it, the future became 'Terra incognita' (*The Chronicle*, 25 June 2016b). In the same vein, another vivid and graphic description of the future ahead was put forward by Carmen Gómez who named 24 June 2016 Gibraltar's particular 'Black Friday' (*Panorama*, 29 June 2016). Furthermore, references to the future were emotionally loaded with the recurrent allusion to 'children' and 'grandchildren', a sentiment which was emphasized with the first-person plural possessive adjective 'our' to call the readers' attention to their most precious assets when deciding on their vote. Examples abound, as in 'We have to do all in Gibraltar's power to make sure our children enjoy that same way of life that we have enjoyed' (Feetham, *The Chronicle*, 22 June 2016a), 'the very serious threats posed to the fundamental interests of Gibraltar and our children and grandchildren' (Caruana, *Panorama*, 21 June 2016), 'will affect the future of our children and grandchildren in years to come' (Daryanani, *The Chronicle*, 22 June 2016), 'Don't kneecap our children's future' (Picardo, *The Chronicle*, 22 June 2016b), and 'for the sake of our children, for the sake of the economic prosperity of generations to come' (Vasquez, *The Chronicle*, 22 June 2016). Even the two housewives in *Panorama*'s Calentita column clearly express their desire for continuity and no change in Gibraltar: '*Eso* (that's it), Brexit or no Brexit, our telephone conversations will carry on regardless. Ciao' (*Panorama*, 27 June 2016b).

Connected to this idea of continuity is that of unity, which in the Gibraltarian press was discursively constructed by means of the personal pronoun 'we' and the lexical repetition of the concept 'unity'. In the opinion pages, Gibraltar was referred to by its official name 'Gibraltar', which represents it as a political entity, and to a lesser degree by the popular term 'the Rock'. However, the most frequent device to refer to Gibraltar was the personal pronoun 'we'. Some illustrative examples are: 'we are good Europeans and deserve special consideration' (García, *Panorama*, 6 June 2016), 'we have worked hard as a community' (Vasquez, *The Chronicle*, 22 June 2016), 'we as a people are no strangers to adversity [...] and together we will again prevail' (Feetham, *The Chronicle*, 25 June 2016b). In these metonymic forms of 'we', the pronoun stands for the whole national body, adding a more human and personal dimension when referring to Gibraltar, at the same time that it builds in-group identity as a united community. Particularly after the result of the referendum confirmed the UK's exit from the EU, appeals to unity became even more frequent and strong, as the article by Gibraltar's Chief Minister himself showed when appealing to that 'spirit of unity' (Picardo, *The Chronicle*, 25 June 2016c).Through the recurrent repetition of the concept of 'unity', the Gibraltarian press presented it as absolutely necessary to overcome the challenges to come.

THE EU REFERENDUM 2016 AND THE SPANISH DIMENSION

Above all, the Gibraltarian press presented the EU referendum not as a British question (that is, not as a question about the position of the UK in the international sphere and the implications for it as a whole), but rather as a local problem, because at the end of the day what really worried this community was 'what is the safest position for Gibraltar' (García, *Panorama*, 6 June 2016), and they voted for what they 'believed was the best path for us to take' (Gómez, *Panorama*, 29 June 2016). The consequences of the UK leaving or remaining in the EU had a direct impact on Gibraltar because of its special status as an overseas dependent territory. Editorials and columnists in the Gibraltarian press were voluble in highlighting both sides of this. That is, on the one hand, they pointed out how it is in the EU that Gibraltar has gained rights and a better standard of living, as presented by Feetham (*The Chronicle*, 22 June 2016a) or Barker (*The Chronicle*, 22 June 2016) among others. In fact, the title of Daryanani's article rightly summarized it as 'Gibraltar needs the EU' (*The Chronicle*, 22 June 2016). And, on the other hand, opinion articles stressed some of the threats for Gibraltar's economy should the UK leave the EU: loss of access to the European single market, restrictions at the border with Spain, exclusion from European air space, and the imposition of taxes, among others (Daryanani, *The Chronicle*, 22 June 2016). But above all, the main threat for the Gibraltarian community was the political consequences that could be derived from a revived Spanish claim for sovereignty; that is, the actions that the Spanish government could take if Gibraltar ceased to be part of the EU. Given that territorial border tensions have been running high since the very beginning of British possession of the Rock, any event that can have even the slightest connection with Spain sounds all the alarm bells in Gibraltar. It is for this reason that 'concern about Spain was one of the main reasons why Gibraltar was expected to turn out in force and vote overwhelmingly for remain on June 23' (Reyes, *The Chronicle*, 17 June 2016a): 'the biggest problem we face if Brexit becomes a reality is that of the insistent pressure we would receive from our neighbours, north of the Border' (Pozo, *The Chronicle*, 23 June 2016). In other words, it all came down to their omnipresent problem, namely, Spain and its irredentist territorial claim. As the former and the incumbent Chief Ministers of Gibraltar put it, 'Here in Gibraltar the real issue is whether Spain can more easily take steps against us if we are in or out of the EU' (Caruana, *Panorama*, 21 June 2016a), and people had to vote remain 'not least because this is the best way to stop Spain playing games about our sovereignty' (Picardo, *The Chronicle*, 22 June 2016b) and represented Gibraltar's only means to 'give Spain no hope' (El-Yabani, *The Chronicle*, 22 June 2016).

Thus, the Spanish dimension was undoubtedly a central issue for Gibraltarians. In fact, 'Spain', together with the word 'sovereignty', was mentioned in every single editorial and opinion article that dealt with the EU referendum, even in the only article that was in favour of the Leave vote (El-Yabani, *The Chronicle*, 22 June 2016). In addition, Spain was negatively represented as it usually collocated with words with negative connotations, as in 'noises from Madrid' (Reyes, *The Chronicle*, 17 June 2016a), 'noises emanating from our neighbours across the frontier (and) at the height of Spanish Foreign Affairs Minister Margallo's psychosis.' (Daryanani, *The Chronicle*, 22 June 2016), 'our oppressive (and) aggressive neighbour' (Vasquez, *The Chronicle*, 22 June 2016), 'Madrid's excesses' (García, *Panorama*, 6 June 2016), and 'Margallo would dearly love to mess Gibraltar up further' (Editorial, *Panorama*, 23 June 2016). And its territorial claim was similarly predicated as a tedious and repetitive 'mantra' (Feetham, *The Chronicle*, 22 June 2016a), that is 'the usual trivia coming from the Spanish camp' (Gómez, *Panorama*, 29 June 2016) that 'we have heard over and again' (Picardo, *The Chronicle*, 22 June 2016b).

Following on from this, the Spanish General Election held on 26 June became an issue in Gibraltar for the direct and obvious consequences that could result for the Gibraltarian community. As Joe García suggested, this election was as important as, if not more important than, the EU referendum itself: 'Whatever way the referendum vote goes, who wins the Spanish elections is bound to have a direct bearing on Gibraltar affairs—whether three days earlier we voted one way or the other' (*Panorama*, 6 June 2016). Similarly, and quite tellingly, *Panorama*'s editorial on 23 June was titled 'What happens at the frontier depends on who wins the Spanish election' (Editorial, *Panorama*, 23 June 2016). Hence, the sovereignty issue remained the central concern in local politics. In such a scenario, it comes as no surprise that words that belong to the semantic field of 'threat', such as 'fear', 'risk' or 'attack' became recurrent lexical choices in the opinion pages of *The Chronicle* and *Panorama* when dealing with the consequences of the EU referendum. Among others, the following examples illustrate this point: 'that is precisely the risk we face in a Brexit' (Feetham, *The Chronicle*, 22 June 2016a), 'The other fear is that the border will close' (El-Yabani, *The Chronicle*, 22 June 2016), 'the border [...] being used as tool by Spain in an ad hoc manner to disrupt our daily lives' (Pozo, *The Chronicle*, 22 June 2016). Indeed, for them, this threat was the only thing that was 'absolutely clear' amidst the extraordinary turmoil caused by the EU referendum (Caruana, *Panorama*, 22 June 2016b).

For its part, what Gibraltar demanded from the EU and from the UK specifically was that they 'protect' Gibraltar's interests and status quo. This idea was much elaborated on throughout the majority of the opinion articles published on the dates analysed, as in the ones by Daryanani ('Britain's ability to protect our interests', *The Chronicle*, 22 June 2016), El-Yabani ('The EU does not protect us from Spain', *The Chronicle*, 22 June 2016), and García ('that Gibraltar is protected by the

UK and will continue to be protected whether we are in the EU or out', *Panorama*, 6 June 2016) among others. And once Brexit was confirmed, that protection became a 'duty', as we can read in 'The Government of the UK (particularly one that is led by Brexiteers) owes a duty to the people of Gibraltar to ensure that we are not left behind' (Feetham, *The Chronicle*, 25 June 2016b). In this new scenario, EU law was presented as a 'shield' (García, *Panorama*, 6 June 2016) against Spain's interests and as 'the only real external impediment to Spain's freedom of action' (Caruana, *Panorama*, 21 June 2016a). To support Gibraltar's call for protection, their Britishness was emphasized, as the illustrative title of Daniel Feetham's article shows, 'Vote remain to preserve British Gibraltarian way of life' (*The Chronicle*, 22 June 2016a) or other frequent references to the 'Britishness of Gibraltar' (Picardo, *The Chronicle*, 22 June 2016b). Furthermore, Gibraltar was generally represented as forming part of a 'family', with its positive connotations of protection, affection and comfort, as constructed in the articles by Picardo in *The Chronicle* (22 June 2016b), Feetham in *The Chronicle* (25 June 2016b) or Gómez in *Panorama* (29 June 2016).

Conclusion

Discursive analysis of opinion articles from the Gibraltarian press published on the dates surrounding the British referendum on EU membership proved useful in understanding the great impact it had on Gibraltar, as well as how the media shaped the representation of this referendum and its subsequent effects. In Gibraltar, the EU referendum was mainly represented not as a British international issue, but as a pre-eminent domestic problem because of the direct consequences which could follow for the Gibraltarian community. On the one hand, the EU referendum was discursively represented as the biggest threat that would challenge the status and way of life that this community had painfully achieved through its 300 years of British history. To face this challenge, appeals to continuity, unity and Britishness were recurrent in the opinion articles analysed. Hence, the Gibraltarian media highlighted the contrast between what they, as a community, had painfully achieved throughout the years, with the uncertainties for their future which Brexit meant. On the other hand, Brexit was represented as an issue of paramount importance for Gibraltar in the light of the continuing threats over sovereignty from Madrid, to the extent that the whole EU referendum issue was presented as having to do more with Spain than with Britain itself. Indeed, at a domestic level, the referendum was instrumentalized as a weapon between Gibraltar and Spain in their endless battle for sovereignty. All in all, it can be concluded that the history of Gibraltar has been peppered with threatening events as important landmarks in its make-up, namely: the Great Siege, the closure of the border, the 2002 referendum on joint sovereignty, the 2006 Constitution. And in this list, the 2016 referendum on British membership of the EU seems to be their latest exacting challenge.

BIBLIOGRAPHY

ACADEMIC SOURCES

Alameda Hernández, A. 2008. Discursive Strategies in the Construction of National Identity: A Critical Discourse Analysis of the Gibraltar Issue in the Printed Media. *National Identities* 10 (2): 225–235.
Fairclough, N. 2003. *Analysing Discourse: Textual Analysis for Social Research.* London: Routledge.
Fowler, R. 1991. *Language in the News. Discourse and Ideology in the Press.* London: Routledge.
Kellermann, A. 2001. *A New, New English. Language, Politics and Identity in Gibraltar.* Heidelberg: Heidelberg SchriftenzurSprache und Kultur.
Kent, S. 2004. 300 Years of Brits on the Rock. *Geographical* 76 (9): 22–26.
Reisigl, M., and R. Wodak. 2001. *Discourse and Discrimination. Rhetorics of Racism and Antisemitism.* London: Routledge.
Stockey, G., and C. Grocott. 2012. *Gibraltar: A Modern History.* Cardiff: University of Wales Press.
Van Dijk, T. 1993. Principles of Critical Discourse Analysis. *Discourse and Society* 4 (2): 249–283.
Wodak, R. 2001. The Discourse-Historical Approach. In *Methods of Critical Discourse Analysis,* ed. R. Wodak, and M. Meyer, 63–94. London: Sage.

NEWSPAPER SOURCES

Barker, Joseph. 2016. Vote Remain—Let's lead, Not Leave, the EU. *The Gibraltar Chronicle,* June 22. http://chronicle.gi (Accessed 22 July 2016).
Calentita. 2016a. Está la cosa de secretos. *Panorama,* June 20. http://gibraltar-panorama.gi (Accessed 22 July 2016).
Calentita. 2016b. El new Bishop se llama como mi primo [...]. *Panorama,* June 27. http://gibraltarpanorama.gi (Accessed 22 July 2016).

Caruana, Peter. 2016a. Where Britain Has Been Strong, and Poor, in Defending Gibraltar. *Panorama*, June 21. http://gibraltarpanorama.gi (Accessed 22 July 2016).

Caruana, Peter. 2016b. It is Right for Our Political Leaders and Others to Point Out Those Things That We Should Rightly Fear. *The Gibraltar Chronicle*, June 22. http://chronicle.gi (Accessed 22 July 2016).

Daryanani, Vijay. 2016. Gibraltar Needs the EU. *The Gibraltar Chronicle*, June 22. http://chronicle.gi (Accessed 22 July 2016).

Editorial. 2016. What Happens at the Frontier Depends on Who Wins the Spanish Election. *Panorama*, June 23. http://gibraltarpanorama.gi (Accessed 22 July 2016).

El-Yabani, Tarik. 2016. In or Out: Will It Make a Difference? *The Gibraltar Chronicle*, June 22. http://chronicle.gi (Accessed 22 July 2016).

Feeham, Daniel. 2016a. Vote Remain to Preserve British Gibraltarian Way of Life. *The Gibraltar Chronicle*, June 22. http://chronicle.gi (Accessed 22 July 2016).

Feeham, Daniel. 2016b. A Positive and Workable Roadmap. *The Gibraltar Chronicle*, June 25. http://chronicle.gi (Accessed 22 July 2016).

García, Joe. 2016. Brexit or Not: Gibraltar Expects England to Do Its Duty. *Panorama*, June 6. http://gibraltarpanorama.gi (Accessed 22 July 2016).

Gómez, Carmen. 2016. Our Black Friday. *Panorama*, June 29. http://gibraltarpanorama.gi (Accessed 22 July 2016).

Picardo, Fabian. 2016a. EU Referendum: A Ministerial Statement by the Chief Minister Fabian Picardo. *Panorama*, April 15. http://gibraltarpanorama.gi (Accessed 22 July 2016).

Picardo, Fabian. 2016b. Do Your Duty: Vote Remain. *The Gibraltar Chronicle*, June 22 http://chronicle.gi (Accessed 22 July 2016).

Picardo, Fabian. 2016c. Gibraltarian Resilience Will Overcome Brexit Challenge. *The Gibraltar Chronicle*, June 25. http://chronicle.gi (Accessed 22 July 2016).

Pozo, Kayron. 2016. "Ludicrous" to Vote Leave. *The Gibraltar Chronicle*, June 23. http://chronicle.gi (Accessed 22 July 2016).

Reyes, Brian. 2016a. The Right Decision. *The Gibraltar Chronicle*, June 17. http://chronicle.gi (Accessed 22 July 2016).

Reyes, Brian. 2016b. Terra Incognita. *The Gibraltar Chronicle*, June 25. http://chronicle.gi (Accessed 22 July 2016).

Reyes, Brian. 2016c. In the Commons, Reassurance Laced With Uncertainty. *The Gibraltar Chronicle*, July 1. http://chronicle.gi (Accessed 22 July 2016).

Vasquez, Gemma. 2016. Tomorrow Gibraltarians Are Called Upon to Vote for Their Future. *The Gibraltar Chronicle*, June 22. http://chronicle.gi (Accessed 22 July 2016).

PART III

European Single Market Countries

Left Versus Right, or Mainstream Versus Margins? Divisions in French Media and Reactions to the 'Brexit' Vote

Thomas Martin and Laurent Binet

INTRODUCTION

The situation of the press in France regarding European integration is somewhat paradoxical. While the French are among the most critical citizens of the European Union (EU), and while the French press is highly politicized (Benson and Halin 2007: 29), there is no major Eurosceptic newspaper in France, and the French media are largely Europhile. As the journalist Bruno Donnet put it on French radio, commenting on the 2016 EU referendum Brexit (UK's exit from the EU) vote, 'at a time where the divorce between the public and the media is more and more discussed, there is, in the coverage of Brexit and the European question,

T. Martin (✉)
King's College, London, UK
e-mail: thomas.1.martin@kcl.ac.uk

L. Binet
Cardiff University, Cardiff, UK
e-mail: laurent1925@free.fr

© The Author(s) 2018
A. Ridge-Newman et al. (eds.), *Reporting the Road to Brexit*,
https://doi.org/10.1007/978-3-319-73682-2_9

145

a substantial incongruity, a discrepancy which needs urgently to be discussed' (Donnet, *France Inter*, 27 June 2016).

This media landscape mirrors the wider political landscape in France, in which parties of the centre-right, centre and centre-left are predominantly pro-EU, while those on the far-right and far-left are more hostile: both see it as undermining national sovereignty, with the far-right linking it to fears around immigration and identity, and the far-left seeing it as imposing the agenda of big business and international finance (Mélenchon 2010; Birnbaum 2012). These divisions on Europe are not new: in 1992, for instance, the Maastricht Treaty was ratified in a referendum in France by 51.04% of voters, but rejected by 92% of Communists and 95% of supporters of the far-right Front National (Guyomarch et al. 1998: 101).

In this chapter, we examine how these dynamics play out in French media reactions to Britain's decision to leave the EU in the referendum on 23 June 2016. We begin by considering the background to the chapter's key theme: Why is there a division in French media coverage of the EU between mainstream and margins? Reactions of France's 'mainstream' press to Brexit in the days following the referendum will then be examined: Do these follow the patterns analysed in the first section? And in what ways are the different sources examined critical of the vote? This discussion refers to three major national newspapers in France, *Le Monde* (centrist), *Le Figaro* (centre-right) and *Libération* (centre-left). Finally, reactions to the vote from non-mainstream sources will be analysed, choosing what we believe to be the most relevant: the iconoclastic online journal of news and investigative journalism *Mediapart*, and the weekly magazine *Valeurs Actuelles*, operating at the intersection of the extreme and mainstream right. Why do they welcome Brexit? How do far-right and far-left reactions differ? And do these reactions reflect a French political climate where the mainstream 'establishment' appears increasingly distrusted?

Context

It is important to start by considering why France's mainstream media are almost uniformly pro-EU. To do this, it is useful to place the question in the context of post-war French history. Before the Second World War, in the 1930s, numerous popular French newspapers were close to the right and the far-right (Charon 2003: 14), displaying strongly nationalistic views. Many of these newspapers took part in collaboration during German occupation, and were therefore targeted in the purges of 1944–1945 following France's liberation. Consequently, after the war, they disappeared to give way to newspapers, either local or national, linked to the Resistance or created in the newly liberated France. Such newspapers often had an editorial line congruent with specific resistance affiliations, for instance communist for *La Marseillaise* and *L'Humanité*, or Christian Democrat for *Ouest-France* and *La Croix*. Additionally, new state rules set after the Liberation, inspired by the Resistance ethos, were designed to produce 'a press system more sympathetic to the viewpoint of the dominant centre-left parties in politics and of progressive forces in society' (Kuhn 2011: 12). This meant in the long run that the pro-European views of the mainstream parties which developed from the early 1950s were largely echoed in the French press as European integration grew, with the notable exceptions of communist and Gaullist newspapers. During the Mitterrand years (1981–1995), meanwhile, the media were seen by both the French government and leading EU figures like Jacques Delors as a means of fostering a new collective European identity. The broadcasting sector received special attention in that respect: in 1992, the Franco-German channel Arte was created with a very pro-European line, which was also the case the following year for the Lyon-based channel Euronews.

As Benson and Halin have noted (2007: 29), French newspapers are 'partisan actors' and have close ties with the political field. As far as European integration is concerned, this has translated into a press overwhelmingly and actively supportive of European integration. It also meant for a long time a tendency to avoid debates about EU membership and to take a 'European approach' when reporting the EU (Williams 2005: 143), in stark contrast with the negative media coverage of the EU in Britain. Past case studies and analyses have suggested that French newspapers and broadcasting coverage in relation to European integration have been biased since the early 1990s, notably during the two EU referendums of 1992 and 2005, when pro-European views were systematically over-represented and Eurosceptic views under-represented (Aboura 2005; Halimi 2005; Laurent and Sauger 2005; Maler and Schwartz 2005; Schwartz 2008). Bertrand Benoit, in his seminal work on the rise of Euroscepticism in France in the 1990s, identified only one press title with a Eurosceptic editorial line, the anti-globalization weekly *Le Monde Diplomatique* (1997: 38). This imbalance between a divided electorate on Europe, and French media overwhelmingly supporting European integration, has, since Maastricht, fuelled an ongoing debate which has resurfaced with the treatment of the Brexit vote result in the French mainstream media.

MAINSTREAM FRENCH PRESS REACTIONS: AN ANTI-BREXIT BIAS?

Having considered the background of France's largely pro-EU national press, it is important to consider the extent to which these positions play out in press reactions to the Brexit vote, drawing out the nuances distinguishing the different shades of mainstream opinion represented in three major newspapers: *Libération*, *Le Monde* and *Le Figaro*. It should perhaps be noted that national newspapers are not read by a mass audience in France: according to the latest figures from the French press observatory Alliance pour les Chiffres de la Presse et des Médias (ACPM), the most read national newspaper is *Le Figaro* with a circulation of 305,701, whereas the most read regional newspaper is *Ouest-France* with 678,860. Nevertheless, the national press remains highly influential, particularly in the seat of political power in Paris, where all three of the newspapers examined in this section are based. They represent furthermore a useful way of examining the different political philosophies competing in the French political arena.

LIBÉRATION: BREXIT AS A THREAT TO THE UTOPIA OF A UNITED CONTINENT

We begin with *Libération*, which, having debuted in 1973 as a journal of the radical left (with Jean-Paul Sartre amongst its founders) gradually came to represent a socially liberal, social democratic centre-left position. Its articles reacting to Britain's decision to leave the EU show consistently pro-EU positioning (in common with its closest political analogue, the French Socialist Party) with a tone showing disappointment and regret at the UK's decision. This tone is set in two leaders by editor Laurent Joffrin: on 24 June, immediately after the vote, Joffrin comments that 'no-one can welcome this result with satisfaction', in that 'the forces of openness, exchange and tolerance' have been defeated by 'distrust', 'solitary sovereignty' and 'fear of foreigners'. The UK, he argues, will become weaker and less prosperous, but the EU also has itself to blame: it has, for Joffrin, no common project, or answers to the major crises it faces, leading nationalism to appear more attractive to those 'left behind' by globalization than a union which appears 'distant, technocratic and elitist'. He concludes that 'the beautiful project of a united, equitable and peaceful continent' is damaged by Brexit and could serve as a precedent for further 'decomposition': reform, therefore, is seen as imperative. In his 27 June column, meanwhile, he addresses the practical consequences of Brexit, rejecting the idea that Britain will be any more 'free' after leaving the EU: this does not apply, he notes, to defence, foreign policy or monetary and financial policy; plus the UK will still have to conform to EU regulations in order to export. It will be able to restrict immigration, but for Joffrin, the emphasis placed on this 'unmasks the real politics behind Brexit' and disproves the discourse of 'sovereignty' and 'democracy' held by Brexit supporters in Europe. Regarding France, he attacks high-profile radical left leader Jean-Luc Mélenchon, who welcomed the vote as a blow to an EU seen as too pro-capitalist and right-wing: Joffrin points out that in doing this, Mélenchon actually supports a decision which restricts immigration and damages workers' rights. As such, *Libération*'s position on Brexit rejects Euroscepticisms of both right and left.

Elsewhere in *Libération*, a guest column addressing Brexit from historian Henry Rousso (26 June 2016) expresses anger at opportunist politicians who made the EU a scapegoat, against 'xenophobic and nationalistic demagogues', and against those who celebrate Brexit without considering political or economic alternatives. Addressing the EU's history and why its potential weakening is to be regretted, he argues that 'its project constitutes one of the last vestiges of a forward-looking conception of time in Western society, a vision of history in which tomorrow is better than yesterday'. Accordingly, the European crisis is seen as a 'crisis of civilization': for Rousso, the EU must urgently be 'refounded', opening a debate on 'the fundamental values we want to preserve'.

'THANK YOU BRITS!': THE CURIOUS CASE OF FRANCE'S PRO-EU PRO-BREXITERS

Meanwhile, the Brussels columnist Jean Quatremer, *Libération*'s most fervent Europhile (to the extent of alienating much of its readership by taking the side of the EU-led Troika over Greece's radical left Syriza Government during the 2015 debt crisis) took a similar ironic tone on Brexit as he had earlier when he had argued that Syriza's programme 'was not worth the paper it was written on' and mocked his readers for seeing this opinion as 'the confirmation of his Europeanist neoliberalism' (Quatremer, *Libération*, 31 January 2015). He also thanked the UK for leaving because, in his view, it only ever had damaging effects for the

EU, in that attempting to accommodate the UK led to the dilution of the EU project. Finally, he thanked Britain for giving the EU a wake-up call: as he put it, 'if one of the four biggest EU states leaving doesn't wake us [the EU] up, if we don't mobilize to relaunch a project which kept peace for seventy years, then we deserve to disappear'. Paradoxically, Quatremer is not alone in being strongly pro-European but supporting Britain leaving the EU: this was also the belief of former Socialist Prime Minister Michel Rocard. Ahead of the referendum, Rocard gave several interviews arguing that the EU would be better off without Britain, which he saw as always having had a detrimental influence on European integration. In the Catholic daily *La Croix* (19 June 2016), for example, he explained that he saw only advantages in Brexit, as he considered that the English (sic), having 'another world in mind', were acting as an unwelcome 'padlock' preventing action on international issues:

> On these questions, there was a negative influence: the English. When they are around a table, it is forbidden to raise the question of reinforcing Europe. They have another world in mind, they dream of a world which is maritime, mercantile and Anglophone. Brexit would make it clear whether this negative 'padlock' will be removed. Me, I only see advantages, on the condition that the Europeans can profit from it.

Similar views backing Brexit for the sake of European unity were also expressed by Christophe Barbier, Editor-in-Chief of the weekly news magazine *L'Express* and regular participant in the popular political debate programme *C dans l'air* on the public television channel France 5. In an opinion piece headlined 'The United Kingdom says yes to Brexit: a chance for Europe!' and with the provocative opening 'Thank you Brits!', he argued that the 23 June vote could act as an electroshock to revive a dying political union (*L'Express*, 24 June 2016).

LE MONDE: A NEWSPAPER REPRESENTATIVE OF FRANCE'S POST-WAR PRO-EU MEDIA

The reaction of *Le Monde* to the UK's decision tells a similar story that of *Libération*. Established in 1944, *Le Monde* is a centrist 'newspaper of record' (Fletcher 1994), often reflecting the positions of the political and media elites of the day (ibid.). Like *Libération*, its editorial line is uniformly pro-EU and anti-Brexit, showing a certain bewilderment at the lack of attention paid to the practical consequences of Brexit, but attempting to contextualize it and understand anti-EU sentiment. An unsigned editorial on 28 June characterizes this focus on the practical issues behind Brexit: the UK, it argues, 'wanted to leave the EU in order to go nowhere', and was 'hardly in the EU to begin with', not participating in the euro or Schengen. The worries which immediately surfaced after the vote, the editorial argues, prove the practicality and value of the EU: farmers no longer knew where financial aid would come from; universities no longer knew about the status of exchanges and European students; bankers no longer knew if they could stay in London; British pensioners no longer knew if they could stay in Europe; and the Irish peace process was immediately thrown into doubt. Further, it attacks the simplistic arguments of Brexit supporters, pointing out that putting into practice 'the will of the people' is incredibly complicated, even leaving aside economic uncertainty and the possibility of a recession; attacks David Cameron and Brexit supporters for 'playing Russian roulette with the UK and the EU' and for 'not having prepared the slightest plan B'; points out the impossible task of simultaneously respecting the vote, not alienating Remain voters and maintaining close economic links with the EU; and ends by attacking the 'irresponsibility' and 'cynicism' of all involved.

Despite this hostility, there is also an attempt to understand Brexit and place it in context. A further editorial on 25 June notes that both far-right and far-left protest movements welcomed Brexit, arguing that this reflects reactions to globalization in the 'rich [global] north'. The EU, it argues, is the 'incarnation' of globalization for many Europeans, being blamed by Brexit voters for opening frontiers and allowing an influx of immigrants, seen as lowering salaries and putting pressure on public services. The same forces are involved, the editorial notes, in the success of Donald Trump in the USA, whose supporters are seen as resembling those of Brexit: white, 50-plus, marginalized, left behind by globalization, and blaming (often out of nostalgia) immigration for their problems. Reacting to this rejection of globalization and immigration, the editorial concludes, must be the principal preoccupation of mainstream parties. The EU itself, a 25 June editorial by Arnaud Parmentier argues, is also to blame for what he calls the current *désamour européen*: the EU, for him, is lacking an 'identity' and a 'project' when faced with 'civilizational challenges'. This leads to a *repli identitaire*, in which nations turn in on themselves and fall back on their perceived 'identity', out of a desire for security, tradition and belonging. The real shock of Brexit, he argues, is that it shows many European populations feel they are better off facing the future alone.

A final piece worth mentioning before moving on from *Le Monde*'s coverage was written by the celebrity 'philosopher' Bernard-Henri Lévy (25 June 2016), also credited as part of the newspaper's supervisory board. Whereas *Le Monde*'s tone was largely measured, Lévy's was astoundingly intemperate: he saw Brexit as a catastrophe; he argued that it represents 'demagogy', 'xenophobia', 'hate', 'the most rancid sovereignism', 'the most stupid nationalism' and 'the dictatorship of the simple'. He deplored what he sees as a victory for the figurehead of France's far-right, Marine Le Pen, and its far-left, Jean-Luc Mélenchon; as well as for radical left party Podemos in Spain, the Five Star protest party in Italy and the populist and nationalist movements of central Europe. It should be noted that Lévy makes no attempt to distinguish these disparate movements and personalities, despite the different political tendencies represented: they are placed beyond the pale by virtue of being critical of the EU. What is more, there is no attempt to understand the motivations of those involved: it is simply a victory for 'boozed-up fascists and hooligans', 'bovine neonationalists' and 'moronic leftists'; a victory of 'ignorance over knowledge' and 'stupidity over thought'. There is a long-standing dichotomy in French political discourse between *civilisation*, represented by France, and *barbarie*, represented by its enemies (Todorov 2008). It could be argued that Lévy, consciously or unconsciously, reproduces this dichotomy here, with the *barbarie* of right- and left-wing populism and nationalism overcoming the *civilisation* of the European project.

To summarize, both *Libération*'s and *Le Monde*'s reactions to Britain's decision to leave the EU supported the idea that France's mainstream press is pro-EU. While tone and emphasis vary, the ideological line taken by the two newspapers was consistent: the UK's decision was regretted, and while there is in most cases an acknowledgement of the EU's failings, it is still supported out of principle rather than expediency, being seen as a valuable project of peace, unity and civilization.

LE FIGARO AND BREXIT: PRAGMATIC CRITICISM OR IMPLICIT SUPPORT?

The case of the final mainstream source to be examined, *Le Figaro*, is however somewhat different. Founded in 1826, *Le Figaro* is France's oldest national newspaper, and can be seen as the standard-bearer of French conservatism, appealing to the upper-middle classes and business elites (Kuhn 1995). While the pro-EU and anti-Brexit tendencies of *Libération* and *Le Monde* are clear, *Le Figaro*'s positioning is more ambiguous, reflecting an ideological divide in the French centre-right between pro-free-market conservatism and populist nationalism.

It is notable that much of the support for the EU in *Le Figaro*'s reaction to Brexit is pragmatic rather than ideological, focused on the dangers Brexit could represent to financial and geopolitical stability. This, it could be argued, is consistent with its position as the newspaper of the establishment and business elites. The headlines in the newspaper's 'analysis' columns in the days following the vote are telling: 'Brexit: the influence of Europe in the world will diminish' (24 June 2016); 'How Brexit will hit the British economy' (26 June 2016); 'The future of Europe in the hands of a weakened Franco-German couple' (24 June 2016a). Similar perspectives are also seen in interviews and guest columns published after the vote, many of which involved establishment conservative figures who see Brexit as unambiguously negative. The former centre-right MEP Jean-Louis Bourlanges (25 June 2016), for instance, argued that 'the British are sacrificing their interests to their fantasies', seeing the vote as irrational, as well as contrary to the UK's conservative traditions, in that the EU is already a zone of free-trade and economic liberalism. For him, Brexit has no advantages and many potential disadvantages for the UK, such as isolation from major partners and export markets, and potentially breaking up the union due to ignoring the interests of Scotland and Northern Ireland. He notes finally that Britain's relationship with the EU was already ideal, and that all the alternatives are 'costly, complicated and unsatisfactory'.

The French business leader Denis Kessler (24 June 2016) argued along similar lines: for him, 'there will be no winners from Brexit'. He predicted that Brexit will negatively impact on commerce, investment and employment, and sees it as a 'foreseeable catastrophe', noting that many business leaders warned against the 'economic, financial, social and political risks' of holding such a referendum. He pointed out that 'markets hate uncertainty' and that Brexit has produced a huge amount of it: it has 'opened Pandora's box'. Accordingly, he sees the need to end such uncertainty as soon as possible, by defining new relationships between the UK and the EU, and giving precise answers to questions such as the status of EU residents in Britain and the UK's place in the European single market. There will be, for Kessler, many more losers than winners from Brexit, and all Europe will suffer the consequences. However, he concluded, we have a choice: either we let the EU disintegrate and waste decades of progress, or we work to refound it. What will happen in the UK, he predicted, will serve as a lesson in France for 'those who believe that there is a future for countries which choose particularism, isolationism and secessionism'. This can be seen as an overt attack on sovereignist movements of the right and left (the most high-profile being the far-right Front National) on anyone who sees these movements as a model to follow, and on anyone who wishes France to follow Britain out of the EU.

In one sense, these columns represent the default position of *Le Figaro*: a pragmatic, conservative Europhilia which sees Brexit as dangerous to the financial and geopolitical stability of Britain, France and Europe. A contrasting position, however, is also widely represented, one which, if not overtly Eurosceptic, is closer to the populist nationalism deplored by Kessler. An editorial by Alexis Brézet (27 June 2016), for example, argued that Brexit demonstrates that Europe must reconstruct and change its philosophy, taking into account the interests of 'the people'. He sees the causes of Brexit as ones felt across Europe: 'uncontrolled immigration, persistent unemployment, the middle classes' loss of social status, a feeling of cultural dispossession, and anxieties about identity'. Here is a major difference between *Le Figaro* and the other mainstream sources examined, one reflecting the French right's contemporary emphasis on immigration and identity, and its closeness in these areas to a discourse resembling that of the Front National, or UKIP in Britain (Noiriel 2007; Cette France-là 2012; Boltanski and Esquerre 2014). It could be argued therefore that even if mainstream conservatives in France are broadly favourable to the EU on pragmatic grounds of stability, or the benefits of the single market, many are sceptical about its current form, seen as harmful to sovereignty and cultural identity. The remainder of Brézet's editorial supported this interpretation: he argued that European peoples have 'never wanted protection [from globalization] so badly', but that 'this Europe of free movement without limits or frontiers' worries them more than it protects them. This leads 'the people' to return to the only worthwhile 'protection': the nation. Some discursive features here are closer to the Eurosceptic margins than they are to *Le Figaro*'s own free-market wing: an emphasis on sovereignty, for example, and claiming to speak on behalf of 'the people'. Brézet is not, he clarified, a Eurosceptic: he sees the EU as 'an irreplaceable community of culture, history and destiny'. However, he argued that it must be substantially reformed, needing 'less federalism, less Commission, fewer directives, less naïve multiculturalism, less dogmatic free tradeism, less abstract universalism', and 'more subsidiarity, more Council, more democracy, more borders, more protection for industry, more respect for identities.

How can this perspective be summed up? It is against the EU as it is (or how it is seen as being), and in favour of the EU as it 'should' be. It shares priorities with Eurosceptic populist movements (immigration and identity) but sees the EU as important and does not want it to break up. In part it can be seen as exemplifying the crossover of mainstream and extreme rights in France. At the same time, however, it should be noted that a perspective like this is not new: Charles de Gaulle, for instance, famously favoured a *Europe des Patries*, whose states would collaborate politically but retain their traditional sovereignty and identity. As de Gaulle put it in 1962 (failing to note, however, that both Dante and Goethe lived before the foundation of Italian and German nation states):

> I do not believe that Europe can have any living reality if it does not include France and her Frenchmen, Germany and its Germans, Italy and its Italians, and so forth. Dante, Goethe, Chateaubriand belong to all Europe to the very extent that they were respectively and eminently Italian, German and French. They would not have served Europe very well if they had been stateless, or if they had thought and written in some kind of integrated [invented languages like] Esperanto or Volapük. (Mahoney 2000: 133)

Le Figaro's divisions on the EU (between conservatism and populism, or between Euroscepticism based on the EU's current state and Europhilia based on its supposed potential) perhaps embodied in the Gaullist conception of Europe, can be seen elsewhere in the newspaper. As a final example, a piece on 24 June by regular opinion columnist Natacha Polony, known in France for her 'sovereignist' views, argued against those who see the Brexit vote as representing racism and xenophobia, and argued for 'a construction of a Europe of peoples and nations'. It is wrong, for Polony, to evoke a divide between supporters of an elitist, pro-free-market EU on one hand, and xenophobic Eurosceptics on the other. This viewpoint, she argued, masks 'the negation of European nations and their history': 'respecting difference', on the contrary, 'is to construct Europe on the articulation of its differences and the freedom of its peoples'. This attack on European federalism is also an attack on globalization, 'the sole programme of the EU', which 'detests difference' and 'accommodates itself badly to the spirit of peoples and the history of nations': the very opposite of the Europe of identity and sovereignty she favours. Again, echoes are audible of both contemporary populism and Gaullist tradition. Perhaps the most intriguing aspect of Polony's argument, however, is its criticism of the EU's emphasis on free markets: she attacks 'those who today sell us a European Union essentially occupied in organizing the free movement of profits into tax havens in Luxembourg, and the free movement of detached workers into locations where social protections are scandalously guaranteed' ('detached workers' are workers from one EU country sent by their employer to temporarily carry out work in another, a practice which critics see as being abused by employers, who bring in skilled foreign labour at wage rates which undercut local workers). Leaving aside her objection to immigrants receiving social protection, it is both surprising and revealing that this argument appeared in a newspaper of the pro-free-market business elite. *Le Figaro*'s reaction to the Brexit vote, it could be argued, illustrates deep ideological divisions in the French right, between supporters of free trade and free markets on one hand, and those who emphasize national autonomy and identity on the other. Whereas the centre and mainstream left in France remain Europhile, as we have seen in *Le Monde* and *Libération*, it is possible in future that the fault line between pro- and anti-EU sentiment will run, as in Britain, directly through the mainstream right.

Few figures better represent the crossover between the world of *Le Figaro* and the world of *Valeurs Actuelles*, the far-right-leaning magazine to be examined shortly, than the journalist and polemicist Eric Zemmour, who contributes to *Le Figaro*, appears at peak time twice a week on RTL, one of France's most popular radio stations, and writes controversial and often best-selling books such as *Le Suicide français* (2014).

Zemmour, an overt supporter of Brexit, operates at the ideological fringes of the mainstream media, but is highly influential in public debate, occupying a unique and controversial position. His views can be described as a French variant of neoconservatism, criticising 'elites', globalization, immigration, socialism, European integration, the free-market economy and progressive ideas which have allegedly caused the decline of France. He regularly denounces minority rights as well as the 'islamization' and 'halalization' of France; is one of the few French journalists to support Donald Trump; and agrees with Marine Le Pen that France's mainstream parties of government (the centre-right Republicans and centre-left Socialist Part) act like a coalition pushing for further European integration despite a façade of opposition. It therefore can be argued that Zemmour is close to the Front National, although he has never publicly called on people to vote for the far-right party. What is clear, however, is that Zemmour is a loose cannon in the French media, and that he is first and foremost 'anti-system'. Many have publicly regretted that Zemmour has been given access to mainstream media, but he claims he is the voice of a 'silent majority' which is otherwise excluded. He therefore claims to represent a defiant grassroots electorate similar to that of Brexit and Donald Trump. As such, his support for Brexit encompassed: criticisms of the economic establishment which predicted negative consequences from Brexit; admiration for the English (sic) who voted despite 'abuse and threats' from globalized elites (30 June 2016b); and emphasis on the key role of ordinary people (*le prolo anglais*). As he put it in one of his RTL broadcasts:

> The *prolo anglais* is detestable; France's political, media, economic, artistic and intellectual elites came down on him with an unprecedented aggressiveness [...] This people's insurrection threatens the Western elites; their privileges, their certainties and their ideals. (28 June 2016a)

Zemmour's prominent place in the mainstream media he claims to despise suggests that his views are no longer fully at the margins, and may well become dominant in the French right, reflecting similar divisions to those of the US right faced with the rise of Donald Trump. At the moment however, similar views are expressed most wholeheartedly in the non-mainstream press, which will be considered in the next section.

FAR-RIGHT AND FAR-LEFT PRESS REACTIONS

In the remainder of this chapter, more sceptical voices from the margins of political debate on the far-left and far-right (both historically hostile towards the EU) will be analysed. For this purpose, two sources will be used. On the right, examples are taken from *Valeurs Actuelles*, a weekly news magazine which lies on the borderline of the far-right and the mainstream right, playing on shared obsessions with immigration and national identity (*Le Nouvel Observateur*, 5 December 2015). On the left, we have chosen to take examples from *Mediapart*, a left-leaning online newspaper which counts 130,000 paying subscribers (*Mediapart*, 9 March 2017) and has become increasingly influential, particularly through its investigative journalism.

Valeurs Actuelles: A Far-Right Celebration of Brexit

We begin with *Valeurs Actuelles* which, of all sources examined, is by far the most enthusiastic about Britain leaving the EU, seeing it as a model that France and other European states should follow. The language used in its headlines makes its position clear: 'Brexit: the storm is only beginning' (4 July 2016); 'Brussels faced with the domino effect' (4 July 2016); or 'Brexit: "Kill the monster"!' (4 July 2016), in which Henri Guaino, a former adviser to ex-President Nicolas Sarkozy (a figure himself favoured by the magazine for placing the issues of immigration and national identity at the centre of political debate) denounces 'German Europe' and demands France 'leave the nightmare of integration and federalism'.

The examples cited from *Valeurs Actuelles* were noticeably written in a style more akin to a British tabloid than to any other sources examined in this chapter, perhaps reflecting better than any of them a French political context in which candidates commonly described as populists (Marine Le Pen on the right and Jean-Luc Mélenchon on the left) received more than 40% of votes in the 2017 presidential election; while even 'mainstream' candidates like the conservative François Fillon emphasized issues of immigration and identity, and presented themselves as representing 'the people' against 'the elites'. Editorialist Raphaël Stainville (30 June 2016), for example, reacted to Brexit by celebrating the end of 'Europe by forced march, with or without the consent of the people', mocking the 'intellectuals and experts' predicting disaster, and the 'religion of a protective Europe, creator of jobs and growth, a veritable heaven on earth for those who know how to profit from the gifts of globalization'. The British, for Stainville, have 'said no to the Europe of Brussels, to its standardizing madness, to foreign workers, to free movement of people and goods, to immigration, to Angela Merkel'. They have 'said no to always more Europe. Not all. But an immense majority.' This is untrue, but in any case, it demonstrates for him that 'peoples are waking up, recoiling, rebelling'; and in France, while mainstream parties 'are in agreement not to have a referendum on a subject as complex as Europe', 'the people are dying to make themselves heard'.

At the heart of *Valeurs Actuelles'* rejection of the EU, however, is immigration. For example, François d'Orcival, argued in an editorial (1 July 2016) that Brexit is not a cause of chaos but a result, caused by the immigration policy of EU leaders. Brexit was inevitable, he implies, because 'England [sic] is no longer an island'. He illustrates his point by namechecking the northern English town of Rotherham, presented as the fearful epitome of a 'multicultural and multi-ethnic model', where 'they speak Polish, Czech, Slovak or Urdu'; where 'gypsies came in their waves', and where 'gangs of Pakistanis indulged in a thousand rapes in just a few years'. When Angela Merkel, he continued, 'opened Germany's doors to mass immigration', the inhabitants of Rotherham 'could see the invasion to come', and from that point, 'Cameron, Obama, Hollande, Merkel, Tusk or Juncker could come up with all the rational arguments, or threats, they wanted, it didn't matter anymore': 68% of voters in Rotherham elected to leave, and 'the town is cracking under the pressure of a violent anti-immigration movement. Because it no longer feels English'. It is not important for the magazine whether the story is exaggerated or untrue, as long as it fits into a narrative reflecting a long-established trope of the far-right: that immigrants profit from globalization to 'invade' Western states with the complicity of political elites (Reynié 2011: 32). Here, the elites involved are those of the EU, already reviled in this worldview for its supposed destruction of sovereignty and national identity.

Valeurs Actuelles, then, rejects the EU in a way consistent with its links to the far-right, emphasizing immigration and identity and celebrating Brexit as a first step towards independence and regained sovereignty for the nations of Europe. In this, it is in tune with the right-wing populists who have gained influence across the Western world in recent years: the magazine's arguments could be repeated verbatim by Marine Le Pen, but also by Donald Trump, Geert Wilders or Nigel Farage. *Valeurs Actuelles*, therefore, places itself within the right-wing narrative of an international populist uprising. At the same time, though, its discourse can be placed within a longer French tradition, France being a pioneer of an exclusionary form of nationalism promoted by late nineteenth and early twentieth-century thinkers such as Charles Maurras and Maurice Barrès.

MEDIAPART AND BREXIT: THE REJECTION OF A NEOLIBERAL AND AUTHORITARIAN EU

This review of French media perspectives on Brexit will end by taking examples from *Mediapart*, enabling us to consider left-wing Eurosceptic perspectives. There is a strong Eurosceptic tradition among France's radical left (Milner 2004), with the EU seen as imposing and enforcing the agenda of 'oligarchies' of big business and international finance, against the interests and wishes of its citizens. It is seen as overriding national governments to force neoliberal capitalism on European states and forbid attempts to control or regulate it, meaning a sustained attack on public services, living standards, workers' rights and job security. This can be seen, for example, in a passage addressing the Lisbon Treaty in the 2012 manifesto of the leftist Front de Gauche. It is seen as 'illustrating all the faults of capitalism today: it imposes "free and undistorted competition" to the detriment of the social rights won by democratic and workers' struggles over the centuries. It encourages free trade to the detriment of the environment and social justice. It continues the European Union's slide towards authoritarianism by concentrating power in the hands of non-elected institutions' (2011: 67).

We have chosen to illustrate this position with examples from *Mediapart* which, despite not being part of the traditional media, is one of the most influential outlets for voices on the left which fall outside the moderate liberal paradigm of *Le Monde*, *Libération* and the Socialist Party, with 130,000 paying subscribers, an admired investigative journalism section, editions in English and Spanish and a well-populated system of blogs and reader contributions.

It may be noted that *Mediapart* sees itself as independent and free-thinking, without a set editorial line: it is not possible, therefore, to talk of the 'opinions' of the site in the same way we have with other sources examined here. What is possible, however, is to review the articles commissioned on a given event, which give an indication of the editorial staff's sympathies on a case-by-case basis. In relation to Brexit, the site's Eurosceptic contributors divide into two categories, one celebrating Brexit as a victory for 'the people' over business and financial elites; the other more circumspect about celebrating due to the negative aspects of the campaign, but welcoming the outcome of the vote in the belief that an EU seen as devoted to an extreme form of capitalism needs to be challenged in order for a more progressive construction to be built.

The first position is represented in a post by Danielle Simonnet of the left-wing Parti de Gauche (24 June 2016). She argued that media coverage of Brexit shows a false dichotomy between two camps, one representing 'the authoritarian ordoliberalism of the German right', and the other the 'xenophobic ultraliberalism of the English right. Iit should be noted that when 'liberalism' is used as pejorative by the French left, it refers specifically to economic liberalism; while 'ordoliberalism' refers to the German model of free-market capitalism. Simmonet uses it as a polemical term to attack Germany's supposed imposition of austerity across Europe, rather than as a reference to a specific political philosophy). On the contrary, she sees the Brexit vote as representing 'the low-paid working class, who suffer the most from [economic] liberalism and austerity policies, unemployment, precarious work and misery'. As such, the main lesson she takes from the vote is that 'a show of strength against European institutions is possible and necessary', which requires a defence of 'sovereignty' and the 'sovereign people'. This is the only way, for Simonnet, to 'break with liberal European treaties, in order to engage other co-operations between peoples, not based on the interests of finance, free trade and the miserable logic of the Transatlantic Trade and Investment Partnership, but the preservation of our ecosystem, of social justice and of democracy'. Arguably, this left-wing Eurosceptic perspective shares the right's preoccupation with sovereignty. However, while the right-wing form values sovereignty as a means of closing borders, controlling immigration and defending national identities, the left-wing form values the possibility of an independent financial policy. Indeed, some on the French left see arguing for reform of the EU as a waste of time: for the leftist sociologist and activist Aurélien Bernier (2014), for example, no left-wing programme is actually possible without leaving the juridical and monetary systems of the EU, as these systems, in conjunction with international trade rules, are designed to prevent states from putting into practice left-wing policies, and tie them into the liberal economic order. A similar logic is followed by fellow *Mediapart* contributor Stathis Kouvelakis (25 June 2016), formerly part of the radical left Syriza Government in Greece. He sees Brexit as 'the end of the current European project', which he regards as 'a project constructed by and for the elites'. It is to be celebrated, furthermore, as 'an opportunity for progressive forces fighting against a neoliberal and authoritarian EU, that is to say, the EU which exists'. His conclusion, therefore, is clear: 'the EU is not reformable, and I think there is no other solution than its dissolution. A true refoundation of Europe necessitates breaking the iron cage of perpetual austerity and neoliberal authoritarianism, and this is only possible by breaking with the institutional machinery of the EU.'

Other contributors, however, are more circumspect about the outcome of the Brexit vote. An editorial by one of the site's founders, François Bonnet, for example, sums up this tendency in its headline: 'Brexit, a welcome catastrophe' (24 June 2016). On one hand, Bonnet is strongly critical of Brexit. It signifies, for him, 'a victory of the worst forces at work in Europe today'. That is, 'it is a victory for the conservative and populist right, it is the victory of the extreme right and the repulsive forces shown in their paranoid frustrations and their dreams of lost empires, bolstered by violent xenophobia and fantastical fears. This can be seen in the fact that the arrival of "hordes of migrants" was the primary argument of Brexit supporters'. On the other hand, however, 'now that the catastrophe has happened, should we cry alongside Jean-Claude Juncker, David Cameron, City bankers and financial markets? Certainly not.' The unsavoury aspects of the 2016 EU referendum campaign, for Bonnet, do not alter the fact that there is a lot wrong with the EU, and he sees its behaviour since the 2008 financial crisis as only having encouraged the rise of far-right and nationalist movements. 'Here we are', he put it, 'at the key moment of a necessary clarification. It has been brutally provoked by the [2016 EU] referendum and it is welcome. The European Union has been confiscated from its citizens. Not only by the markets and financial oligarchies. But also by a remote political class, living according to principles of irresponsibility and impunity.' Elsewhere, he criticized an EU which has become 'deaf to the aspirations of its citizens, blind to the issues facing the planet, impotent in resolving crises and a vassal of financial powers'. As for possible solutions, he appears pessimistic. He took some heart from the emergence of new progressive left movements like Syriza in Greece, Podemos in Spain and, more ambiguously, the Five Star movement in Italy; seeing them as the basis of a potential reconstruction of the European left. However, 'this reconstruction is in its infancy, fragile, made from both advances and setbacks. The failures are numerous, the victories uncertain'. As a perspective on the future, this is a long way from the enthusiasm of *Valeurs Actuelles* on the far-right.

Conclusion

Summing up, we have considered the extent to which the historic divide on Europe within the French press (between a Europhile mainstream and Eurosceptic margins) remains valid in the case of their reactions to the Brexit vote. For the most part, we find, it does; the least ambiguous cases being the centrist *Le Monde* and the centre-left *Libération*. Both of these newspapers deplore Brexit and are committed to the EU out of principle: even though they may admit that it is imperfect, they present the EU as a valuable project of peace, unity and civilisation. Divisions, however, appear elsewhere. The conservative *Le Figaro*, while never explicitly pro-Brexit or anti-EU, is dragged in several different directions by: its support for free markets; the influence of contemporary right-wing populism; and the nostalgic aura of a Gaullist *Europe des Patries*. As such, reflecting wider divisions on the mainstream right in France and elsewhere, it is divided between pragmatic support for the EU based on its value to business, and a desire to substantially reform it in a more conservative direction that emphasizes the strengthening of borders, the reduction of immigration and a greater respect for national identities and specificities. The two non-mainstream sources examined, meanwhile, are more sceptical towards the EU. However, the reasons for this differ substantially. On the border of the far-right and the mainstream right, *Valeurs Actuelles* is by far the most enthusiastic about Brexit amongst the sources examined, presenting it as a liberation from a dictatorial empire imposing mass immigration and destroying national identity, and hoping fervently that other European states will follow suit. The radical left-inclined contributors to *Mediapart*, on the other hand, are divided between celebrating Brexit as a victory for 'the people' against financial and business elites and regretting the xenophobia of the Brexit campaign. They also cautiously welcome the vote on the grounds that an EU seen as hyper-capitalist needs to be brought down if something better is to be built in its place. The division between mainstream and margins in French media positioning on Europe shows a clear parallel with wider divisions in the French political landscape, as reflected by the presidential election campaign in 2017. The eventual winner, the pro-EU Emmanuel Macron, was backed by moderates of the centre, centre-right and centre-left. Euroscepticism, meanwhile, remained on the ideological margins, appearing principally in the campaigns of the far-right Marine Le Pen and the far-left Jean-Luc Mélenchon. The strong showings of Le Pen and Mélenchon, however, suggest that this 'marginal' position is becoming more and more influential.

BIBLIOGRAPHY

Aboura, S. 2005. French Media Bias and the Vote on the European Constitution. *European Journal of Political Economy* 21 (4): 1093–1098.

Benoit, B. 1997. *Social Nationalism: An Anatomy of French Euroscepticism.* Aldershot: Ashgate.

Benson, R., and D.C. Hallin. 2007. How States, Markets and Globalization Shape the News: The French and US National Press, 1965–97. *European Journal of Communication* 22 (1): 27–48.

Bernier, A. 2014. *La gauche radicale et ses tabous.* Paris: Éditions du Seuil.

Birnbaum, P. 2012. *Genèse du populisme: Le peuple et les gros.* Paris: Fayard/ Pluriel.

Boltanski, L., and A. Esquerre. 2014. *Vers l'extrême: Extension des domaines de la droite.* Bellevaux: Éditions Dehors.

Cette France-là. 2012. *Xénophobie d'en haut: le choix d'une droite éhontée.* Paris: La Découverte.

Charon, J.M. 2003. *Les médias en France.* Paris: La Découverte.

Fletcher, J. 1994. Le Monde: Anatomy of a Newspaper. *French Cultural Studies* 5 (13): 57–71.

Front de Gauche. 2011. *L'humain d'abord.* Paris: Librio.

Guyomarch, A., H. Machin, and E. Ritchie. 1998. *France in the European Union.* Basingstoke: Palgrave Macmillan.

Halimi, S. 2005. *Les nouveaux chiens de garde.* Paris: Liber-Raisons d'agir.

Kuhn, R. 1995. *The Media in France.* London: Routledge.

Kuhn, R. 2006. *The Media in France.* London: Routledge.

Kuhn, R. 2011. *The Media in Contemporary France.* Berkshire: Open University Press.

Laurent, A., and N. Sauger. 2005. *Le référendum de ratification du Traité constitutionnel européen: comprendre le 'Non' français.* Paris: Centre de Recherches Politiques de Sciences Po.

Mahoney, D. 2000. *De Gaulle: Statesmanship, Grandeur and Modern Democracy.* New Brunswick: Transaction Publishers.

Maler, H., and A. Schwartz. 2005. *Médias en campagne. Retours sur le référendum de 2005.* Paris: Editions Sylleps.

Mélenchon, J.-L. 2010. *"Qu'ils s'en aillent tous!" Vite, la Révolution citoyenne.* Paris: Flammarion.

Milner, S. 2004. For an Alternative Europe: Euroscepticism and the French Left Since the Maastricht Treaty. *European Studies: A Journal of European Culture, History and Politics* 20 (1): 59–81.

Noiriel, G. 2007. *À quoi sert 'l'identité nationale'*. Marseille: Agone.

Reynié, D. 2011. *Populismes: la pente fatale*. Paris: Plon.

Schwartz, A. 2008. Bonne Europe et mauvaise France. Les éditorialistes français interprètent la victoire du « non » au traité constitutionnel européen. *Politique et Sociétés* 27 (2): 137–159.

Todorov, T. 2008. *La peur des barbares: au-delà du choc des civilisations*. Paris: Laffont.

Williams, K. 2005. *European Media Studies*. London: Hodder Arnold.

Zemmour, E. 2014. *Le suicide français*. Paris: Albin Michel.

NEWSPAPERS AND WEBSITES

Adler, A. 2016. Brexit: la tempête ne fait que commencer. *Valeurs Actuelles*, July 4. http://www.valeursactuelles.com/la-tempete-ne-fait-que-commencer-63175.

Alliance pour les Chiffres de la Presse et des Médias. 2017. www.acpm.fr.

Barbier, C. 2016. Le Royaume-Uni dit oui au Brexit: une chance pour l'Europe! *L'Express*, June 24. http://www.lexpress.fr/actualite/monde/europe/le-royaume-uni-dit-oui-au-brexit-une-chance-pour-l-europe_1805702.html.

Bonnet, F. 2016. Brexit, une catastrophe bienvenue. *Mediapart*, June 24. https://www.mediapart.fr/journal/international/240616/brexit-une-catastrophe-bienvenue?onglet=full.

Bourlanges, J.-L. 2016. Les Britanniques sacrifient leurs intérêts à leurs fantasmes. *Le Figaro*, June 25. http://www.lefigaro.fr/vox/monde/2016/06/25/31002-20160625ARTFIG00050-jean-louis-bourlanges-les-britanniques-sacrifient-leurs-interets-a-leurs-fantasmes.php.

Brézet, A. 2016. L'éditorial d'Alexis Brézet: reconquérir les peuples. *Le Figaro*, June 27. http://www.lefigaro.fr/vox/monde/2016/06/26/31002-20160626ARTFIG00172-reconquerir-les-peuples.php.

Cheyvialle, A. 2016. Comment le Brexit va frapper l'économie britannique. *Le Figaro*, June 26. http://www.lefigaro.fr/conjoncture/2016/06/26/20002-20160626ARTFIG00138-comment-le-brexit-va-frapper-l-economie-britannique.php.

Colonna, A. 2016. Bruxelles face à l'effet domino. *Valeurs Actuelles*, July 4. http://www.valeursactuelles.com/bruxelles-face-a-leffet-domino-63114.

d'Orcival, F. 2016. L'Europe des aveugles .... *Valeurs Actuelles*, July 1. http://www.valeursactuelles.com/leurope-des-aveugles-63101.

Donnet, B. 2016. Editorial on France-Inter radio. *France-Inter*, June 27. https://www.youtube.com/watch?v=_KyiRYWPxLE.

Guaino, H. 2016. Brexit: Tuer le monstre! *Valeurs Actuelles*, July 4. http://www.valeursactuelles.com/tuer-le-monstre-63173.

Ifop-Fiducial. L'élection présidentielle en temps réel, 30 mars 2017, opinion poll. http://dataviz.ifop.com:8080/IFOP_ROLLING/IFOP_30-03-2017.pdf.

Joffrin, L. 2016a. Brexit: l'écran de fumée souverainiste. *Libération*, June 27. http://www.liberation.fr/planete/2016/06/27/brexit-l-ecran-de-fumee-souverainiste_1462431.

Joffrin, L. 2016b. Une révolte populaire et une cinglante défaite. *Libération*, June 24. http://www.liberation.fr/planete/2016/06/24/une-revolte-populaire-et-une-cinglante-defaite_1461674.

Kessler, D. 2016. Il n'y aura pas de gagnants au Brexit. *Le Figaro*, June 24. http://www.lefigaro.fr/conjoncture/2016/06/24/20002-20160624ART-FIG00374-denis-kessler-il-n-y-aura-pas-de-gagnants-au-brexit.php.

Kouvelakis, S. 2016. L'UE n'est pas réformable. *Mediapart*, June 25. https://www.mediapart.fr/journal/international/250616/stathis-kouvelakis-l-ue-n-est-pas-reformable?onglet=full.

Laserre, I. 2016. Brexit: l'influence de l'Europe dans le monde va s'éroder. *Le Figaro*, June 24. http://www.lefigaro.fr/international/2016/06/24/01003-20160624ARTFIG00354-brexit-l8216influence-de-l-europe-dans-le-monde-va-s-eroder.php.

Lévy, B.-H. 2016. Étrange défaite à Londres. *Le Monde*, June 25. http://www.lemonde.fr/idees/article/2016/06/25/bernard-henri-levy-etrange-defaite-a-londres_4958066_3232.html.

Parmentier, A. 2016. Le "Brexit" n'aura pas lieu. *Le Monde*, June 25. http://www.lemonde.fr/idees/article/2016/06/25/le-brexit-n-aura-pas-lieu_4957905_3232.html.

Plenel, E. 2017. Mediapart a neuf ans: nos comptes, nos résultats. *Mediapart*, March 9. https://blogs.mediapart.fr/edwy-plenel/blog/090317/mediapart-neuf-ans-nos-comptes-nos-resultats.

Polony, N. 2016. Encore un coup des xénophobes! *Le Figaro*, June 24. http://www.lefigaro.fr/vox/monde/2016/06/24/31002-20160624ART-FIG00285-encore-un-coup-des-xenophobes.php.

Quatremer, J. 2015. Le programme de Syriza ne vaut pas même pas le papier sur lequel il a été écrit! *Libération*, January 31. http://bruxelles.blogs.liberation.fr/2015/01/31/le-programme-de-syriza-ne-vaut-meme-le-papier-sur-lequel-il-a-ete-ecrit-/.

Quatremer, J. 2016. Brexit: amis anglais, merci pour votre sacrifice! *Libération*, June 27. http://bruxelles.blogs.liberation.fr/2016/06/24/brexit-amis-anglais-merci-pour-votre-sacrifice/.

Rocard, M. 2016. Brexit: L'enjeu est l'entité politique de l'Europe. *La Croix*, June 19. http://www.la-croix.com/Monde/Europe/Brexit-L-enjeu-entitepolitique-Europe-Michel-Rocard-ancien-premier-ministre-PS-2016-06-19-1200769809.

Rousso, H. 2016. No future? *Libération*, June 26. http://www.liberation.fr/debats/2016/06/26/no-future_1462191.

Simonnet, D. 2016. Brexit, l'oligarchie panique en découvrant que le peuple existe! *Mediapart*, June 25. https://blogs.mediapart.fr/danielle-simonnet/blog/240616/brexit-l-oligarchie-panique-en-decouvrant-que-le-peuple-existe.

Stainville, R. 2016. Brexit ... Demain la France? *Valeurs Actuelles*, June 30. http://www.valeursactuelles.com/demain-la-france-63108.

Unknown author. 2016a. L'avenir de l'Europe entre les mains d'un couple franco-allemand affaibli. *Le Figaro*, June 24. http://www.lefigaro.fr/international/2016/06/24/01003-20160624ARTFIG00376-l-avenir-de-l-europe-entre-les-mains-d-un-couple-franco-allemand-affaibli.php.

Unknown author. 2016b. "Brexit": le vote des malmenés de la mondialisation. *Le Monde*, June 25. http://www.lemonde.fr/idees/article/2016/06/25/le-vote-des-malmenes-de-la-mondialisation_4958072_3232.html.

Unknown author. 2016c. L'Europe existe, les Anglais l'ont rencontrée. *Le Monde*, June 28. http://www.lemonde.fr/idees/article/2016/06/28/l-europe-existe-les-anglais-l-ont-rencontree_4959533_3232.html.

Vaton, M. 2015. "Valeurs Actuelles": enquête sur une extrême droitisation. *Le Nouvel Observateur*, December 5. http://teleobs.nouvelobs.com/actualites/20151201.OBS0468/valeurs-actuelles-enquete-sur-une-extreme-droitisation.html.

Zemmour, E. 2016a. *RTL*, June 28. Broadcast accessed at http://ericzemmour.blogspot.co.uk/2016/06/rtl-chronique-eric-zemmour-28juin-brexit.html.

Zemmour, E. 2016b. *RTL*, June 30. Broadcast accessed at http://ericzemmour.blogspot.co.uk/2016/07/eric-zemmour-sur-rtl-brexit-philippe.html.

CHAPTER 10

The 2016 EU Referendum Stories in Austrian, German, and Swiss Media: Catastrophes, Characterizations, Challenges

Klaus Peter Müller

Introduction

Whenever we try to make sense of life and detect meaning in it, we construct stories or adopt those offered by our culture and media. Storytelling is in fact a cognitive schema; that is, a firm part of the human mind, whose relevance has been confirmed by the cognitive sciences and whose functioning is described by narratology (see, for example, Eysenck 2012; Herman 2013). This analysis of the stories told about the 2016 European Union (EU) referendum in Austrian, German and Swiss media will use the basic categories of stories which we also apply in our everyday lives, where we speak of people (characters), what they do (action), where we meet them (setting), why we think they act in a particular way (reasons), and what effects this has had on us (results and conclusions).

K. P. Müller (✉)
Johannes Gutenberg-University Mainz, Mainz, Germany
e-mail: kmueller@uni-mainz.de

© The Author(s) 2018
A. Ridge-Newman et al. (eds.), *Reporting the Road to Brexit*,
https://doi.org/10.1007/978-3-319-73682-2_10

The vast amount of media texts on the referendum can be usefully subdivided in this way and offer new perspectives as well as intriguing insights. Descriptions of Brexit (Britain's exit from the European Union) as a tragedy or catastrophe instantly deliver a meaningful story to people, who, however, may also see Brexit as a positive result, a comedy or liberation. Important information is provided by finding out which of the German-speaking media regarded the referendum in any of these ways, or as a farce, or some other kind of story genre. Which of them saw David Cameron as a tragic character or a trickster, the British people as fighting for more justice or being deluded by political liars? One instantly knows the story told when both David Cameron and Nigel Farage are described as the 'biggest rat deserting a sinking ship', and it is revealing to find out that this was not only a headline in the Swiss tabloid *Blick* but also used by respected media such as the *Wiener Zeitung* in Austria or the weekly magazine *Spiegel* and the ARD (the first public-service channel) in Germany.

The rat example instantly highlights the significance of language, still the essential human medium, which is why a linguistic approach will also be used in order to detect the key words that give stories a particular characteristic. Is Brexit a divorce with the usual strong emotions involved, or a fairly rational ending of political and economic relationships and contracts? It is not surprising that metaphors (like 'rat') predominate among the key words, because of their extreme usefulness in helping people quickly understand difficult situations (see Lakoff and Johnson 2003; Wittgenstein 2009). But are they used differently in tabloids, broadsheets, on TV or radio, or across the countries investigated?

A total of 2112 media texts were analysed, as follows (including their abbreviations, characteristics, and the number of texts on the referendum):

Austria

Heute (www.heute.at) (daily tabloid)	34
Krone (www.krone.at) (daily tabloid)	27
Standard (www.derstandard.at) (daily broadsheet)	207
Wiener Zeitung (*WZ*) (www.wienerzeitung.at) (daily broadsheet)	108
Österreich 1 ORF 1 (http://oe1.orf.at) (radio)	59
ORF (http://tv.orf.at/) (TV)	28

Germany

Bild (www.bild.de) (daily tabloid)	32
Handelsblatt (*HB*) (http://www.handelsblatt.com) (daily business broadsheet)	53

Frankfurter Allgemeine Zeitung (FAZ) (http://www.faz.net) (daily broadsheet)	215
Spiegel (http://www.spiegel.de) (weekly quality magazine)	147
Süddeutsche Zeitung (SZ) (http://www.sueddeutsche.de) (daily broadsheet)	145
tageszeitung (taz) (http://www.taz.de) (daily broadsheet)	24
Welt (http://www.welt.de) (daily broadsheet)	233
Zeit (www.zeit.de) (weekly quality paper)	171
ARD (www.ard.de) (TV and radio)	155
ZDF (http://www.zdf.de) (TV)	82
Deutschlandfunk (DLF) (http://www.deutschlandfunk.de) (radio)	63
Switzerland	
Blick (http://www.blick.ch) (daily tabloid)	47
Handelszeitung (HZ) (http://www.handelszeitung.ch) (business daily)	21
Neue Zürcher Zeitung (NZZ) (http://www.nzz.ch) (daily broadsheet)	86
20 Minuten (20Min) (http://www.20min.ch) (daily tabloid)	89
SRF Schweizer Rundfunk (http://www.srf.ch) (radio & TV)	86

Quality daily newspapers and weeklies provided the majority of the material. The referendum got much wider coverage in these sources, and it was dealt with in different sections, instantly providing dominant categories, ranging from politics, business and the stock exchange to topics such as sport and literature. Tabloids have also been used as well as representative TV and radio programmes. In most cases, the media's online versions have been investigated. The determining factors for the choice of the media have been their circulation (and thus their importance for the public), their specific interests (for example, general information or business focus), political leanings (for example, *taz* with a left of centre position, *FAZ* right of centre), and the recipients addressed. In this way, all important parts and opinions of the respective nations studied have been included for an analysis of the different scopes and ways of presenting the referendum in the media.

What follows is the gist of an extensive analysis that highlights the main results of this investigation, focusing first on the protagonists in the referendum stories, their actions and motives. The second section analyses stories that detect reasons for the referendum and its result and attribute responsibilities. The third section discusses the stories of consequences, the immediate and long-term effects of the referendum. The plural term 'stories' indicates that variations quickly occur through minor changes, but it is a significant result of this investigation that the basic elements in the stories are surprisingly the same in all media. These and national varieties will be pointed out with references to typical examples and representative sources. The statements made and conclusions drawn are of general validity and extreme importance. They reflect what the media express and are an enormous challenge to the public.

There are a few formal differences between the presentational style of this chapter and that found elsewhere in this book. First, given the storytelling approach adopted here, I have opted to use the historic present rather than the past tense throughout in order to capture the vividness of the narratives analysed. Second, since such an approach generates a very large number of citations, only abbreviated in-text references are supplied without corresponding detailed entries in the Bibliography.

THE MAIN CHARACTERS' STORIES

SZ (11 June 2016) presented a list of who, at that time, it thought to be the 11 most important British figures in what became known in the German-language media as the *Brexit-Streit* (variously translatable as 'Brexit argument/row/dispute/quarrel/contention/strife/clash/struggle/controversy/fight/battle/conflict'). *Streit* is a key word, very often used, with all of the shades of meaning of the English words selected here. The word instantly sets the scene where opponents meet, and *SZ* puts them directly into the respective camps, either 'Pro-Brexit' or 'Pro-Europe'. The main action is also evident, but its form can vary with the protagonists. The list is a good starting point for a description of the stories widely told in German-speaking media about the British protagonists of this encounter. I will begin with the person who was politically in charge of Britain at that time, Prime Minister (PM) David Cameron. However, it is interesting to note that Cameron was presented by *SZ* as of merely secondary importance to Boris Johnson, Cameron's referendum rival and long-standing Tory colleague.

THE DAVID CAMERON STORIES

His 'status: PM in a double role' instantly defines Cameron as 'being on the horns of a dilemma', having brought about the referendum and being forced to convince everybody of the merits of the EU. He has not been very successful, as he used to blame the EU for everything that did not work well in Britain (*SZ*, 11 June 2016). Cameron has thus not only manoeuvred himself into a quagmire, but is also completely unconvincing, and the public does not believe him. The 'inconsistencies' in his actions are too plainly visible (DLF, 23 June 2016).

All media agree that the reasons why Cameron promised the referendum were party-political ones, not for public benefit (*SZ*, 28 June 2016). *NZZ* (4 July 2016) plainly says that Cameron took the risk in order to increase the chances of his party winning the next election. Born a 'lucky fellow, he gambled with his country's future for the benefit of his career and his party, and lost'. His actions are therefore often described as gambling or 'playing poker' (*HB*, 16 June 2016; *WZ*, 24 June 2016; *FAZ*, 26 June 2016; *Krone*, 27 June 2016), and his intention of calming down the Eurosceptics in his party has only led to a still greater division among the Tories (*NZZ*, 22 June 2016), even a 'disastrous schism' in the entire country (*Zeit*, 14 June 2016). Failing to understand the dangerous dimensions of the referendum, Cameron has taken the UK into a serious crisis, a 'gaping abyss', and his government has 'gambled with the destiny of Europe' (DLF, 17 June 2016; *HB*, 25 June 2016; 26 June 2016). He has 'pushed his luck to the limit' and lost a 'battle'. Cameron's gamble turned out to be what *HB* already feared on 17 June 2016: a 'suicide mission'.

SZ (25 June 2016) expresses the general verdict on Cameron in this way: 'He has bequeathed a result to us that will leave Europe irrevocably weakened and possibly break up the UK. What a terrible legacy'. *NZZ* (4 July 2016) puts the Cameron story in a nutshell: 'Cameron will enter history as a gambler and loser.'

The Boris Johnson Stories

Johnson is first in the *SZ* list (11 June 2016), '*Status: Zausel-Rhetoriker*', a Bavarian term for Johnson's rhetorical quality, defined as being 'both sharp-tongued and unfair'. Other papers describe it as a 'cocktail of humour and crude exaggerations', while he is 'the man who never believes what he says' (*FAZ*, 3 July 2016). *WZ* (30 June 2016) spoke of Johnson's 'rhetorical pirouettes'. *FAZ* (5 June 2016) called him 'Mister Brexit', 'Britain's most jarring politician, trying to drive his country out of the EU with anti-German tirades—but there is another plan behind this'.

Johnson's comparison of the EU with Nazi Germany was called a 'new low-point' of the EU referendum (*NZZ*, 17 June 2016), with *HB* (17 June 2016), *SZ* (22 June 2016) and *Zeit* (24 June 2016) fearing that the UK was 'getting hysterical'. Dominic Johnson (*taz*, 30 June 2016), a Brit strongly in support of the British union and against Scottish independence, describes Boris as a 'ruthless improviser', who 'failed with panache', but has 'more political instinct than many of his colleagues'. *NZZ* (4 July 2016) uses a boxing metaphor: Boris 'throws in the towel' and gives up the fight to become Prime Minister. For all media, this was the plan behind Johnson moving into the Brexit camp and contradicting his many earlier praises of the EU (DLF, 3 July 2016; *HB*, 10 June 2016; *Zeit*, 16 June; 22 June 2016; *SZ*, 24 June 2016). 'Personal power-political calculations' (*NZZ*, 4 July 2016) are unanimously regarded as the main reason for Johnson's actions. This 'egomaniac populist', they say, has failed because of his 'burning ambition, gambling nature', and complete 'lack of moral concern'.

After the referendum result, *HB* (24 June 2016) spoke of 'King Boris', as they (like *MM*, 24 June 2016) assumed he would be the next Prime Minister. But they also called him an 'entertainer' and 'clown' (*MM*, 21 June 2016). He was described as a 'coward' and 'deserter', leaving it up to others to 'clean up his mess' (*20Min*, 30 June 2016; *Spiegel*, 1 July 2016), pulling the 'ripcord before buzzing off' (*FAZ*, 30 June 2016, three different articles), a 'happy-go-lucky-guy' (ARD, 30 June 2016), who has won a 'pyrrhic victory' (*20Min*, 28 June 2016; SRF, 30 June 2016; *WZ*, 6 July 2016). Alexander Graf Lambsdorff, vice-president of the EU Parliament, claims that 'Boris Johnson lives in a parallel universe' (*FAZ*, 28 June 2016), making empty promises (*Spiegel*, 27 June 2016). *MM* (30 June 2016) says that he 'with fibs constructs a world that suits him' and it exposes 'five of his main lies' and fantasies (with a link to https://qz.com/717412/boris-johnsons-telegraph-column-on-brexit-is-made-of-lies-half-truths-omissions-and-magical-thinking/).

Johnson's story in the media is that of an even 'bigger opportunist than Cameron' (*SZ*, 17 June 2016), a representative of the current 'populist model' (*Standard*, 30 June 2016). A good short description of his story is expressed in *Zeit* (1 July 2016), calling him 'Britain's spoiled son', almost a story genre of its own, making instant sense. A longer characterization is given by *Spiegel* (24 June 2016): he is 'the man responsible for Brexit', based on 'sheer foolishness', and a 'typical representative of the elite'. When he and other members of Oxford's Bullingdon Club had trashed a restaurant, 'they paid for their vandalism the next day. This time is different. The whole country will have to pay the bill, probably most those left behind who have voted for him'.

THE MICHAEL GOVE STORIES

Gove is third in the *SZ* list (11 June 2016), 'status: head of the [Leave] campaign'. He is the 'living proof of the enormous divisions in the Tory party', being Cameron's justice secretary in complete opposition to the Prime Minister. 'That would be impossible in Germany, but Brits are wired differently.' Nothing more on him there, and quite generally Gove received less than 30% of the coverage of Johnson, Cameron and Farage. He got into the headlines, however, when he thought it a good idea to defy expert opinion against Brexit with reference to German expert scientists denying Einstein's achievements. He later apologized for his 'inept statement' (*SZ*, 24 June 2016).

He was, nevertheless, generally regarded to be at the pinnacle of his career after the referendum and a strong candidate for the premiership (*SZ*, 24 June 2016; *Standard*, 30 June 2016; ARD, 1 July 2016). But then he came to be presented as the person 'betraying' Johnson in the run-up (*NZZ*, 4 July 2016), 'catapulting' himself with a 'sensational backstabbing' among the competitors. His is the 'most radical position with no interest in the EU market' (*WZ*, 30 June 2016). His story is neatly characterized by *NZZ* (30 June 2016) saying Gove will be presented 'in the history books as a shameless traitor', 'stabbing first Cameron then Johnson in the back'. A single word also instantly expresses his story when he is called Johnson's 'Brutus' (*20Min*, 30 June 2016; *Bild*, 30 June 2016; *Spiegel*, 1 July 2016).

THE NIGEL FARAGE STORIES

Farage was only eighth in the *SZ* list (11 June 2016), 'status: Game Changer', connected with him leaving the Conservatives in 1992 because of Maastricht, then being one of the founders of the United Kingdom Independence Party (UKIP) in 1993, its leader since 2006. He is described as the 'grubby urchin', the 'pariah nobody in the Leave group wants to have anything to do with'. He himself, however, says he has 'single-handedly brought the referendum about' and highlights the importance of his role in this 'game'. While *SZ* only insinuates that Farage is a rather conceited man, other texts are much more direct: *Standard* (24 June 2016) describes Farage as a 'lout' and a 'turkey' (Austrian for 'peacock', 4 July 2016), and *Spiegel* (24 June 2016) calls him 'a blockhead' who thinks his 'nicotine dependence is already an act of non-conformism and resistance'. For *Zeit* (4 July 2016), he is a 'pub politician', a 'right-wing populist' (*FAZ*, 24 June 2016), a 'nationalist' (*MM*, 21 June 2016), or simply a 'moaner' (*FAZ*, 8 June 2016). The well-known Austrian actor Christoph Waltz, a London resident for 15 years, called Farage the 'head rat deserting the sinking ship' (*Spiegel*, *WZ*, 5 July 2016). Like the entire Brexit group, Farage lied to the people and made promises he knew he could not keep (*FAZ*, 24 June 2016; *SZ*, 17 June 2016).

However, he is also the 'clear winner of the referendum', having 'fulfilled his political life', the 'man the British people decided to follow' (*SZ*, 24 June 2016, referring to the *Daily Telegraph* headline of the same day). An essential reason why people listened to him, not to the pro-Europe group, becomes instantly visible in a *FAZ* (8 June 2016) description of the TV encounter between Cameron and Farage: while Cameron pointed out that 'the UK would lose its international influence', Farage emphasized 'national pride', saying 'we Brits deserve better'. The battle was indeed won through emotions, not rational arguments, and Farage managed to stir people's feelings profoundly. His declaration of 'Britain's independence day' was accordingly repeated in all media (*Bild*, *Krone*, *Spiegel*, *SZ*, 24 June 2016).

NZZ (4 July 2016) is convinced that there would not have been a referendum without Farage, but he is a winner 'now skulking off', and ('like all other factions in the Brexit camp') he has 'no plan of what to do now'. Unlike others, he 'did not shy away from inciting xenophobic and anti-immigrant feelings', and he has 'only one-and-a-half issues: rejection of the EU and of uncontrolled immigration'. But he is 'triumphant in the EU Parliament' (*NZZ*, 28 June 2016; *SZ*, 28 June 2016), predicting the 'EU's slow death' (*WZ*, 6 July 2016), asking all parliamentarians, those who had made fun of him for years, 'Isn't it funny?' (*FAZ*, 29 June). What fun for somebody who has been the media's figure of fun and 'whipping boy' (SRF, 4 July 2016).

Like the other characters, Farage is a well-known type in human history. His story is that of a man adopting roles that suit his character and help him achieve his ends. His joviality allows him to appear as a common man or a clown, he likes the pub like many others, and can easily disguise that he is part of the elite he pretends to oppose. There is not a single indication in any of the media texts about him that he really cares for others. The peacock or Austrian turkey metaphor thus quite usefully expresses a key element in his story.

The Stories of Continental European Politicians

The settings in these stories change from London and other British places to Brussels, Berlin, Vienna and Zurich. The main characters are the top EU representatives Jean-Claude Juncker, Martin Schulz and Donald Tusk, as well as the representatives of Austria, Germany and Switzerland. They are presented in their official functions, and the EU politicians berate Cameron, Farage and Johnson for what they think is a 'disastrous result' (*Spiegel*, 5 July 2016). But the same politicians are also shown as responsible for Brexit (especially Juncker and Merkel), as having learned nothing, and they should, therefore, step down rather than go on living in the past or adopting desperate measures such as expanding the eurozone (*FAZ*, 26 June 2016 in two different articles; *FAZ*, 24 June 2016 on Juncker). For *Standard* (28 June 2016) and *WZ* (4 July 2016), Juncker is indeed 'part of the problem' and should 'resign'. While Juncker is afraid of further referendums (*FAZ*, 21 June 2016; 25 June 2016), the Austrian government is clearly against an '"Öxit" [Austrian exit] Referendum' (*Krone*, 24 June 2016; *WZ*, 24 June 2016; ORF, 4 July 2016), and their Finance Minister Hans Jörg Schelling even thought that the UK will remain an EU member, perhaps only with its Scottish and Northern Irish parts in a 'Brexit-light' version (*HB*, 4 July 2016; *Spiegel*, 5 July 2016; *Zeit*, 5 July 2016). Merkel, on the other hand, quickly said that 'Brexit is irreversible' (*Zeit*, 29 June 2016). All stories reflect the numerous difficulties of the EU and the UK, further described in the following sections.

Stories of Causes and Responsibilities

These stories are of particular significance for our understanding of what has happened in European history and what we are dealing with today. Who or what are the reasons for the referendum and its result? Who or what is responsible? The answers given in the stories are manifold only at first sight. Then a fairly clear picture emerges which offers useful insights into the complexity of contemporary societies, the main powers behind the apparent diversity, and their reflections in the media. The absolute majority of stories on the referendum are in explicit opposition to Brexit. Those expressing support make up only 2% and reflect the positions of either right-wing populist nationalists or supporters of neoliberalism. The remaining 98% of media stories will be focused on next.

For the Swiss tabloids *20Min* (25 June 2016) and *Blick* (26 June 2016), Cameron, Merkel and the free movement of people are responsible. Migration evidently was a key issue in all countries (*Standard*, 29 June 2016), but it is just one element in a long list of reasons, not the most important one, but prominent in the headlines. The Swiss tabloids' focus was not repeated in other media or countries.

An essential cause is how problems are dealt with, and problem solving has not been among the EU's and UK's best abilities. The EU disastrously failed to find a united solution for the refugees, and the UK was among the nations refusing to co-operate, joining nationalist Poland and Hungary (*HB*, 30 June 2016). A cluster of reasons was explicitly mentioned for this: London's Mayor Sadiq Khan is often quoted blaming Johnson for a campaign based on 'hatred' (*Zeit*, 22 June 2016), the 'force of shrill lies' is outlined (*Zeit*, 17 June 2016), the 'new impetus of nationalism' and the power of its 'most important weapons, rage and indignation' (*Zeit*, 27 June 2016). Any open exchange of rational arguments ended far too quickly (*Zeit*, 5 June 2016). When, for instance, Mark Carney, head of the Bank of England, spoke of serious dangers to Britain's financial system, demands for his resignation were raised rather than counterarguments used (*HB*, 17 June 2016). One of the strongest factors in this lack of rational communication is the media, which is why *Zeit* (5 July 2016) claims that 'Brexit was written up by the British media'.

Many texts support this, such as *SZ* (28 June 2016), quoting Raymond Geuss, Professor Emeritus of Philosophy at Cambridge University, who speaks of 'the uncomfortable truth that we, the Brits, not Angela Merkel, are responsible for the refugee problem due to our continued wars in the Middle East'. This lack of open communication, discussion of relevant contexts, and knowledge of historical facts went together with the propagation of lies and myths, such as the one about regaining autonomy and taking back control. How can any state claim autonomy in a global world? *Zeit* (1 July 2016) made this very visible by showing a picture of a Syrian woman with a small child in her arms in a refugee camp in Greece, alongside the headline 'What has this woman got to do with Brexit?' Everything, they then showed.

Globalization and the insecurities it creates are key reasons behind a 'deluge of misinformation' (*Zeit*, 23 June 2016). People take refuge in myths and illusions (*NZZ*, 10 June 2016), individuals and countries 'run amok', 'for they know not what they do' (*SZ*, 21 June 2016; *Zeit*, 26

June 2016, referring to Luke 23: 34). British historian Timothy Garton Ash is '100% convinced that Brexit is also a vote of protest against globalization' (*HB*, 7 July 2016). It is surprising that no text sees globalization in the context of humanity moving out of the industrial into a post-industrial world, driven by digitalization and artificial intelligence, but still undefined. This is such a radical change that nobody should be surprised about people being confused and desperate about losing the world they have grown up with, not knowing which world they are now entering. Brexit in this context is a solution of the past.

The most basic cause for Brexit mentioned in the media is, therefore, the loss of identity. They do not, however, point out that Britain lost its identity with the Suez Crisis in 1956 and had already been called upon to find a new one by the US politician Dean Acheson in 1962 (cf. Müller 2013; Harrison 2009). But in connection with the EU the sense of having lost one's identity has become evident, at least strongly felt by many British people, and the 'EU has become the symbol of this loss of identity, sovereignty and the idea that one can decide one's fate oneself'. This is Britain's 'tragic illusion: to think that these characteristics can be defended by going it alone'. A 'completely irrational' assumption and also 'not what Britain practises in NATO, the IMF etc.' (*HB*, 17 June 2016). The strong emotions during the referendum are connected with this 'serious identity crisis' (*HB*, 11 July 2016), a strong sense of 'emotional insecurity' (*Zeit*, 23 June 2016), and while 'the Brits are looking for their identity, Europe is just their victim' (*SZ*, 22 June 2016). The new English nationalism, right-wing populism, and the 'meltdown of political parties' are 'manifestations of this severe identity crisis' (*HB*, 20 June 2016; 26 June 2016; 27 June 2016; 11 July 2016; *NZZ*, 26 June 2016). Whatever the result of the referendum, 'this question will persist and must be answered by Britain: who are we? And who do we want to be in the 21st century?' *SZ* (22 June 2016) hoped there would be an 'exemplary debate at the highest level' about this question in Britain. But are there any signs of this actually taking place?

The EU also faces a serious identity crisis (*HB*, 20 June 2016; 27 June 2016; 1 July 2016), and starts from an even weaker position, as a nation basically does not need to justify its existence, usually already established by history, whereas a union of nations must make its usefulness evident (*HB*, 28 June 2016). The EU, however, has even failed to deliver sound, basic economic results: 'since the financial crisis an additional 8 million Europeans are threatened by poverty, Europe has no economic growth strategy at all', nor any efficiency in increasing employment (*HB*, 26 June 2016; 27 June 2016; 7 July 2016). It is seen as supporting big business but doing nothing for the common people (*HB*, 7 July 2016; 14 July 2016), as betraying the widely applauded 'European project', the essential 'European idea' (*HB*, 26 June 2016; *Zeit*, 2 July 2016), that is its original intention of securing peace and prosperity in Europe. This betrayal of the EU's original identity is regarded as an essential reason for Brexit and often criticized (*SZ*, 21 June 2016; 24 June 2016; 25 June 2016; *HB*, 30 June 2016; 1 July 2016; *Spiegel*, 1 July 2016). There was, therefore, widespread agreement that the EU must redefine itself (*MM*, 10 June 2016; *Spiegel*, 10 June 2016; *Standard*, 24 June 2016; *FAZ*, 25 June 2016; *NZZ*, 26 June 2016; *HB*, 1 July 2016; ZDF, 4 July 2016).

STORIES OF CONSEQUENCES

Predictable Consequences

There are the predictable consequences with stories speaking of 'shock' (ARD; ZDF; *Zeit*, 24 June 2016), the 'big bang' (*Spiegel*, 24 June 2016), the 'greatest catastrophe' (*Standard*, 28 June 2016), 'Black Friday on the stock exchange' (*MM*; *Spiegel*, 24 June 2016), or the 'ultimate MCA' (maximum credible accident) (*Zeit*, 27 June 2016), followed by great 'insecurity' (*NZZ*; SRF, 24 June 2016; *Standard*, 24 June 2016; 1 July 2016; ORF 1, 30 June 2016), and the feeling that 'the sun is setting on Europe' (ORF 1, 29 June 2016). Only one financial expert calls Brexit a 'Non-Event' (*FAZ*, 20 June 2016).

National Consequences

Austrian Chancellor Christian Kern's remark that 'this is not a good day for our country. Europe's importance will decline' links the nation in question and Europe (*Heute*, 24 June 2016) and addresses national consequences. All countries quickly hope they might profit from Brexit economically (SRF, 25 June 2016): 'Austria wants to profit' (ORF, 30 June 2016; 5 July 2016), but the effect on its economy is 'uncertain' (*Standard*, 24 June 2016). As the EU's preoccupation with Brexit will diminish the nation's influence on Brussels, Switzerland sees itself in the 'most remote orbit' (*NZZ*, 26 June 2016). No such fear is expressed in Austria, which highlights not so much this country's size, political or economic powers but rather the importance of being an EU member.

Hard or Soft Consequences

There are quite a few surprising similarities between the EU and UK: while the UK wondered about a hard or soft Brexit, the EU has been pondering hard or soft consequences. 'No cherry picking' is the slogan for a hard line, expressed in the official statement by Juncker, Tusk and Schulz and media reports on it (*FAZ*, 24 June 2016; 28 June 2016; *Standard*, 28–29 June 2016). Merkel is sometimes presented as supporting this attitude (*FAZ*, 28 June 2016), but also as adopting a position that gives the UK more time, acknowledges the need for future close links, being in this way different from Juncker and Hollande (*HB*, 7 July 2016). Soft measures are favoured by most business, liberal or left-leaning media (e.g. *NZZ*, *SZ*, *taz*, *Zeit*), hard ones by sources like *Standard* (e.g. 27 June 2016).

Demand for Unity

The second remarkable similarity and the fourth consequence is the demand for unity in the EU as well as in the UK (*taz*, 21 June 2016; *Standard*, 24 June 2016; ARD, 29 June 2016; *HB*, 7 July 2016;). The media often pointed out the 'dis-united kingdom', the enormous split among people as well as the British nations (*SZ*, 24 June 2016). During the referendum, the UK was 'miles away from the traditional British communicative culture'. 'The first casualty of Brexit is the precondition of truth, open discussions' (*Zeit*, 5 June 2016). The remarkable 'increase in racist incidents in the UK' (*Standard*, 28 June 2016) is another consequence of Brexit and the divisions it has created. There is much irony in the fact that politicians who have produced a 'divorce' and wanted a 'radical separation' (ARD, 24 June 2016; *NZZ*, 24 June 2016; 27 June 2016; *FAZ*, 24 June 2016; 28 June 2016; *HB*, 28 June 2016; *Standard*, 28 June 2016) now underline the need for coming together again. Or is this rather a sign of schizophrenia, of the sickness of the world we live in?

Good Planning

The fifth consequence and third similarity is the need for good planning. *Zeit* (4 June 2016) claimed early on that 'Merkel and Hollande need a Brexit-Plan'. It was generally assumed that they really had one (*FAZ*, 11 June 2016; 4 June 2016; 23 June 2016; SRF, 23 June 2016; *HB*, 25 June 2016; 1 July 2016), but all media were sure that the pro-Brexit group had no clear plan at all, simply hopes, intentions and ambitions (*Zeit*, 27 June 2016; *Standard*, 28 June 2016; DLF, 4 July 2016; *WZ*, 6 July 2016). 'British industry' was particularly afraid of this and is quoted as saying 'our government has no plan' (*FAZ*, 24 June 2016; 28 June 2016; 30 June 2016, two articles). *Standard*, *SZ*, and *Zeit* (15 June 2016) presented the 'exit plan' of the pro-Brexit group and highlighted their intention of 'passing a bill that would immediately end the rogue European Court of Justice's control over national security' (with a link to http://www.voteleavetakecontrol.org). 'Scotland's plan for a second referendum', securing independence and a place in the EU, was often mentioned, mostly favourably (but not in *Standard*), occasionally in connection with the Northern Irish vote against Brexit (*SZ*, 24 June 2016; SRF, 24–25 June 2016; *WZ*, 24–25 June 2016; ARD, 24 June 2016; 27 June 2016; 29 June 2016; 3 July 2016; *Welt*, 25 June 2016; *Zeit*, 25 June 2016; 29 June 2016; *Spiegel*, 26 June 2016; 28 June 2016; 30 June 2016; *Standard*, 26 June 2016; 29 June 2016; 3 June 2016; ORF 1, 27 June 2016; 30 June 2016). George Osborne's 'Brexit emergency plan' (ORF 1, 27 June 2016; ARD, 1 July 2016) was used as another indicator of the negative results of Brexit.

The Austrian *Standard* (27 June 2016) was most explicit in its criticism of the pro-Brexit group having no plan at all, being 'totally irresponsible', 'completely unrealistic', and revealing a 'dangerous degree of an exaggerated opinion of themselves'. Those in charge showed a 'despicable attitude', and Britain should now be treated like a 'grumbling football player, refusing to play well, demanding a transfer, but staying on the bench. That player must instantly leave. Britain must go as quickly as possible.'

THE NEED TO DEFINE IDENTITIES

The football comparison makes instant sense and invites every footballer's agreement, but it completely fails to grasp the dimensions of the problems we are dealing with. I am emphasizing the similarities between the UK and the EU, in order to point out what we all have in common: all of these problems. They are inseparable from each other and from the biggest problem, the sixth consequence and fourth similarity, at the same time also one of the causes of Brexit and indeed the referendum: namely, the need to openly define the identities of the UK and the EU. Carwyn Jones, the Welsh First Minister, expressed this need for his nation in his first response to the referendum result when he said, 'however people may have voted, all of Wales now needs to think about its future and unite' (*SZ*, 24 June 2016). This was more than just another appeal to unity, it required a definition of unity and what the unity is for. Thinking about one's identity has taken place in Scotland much more explicitly than in Wales because of the Scottish 2014 referendum. It will now necessarily also commence in Northern Ireland, where nobody wants a new border with the Irish Republic. It will most urgently have to begin in England (see Müller et al. 2013; MacWhirter 2014; Müller 2015; and Lodge et al. 2012). All nations must keep this in mind: 'if identity is to become a recognisable part of our national life, it will have to be educated into our consciousness and into the consciousness of successive generations, as surely as it has been educated out' (Macdougall 2001: 196).

The tabloids do not address this consequence in any remarkable way, and the quality media tend to discuss only some aspects of this key issue when they, for instance, agree on the urgent need for decisive actions, especially with regard to defence, EU borders, and so on (*Zeit*, 29 June 2016; *Standard*, 29 June 2016; 1 July 2016). Europe, however, must wake up from its 'lethargy and complacency', redefine its identity, and in the same process improve its 'weak democracy' (*Standard*, 28 June 2016).

The Need to Define and Practise Democracy

Democracy is a much discussed issue: there is too little of it everywhere, much more is urgently needed to save the EU, which constantly fails to be democratic (*FAZ*, 24 June 2016; *NZZ*, 30 June 2016; *Zeit*, 5 July 2016). The solution most often presented is that 'Europe must be citizen-oriented', its democracy visible, and practicably present locally, not far away and theoretical (*Zeit*, 25 June 2016). During the referendum, 'British democracy failed disastrously', as the necessary 'control mechanisms used in other countries, such as Switzerland', were simply not there. The referendum was thus the expression of 'momentary feelings' of 'only 36% of the electorate' with 'no idea of what was at stake' and 'no knowledge of the consequences' (*Standard*, 26 June 2016). Referendums like this one are therefore not really an expression of democracy, 'nor a means of improving it'. 'Demagogues love them, as results can be easily influenced by hate campaigns.' Their 'most important weapons are rage and indignation' (*Zeit*, 27 June 2016; 5 July 2016). They are a way of expressing fear, frustration, insecurity, a 'rejection of the complexity' of the world we live in, where economic, political, and social conditions seem to be 'out of control'. The solution suggested is indeed a 'local organization' of these areas of society, producing local democracy (*Standard*, 27 June 2016).

THE ROLE OF THE STATE

The new nationalist populism is often regarded as the most serious threat to democracy. But this populism is not the cause of the weakness of both democracy and the state. It is the other way around: the weak state, experienced by many people as incapable of giving them protection, security, jobs, of solving problems and so on, in connection with a democracy that appears non-existent or completely inefficient, are the reasons for the rise of nationalist populism. It is thus not only democracy that is seriously endangered but also the state as the predominant traditional institution providing safety and identity (see the excellent article in *Zeit*, 3 June 2016), available in English at http://www.zeit.de/2016/24/democracy-end-crisispopulism-authoritarians, and the equally illuminating texts in *HB* (20 June 2016; 26 June 2016). Diller (2016) and Müller (2016) describe the state threatened by 'the Land of Google'. See also Nelson (2006), Cudworth (2007), and O'Neil (2016).

The British way of turning the referendum result into political practice reveals that the state itself has a rather weak notion of democracy. The government simply follows the British first-past-the-post tradition: as 51.9% voted for Brexit, 48.1% against, only the majority counts, and the minority, almost half the population, are completely disregarded. Democracy would require a 'coalition' or some kind of compromise between these two parties. What we have instead is part of the feudal and 'essentially monarchical' tradition that Hutton (2015: 213) has repeatedly described. Stephan Richter, Editor of the *Globalist*, uses another expression for the same phenomenon in connection with the referendum by calling it the 'Diktat of the respective prime minister' (*HB*, 11 July 2016). In this context, he continues, 'serving the public interest is irrelevant', Parliament becomes the 'playground of conceited individuals'. But the key point is that 'Brexit is the testimony of the depth of the British identity problem.' A different understanding and practice of democracy and the state is one of the key things that need to be learned while developing a new identity. It is therefore not surprising that the consequences pointed out here have gained in significance: see Reybrouck (2016), for whom 'sortition' is a possible remedy, and Brennan (2016: viii, 204ff) who, 'in light of widespread voter incompetence', emphasizes the importance of knowledge and favours 'epistocracy, The Rule of Knowers'. It is fitting in this context that *SZ* (24 June 2016) described Brexit as 'an answer from the wrong century', from the past, a 'parochial' narrow-minded answer, 'unsuitable for the 21st century'.

The Need for New Ideas

Nationalism is an outdated concept that people and politicians fall back on for an illusion of security or an increase of power. New ideas are urgently needed. Europe is at a 'crossroads' after the 'watershed' event of the referendum, which can result in 'nation states fighting against each other' again or (as a result of the redefinitions) a 'stronger, more social Europe' (*HB*, 27 June 2016). One intriguing suggestion is to 'abolish the nation states' and to increase 'people's participation' in all important decisions on a local level. A 'European Republic' could be created in this way, where the dominance of national interests is avoided and a 'post-nationalist democracy' is created by people, not by nations. Why should people not manage to achieve another powerful 'revolution like the one in 1989' that put an end to the Eastern bloc? A 'Utopia' indeed, but of the kind urgently required (*SZ*, 21 June 2016).

The Final Consequence: Successful Evolution Requires Thoughtful Creativity

Brexit is just one of many huge changes taking place in the world. This final conclusion begins with the important reminder that human evolution continues relentlessly and human beings must try to determine at least part of its direction. Creativity is required, and people's lives urgently need to be improved. Almost all media agree that things cannot continue in the old ways, but at the same time, there is a predominance of old concepts, nationalism being the most visible one. The quality media investigated draw a fairly comprehensive picture of the agents, causes, characteristics and consequences of the 2016 EU referendum, while the tabloids turn evident characteristics and key words into eye-catching headlines.

Solutions to the urgent problems connected with Brexit cannot be expected from the media. The media reveal, however, that the dominant political and economic powers have no convincing ideas either, they tend to favour traditional concepts that only maintain or increase old influences. As new ideas also hardly come from universities, where could they originate? The only hope expressed in the media is their creation among people frustrated with the current conditions, who cannot expect to have their lives improved. Such people must improve their worlds themselves with new ideas created in local communities, resulting in action, practical democracy that changes life there, and then spreads to further regions. A utopian idea, but in my opinion the only one that promises any improvement. This requires more knowledge among people, therefore better education, and a stronger ability to live together without tribal fears and old concepts. Nationalism has given us two world wars and was then supposed to be replaced by the idea of a united Europe. A wonderful idea, now made even more difficult with Brexit. Humanity, however, will only survive united. It would be much better if the UK and the EU addressed the consequences mentioned above together rather than separately.

Acknowledgements As regards the survey of the media, student assistants Sarah Poschen and Andrea Schlotthauer as well as my colleague Lothar Görke helped me collect this material, and I owe them special thanks.

REFERENCES

Brennan, J. 2016. *Against Democracy*. Princeton: Princeton University Press.
Cudworth, E. 2007. *The Modern State: Theories and Ideologies*. Edinburgh: Edinburgh University Press.
Diller, B. 2016. We're All Serfs in the Land of Google. Bloomberg, June 28. https://www.bloomberg.com/news/videos/2016-01-27/barry-diller-we-re-all-serfs-on-the-land-of-google (Accessed 31 March 2017).
Eysenck, W. 2012. *Fundamentals of Cognition*, 2nd ed. Hove: Psychology Press.

Harrison, B.H. 2009. *Seeking a Role: The United Kingdom 1951–1970.* Oxford: Clarendon.

Herman, D. 2013. Cognitive Narratology. In *Handbook of Narratology*, ed. P. Hühn, J. Pier, W. Schmid, and J. Schönert, 30–43. Berlin: de Gruyter. http://www.lhn.uni-hamburg.de/article/cognitive-narratology-revised-version-uploaded-22-september-2013 (Accessed 31 March 2017).

Hutton, W. 2015. *How Good We Can Be. Ending the Mercenary Society and Building a Great Country.* London: Abacus.

Lakoff, G., and M. Johnson. 2003. *Metaphors We Live by*, 5th ed. Chicago: University of Chicago Press.

Lodge, G., R. Wyn Jones, A. Henderson, and D. Wincott. 2012. *The Dog That Finally Barked: England as an Emerging Political Community.* London: Institute for Public Policy Research. http://www.ippr.org/publications/the-dog-that-finally-barked-england-as-an-emerging-political-community (Accessed 31 March 2017).

MacDougall, C. 2001. *Painting the Forth Bridge. A Search for Scottish Identity.* London: Aurum.

MacWhirter, I. 2014. *Disunited Kingdom: How Westminster Won a Referendum but Lost Scotland.* Glasgow: Cargo.

Müller, K.P. 2013. Narration und Kognition britischer Geschichte transmedial. Medienkonvergenz im britischen Fernsehen. In *Medien. Erzählen. Gesellschaft. Transmediales Erzählen im Zeitalter der Medienkonvergenz*, ed. K.N. Renner, D. von Hoff, and M. Krings, 301–340. Berlin: de Gruyter.

Müller, K.P. (ed.). 2015. *Scotland 2014 and Beyond—Coming of Age and Loss of Innocence?* Frankfurt: Lang.

Müller, K.P. 2016. Scottish Media: The Evolution of Public and Digital Power. *Scottish Studies Newsletter* 46, pp. 14–41. http://www.fb06.uni-mainz.de/anglistik/Dateien/SSN_46.pdf or http://ow.ly/d/4vp2 (Accessed 31 March 2017).

Müller, K.P., B. Reitz, and S. Rieuwerts (eds.). 2013. *Scotland's Cultural Identity and Standing.* Trier: Wissenschaftlicher Verlag.

Nelson, B.R. 2006. *The Making of the Modern State: A Theoretical Evolution.* London: Palgrave Macmillan.

O'Neil, C. 2016. *Weapons of Math Destruction: How Big Data Increases Inequality and Threatens Democracy.* London: Allan Lane.

van Reybrouck, D. 2016. *Against Elections: The Case for Democracy.* London: Bodley Head.

Wittgenstein, L. 2009. *Philosophical Investigations*, 4th ed. Chichester: Wiley-Blackwell.

CHAPTER 11

It's the Economy, Stupid: Coverage of the British EU Referendum in Norway

Birgitte Kjos Fonn

INTRODUCTION

Political and economic chaos. Breakdown. Crash. A seriously weakened Europe. If you followed the news in Norway in the days around the British EU referendum in 2016, you had every reason to be worried. Admittedly, most sources and commentators did not really believe that a 'Brexit' (Britain's exit from the EU) could happen, and in the days before the referendum, polls pointed slightly in the direction of a 'Bremain' (Britain remaining in the EU) vote. But the bleak prospects of a Leave victory were discussed, and the headlines were loud. When the outcome of the referendum was finally clear, it was described as both a shock and an expected disaster. Some even claimed it could be the beginning of a crisis on a world scale. Media consumers in a country that has voted no to Norwegian EEC/EU membership twice had to ask themselves what on earth the Brits were thinking about—had they gone completely mad?

B. K. Fonn (✉)
Oslo Metropolitan University, Oslo, Norway
e-mail: birgitte@oslomet.no

© The Author(s) 2018   189
A. Ridge-Newman et al. (eds.), *Reporting the Road to Brexit*,
https://doi.org/10.1007/978-3-319-73682-2_11

Obviously, it is not the aim of this chapter to answer that question, or what the effects of Brexit will be. Rather, it aims to be a systematic study of some major Norwegian news media in order to reveal underlying patterns, discover major and competing frames (Entman 1993), and attempt to assess how the selection of sources determines what become dominant views in a case like this. The chapter is an analysis of four Norwegian outlets; three daily newspapers and the online service from the public-service Norwegian Broadcasting Company NRK. It also includes a short glimpse into the social-media debate among some journalists, academics, politicians and other commentators.

NATIONWIDE WITH A BROAD REACH

The newspapers, *Aftenposten*, *Dagens Næringsliv* and *Klassekampen* have been selected for three reasons. They are the top three papers when searching for the word 'Brexit' in the database of the Norwegian media-monitoring agency Retriever, Brexit being the most commonly used word in Norway when referring to the referendum. There is also an interesting spread of political stances among these four outlets altogether: whereas NRK is a state-run national broadcaster with a duty to give a balanced view of the world, *Aftenposten* has a pro-EU stance in editorials but is Norway's largest newspaper and also seeks a balanced news coverage. *Dagens Næringsliv* is Norway's major financial newspaper, economic liberalist in editorials and business-leaning in news reporting, but has over the years become the country's fifth largest daily and appeals to readers far beyond the business community. *Klassekampen* is a former fairly sectarian left-wing newspaper whose editorials currently mainly support the political centre-left, but this paper also has extended its readership substantially over the last decade because of its high journalistic quality.

Together these outlets should give a fair idea of what Norwegian quality journalism, but also with a broad reach as far as readership is concerned, looked like in the weeks surrounding the British EU referendum from 3 June to 3 July 2016. I have studied the print versions of the newspapers because they give better information about newsroom priorities, but for pragmatic reasons I have chosen the online (text) version of the broadcaster.

NORWAY LOVES BRITAIN

First, a central fact must be established: many Norwegians have a life-long love affair with Britain. Many Norwegians hold affection for prominent cultural symbols in Britain like Old Trafford, Oxford Street and the Royal Mile. They revere Regent Street (which Norway literally owns a share of, through the so-called Oil Fund) and enjoy British popular culture, from *Downton Abbey* to *Harry Potter*. The cultural and political ties between Norway and Britain have been close across the countries' significant histories. Both have been seafaring nations with only the North Sea between them. During the Second World War the Norwegian government was given a safe haven in London, and the state-run public broadcaster NRK sent its illegal radio broadcasts from Bush House, which remains an important part of Norwegian media history. When Britain's Foreign Secretary Ernest Bevin in 1948 proposed the creation of a Western defence alliance (later the North Atlantic Treaty Organization), Norway was one of the first countries to join. Norway and Britain were furthermore two of the original European Free Trade Association (EFTA, the precursor to The European Economic Area, EEA) members, established in 1960. The Treaty of Rome, which established the European Economic Community (EEC), came into effect in 1958. However, both Britain and Norway decided against engaging with the treaty talks that led to the EEC. When Britain changed its mind a few years later, Norway's first attempts to join the EEC followed suit. Charles de Gaulle's 'no' to Britain in 1967 put a preliminary end to the Norwegian plans as well.

These shared historical factors mean British politics still has an important place in the Norwegian mind-set and its media, and the coverage of a major event such as this referendum was therefore significant. According to the Norwegian News Agency NTB (5 July 2016), the EU referendum across England, Northern Ireland, Scotland, and Wales was the news story that made the most significant impact on Norwegians during the entire first half of 2016.

Norway's and Britain's paths parted, however, when the question over whether to join the EEC was raised again in the early 1970s, after de Gaulle's death. In Norway, the issue had in the meantime become so controversial that a referendum was called, and thereafter Norway voted 'no' (albeit with a relatively small majority) to the EEC and EU twice—in 1972 and 1994. In 1994 the turnout was the highest in any election since universal suffrage was introduced in 1913 (Jenssen and Valen 1995).

Like Britain, Norway can therefore be said to be a 'divided' country. But it has traditionally been divided in a slightly different way, as the Eurosceptics in Norway and Britain are rather different. In Norway, Eurosceptics have mostly been centre-left. Whereas a strong right-wing lobby in the British Conservative Party regards the EU as too eager to regulate business, parts of the centre-left in Norway may rather characterize the EU as a neoliberal machine, and also a threat to democracy. The Norwegian Conservatives have always been the most EU-loyal party. After the financial crisis, however, opposition to the EU among Norwegian voters has increased to an average of 70%, and even among the Conservative Party's voters it is currently high at 60%.

All this contributes to Britain being a country Norwegian media consumers are interested in and can identify with; a well known mechanism determining the amount of coverage any event gets. A second important factor that has been believed to determine the frames in the coverage of foreign news events is what the event looks like from home; the world is often seen through the glasses of dominant national opinions, concerns and debate (Eide and Simonsen 2008).

STAY OR GO—AND WHY?

A first superficial look at the referendum coverage in Norway indicates that the question was simply about whether Britain should stay or go. When systematically going through the material chosen for this chapter, however, one interesting thing immediately springs to mind: there were four competing frames, and all were about a possible leave vote. Two of them were about the possible *consequences* of a Leave vote, two about the possible *reasons* for a Leave vote. The consequences were presented either as negative, or not particularly negative; in some cases positive, or more often business as usual. We can call these respectively the 'negative-effects' frame and the 'no-catastrophe' frame, as this last seems to be the overall message in the articles where the sources did not believe in negative effects. The reasons why there might be (and eventually was) a Leave vote were presented either as a revolt against increased social and economic inequality, lack of housing and jobs, or as a result of the voters' wish to curb immigration or even of their racist inclinations. These can be called respectively the 'inequality' frame and the 'immigration' frame. Only the first two frames are fully mutually exclusive.

I started off with 763 Retriever matches in all four outlets altogether. I primarily wanted to study news, so I omitted editorials, op-eds, debate and fact boxes, and also a number of irrelevant stories: stories about the other 'Brexit', England's exit from Euro 2016, or stories where reference to the referendum was just used as a peg. I let print stories that also hit the front pages count as two. All in all this gave a corpus consisting of 408 relevant articles.

Among these there were naturally a number of neutral articles, for example about the mutiny against Jeremy Corbyn or the battle for the new leadership in the Conservative Party. As a whole, an average of approximately 38.5% of the stories were neutral (as NRK and *Dagens Næringsliv* had a larger share of the articles than the others, all numbers in this chapter are averages).

The next major group was the negative-effects frame, with an average of 31.5%, followed by the immigration frame with a little over 12%, the inequality frame (9.5%), and the 'no-catastrophe' frame (7.5%). The numbers hide some differences between the four outlets, but the patterns are the same in all but *Klassekampen*, where the inequality frame was the second largest after the neutral frame, followed by respectively negative-effects, no-catastrophe and finally immigration.

But as indicated above, the ordinary Norwegian media consumer did not come out of the referendum period with the impression that the coverage had been particularly neutral. One reason is clearly the fact that the neutral frame was not very popular front-page material, nor did it spark much debate. So I will concentrate my analysis on the articles with a clear framing; after all, they were the main competitors here.

When doing so, the picture changes visibly, and the negative-effects frame increases to constitute an average of almost 49.5% of the matches; very close to half. The immigration frame is furthermore found in 20.5% of the articles, inequality in a little over 17% and the 'no-catastrophe' frame in 12.5%. Note that the two dominant frames differ in the respect that one was about the consequences of a leave vote, the other about the reasons for a leave vote.

The first finding is, in other words, that the impression of a strong focus on the possible negative effects turns out to hold true. The fact that DN and NRK had a larger share of the overall articles contributes to this impression, with respectively 71% and 52% of articles with a negative-effects frame. *Klassekampen* had the lowest amount, 27%, *Aftenposten* 47.5%.

CHRONICLE OF A DISASTER FORETOLD

During the last week before the referendum, polls were shifting from Remain to Leave almost from one day to the next, but most of them predicted that Britain would remain. The various experts who were quoted in the Norwegian media predicted a Remain vote with even more certainty. The warnings about what would happen if Britain left were however becoming more and more frequent as the day of the referendum approached. Words and phrases like 'fearing', 'warning against', 'catastrophe', 'threatens' and 'frightens' characterize many of the articles. Headlines contained things like 'Fears the consequences of Brexit' (Brekke, 22 June), 'Fears for world growth rates' (Berger, 21 June) and 'Brexit can result in a weakened world' (Sættem and Søhusvik, 22 June). A collection made by *Klassekampen* (Kihl, 22 June) shows similar headlines outside this corpus, like '[Experts] predict panic and chaos' and 'Catastrophe for all of us if we say no' ('we' here being the British; examples from newspapers *Dagsavisen* and *VG*, both from 20 June).

With some knowledge of the general EU debate, one could expect that what the sources feared was the dissolution of a union that is said to have secured peace in Europe over the last 60 years. Or it could have been the withering-away of European solidarity, or maybe concern for human rights if Britain should also leave the European Convention on Human Rights, which was also an issue at the time of the referendum. Some did fear these things, too. But out of all the articles with a negative-effects frame, an average of almost 70% were about the possibly devastating *economic* effects of a Brexit on the world economy, the European economy, the British economy and the Norwegian economy.

The whole referendum was however about to take an extraordinary turn when, on 16 June, the Labour MP and 'Bremainer' Jo Cox was suddenly killed outside a library in her constituency by a man who shouted the name of a small extreme-right party as he attacked her. This detestable deed, the killing in broad daylight of a respected politician and the mother of young children was believed to turn quite a few voters away from the Leave camp, thereby making a victory for the Remain camp more likely. Although despicable, almost immediately after Cox's death, the press reported that stock exchanges rallied at the news of the killing. This was referred to in cold detached language: 'Stock prices were up in Europe and Asia, and the pound made gains, after the killing of the British politician Jo Cox' (Sandberg, 18 June).

In fact, this (some would say rather inappropriate) celebration of the result of a murder points to the second striking feature of the coverage: that the short-term ups and downs of the financial markets were covered with almost the same eagerness as a possible long-term economic crisis. There was also room for even more prosaic (proseccic) anxieties: 'Brexit creates Prosecco fear in Italy' (NTB-AFP, 22 June).

The only outlet where this feature was almost entirely absent was *Klassekampen*, whose rather few articles on negative effects altogether were more likely to concentrate on things like George Osborne's announced budgetary cuts, or the head of the Norwegian employers' union, Kristin Skogen Lund, warning the British that a future in the EEA would solve no problems (Tilseth, 18 June).

Despite all the fear and warnings beforehand, when it turned out that a majority had voted for leaving the EU, the Norwegian media immediately went into a state of simultaneous shock and disbelief, at least if one is to believe the headlines now predicting even more chaos and destruction. One headline read 'Major bank warns against major downturn' (Buanes, Gjerstad and Ånestad, 27 June), another 'This can be the beginning of a crisis in the whole world' (Åsnes, 24 June). Even Norwegian media which had taken a clear stance against Norwegian EU membership used the word 'shock'; for example, *Klassekampen* on its 25 June front page.

Eventually the press started to concentrate on issues such as when British withdrawal from the EU might actually take place. Jo Cox's death, on the other hand, did not seem to have a lasting impact in Norway. From the day of the referendum, 23 June, until 14 July, the day Theresa May took over as Prime Minister, Jo Cox's name was mentioned 16 times in well over 2000 'Brexit' matches in all Norwegian print media registered by Retriever.

A 'REPUBLICAN' STANCE

One reason for the relatively unanimous reaction to the result of the referendum is of course that it was both sensational and spectacular: nobody had voted to actually leave the EU before. Britain is furthermore a large and important country, almost in every respect. But it does not explain why the coverage by major media in a country where in opinion polls 70% of those questioned state that they are against Norwegian membership of the EU leaned so heavily on sources that feared the results of a Leave vote.

To understand this, we first need to take a step back and look at Norway's EU history (see for example Bjørklund 1982; Jenssen and Valen 1995). In both Norwegian referendums the 'no'-camp was to a degree a counter-cultural phenomenon, consisting of blue-collar workers, small farmers, environmental activists and so on, but also voters with what Bourdieu (1995) describes as more cultural than economic capital: civil servants, academics and artists. The EU stance did not necessarily follow party lines. The Conservatives were mostly pro-EU, but many other parties had (and still have) severe internal cleavages between business-friendly wings and 'grassroots' which feared for both democracy and job losses. The Labour Party has, for example, been split between an anti-EU and a pro-EU camp, the pro-camp (in later years with similarities to Britain's 'New Labour') often represented by the party leadership. Parties in the political centre which have normally considered themselves non-socialist have often sided with Labour's left wing in their EU opposition.

This centre-left dimension, already noted by the political scientist Stein Rokkan more than half a century ago (Rokkan 1967), is still an important dividing line in Norwegian society, and on far more issues than just the EU. Rokkan found a main dividing line, as important as class differences, between the centre and the periphery, between the cities on the one hand and the countryside and the remote coastal areas on the other; in simple terms, one could say between the establishment and the rest. Add the various representatives of the so-called 'counter-expertise' living in the centre (for example, economists questioning mainstream economics) and you have a quite viable opposition to the establishment positions.

The Euroscepticism that unites these different groups can, to an extent, be explained by the deep-rooted opposition to being under foreign supremacy dating all the way back to the so-called 'dark centuries' as a Danish province. Altogether, Norway was under Danish or Swedish kings for 500 years, until the country finally gained full independence in 1905. Norway's constitution, written in 1814, was heavily influenced by both the French Revolution and the American

Declaration of Independence. Accordingly, it was also permeated by the idea of 'Republicanism', here meant as the people's opposition against any autocratic rule (Pettit 1997), not as the more or less half-hearted discontent with monarchy one can find in modern democracies. But this again underlines the difference between Norwegian and British Euroscepticism, as some national elites also came to be associated with foreign rule. Today one could say that Norway clings to its independence for fear of being swallowed up by another European empire again, whereas evil tongues will have it that Britain clings to its independence because it still sees itself as a European empire. This way Norway has far more similarities with Scotland, reluctantly under British rule for centuries and constantly discussing whether to break out of the UK; but while the majority in Scotland feels freer within the EU, the majority in Norway feels freer outside.

However, the interesting thing is that not only does the establishment hold a pro-EU stance, but, in large part, so too does the Norwegian press. In 1972 this contributed to totally uprooting the current press system, as the referendum marked a sudden shock that eventually led to the dissolution of the party press. The party press in Norway was shared between four major political parties and rested on the belief that the audience would do as their editors thought best, and subsequently the papers failed to see the resistance that was building up among the general public (Bastiansen 2009). Another way of describing it is that the elites did not understand the people, and there was virtually nobody there to inform them, as the press was part of the elite.

By 1975, the Norwegian Union of Journalists had discarded its old role as a mouthpiece for power and adopted a new set of ethical rules, stating that the journalist's mission was to be the *vox populi* and otherwise give a balanced account of differing views in their news reporting. The level of conflict was so high among the public that the EU membership question was not raised again until 1994. By then the party press was more or less phased out and a commercial press had emerged. Norwegian journalists had professionalized their work and refined their role as an 'ombudsman' for 'the little man in society'.

Despite the fact that anti-EU organizations mobilized heavily, pro-EU arguments were still more often cited in the media than the arguments against (Jenssen and Valen 1995). The major newspapers had given up their party affiliations and thereby their roles as political missionaries, but most of the pro-EU sources were still elite persons of the kind who have easy access to the media: politicians, employers' organizations, business leaders. Again the pro-camp won the media debate. But to no avail; again the answer from the public was 'no'.

'THE WORLD SEEN FROM THE BANK'

Over 20 years later, the idea of non-partisan journalism has long since been internalized. All newspapers in this study, although openly political in editorials, adhere strongly to the idea of objective and balanced journalism. The national broadcaster NRK has to be balanced and is supposed to appeal to the whole country, to high and low alike. The political parties furthermore no longer have unlimited access to the media, a fact that is quite visible when one examines the use of sources in the referendum coverage: on average only 21.9% of the sources in all articles with one of our four frames were politicians. Among these, 63% were Norwegian politicians, which of course reflects the fact that this was not an internal Norwegian matter (and that foreign politicians are often only a tweet away). But on the other hand, most of the politicians quoted (both Norwegian and foreign) were pro-EU or spokespersons for the EU in one way or another, and it is quite likely that this influenced the coverage.

Who are the other 80% or so? Other representatives of the authorities, bureaucrats, university researchers and representatives of think tanks were few in number. Taken together, these diverse groups accounted for only 12.5% of the sources. The trade unions were represented by well under 1%, so they cannot be said to have had much influence. Other news media accounted for another almost 12% (but this is an unreliable figure, since we know that other news media are frequently used without being quoted). As most voters are 'ordinary people', we also have a look at this group, but it turns out they constitute only 11.5% of all sources. In other words, none of these groups (including a small, diverse group of 'others') is of such a size that they are likely to determine the outcome of the coverage, at least not on their own.

In fact, the largest group turns out to be representatives of the business community, with an average of almost 35% of the sources. As a fair share of politicians also spoke about economic issues, this gives a strong impression of the issue being primarily regarded as an economic one. And what is more, it turns out that a little over 50% of the business sources in one way or another represent the finance sector or the 'market'.

In some cases the market itself even plays the role of the most important source of information. This is very illustrative of how a particular discourse has become internalized in journalistic media over the past decades; the discourse of what is good or bad not only for business life (which has also increased considerably), but for financial institutions and the finance markets as well (Kjær and Slaatta 2007; Bjerke et al. 2016). What a number of scholars (for example, Epstein 2005) have called a 'financialization' of the world economy has also, to some extent, led to a financialization of the news media. But this also means that the reduction of the voice of politicians in the news media has not necessarily led to a reduction of elite sources; rather, the business sector has gained more influence at the expense of others. From the point of view of an onlooker, the Norwegian economist Erik Reinert characterized the coverage of the British EU referendum as 'the world seen from the bank' (Ekeberg, 29 June).

Well over 80% of the sources were elite persons (politicians, experts, business heads, analysts and so on), elite institutions (brokerages, organizations) or other news media. All journalism is of course dominated by elite sources, but an overview of Nordic economic journalism studies shows that the amount of elite sources is even higher in this field—not only in major, nationwide, niche outlets, but also in mainstream media at all levels (Bjerke et al. 2016).

The financialization of media has both given economic journalism a more important role in society *and* given the kind of sources that were traditionally reserved for the business press an increasingly strong position in mainstream media. This means that representatives of business firms, brokers, analysts and chief economists, who may in fact have vested interests in the outcome, have increasingly come to be used as 'experts', at the expense of not only politicians but also university economists (as this material also indicates). At the same time this field is, more than most other journalistic fields, at the mercy of the experts. The result is often a journalism where the worldviews of the business and finance communities are reproduced more or less uncritically (Bjerke et al. 2016). What is more, the business elites are the most international of the national elites, and the international business elites are also more available now than they were a couple of decades ago, through everything from online reports to social media. This may influence the coverage of an issue like the British referendum profoundly, so that the national angles noted by Eide and Simonsen (2008) are becoming far less important.

The particularly high level of elite sources of course also stems from the fact that this *is* foreign news, another journalistic field known for its high elite factor. But the share of sources representing business and, to be particularly noted, the financial sector supports the view that the issue is largely regarded as economy news as well.

When dealing with economic news, there is however one question that journalists often do not ask: Whose economy is it? When sources 'fear' for profits, crises, interest rates or stock prices, journalists are not always aware that they contribute to masking deep conflicts of interest in society. It is of course the duty of political leaders to make sure their country does not lose out in the world economy, and the same could be said about companies and industries that have responsibility for employment, wages, and feeding the treasuries that finance the European welfare states. But the striking aspect of this coverage is how it also legit-imized the concerns of private and institutional investors whose main business is to move money around in a way that was very seldom seen a little over 30 years ago (Kjær and Slaatta 2007).

It must be said, though, that business and finance community sources also contributed to the (far fewer) no-catastrophe frame, as this frame was a kind of mirror image of the negative-effects frame, but mostly in the business daily. Originally a shipping paper, *Dagens Næringsliv* is still the Norwegian newspaper with by far the most comprehensive coverage of business life in London. It was therefore not surprising to find British or Britain-based sources in *Dagens Næringsliv* who did not oppose a Leave vote because they believe that the EU regulates busi-ness far more zealously than they think Britain would do on its own. Or that they would definitely find a way to reap the benefits if Britain left (Aartun, 12 June; Berger and Bjørndal, 28 June).

'A Basket of Deplorables'

The intriguing aspect of the public legitimizing of concerns for private economic gain or loss is, however, that this does not apply to all the sources featured in the coverage. This is quite apparent in the articles with an inequality or immigration frame. The two frames trying to give a reason for a potential Leave vote were the only articles where 'ordinary people' had a clear voice: approximately 11.5% of the sources. Of these, almost 85% (a little less than one of ten in the whole material) appeared to be British citizens (regardless of descent), and subsequently British voters. The remainder were citizens of other EU or EEA countries.

Some 45% of the voters interviewed were Leave voters. When examining what they actually said, however, one particularly interesting feature appears: only half the Leave voters mentioned immigration as a reason for their vote. This is of course no accurate poll, and the proportion could be different in other media (and all interviewees may not even have been honest about their motives). But considering the fact that the immigration frame was the second most salient (and also very frequent in op-eds, TV debates and so on), this is still quite striking. There were far more elite sources interpreting opposition to British EU membership as an immigration issue than voters actually saying this was their main concern.

There is of course no doubt that the Leave campaign was partly about immigration, and maybe even about racism. The United Kingdom Independence Party's (UKIP) Nigel Farage was one of the most visible and most quoted politicians, a fact that probably influenced the coverage considerably. On the other hand, it seems unlikely that experienced public debaters were unaware that over 17 million Britons could not possibly be racists. One communications professor was probably close to the truth when he said that of course all Leave voters were not racists, but most racists were Leave voters; nevertheless an important difference (Pletten, 18 June).

The fact that ordinary people could have legitimate reasons for voting Leave was however largely overshadowed by the immigration frame. In fact, *Klassekampen* (which is both Eurosceptic and at the same time openly pro-immigration and staunchly anti-racist) was the only one of the four outlets where the immigration frame did not occupy much space. The reason was probably that *Klassekampen* has a policy of acknowledging the economic concerns of the 'little man in society' as legitimate, which perhaps makes it less inclined to jump to conclusions about the motives of all Leave voters.

How the Other Half Lives

The Leave voters featured in the articles can be placed in three categories. One was the obviously immigration-hostile group, some even UKIP members, but they were only ten sources altogether. The next consisted of losers in the job market, often resident in areas with severe social problems, who had gained little from globalization and who also felt marginalized due to immigration and other kinds of foreign competition. Third, there were the job-market losers living in problem areas who did not mention immigration at all. The social problems and unemployment in pro-Leave areas were also emphasized by some Remain voters.

One of the (relatively few) decidedly sympathetic reports from the disadvantaged suburbs was published in *Aftenposten* on 27 June. The main character was a woman in her early 40s living in a council house, who said she had tried everything to get a proper job, but in her own words had reaped only humiliation. Her 22-year-old son made less than £8 an hour in a factory, and did not see how he could afford either a place to live or an education. The surrounding area, a run-down former seaside resort, was full of alcoholism, poverty and despair.

In quite a few cases the concern for private economic loss, for dwindling incomes, for losing or not getting a job, was in some sense delegitimized by the frame chosen in the articles, or by other features that gave the impression that Leave voters were either racists or undeserving people living off other people's contributions to welfare benefits, or both. In some articles the characteristics of Leave voters were directly derogatory. As one British golf club director put it when *Dagens Næringsliv* looked him up on the golf course the day after the referendum: 'These are little Englanders' (Ånestad, 26 June). Another director, encountered in her cabriolet with her husband on a trip to digest the result of the referendum, commented on the Leave victory this way: 'I'd rather hire a hard-working Pole than a lazy Englishman' (Buanes, 27 June). A young Polish resident in Aberdeen said she doubted that 'people who spend their days on their couch claiming benefits' wanted to work even if they could (Kløvstad-Langberg and Pletten, 26 June).

LITTLE ACCEPTANCE FOR XENOPHOBIA

In Norway, the discussion about immigration, even the more challenging parts, has been fairly decent. There has for some years been a growing anti-immigration sentiment, and there is an opinionated debate about Islam going on in social media and on certain websites. But the only political party with a really harsh kind of rhetoric on the issue is the so-called Progress Party (FrP), Norway's only right-wing populist party.

In general, there is however less acceptance for a harsh immigration debate in Norway than in many other countries, and the Progress Party is regularly criticized for creating a poisonous atmosphere. It was therefore not surprising that the open hostility towards immigration from UKIP representatives led to reactions among the Norwegian press.

But the coverage also blurred the distinction between racism and the fear of everything from unemployment to social dumping, a distinction otherwise well-known in the Norwegian debate. The fact that unemployment, lack of housing or social dumping might be just as detrimental to British people of African and Asian descent was also overlooked, whereas the fear among well-educated white citizens from other European countries of losing jobs in the UK was accentuated (Kløvstad-Langberg and Pletten, 26 June). The same thing happened when white British citizens feared losing good jobs in Brussels (Ånestad, 23 June).

Except for the fact that the contents of social media are not easily quantifiable (a fact that should also be noted whenever journalists point to 'social media' as a source), the debates on Facebook and Twitter can also be a good measure of what leading debaters, academics, politicians and journalists regard as being at stake. The immigration issue was heavily commented on, both among those who regret xenophobic sentiments and those (far fewer) who are more anti-immigration. Furthermore, many Norwegian Eurosceptics were so reluctant to be associated with immigration-hostile forces that they found it hard to enjoy the result; a point that was also noted in the press (Kihl, 28 June).

The possibility that the Remain camp and its supporters benefited greatly from the idea that all Leave voters were racists was furthermore not questioned at all in this material. Norway's Conservative Prime Minister Erna Solberg, in her fourth year in a coalition government with the Progress Party when this chapter was written, was even quoted as saying that she feared the rise of populism; this, without being asked a single critical question (Brekke, 22 June; Sættem, 22 June).

CONCLUSIONS

In the weeks and months after the 2016 EU referendum, mainly beyond the period examined for this chapter, there has been far more attention brought to the fact that there are both winners and losers in the game of globalization. One important question that arose slowly as the distance from the referendum increased was whether the referendum was about the EU at all. Commentators have also raised doubts that leaving the EU is going to change anything for unhappy voters. Jonas Gahr Støre, Labour leader and thus representing the Norwegian centre-left (but also himself pro-EU) was one of the few persons in the Norwegian debate who at an early stage argued that the Leave vote might not have as much to do with the EU as with the unfortunate consequences of globalization. He pointed to the deteriorating conditions for the unemployed, the growing 'precariate' and other kinds of working poor. All in all, the coverage of the referendum revealed severe cleavages between different social groups in the British society, but also interesting differences when it comes to whose voices are heard and taken seriously in major Norwegian media.

BIBLIOGRAPHY

ACADEMIC SOURCES

Bastiansen, H.G. 2009. Lojaliteten som brast. Partipressen i Norge fra senit til fall 1945–2000. *Pressehistoriske skrifter,* No. 11.

Bjerke, P., B.K. Fonn, and E.S. Strømme (eds.). 2016. *Økonomijournalistikk. Perspektiver og metoder.* Bergen: Fagbokforlaget.

Bjørklund, T. 1982. *Mot strømmen. Kampen mot EF 1961–1972.* Oslo: Universitetsforlaget.

Bourdieu, P. 1995. *Distinksjonen. En sosiologisk kritikk av dømmekraften.* Oslo: Pax.

Eide, E., and A.H. Simonsen. 2008. *Verden skapes hjemmefra.* Oslo: Unipub.

Entman, R. 1993. Framing. Towards Clarification of a Fractured Paradigm. *Journal of Communication* 43 (4): 51–58.

Epstein, G.A. 2005. *Financialization and the World Economy.* Cheltenham: Edward Elgar.

Jenssen, A.T., and H. Valen (eds.). 1995. *Brussel midt imot.* Oslo: Ad Notam Gyldendal.

Kjær, P., and T. Slaatta (eds.). 2007. *Mediating Business.* Copenhagen: Copenhagen Business School Press.

Pettit, P. 1997. *Republicanism. A Theory of Freedom and Government.* Oxford: Oxford University Press.

Rokkan, S. 1967. Geography, Religion and Social Class. Crosscutting Cleavages in Norwegian Politics. In *Party Systems and Voter Alignments,* ed. S.M. Lipset and S. Rokkan, 367–444. New York: Free Press.

News Sources

Aartun, Jorun Sofie F. 2016. Sweet and Sour EU Scepticism. *Dagens Næringsliv*, June 13.

Ånestad, Morten. 2016a. Brexit Scares Brussels. *Dagens Næringsliv*, June 23.

Ånestad, Morten. 2016b. Change of Citizenship Sought. *Dagens Næringsliv*, June 25.

Anon. 2016. The Shock. *Klassekampen/Front page*, June 25.

Åsnes, Alexander. 2016. This Can Be the Beginning of a World-Wide Crisis. *NRK*, June 27.

Berger, Erik. 2016. Fears for World Growth Rates. *Dagens Næringsliv*, June 21.

Berger, Erik, and Bente Bjørndal. 2016. Confidence in Good Times Ahead in London. *Dagens Næringsliv*, June 28.

Brekke, Ingrid. 2016. Fears for the Consequences of Brexit. *Aftenposten*, June 22.

Buanes, Frode. 2016. Ready for a New Scottish Liberation Struggle. *Dagens Næringsliv*, June 27.

Buanes, Frode, Tore Gjerstad, and Morten Ånestad. 2016. Major Bank Warns Against Major Downturn. *Dagens Næringsliv*, June 27.

Ekeberg, Emilie. 2016. The World Seen from the Bank. *Klassekampen*, June 29.

Sættem, Johan B. (2016). 'Fears for a More Nationalistic Europe'. *NRK*, June 22.

Sættem, Johan B., and Lilla Søhusvik. 2016. Brexit Can Result in a Weakened World. *NRK*, June 22.

Sandberg, Hallvard. 2016. Belief that Cox Killing Will Keep the Country in the EU/Notice. *NRK*, June 18.

Tilseth, Trond Ola. 2016. Skogen's "Cold Shower". *Klassekampen*, June 18.

CHAPTER 12

Spanish Media and the EU Referendum 2016: The Assault on an Enlightened Project

Fernando León-Solís, Enric Castelló and Hugh O'Donnell

Introduction

Spain is no country for Eurosceptics. The country's accession to the then European Economic Community (EEC) in 1986, eleven years after the final collapse of the Franco regime (1939–1975), was rather experienced as an 'ascension' to a higher historical stage after almost forty years of dictatorial isolationism: an ascension which, as we will see, involved moving beyond an unspeakable but still haunting irrational past for which Brexit (Britain exiting the European Union [EU]) operated as a highly

F. León-Solís (✉)
University of the West of Scotland, Paisley, Scotland
e-mail: Fernando.leon-solis@uws.ac.uk

E. Castelló
Universitat Rovira i Virgili, Tarragona, Spain
e-mail: enric.castello@urv.cat

H. O'Donnell
Glasgow Caledonian University, Glasgow, Scotland
e-mail: H.ODonnell@gcu.ac.uk

© The Author(s) 2018   207
A. Ridge-Newman et al. (eds.), *Reporting the Road to Brexit*,
https://doi.org/10.1007/978-3-319-73682-2_12

malleable proxy. And the original enthusiasm does not seem to have substantially waned. Despite acknowledgment of the shortcomings of the EU (it is accused in the Spanish press of mismanagement of the migration and economic crises [*El País* 2016a], of forfeiting its social dimension [*El País* 2016f] and of being ossified [de Quirós, *El Mundo*, 19 June 2016]), the EU, often conceptualized as the 'Common Home' or 'the common project', continues to be regarded across the Spanish media and the political spectrum as the best guardian of representative democracy, as a guarantor of the orderly process of globalization, of productive economy and of social cohesion (*El País* 2016c; Piqué, *El Mundo*, 27 June 2016). This redemptive view of Europe is not shared by all; some dissenting voices, particularly on the left, have protested against the neoliberal austerity measures implemented to solve the economic crisis and against the political dynamics of the institution, but rarely against the Union itself.

Together with this perception of the EU, Spain's close links with, and its exposure and vulnerability to the vicissitudes of the British economy constituted a major influencing (and worrying) issue in the media handling of the campaign and its final result: in fact, the Spanish Stock Exchange (Ibex-35) suffered the worst fall of all European markets (12.5%) after the 2016 EU referendum result was announced. However, one of the most salient factors in understanding the Spanish media coverage is domestic: after six months of inconclusive party negotiations following the December 2015 elections, the Spanish electorate was called to choose a new government on 26 June 2016.

Unsurprisingly, the 2016 EU referendum featured highly in the Spanish campaign, not only because of its potential impact on Spain and the whole of Europe, but also in relation to the broader discussion of the appropriateness of referendums and 'going to the people' as political instruments in modern representative democracies. The debate must also be considered in the context of the demands for a referendum on independence by the ruling nationalist coalition in the Catalan Parliament, demands which are supported by almost 75% of Catalans (Moldes, *Ara*, 30 March 2017) but were ruled unconstitutional and opposed by the Central Government in Madrid and by most of the Spain-wide parties. Another key feature of the electoral campaign was the growing ascendancy of the newly formed, left-wing multi-party coalition Podemos, the only major Span-wide political grouping to support an independence referendum in Catalonia. Podemos is regarded by many as anti-establishment and 'populist'; another concept which, as will be seen in this chapter, became pivotal in the political and media interpretation of the EU referendum.

This chapter investigates the coverage of the referendum in the op-ed columns and news reports in four dailies: two Madrid-based, *El País* and *El Mundo*, and two based in Barcelona, *La Vanguardia* and *Ara*. The time frame covers the period 15 June–3 July 2016. The analysis considered all pieces dealing with the EU referendum, a total of 166 in *La Vanguardia*, 94 in *Ara*, 174 in *El País* and 187 in *El Mundo*.

The project started with a basic analysis to quantify the key themes, which as Van Dijk suggests ought to be the first step in studies with extensive corpora (1988: 169). Special attention was paid to metaphors which, as Wilson (1990) and Charteris-Black and Musolff (2003) point out, can facilitate the comprehension of complex issues while also containing a strong ideological component. Mio (1997) and Musolff (2004) have studied metaphorical language in political discourse; and authors such as Cammaerts (2012), León-Solís (2013) and Castelló and Capdevilla (2015) have carried out insightful studies of the use of metaphor in media and political reporting. The categorization of repeated elements allowed us to identify the most salient themes which, in turn, shaped a series of discourses which on occasions overlapped but very often clashed, depending on the editorial stance of the dailies.

The EU and Spain's (Returning) Hour of Darkness

The Spanish Madrid-based media agreed on the high stakes set in play in Britain and Europe by the referendum which, unsurprisingly, was often conceptualized as a 'crucial vote' (Sahuquillo, *El País*, 2016c) and a 'turning point' in a moment of 'existential crisis' for the EU (*El País*, 2016f; De Quirós, *El Mundo*, 19 June 2016). In the days leading up to the vote the possibility of a Leave campaign victory was presented as a threat (Fresneda, *El Mundo*, 19 June, 2016) and its possible effects as a 'convulsion' (*El País* 2016b). As will become clear in our analysis, this 'convulsion' was not seen simply as a political one: on the contrary, for the Spanish media it had a very clear *philosophical* dimension which endowed it with existential rather than (merely) geopolitical meaning. In Europe's returning hour of darkness, it signalled the catastrophic end of the triumph of reason over irrationality and even superstition in the form of dread of the unknown. As a result, a sense of foreboding and doom was disseminated, and an atmosphere of uncertainty and nervousness was created. It would be a 'blow' for the European project, *Ara* predicted (15 June 2016a), and it would place the whole of Europe in 'check' (Navarro, *La Vanguardia*, 21 June 2016). The impact could be 'brutal', *El País* warned on the eve of the 2016 EU referendum (2016a).

The actual result was accepted by all, but also interpreted in calamitous and ominous terms as a 'disaster' leading Britain and Europe to the edge of a 'dangerous abyss' (*El País* 2016d); and as a 'tragedy' that had created 'a gaping breach' (Ramos, *La Vanguardia*, 27 June 2016). In accordance with the conceptualization of the EU as a family, Brexit was frequently constructed metaphorically as a 'divorce' (Aranda, *Ara*, 2016a; López, *La Vanguardia*, 28 June 2016); in line with the image of Europe as a 'Common Home', the allegory of a petulant Britain exiting Europe and slamming the door was widespread (for instance, in the editorial of *La Vanguardia* [25 June 2016]) and graphically represented by the image of 10 Downing Street's closed door occupying *Ara's* front page (25 June 2016).

These catastrophic tones were further maintained through a wealth of metaphors of natural disasters used to conceptualize the result, among others: a 'tsunami' (González and Maqueda, *El País*, 24 June 2016); 'earthquake' (Aranda, *Ara*, 2016b; Naím, *El País*, 27 June 2016; Ramos, *La Vanguardia*, 27 June 2016); 'gale' (*El País* 2016g); 'wave' (Ahrens, *El País*, 28 June 2016; Aranda 2016c).

THE EU AND ITS FOES

In all four dailies analysed, explanations for the momentum and final victory of the Brexit option were offered. For example: Méndez, in *El País*, put it down to the alleged averseness among British people to dual (British-European) identity (17 June 2016); whereas others saw the inequalities caused by globalization and the fears it generates as reasons for the pro-Leave momentum (Pérez, *La Vanguardia*, 26 June 2016). In *La Vanguardia* (28 June 2016), former Swedish Prime Minister Carl Bildt castigated British leaders' historically lukewarm support for an integrated Europe and their failure to present the EU in a more positive light; other authors attributed the result to downright Euroscepticism since the Thatcherite years (Masdeu, *Ara*, 26 June 2016), 'fuelled by public schools' (Colomina, *Ara*, 27 June 2016).

One of the salient features of the media coverage was the dissemination of a discourse in which globalized liberal democracy, represented by the EU, was assaulted by and finally left reeling under the attack of populism. This was in particular a feature of the Catalan press: as stated by the editor of *Ara*, Brexit was the consequence of anti-immigrant populism and the revolt against the elites (Vera, 26 June 2016). In *La Vanguardia*, the result was due to an 'explosive cocktail' formed by populism, immigration and poor economic growth (Ramos, 27 June 2016) and to xenophobic populism (Foix, 29 June 2016).

The Madrid-based press offered a different view: populism was seen as accompanied by nationalism of all types. In fact, more often than not these two political enemies were seen as one entity, forming a two-headed foe which was defined by *El País*, for instance, in these terms: 'populisms, that is, often ultra and xenophobic nationalisms, that have transited from Euroscepticism to Europhobia' (2016a). As will be argued in this chapter, the link between nationalism and populism must be considered in the context of the strength of pro-independence Catalanism and the threat it was perceived to represent to the territorial structure of Spain. Even though Catalan nationalism cannot in any way be described as Eurosceptic or Europhobic, the demands for a Catalan independence referendum (regarded as a weapon of populism in the Madrid-based press, as will be seen) appeared to be enough to establish the connection.

REALITY-BASED RATIONALITY VERSUS DECEPTIVE EMOTION

A conspicuous feature of the Madrid-based press (not so prominent in the Catalan dailies) was the interpretation of both camps using binary contrasts. In *El Mundo* and *El País*, the two battling entities, the EU and nationalist populisms (represented in Britain by Brexiters) were assigned contrasting values following a clear binary system, respectively: young versus old; more apathetic versus more committed (*El País* 2016e); in class terms with the wealthier, professionals, intellectuals and urbanites versus the unemployed, benefit-dependants and workers who see themselves as the victims of globalization (Tubella, *El País*, 25 June 2016); and, in geographical terms with dynamic and cosmopolitan London versus the rest of the country; and England and Wales on the one hand against Scotland and Northern Ireland on the other (Piqué, *El Mundo*, 27 June 2016).

One noticeable binary contrast in *El Mundo* and *El País* was the dichotomy of 'reality-based rationality' versus 'deceptive emotion'. This dual system was in turn grounded on the idea of the EU as 'the most successful common project in the history of Europe' (*El País* 2016c), which provides a 'framework of progressiveness' (Martínez-Bascuñán, *El País*, 25 June 2016) characterized by its 'open-mindedness and liberating spirit' (Alcover, *El Mundo*, 19 June 2016), and its 'solidarity' (Martínez-Bascuñán, *El País*, 25 June 2016). The ideas of 'framework' and 'project' are essential as they constructed the EU as a solid, forward-looking, long-term endeavour based on the principles of progress, and, very importantly, of reality-based reason; that is, the enduring values of the Enlightenment.

Six days before the 2016 EU referendum, with opinion polls indicating an increase in the support for the Leave camp, a concerned *El País* put its trust in 'the rationality' of its 'British fellow citizens' (2016a). In contrast, the Leave (nationalist and populist) leaders were portrayed as looking for short-term fixes, playing with people's vulnerabilities generated in moments of crisis (Tortella, *El Mundo*, 25 June 2016; Alcover, *El Mundo*, 19 June 2016) and driven by illusion, emotion and mendacity. Nigel Farage, Boris Johnson et al. were portrayed as demagogues with no scruples who employed 'flea-market selling rhetoric' (*El País* 2016g) to manipulate people's emotions (Alcover, *El Mundo*, 19 June 2016). Their arguments were condemned as 'deceptively simple solutions for complex problems' (Tortella, *El Mundo*, 25 June 2016); and, very prominently, as lacking in accuracy and veracity.

Immigration was one the key battlegrounds for the fight over truth in the Madrid press. Thus, the argument for the need for border controls was regarded as an 'alarmist message' (Guimón, *El País*, 2016b); that is, exaggerated and not evidence-based. Farage's immigration proposals were 'toxic harangues'—the Spanish term used to describe their aim being *soflama*, indicating an intention to stir up the audience, to rouse its passions (Sahuquillo, *El País*, 2016a). Raising the accusation to the level of mendacity, Carlin suggested that pro-Brexit politicians 'lied' (*El País*, 25 June 2016) and other *El País* roving reporters sent around Britain to take the pulse of the voters condemned these 'fabrications' on immigration as 'exaggerated and *unreal* ideas based on the anti-immigration discourse of Brexit supporters that exploits the *false* argument that immigrants abuse the British benefit system when *in reality* only 7% of them receive any benefit' (Sahuquillo, *El País*, 2016d, our italics).

The other main arena for scrutiny (and attack) of the 'emotional', 'deceptive' and 'simplistic' Brexit rhetoric was the economy, which (presumably because of its quantifiable nature) was presented as the rational arena in which to counteract the anti-EU movement (Guimón, *El País*, 2016a) whose arguments were 'of a more visceral nature' (Méndez, *El País*, 17 June 2016). After a long presentation of the possible effects of Brexit, de Quirós wrote in *El Mundo*: 'the rational thing for the United Kingdom is to stay in the Union and it should be expected that British pragmatism will prevail on 23 June' (19 June 2016). On occasions, the economic figures and statistics of the Leave camp were presented as a myth and denounced as 'unlawful, unfair and unreasonable' (the Spanish term used to describe them being *torticeras*, meaning 'unfair, contrary to the laws or reason'). Most notable among these was the claim that the UK would save £350 million a week by coming out of the EU, money that would be used to fund the cash-strapped NHS (Sahuquillo, *El País*, 2016b). In contrast to the Brexit camp's 'more irrational' 'sentiments of belonging or identity', the Remain movement was constructed as moved by 'tangible' economic arguments (Sahuquillo, *El País*, 2016d).

As opposed to the cosmopolitan, globalized image of the world represented by the EU, the idea of 'national control' was criticized by *El Mundo* and *El País* as a combination of conservatism with nostalgia for a world that is not real any more. In this view, nationalist populisms (left-wing and right-wing) were characterized as movements of 'political melancholy' steeped in conservative 'reactionary' ideology (Martínez-Bascuñan, *El País*, 25 June 2016) whose restricted framework of reference is that of the 'fatherland', with a vision of 'withdrawal', designed to 'armour plate the country' (Sahuquilllo, *El País*, 2016b). The motto 'Let's gain back control' was regarded in *El Mundo* as an 'old slogan' (Fresneda, 19 June 2016); but it was also seen as an 'illusion' as much for the impossibility of its realization in a globalized world as for its reference to the past (Naím, *El País*, 27 June 2016). In line with this, the Leave camp was seen to be fed by the 'nostalgia of the elderly' (Gil, *El Mundo*, 19 June 2016); Brexiters were regarded as morose and obsessed by an 'absurd imperial nostalgia' (Carlin, *El País*, 25 June 2016), and as 'nostalgic for Empire' for thinking that by 'leaving the EU the United Kingdom will regain the sovereignty and grandeur of the times of the Empire' (González, *El País*, 17 June 2016). This idea of 'imperial nostalgia' was echoed in *La Vanguardia* (Buj, 28 June 2016); and, very importantly, was seen as tingeing Brexiters' perception of 'their present with negativity' (Carbajosa, *El País*, 28 June 2016), a notion that runs contrary to the joy of forward-looking Reason-led projects driven by the spirit of the Enlightenment.

These fake, deceptive, illusionary ideas were exposed (that is, reality-checked) right after the announcement of the referendum result, hailed as an 'irrational decision' (*El Mundo*, 24 June 2016). With the sudden fall in the value of sterling the warnings given prior to the referendum were vindicated by the facts. By way of example, consider the contrast established between evidence and trickery:

> The devastating results of this search for 'control' did not take long to appear. The most dramatic is that the devaluation of the currency, which dragged the pound down to 1985 levels, has made the economy contract dramatically [...] 'To gain back control' is proving to be prohibitively expensive for the Brits. And even more so because it is a false illusion. In today's world the control promised by demagogues does not exist. This might be one of the first lessons Brexit will teach us. (Naím, *El País*, 27 June 2016)

As noted above, this was a noticeable feature of the Madrid-based press. On only one occasion did this attack on the 'populist' discourse of 'mendacity', 'emotion' and 'closed nationalism' evoke some resonance in *La Vanguardia* in an article penned by José Antonio Zarzalejos, sometime editor of the Madrid-based daily *ABC* (2005–2008), one of the most conservative national dailies in Spain: 'The worst English supremacist nationalism has won, along with its emotive and isolationist arguments' (Zarzalejos, 26 June 2016). In *Ara*, the emphasis on the dichotomized view that orders the world into nationalists and non-nationalists was not only avoided but also criticized (Culla, 26 June 2016).

Opportunities and Lessons: A European Catastrophe

The consequences for the EU of a Brexit vote (before and after the referendum) were expressed using a wealth of metaphors conveying a sense of vulnerability, including references to a 'house of cards' (the disintegration of the EU), 'the domino effect' on other countries; or the more medical 'contagion'. The actual result was received with shock and consternation in the Spanish media and across the political spectrum, with concern for the uncertain future of Britain ('The UK jumps onto rollercoaster', Aranda, *Ara*, 2016d) but most importantly for the future of the EU.

However, almost concurrently with the announcement of the result, an uplifting narrative became dominant: what was felt as a disaster could be turned into 'an opportunity for the future' (*El País* 2016d). The four main political parties involved in the immediately preceding round of Spanish General Elections advocated stronger economic and political European integration in the face of Brexit (González and Maqueda, *El País*, 24 June 2016) with the centre and centre-left parties more concerned with the development of a more civically minded, socially aware, reformist EU focused on re-enforced social democratic principles of equality (*El País* 2016f, h), the abandonment of which was seen as the cause of the ascendancy of populisms represented in Britain by the Brexit camp. The pro-independence Catalan newspaper *Ara* not only viewed the result as an opportunity to rebuild a more unified Europe with greater integration into the United States of Europe (Font, 23 June 2016), but also celebrated the prospect for Scotland to hold a new independence referendum.

THE 2016 EU REFERENDUM: A BONE OF CONTENTION

As noted above, the discussion on the suitability of referendums as a political tool to solve constitutional issues was central to the debate. For *Ara*, despite the unexpectedly adverse result, referendums were still 'the best way of reaching collective decisions' (Vera, 26 June), and Catalonia should enjoy the same rights as Scotland in this respect. It argued that 'in due time, Europe will see that neither Scotland nor Catalonia are the problem, but the idea of democracy that prevails in Spain' (30 June 2016b).

In contrast, for *El Mundo*, *El País* (and to a certain extent *La Vanguardia*), popular plebiscites were per se a threat because of their potential misuse by populist movements. Thus, the solution put forward to protect the European Project against 'the populist onslaught' (*El País* 2016h) was to undermine the very notion of the referendum. (An aversion to referendums is not in itself a peculiarly Spanish feature; see, for example, Leonard, *El País*, 30 June 2016.) This attitude was adopted by all the Spain-wide political parties except for the left-wing coalition Podemos. In Madrid, referendums were rejected on three main grounds:

- For what was seen as their uncontrollable ability 'to open the flood-gates to xenophobic populism and the worst type of nationalism' (*El País* 2016b); that is, for their knock-on, copycat effect across Europe (*El País* 2016g; de Quirós, *El Mundo*, 19 June 2016; Suanzes, *El Mundo*, 24 June 2016).
- For the irreversibility of the result (*El País* 2016c), which renders political negotiation impossible.
- For the binary nature of referendum questions, which makes them inappropriate for complex issues (Sahagún, *El Mundo*, 24 June 2016).

The assistant editor of *Ara* rightly argued that 'David Cameron will most likely become enemy number one of the Spanish political class' (Miró, *Ara*, 25 June 2016) for having called not one but two referendums (on Scottish independence and Brexit). In fact, the process of Cameron's demonization had started before polling day. For *El País*, the Tory leader had embarked on a 'frivolous and dangerous' adventure (2016b) to sat-isfy his political and personal interests. After the result, the British Prime Minister was accused of 'temerity' (*El Mundo*, 24 June 2016) and irre-sponsibility (Piqué, *El Mundo*, 27 June 2016). In both Madrid-based papers and the Catalan daily *La Vanguardia* he was held responsible for Brexit (*El País* 2016d; Sahagún, *El Mundo*, 24 June 2016; Carol, *La Vanguardia*, 25 June 2016).

The rejection of referendums as a suitable political instrument and the defence of the EU in the Madrid-based papers and *La Vanguardia* went hand in hand with the defence of representative democracy. For Sáenz de Santamaría, the Conservative Spanish Deputy Prime Minister, referendums should not be called to make 'important decisions. Mainly because the political representatives are there to deal with and manage critical issues precisely because citizens elect them in democratic elec-tions' (Segovia and Cruz, *El Mundo*, 24 June 2016). This was echoed by the then Socialist candidate to the post of Prime Minister, Pedro Sánchez, who noted (claiming clear ownership of the process): 'We are now seeing what referendums produce, they transfer to the citizens solu-tions that political parties must offer. Politics, like life, is not all or noth-ing. We need to reinforce representative democracy' (*El País* 2016e). In the press, this idea was encapsulated by *El País* in its 23 June editorial: 'the time-honoured British parliamentary system proves that represent-ative democracy has the virtue of making reversible decisions, which is more difficult in a referendum, vulnerable as these are to base passions, reductionism and populism' (2016c). This stance must be considered in the context of the rejection of a Catalan referendum on independence on the part of the Madrid-based media and most Spain-wide political parties except Podemos; it should be seen as a strategy to link together and delegitimize referendums, populism and nationalism.

CONCLUSION

The amount of coverage of the 2016 EU referendum provided by the dailies analysed in this chapter (and by the Spanish media in general) was truly remarkable. This is hardly surprising as Brexit potentially jeopardized what was seen as an enlightened project celebrated almost unanimously (albeit in different degrees and with variations) for having delivered countless political and economic benefits to Spain. However, this must also be seen in relation to the internal political life of the country. Thus, the Madrid-based press's stance against 'populist nationalism' should be regarded as a reaction against the left-wing coalition Podemos, on the one hand, and Catalan nationalism on the other. In this account, both had simplistically found an enemy whose elimination would solve all societal problems: 'the establishment' in the case of Podemos and the Spanish state in the case of the nationalists. And both were denounced for their defence of the referendum as a means to solve the independence question in Catalonia. In line with the official position of the Spanish government and most political parties, *El País* and *El Mundo* sustained a defence of representative democracy and steadfastly upheld the notion of the unsuitability of referendums for the resolution of constitutional questions. In response to the Brexit result, *El País* claimed that 'contrary to the idea disseminated by nationalist politicians (irredentist nationalisms, such as the Catalan one), direct consultations of the people constitute a serious mistake as they see themselves forced to choose between situations that produce complex consequences' (2016g). The same applied to Podemos, the only Spain-wide political grouping in favour of holding an independence referendum in Catalonia.

La Vanguardia adopted an intermediate position: while aligning itself with the Madrid press in regards to referendums, it avoided establishing a direct link between populism and nationalism. Finally, albeit lamenting the results and their consequences for the European project, the pro-independence and pro-referendum Catalan newspaper *Ara* main-tained an unwavering defence of referendums as a legitimate mechanism which respected the democratic convictions of the people.

This study has shown that the coverage of the EU referendum in Spain constituted a striking example of the 'domestication of the news' (Gurevitch et al. 1991); that is, the interpretation of foreign or global events using domestic frames which, on the one hand, bring the news experientially closer to the reader but also (as was the case here) facilitate the use of those events as substitutes for national debates. This chapter has shown that 'domestication' did not imply one homogeneous Spanish view, but a range of ideologically grounded interpretations in which the independence of Catalonia featured as highly as the future of the EU. 'Home', as several journalists point out, is after all the 'Common European Home', the 'common project' which can reject the parochial, the atavistic, the emotional and the irrational and nourish opposing views within a superordinate rational frame: the frame of Enlightened European modernity.

Acknowledgements This article is part of the research project "The role of the metaphor in the definition and social perception of conflict issues: institutions, media and citizens", funded by the Spanish Ministry of Competitiveness, CSO-2013-41661-P.

References

Primary Sources

Ahrens, J.M. 2016. El peso mexicano sufre la devastadora ola del Brexit, June 28. http://economia.elpais.com/economia/2016/06/28/actuali-dad/1467074486_755229.html (Accessed 27 March 2017).

Alcover, Antonio. 2016. Cuando el corazón manda…. *El Mundo*, 19 June. http://www.elmundo.es/baleares/2016/06/19/5766eed046163faf458b468d.html (Accessed 27 March 2017).

Ara. 2016a. Les incògnites econòmiques del Brexit, June 15, p. 3.

Ara. 2016b. Escòcia i la UE: Europa té un dilema i Rajoy un problema, June 30, p. 3.

Aranda, Quim. 2016a. L'hora del divorci entre el Regne Unit i Europa? *Ara*, June 22, p. 12.

Aranda, Quim. 2016b. Terratrémol Brexit. *Ara*, June 25, p. 4.

Aranda, Quim. 2016c. Cameron cau víctima d'ell mateix. *Ara*, June 25, p. 7.

Aranda, Quim. 2016d. El Regne Unit s'aboca a la muntanya russa, June 27. http://www.ara.cat/internacional/Regne-Unit-saboca-muntanya-russa_0_1603039693.html.

Bildt, Carl. 2016. Gran Bretaña a la deriva. *La Vanguardia*, June 28, p. 6.

Buj, Anna. 2016. Nostalgia Imperial. *La Vanguardia*, June 28, p. 8.

Carbajosa, Ana. 2016. El UKIP busca su razón de ser tras el "Brexit", June 28. http://internacional.elpais.com/internacional/2016/06/26/actualidad/1466968949_812813.html (Accessed 27 March 2017).

Carlin, John. 2016. Inglaterra, país 'hooligan', June 25. http://internacional.elpais.com/internacional/2016/06/24/actualidad/1466785517_980774.html (Accessed 27 March 2017).

Colomina, Carme. 2016. Referéndums. *Ara*, June 27, last page.

Culla, Joan B. 2016. La sort dels no-nacionalistes. *Ara*, June 26, p. 47.

De Quirós. 2016. Los costes europeos, June 19. http://www.elmundo.es/economia/2016/06/19/57618eb9468aebfb318b45bb.html (Accessed 27 March 2017).

El Mundo. 2016. Brexit: un desastre imprevisto para ellos y para nosotros, June 24. http://www.elmundo.es/internacional/2016/06/24/576cdcac46163f59078b45d4.html (Accessed 27 March 2017).

El País. 2016a. Británicos y europeos, June 17. http://elpais.com/elpais/2016/06/16/opinion/1466092718_157168.html (Accessed 27 March 2017).

El País. 2016b. España contra el Brexit, June 20. http://elpais.com/elpais/2016/06/19/opinion/1466356157_010695.html (Accessed 27 March 2017).

El País. 2016c. Mejor dentro que fuera, please, June 23. http://elpais.com/elpais/2016/06/22/opinion/1466619583_470263.html (Accessed 27 March 2017).

El País. 2016d. Tocados, no hundidos, June 24. http://elpais.com/elpais/2016/06/24/opinion/1466783949_809873.html (Accessed 27 March 2017).

El País. 2016e. Referéndum del 'Brexit': ¿Cuándo habrá resultado? ¿Dónde primero? June 24. http://internacional.elpais.com/internacional/2016/06/23/actualidad/1466672978_809482.html (Accessed 27 March 2017).

El País. 2016f. España ante el reto europeo, June 25. http://elpais.com/elpais/2016/06/24/opinion/1466785960_226429.html (Accessed 27 March 2017).

El País. 2016g. Un retroceso económico e institucional, June 26. http://economia.elpais.com/economia/2016/06/24/actualidad/1466778320_658628.html (Accessed 27 March 2017).

El País. 2016h. Más, mejor Europa, July 3. http://elpais.com/elpais/2016/07/02/opinion/1467467588_593199.html (Accessed 27 March 2017).

Foix, Lluís. 2016. Nuevas formas de demagogia. *La Vanguardia*, June 29, p. 26.

Font, Alex. 2016. Una oportunitat per construir els Estats Units d'Europa. *Ara*, June 23, p. 14.

Fresneda, Carlos. 2016. Europa sin Reino Unido… y viceversa: Diez víctimas del "no" a la UE, June 19. http://www.elmundo.es/economia/2016/06/19/5 764298e22601d32498b45e5.html (Accessed 27 March 2017).

Gil, Iñaki. 2016. Cameron, el amigo invisible de Trump y Puigdemont, June 19. http://www.elmundo.es/cronica/2016/06/19/5765ec23268e3ed0138b464b. html (Accessed 27 March 2017).

González, Miguel. 2016. Cameron y Picardo agitan la 'amenaza española' a Gibraltar para frenar el "Brexit", Junio 17. http://politica.elpais.com/ politica/2016/06/16/actualidad/1466104691_675013.html (Accessed 27 March 2017).

González, Miguel, and Antonio Maqueda. 2016. Todos los partidos coinciden en pedir "más Europa" pero discrepan en cuál, June 24. http://politica. elpais.com/politica/2016/06/24/actualidad/1466761652_431537.html (Accessed 27 March 2017).

Guimón, Pablo. 2016a. Las empresas británicas defienden los beneficios a largo plazo de permanecer en la UE, June 17. http://internacional.elpais. com/internacional/2016/06/16/actualidad/1466096569_591922.html (Accessed 27 March 2017).

Guimón, Pablo. 2016b. El voto contra el "Brexit: cobra vigor a tres días del referén-dum, June 23. http://internacional.elpais.com/internacional/2016/06/20/ actualidad/1466423012_493317.html (Accessed 27 March 2017).

La Vanguardia. 2016. Europa, ahora o nunca, June 25, p. 26.

Leonard, M. 2016. Un tsunami de plebiscitos en Europa, June 30. http://elpais. com/elpais/2016/06/28/opinion/1467138323_672597.html (Accessed 27 March 2017).

López, María-Paz. 2016. El divorcio británico se complica. *La Vanguardia*, June 28, p. 3.

Martínez-Bascuñán, Miriam. 2016. Primavera patriótica, June 25. http://elpais. com/elpais/2016/06/24/opinion/1466761189_100214.html (Accessed 27 March 2017).

Masdeu, Jordi. 2016. Una decisió lògica però en el pitjor moment. *Ara*, June 26, p. 23.

Méndez, Carlos. 2016. ¿Y si hay 'Brexit'? June 17. http://politica.elpais.com/ politica/2016/06/17/actualidad/1466185756_160796.html (Accessed 27 March 2017).

Miró, David. 2016. Cameron, enemic públic número 1. *Ara*, June 25, p. 17.

Moldes, Aleix. 2017. Gairebé el 75% dels catalans participarien en un referen-dum unilateral, segons el CEO, March 30. http://www.ara.cat/politica/

catalans-partidari-referendum-votaria-independencia_0_1768623247.html (Accessed 31 March 2017).

Naím, Moises. 2016. Brexit y el Stalingrado italiano, June 27. http://internacional.elpais.com/internacional/2016/06/25/actualidad/1466865527_079527.html (Accessed 27 March 2017).

Pérez, Manel. 2016. Golpe Global. *La Vanguardia*, June 26, p. 81.

Piqué, Josep. 2016. Es la política, estúpido, June 27. http://www.elmundo.es/internacional/2016/06/27/576fa60f268e3e5d6f8b4614.html (Accessed 27 March 2017).

Ramos, Rafael. 2016. El nuevo orden post-'Brexit'. *La Vanguardia*, June 27, p. 3.

Sahagún, Felipe. 2016. Los británicos eligieron el limbo, June 24. http://www.elmundo.es/internacional/2016/06/24/576cfc59e5fdea88428b463e.html (Accessed 27 March 2017).

Sahuquillo, María. 2016a. Los pescadores británicos enarbolan la bandera del "Brexit", June 20. http://internacional.elpais.com/internacional/2016/06/18/actualidad/1466287179_996195.html (Accessed 27 March 2017).

Sahuquillo, María. 2016b. Financiada por Europa pero partidaria del "Brexit", June 21. http://internacional.elpais.com/internacional/2016/06/20/actualidad/1466396907_989722.html (Accessed 27 March 2017).

Sahuquillo, María. 2016c. Partidarios del "Brexit" y la permanencia luchan voto a voto a horas de la consulta, June 22. http://internacional.elpais.com/internacional/2016/06/22/actualidad/1466594667_659472.html (Accessed 27 March 2017).

Sahuquillo, María. 2016d. El vértigo de la decisión más importante de una generación, June 23. http://internacional.elpais.com/internacional/2016/06/21/actualidad/1466533523_092880.html (Accessed 27 March 2017).

Segovia, Carlos, and Marisa Cruz. 2016. El Gobierno pide un voto en España a "la estabilidad" tras el Brexit, June 24. http://www.elmundo.es/espana/2016/06/24/576cd5b546163f546a8b4576.html (Accessed 27 March 2017).

Suanzes, Pablo. 2016. La ultraderecha, eufórica, pide referéndum en Francia, Italia y Holanda, June 24. http://www.elmundo.es/internacional/2016/06/24/576cccacca4741f7408b4600.html (Accessed 27 March 2017).

Tortella, Gabriel. 2016. "Hooligans" al poder, June 25. http://www.elmundo.es/espana/2016/06/25/576d9199e5fdea82428b4645.htm (Accessed 27 March 2017).

Tubella, Patricia. 2016. Los laboristas críticos se rebelan contra Corbyn tras el "Brexit", June 25. http://internacional.elpais.com/internacional/2016/06/24/actualidad/1466777886_675195.html (Accessed 27 March 2017).

Vera, Esther. 2016. La revolta contra les elits. *Ara*, June 26, p. 3.

Zarzalejos, Antonio. 2016. La primavera de los patriotas. *La Vanguardia*, June 26, p. 40.

SECONDARY SOURCES

Cammaerts, Bart. 2012. The Strategic Use of Metaphors By Political and Media Elites: The 2007–11 Belgian Constitutional Crisis. *International Journal of Media & Cultural Politics* 8 (2–3): 229–249.

Carol, Marius. 2016. La puerta de salida. *La Vanguardia*, June 25, p. 2.

Castelló, Enric, and Arantxa Capdevila. 2015. Of War and Water. Metaphors and Citizenship Agency in the Newspapers Reporting the 9/11 Catalan Protest in 2012. *International Journal of Communication* 9: 612–629.

Charteris-Black, Jonathan, and Andreas Musolff. 2003. "Battered Hero" or "Innocent Victim"? A Comparative Study of Metaphors for Euro Trading in British and German Financial Reporting. *English for Specific Purposes* 22 (2): 153–156.

Gurevitch, M., M.R. Levy, and I. Roeh. 1991. The Global Newsroom: Convergences and Diversities in the Globalization of Television News. In *Communication and Citizenship: Journalism and the Public Sphere in the New Media Age*, ed. P. Dahlgren and C. Sparks, 195–216. London: Routledge.

León-Solís, F. 2013. El Punt/Avui+ y la selección del "Estado agresor". *Ámbitos, Revista International de Comunicación* 22.

Mio, S.J. 1997. Metaphor and Politics. *Metaphor and Symbol* 12 (2): 113–133.

Musolff, A. 2004. *Metaphor and Political Discourse. Analogical Reasoning in Debates About Europe*. New York, NY: Palgrave Macmillan.

Van Dijk, T. 1988. Semantics of a Press Panic: The Tamil "Invasion". *European Journal of Communication* 13: 167–187.

Wilson, J. 1990. *Politically Speaking: The Pragmatic Analysis of Political Language*. Oxford: Basil Blackwell.

CHAPTER 13

Discursive Dimensions of the EU Referendum 2016 Press Coverage in Portugal

Isabel Simões-Ferreira

INTRODUCTION

Even though the European Union (EU) is a 60-year-old political project (Treaty of Rome 1957) continually moving towards an ever closer integration, grass-roots support for its maintenance seems to be waning. The victory of Brexit (Britain's exit from the EU via the 2016 EU referendum) campaign, seen as a backlash against this process of Europeanization, represents a watershed in Europe's recent troubled history. Apart from the various reasons that may have accounted for such a victory, the role of the media in constructing or deconstructing Europe cannot be neglected. Media coverage can have a powerful effect on the way citizens perceive the EU market and polity-building project, and on how they perceive the rightness or wrongness of the decision of one of

I. Simões-Ferreira (✉)
Escola Superior de Comunicação Social,
Instituto Politécnico de Lisboa, Lisbon, Portugal
e-mail: iferreira@escs.ipl.pt

© The Author(s) 2018
A. Ridge-Newman et al. (eds.), *Reporting the Road to Brexit*,
https://doi.org/10.1007/978-3-319-73682-2_13

its member states to hold a referendum on whether to leave or remain in the EU.

A significant body of research (de Vreese 2007; Valentini and Nesti 2010; Papathanassopoulos and Negrine 2011; Lloyd and Marconi 2014) argues that so far there has not been a dedicated European news agenda focused on fostering citizen engagement with EU affairs so as to build a sense of Europeanness or, to use Benedict Anderson's words (1991), a sort of Europeanized 'imagined community'. Reporting the EU has mainly lacked stories that could have made it immediately newsworthy in the eyes of journalists when compared with domestic issues. Many explanations have been provided for this state of affairs. The EU's decision-making arrangements are said to be too complex to be easily understood by ordinary citizens, or even by many journalists unfamiliar with EU procedures. Moreover, party politics are organized differently. EU-wide political parties do not exist, which makes discussion and political confrontation potentially less attractive for journalistic coverage.

Ideally, the European public sphere, according to Philip Schlesinger, 'would be composed of transnational citizens who have (a) an equal and widespread level of communicative competence, (b) relatively easy access to the full range of the means of communication, and (c) a generalized communicative competence that embodies sufficient background, knowledge, interest, and interpretative skills to make sense of the EU and its policy options and debates' (1999: 129–130).

However, the nature of this public sphere, drawing on Habermas's (2005) rational-critical debate model, has been largely usurped and replaced by infotainment and market forces leading to the sameness of information and the pervasiveness of strategic news reporting. This means that quite often the news focus is put on horse-race politics, game framing and storytelling techniques such as personalization, simplification and polarization rather than on policy-issue framings in order to capture large audiences (Strömbäck and Kaid 2008).

Set against this backdrop, the EU referendum (2016) in the United Kingdom (UK) may not have triggered a rational or enlightened public debate such as that advocated by Schlesinger, but it undoubtedly unleashed a wave of renewed and emotional interest in (un)European issues, whose lack of '"emotional shine"' (Aart de Geus in Merritt 2016: 24) is said to be one of the causes of their comparatively diminished news value.

If it is true that the 2008 financial crisis had already prompted a surge of unprecedented attention on the part of editors and broadcasters, Britain exiting the EU has generated a widespread wave of dramatic news coverage. 'Shakespeare's will', the headline of an opinion article run by *Expresso* (Pinto, 18 June 2016: 33) poignantly signalled the potential for real drama. Indeed, the 2016 EU referendum presented real actors using enticing language, disaster (Jo Cox's murder) and numerous political twists and turns (David Cameron's sudden resignation, anti-Corbyn leadership opposition, Scotland's and Northern Ireland's determination to fight for a new political settlement regarding the EU and Westminster).

In Portugal the idea of Britain leaving an EU facing diverse challenges not only from the outer world but also from within (particularly from the European far-right and far-left parties) produced massive media coverage: hundreds of news articles, opinion columns, leaders and special reports were published in the press. In order to assess the average extent, weight and character of this coverage, we analysed the print editions of three of the most well-known Portuguese titles, two dailies (*Correio da Manhã* and *Público*) and one weekly (*Expresso*), published between 4 June and 4 July 2016. *Correio da Manhã*, a mid-market tabloid, has the highest circulation of all Portuguese newspapers and reaches various strata of the population. According to the latest data (2015) from the Portuguese Association for Auditing Circulation (APCTC), its average daily circulation amounts to 108,997 copies. *Público* is one of the leading quality dailies, targeting mainly a middle and upper-middle class readership. Its average daily circulation is 21,376 copies. *Expresso*, the most widely read weekly broadsheet, is a reference title with an estimated weekly circulation of 78,932 copies. Taken as a whole, this study is based on a corpus of 284 news items: 33 articles and 65 news-in-brief items in *Correio da Manhã*, 132 articles in *Público* and 54 in *Expresso*. Despite the equally extensive media coverage given to the 2016 UEFA European Championship, all these newspapers revealed heightened coverage between 17 and 25 June 2016 (Jo Cox's murder and the unexpected final count of the referendum vote). Throughout the four-week period under study, we came across 9 cover stories (1 in *Correio da Manhã* and 8 in *Público*) and 5 full front pages dedicated to the 2016 EU referendum (3 in *Público* and 2 in *Expresso*).

Articles were then subjected to a critical discourse analysis. Like many social theorists (Foucault 1990; van Dijk 1988; Fairclough 1995; Wodak and Meyer 2001), we take the view that discursive practices comprise three important interrelated phenomena: systems of knowledge, social relations and cultural identity. Language use is therefore political and ideological in the sense that it shapes worldviews and recontextualizes competing and existing discourses, giving them uneven and differentiated emphases.

Hence our main focus of analysis is on transitivity. According to Michael Halliday (2014), transitivity is the cornerstone of representation. It brings to the forefront agency and responsibility for actions and describes circumstances and processes of being, doing or understanding.

Accordingly, some of the central questions used to analyse the news items were: How did Portuguese journalists and columnists/opinion-formers represent agency with regard to the referendum 'battle'? Which actors were given lesser or greater prominence? Were they against the movement or arguments leading to Brexit, or were they in favour of it? Which frames and grammatical or lexical realizations were given preference? What levels of discursive concreteness or abstraction did they use in order to explain or contextualize the opposing forces?

THREE CONTENDERS: EU REFERENDUM CAMPAIGN

From the point of view of transitivity, when we analyse agency (who does what to whom) and action (what gets done), we have to consider two key categories: the so-called 'doers' and 'done-tos', that is to say, 'those who are at the receiving end of action' (Machin and Mayr 2012: 104). On one side we had David Cameron, the person responsible for the decision to hold a referendum on the EU along with his adversaries, Boris Johnson and Nigel Farage; while, on the other, there was the EU, which was represented as being the most affected by the impact of the UK leaving the EU.

Let us then start with the former. Of all the social actors who actively participated in the campaign, the former Prime Minister, David Cameron, was the person most frequently represented by the newspapers from both a visual and a verbal perspective. When compared to the other actors, he had greater framing power. The discursive register of the newspapers was predominantly serious and deferential, highlighting the authority that emanates from his position and the primacy of his arguments in favour of remaining. His emphasis on subjects of an economic nature was particularly worth noting. His picture was accompanied by headlines, some of which were prominently positioned on the front page: 'Cameron appeals to the British not to give up on Europe' (*Público*, 2016b: 1), or 'Cameron asks people to vote for the EU' (*Correio da Manhã*, 2016b: 29). Even in a report on the social profile of Leave supporters, '"They are Boris" people and want to "save democracy"', the sentence printed in bold in the body of the text referred to Cameron's warning: 'There's no turning back' (Pereira, *Público*, 2016a: 1).

By contrast, the voices of his more direct opponents (Boris Johnson and Nigel Farage) were clearly relegated to second place in quantitative terms and did not enjoy front-page coverage. They appeared in articles that, thematically, tended to exploit the up-and-down swings of opinion polls or bookmakers through what is known, in matters of election coverage, as 'game framing' with titles such as: '"If it goes wrong, I apologise"' (*Correio da Manhã*, 23 June 2016c: 29) or 'Boris Johnson calls for "Independence Day"' (F., *Correio da Manhã*, 22 June 2016: 29).

As can be seen in the above examples and other similar cases, the newspaper's voice insisted on marking its critical distance from Boris Johnson's voice by using quotation marks, thus avoiding using indirect speech. Jokingly nicknamed 'Blondie' by a Portuguese Member of the European Parliament (MEP) and *Público* columnist ('The false Pax Britannica' [Rangel 2016a: 46]), which removed substance and seriousness from his opinions, Johnson was also subjected to a vehement attack on his lack of character by a columnist from *Expresso* (Alves, 25 June 2016: 3). 'Dear Boris' (a chronicle written in an epistolary style) not only deconstructed the 'insane' nostalgia for getting the country back again, invoking for this purpose an article written by A. A. Gill in the *Sunday Times* on 12 June 2016, but it also denounced the incoherence of the anti-immigration policy advocated by Alexander Boris de Pfeffel Johnson considering his multi-ethnic background.

As for Nigel Farage, the three newspapers resisted reproducing his voice in headlines, whether in direct or indirect speech. The United Kingdom Independence Party (UKIP) leader was described, moreover, by Rangel in his *Público* article as a 'little tinpot dictator' (Rangel 2016a: 46). The editorial voice of *Público* corroborated the scathing nature of this type of criticism in 'Farage vs Cox Equation' (*Público*, 2016a: 64), likening him to Hitler because of the xenophobic fanaticism of his political propaganda.

Despite Euroscepticism's dislocation from the margins to the centre with the onset of the Eurozone crisis which led to the transnational concertation of anti-Europeanist voices and the increase of a progressively hostile rhetoric by some media and traditionally pro-European parties (Brack and Startin 2015), the reality is that the main Portuguese political parties (Social Democratic Party [PSD] and the Socialist Party [PS]) remain committed Europeanists with the Communist Party (PCP) and the Left Bloc (BE) being the exceptions. Following the demise of the Portuguese colonial empire, the Portuguese elite realized that the key to their future economic development and political stability lay in joining the then European Economic Community (1986), a view that is still held today.

It is not to be wondered at, therefore, that in the struggle between the Leave and the Remain supporters the newspapers gave a favourable voice to the calls to remain and then expressed sadness and anxiety about the result. 'Stay with us, Tusk and Costa ask', wrote *Correio da Manhã* (2016a: 36), foregrounding the wishes of the President of the European Council and the Portuguese Prime Minister. In a similar vein, the plea 'Please, don't go' (*Público*, 2016c: 6) shows how Teresa de Sousa used one of the headlines from *Der Spiegel* to reinforce the call to remain. 'A sad day', the editorial headline in *Público* (2016c: 3) declared a few days later. 'Keep calm? But how?' asked Guerreiro in *Expresso* (25 June 2016: 2).

UNREPORTED ISSUES AND THEIR CONSEQUENCES

However, the game framing based on the two-sided struggle between Cameron and his adversaries (Johnson/Farage) in the name of the UK leaving or remaining in the EU conferred on Cameron, in view of the above, a sense of responsibility supposedly inherent to a statesman as opposed to the demagogic manoeuvres of ambitious politicians. This then showed how the Portuguese press neglected or simplified to a large extent their representation of David Cameron, the politician par excellence, and the Conservative Party's intraparty manoeuvres for power.

In fact, there exist an editorial, 'Yes or no? In or out? Cameron or Johnson?' (*Público*, 4 June 2016d: 2) and a few opinion articles which denounced Cameron's egocentricity and his struggle for political survival. Examples of this are: 'Brexit: Shakespeare in London and Lisbon' (Rangel, *Público*, 2016b: 44), 'Brexit and national egotism' (Pisco, *Público*, 21 June 2016: 47) or 'David Cameron, the European' (Sousa, *Público*, 2016d: 4), a deeply ironical headline that succinctly revealed the former British Prime Minister's political hypocrisy and cynicism. These headlines, however, serve as specific examples of a much wider series of articles on the 2016 EU referendum. In fact, the thematization of the 'battle' between Leave and Remain supporters effaced the intra-party struggle between 'the Brexit ringleaders [...] Neros with an Eton accent' (*Público*, 3 July 2016: 44), to use Alexandra Coelho's sarcastic expression.

What was hardly thematized at all was, first, how the Conservative Party had been 'captured' by Eurosceptics, especially since William Hague's leadership, which was a path Cameron also followed although he was not able to stem the flow of Conservative voters deserting to UKIP. Then the devastating negativity of the English tabloid press towards Europe also went unreported. We are talking about a power against which British politicians, according to David MacShane (2016), do not know, as a rule, how to react for fear that the powerful Rupert Murdoch and other press magnates will not support them in future parliamentary elections. And, lastly, a topic that was significantly back-grounded was the so-called British 'awkwardness'; an expression used by Andrew Geddes (2013: 28) to designate, among other things, Britain's vacillation and backtracking in relation to various European policies from the very first moment it joined in 1973. The non-salience of these issues did not help readers to form a proper opinion of either the importance of the domestic intraparty struggles or the UK's special relationship with the EU.

In this respect, it is worth noting that *Correio da Manhã* ranked first for the non-existence of any contextualization or historical allusion to the intraparty struggle. In fact, the 'Brexit' theme only acquired news value from 17 June 2016 onwards owing to the murder of Jo Cox. Hatred, betrayal and fear are the common denominators of a predominantly sensationalist frame that fed off exploiting the emotions of its readership.

The scarcity of historical framings and/or contextualizations by the press, even though *Correio da Manhã* was in this respect an exceptional case, ended up causing an ideological dislocation; in other words, it blurred the complexity of Britain's singularity and refocused the readers' attention with redoubled emphasis on the dual conflict between the sovereign will of a nation state and the European project's supranationalism (UK vs EU), which could be exploited on another geographical level with direct implications for Portugal's current situation and its relationship with the EU, a subject we shall return to later.

In addition, problematizing Brexit as a political phenomenon is emotionally exploited through using future catastrophic scenarios of the break-up of the EU as well as of the UK itself. 'Earthquake', announced Gonçalves in *Correio da Manhã* (2016: 27). 'Disunited states in Europe [...] What comes next in Europe's life now the United Kingdom has changed history', wrote *Expresso* (2016b: 1) with a full-cover Union Flag on its front page. 'The major earthquake Europe has long feared', declared *Público* (Pereira 2016b: 2), with the front page showing the EU flag with one of the stars in free fall.

EUROPE: CAUSE AND VICTIM OF A CATASTROPHE

Having reached this point, the question mentioned previously needs to be (re)addressed: What is the representation of the journalistic coverage of those who are suffering the impact of David Cameron's January 2013 decision to go ahead with the referendum? Here we are of course referring to the so-called 'done-tos' in the process.

In this domain, Europe was undoubtedly represented as the principal victim hit by the action that had been triggered. 'The destiny of Europe is at stake in the British referendum', claimed *Teresa de Sousa in Público* (2016a: 4). 'The future of Europe begins in five days' time', announced *Expresso* (2016a: 1) on 18 June. And Ribeiro later asked in the same weekly: 'What now, European Union?' (2 July 2016: 28), pointing in an elliptical way to the challenges that the EU finds itself facing, ranging from the populisms that threaten to tear it apart to the effects of the financial crisis and lack of growth that persist in the eurozone.

Nonetheless, the centrality of Europe, whether in the body of the text or in the headlines, did not prevent it, somewhat paradoxically, from being constructed as 'Other'; that is to say, as a non-democratic power, a foreign power external to the UK and Portugal as well as to the other member states. This is therefore equivalent to saying that Europe appeared represented not only as one of the main passive agents ('done-tos'), but also as an active agent (a 'doer') responsible for the result of the 2016 EU referendum. This double representation, to a great extent motivated by the debt situation in which Portugal finds itself, results in an evaluative discourse which one moment blames the UK, or praises it for its courage, and the next moment applauds the vision of the European project, or condemns the EU for its lack of solidarity and democratic governance.

It is therefore a good idea to look at the interpersonal dimension of journalistic discourse, or the evaluative attitude that establishes the balance of power and/or causality between the facts and the principal social actors (UK vs EU). The arguments of those who criticized England were divided between those which censured its nostalgia for the demise of its imperial rule and delusions of grandeur when faced with the present and those who admonished it for precisely the opposite, for its parochialism and insular narrow-mindedness that had led John Bull to be concerned 'more about his own backyard than with the European avenue' ('Chronicle of the small island', Cachão, *Correio da Manhã*, 21 June 2016: 2).

The argumentation used by the side who praised England sought to emphasize the fact that the legacy of the Magna Carta and the Glorious Revolution means that England does not need to receive 'lessons in democracy from anyone. [...] As a European, I hoped that the UK might have decided to stay. As an anglophile, I admire the English and their sovereign will' wrote Mexia in *Expresso* (25 June 2016: 106).

In other words, the above eulogies all evoked British parliamentarianism as an asset or a political weapon to criticize Europe's current mismanagement. There are even commentators who exhorted England to show us the way in 'A lamp leading the way' (Oliveira, *Expresso*, 18 June 2016: 33), a headline that draws on intertextuality with the Portuguese proverb 'A lamp leading the way sheds its light twice'.

Thus, sovereignty seen as a desirable weapon of independence and not of demagoguery stood out as one of the arguments that served precisely to criticize the EU's oppressive and anti-democratic drift. Note the dramatic tone of some of the headlines printed: 'Europe divided between punishing the British and calming the waters' (Ribeiro, *Público*, 26 June 2016: 8), 'Brexit and Europe's guilt' (Barrinha, *Público*, 30 June 2016: 55). Similarly, the exploitation of the intertextual game with the term given to the parliamentary majority governing Portugal at the time of the referendum, 'The European *geringonça* [fragile contraption]' (Sá, *Público*, 2 July 2016: 53), also had a clearly negative connotation, putting the blame on Europe.

This leads to a series of antonyms whose ideological strategy is obvious: freedom vs tyranny, democracy vs bureaucratic oppression or despotism, the benefits resulting from the supremacy of the nation state vs the constraints and castrating hegemony of European supranationalism.

The predominance of this negative strategic framing in relation to the EU was denounced in a remarkably concise way through a headline in *Público*: 'The goat [the EU] is tired of being scaped' (30 June 2016: 56). By representing the European Union as 'Other', readers found themselves confronted, as Andrew Geddes (2013: 38) puts it, with 'intra-EU squabbles and conflicts, rather than "Europe vs the world" stories that could inculcate the "we-feeling" among Europeans'.

The reality is that the interests and political culture of the nation state, dramatically foregrounded by the 2016 EU referendum coverage, persist in providing, even for a country like Portugal where no referendum on Europe is likely to be held, the mental framework of reference for the polyphonic discourse of newspapers, represented by the confrontation of ideas and/or party struggles between opinionmakers of the left and the right. Some are committed to condemning the austerity policies imposed on Portugal and highlight the 'failure' of the single currency; others are committed to advocating the advantages of remaining in the EU, although not always totally uncritically.

As one PSD deputy warned: 'The British referendum could serve the BE and the PCP, who are calling for Portugal to leave the euro and the EU, [...] to tell the truth about what the Portuguese might stand to gain and lose with an isolationist policy if they turned their back on Europe' (Ferreira, *Correio da Manhã*, 23 June 2016: 2).

Even though this left-right politicization might not conform to the EU's so-called 'consociational nature' (Papadopoulos and Magnette 2010), the coverage in Portugal of the UK's EU referendum was heavily influenced by a left-right partisan view, often figuring as a pretext to talk about Europe as a normative centre and its lack of solidarity with the indebted countries of Southern Europe.

However, if being European today in fact means, according to Teresa de Sousa, discussing Europe and weighing up the advantages and disadvantages of referendums of this type ('What does being pro-European mean? It means discussing Europe', *Público*, 2016b: 62), journalists must not lose sight of the difference between politics/politicking and policies. The politicization of the European public sphere, especially visible in moments of crisis after the signing of the Treaty of Maastricht (1992), allowed itself in this case to be driven more by game framings (horse-race politics) or passion framings (putting the emphasis on the emotionalism of political rhetoric and people's hatreds and fears) than by macro-economic or geopolitical framings, a tendency whose effects could result in an 'information diet' harmful to citizens.

ABSTRACTION VS CONCRETENESS

On the other hand, the levels of discursive abstraction or concreteness of the arguments used to defend the UK or to put the relationship between the UK and the EU into perspective also deserve our attention. The polarization of the arguments based on the antonyms mentioned above to support the UK or to blame the EU refers us either to ethically unquestionable, universal values of an abstract nature (democracy, freedom, independence, human rights under the logic of the nation state) or to power relations rooted in an ideological framework of Marxist reference (oppressors/the EU vs the oppressed/its member states) without taking into consideration, for example, the realities imposed by globalization and the inexorable pace of technological development. As John Pilger (1996: 4) reminds us, journalists are used to 'parroting' words like 'democracy' and other buzzwords. It is necessary, however, to deconstruct or contextualize these types of words in the light of contemporary co-ordinates of time and space/place. This means, in other words, that the geopolitical framings and the 'cosmopolitan discourse' (Heikkila and Kunelius 2006: 72) that might provide readers with substantive material to understand the economic dynamics and multipolarity of world politics are, save for some notable exceptions, manifestly scarce.

The very use of the term 'Europe' and/or EU needs disambiguation. The generalization of their undifferentiated use by journalists and columnists, at times without our knowing exactly what they are referring to, taking, from a metonymic point of view, the 'faceless' whole for its parts (too often in a confrontational attitude), does not favour informed debate on the relationship between the EU's specific institutions and its member states and respective representatives.

It can be seen, however, that the levels of discursive abstraction mentioned above alternate with levels of considerable concreteness, some of a seemingly caricature-like sensationalist nature, while others are of a purely pragmatic nature to explain the presumable effects of Brexit.

On the front page of the 25 June edition of *Correio da Manhã*, there was a cover story right below the banner headline announcing: 'Brexit. Mourinho loses 700 thousand euros a year.' Further on one can read:

> The announcement that the United Kingdom will leave the EU made sterling fall and also Mourinho's income. He signed a contract in May with Manchester United for an annual salary of 10 million pounds. In May, that was worth 13,175 million euros, but at yesterday's exchange rate this fell to 12,477 million euros (698 thousand euros less). (*Correio da Manhã*, 2016d: 30)

The repercussions of Brexit were personalized in this way using football's celebrity culture. This favours the economic dividends the paper can extract from a process of affective construction with its readers. No other news item equals the degree of tabloidization here. What is more, despite the differences in style, when it comes to dealing with the impact of Brexit on Portugal, all three newspapers focused their attention on themes that visibly laid bare the national interest and showed the degree of discursive concreteness, whether this concerned the fears of Portuguese immigrants in the UK, advice about measures for their future legalization or economic estimates of the repercussions of Brexit on the tourist industry.

According to Philip Schlesinger (1999: 277–278), if it is true that for a European public sphere to truly exist it must presuppose 'the dissemination of a European news agenda' and constitute 'a significant part of everyday news-consuming habits of European audiences' cemented by an 'affective dimension', it is no less true that there is a need to reflect on the nature of this affective dimension and make a clear distinction between matters that galvanize the interest of the public and matters of interest to the public.

The coverage of the 2016 EU referendum by the newspapers under analysis certainly managed to interest and alarm the public, but much of the time it did not manage to provide people with material for reflection, for example about some of the motives behind Brexit (the intraparty struggle within the Conservative Party), the pros and cons of European supranationalism as a political project, or the myth of immigration as an instrument for displacing or excluding local workers in the globalized knowledge society.

CONCLUSION

The first news about Brexit reached *Correio da Manhã* readers by way of emotion and crime (Jo Cox's murder). Since it is the newspaper with the highest circulation in Portugal, one could say that the EU continues to be treated as a subject that is somewhat distant from the concerns of most citizens unless directives coming from Brussels interfere directly with their everyday lives.

Although cosmopolitan discourse does not lie within its editorial preferences, the reality is that its attitude was pro-Europeanist. It highlighted Cameron's appeals for the UK to remain in the EU. It adopted a classic professional discourse (Heikkila and Kunelius 2006: 72) centred on reproducing the arguments put forward by the highest democratically elected representative of the UK rather than on the political rhetoric used by his main opponents (Boris Johnson and Nigel Farage). From the perspective of the wider picture of relations between the participants in the ongoing referendum process (UK vs EU), the accountability and/ or the culpability of the EU were neutralized in the face of criticism of British insularity and the hegemony of 'Little England'.

The monologic orientation of the discourse in *Correio da Manhã* contrasted, in this respect, with the dialogism of *Público* and *Expresso* when representing political agency. The ambiguity of the criticism directed at the principal political actors involved (UK vs EU) was governed by a confrontational framing which largely blamed the EU's lack of leadership and despotism for the current state of affairs. At times, the alterity with which the EU was described means that it appeared represented simultaneously as the recipient of the political action triggered by Cameron/England ('done-to') and as one of the active political agents ('doer') of the process that led to the victory of Brexit. This double representation was not unrelated to the left-right politicization or the Portuguese recontextualization of the theme as a result of both the austerity policies imposed on Portugal and the European Commission's much publicized lack of solidarity towards the indebted countries of Southern Europe.

In all cases, regardless of differences in style, the domestic framing was predominant. When it comes to reporting EU-related subjects, most newspapers, as J. Lloyd and C. Marconi point out, 'bring their nation with them [...]. "Europe" thus becomes an adjunct to the nation, and is simply another chamber in which the latter "speaks to itself"' (2014: 5). Hence there is the risk of disinformation and simplifying the complexity of the theme(s) covered.

In the case of the representation of the UK vs EU conflict and voices from *Público* and *Expresso* overvaluing the legacy of British parliamentarianism as the expression of the sovereign will of the people and their right to 'get their country back again', in the sense of devolving power and security to those disenfranchised by globalization, what was not mentioned in fact was the contribution made by the UK itself to the actual process of globalization, in particular the expansion of neoliberalism and deregulation of the financial markets (Harvey 2007). These were certainly responsible for the discontent felt by various sectors of the population who voted in favour of Brexit.

If we take into account that the EU, besides being a territorial and political construct, is itself also a discursive construct, the press and the media in general must rise to the challenge that is placed before them so that citizens and voters may in all conscience and with informed knowledge participate in this collective process of construction or deconstruction.

REFERENCES

ACADEMIC SOURCES

Anderson, B. 1991. *Imagined Communities.* London: Verso.

Brack, N., and N. Startin. 2015. Introduction: Euroscepticism, from the Margins to the Mainstream. *International Political Review* 36 (3): 239–249.

de Vreese, C. 2007. A Spiral of Euroscepticism: The Media's Fault? *Acta Politica* 42 (2/3): 271–286.

Fairclough, N. 1995. *Media Discourse.* London: Edward Arnold.

Foucault, M. 1990. *L'Ordre du Discours.* Paris: Gallimard.

Geddes, A. 2013. *Britain and the European Union.* Basingstoke: Palgrave Macmillan.

Habermas, J. 2005. *The Structural Transformation of the Public Sphere,* 7th ed. Cambridge: Polity Press.

Halliday, M. 2014. *An Introduction to Functional Grammar,* 4th ed. London: Hodder Arnold.

Harvey, D. 2007. *A Brief History of Neoliberalism,* 2nd ed. Oxford: Oxford University Press.

Heikkila, H., and R. Kunelius. 2006. Journalists Imagining the European Public Sphere. *Journal of the European Institute for Communication and Culture.* 13 (4): 63–80.

Lloyd, J., and C. Marconi. 2014. *Reporting the EU.* London: I.B. Tauris.

Machin, D., and A. Mayr. 2012. *How to Do Critical Discourse Analysis.* London: Sage Publications.

MacShane, D. 2016. *Brexit.* London: I.B.Tauris.

Merritt, G. 2016. *Slippery Slope.* Oxford: Oxford University Press.

Papadopoulos, Y., and P. Magnette. 2010. On the Politicisation of the European Union. *West European Politics* 33 (4): 711–729.

Papathanassopoulos, S., and R. Negrine. 2011. *European Media.* Cambridge: Polity Press.

Pilger, J. 1996. The Hidden Power of the Media. *Socialist Review.* 200: 1–5.

Schlesinger, P. 1999. Changing Spaces of Political Communication. *Political Communication* 16 (3): 263–279.

Strömbäck, J., and L. Kaid. 2008. *The Handbook of Election News Coverage Around the World.* London: Routledge.
Valentini, C., and G. Nesti. 2010. *Public Communication in the European Union.* Newcastle upon Tyne: Cambridge Scholars Publishing.
van Dijk, T. 1988. *News as Discourse.* Hillsdale: Lawrence Erlbaum Associates.
Wodak, R., and M. Meyer. 2001. *Methods of Critical Discourse Analysis.* London: Sage.

NEWSPAPER SOURCES

Alves, C. 2016. Dear Boris. *Expresso,* June 25, p. 3.
Barrinha, A. 2016. Brexit e a culpa europeia. *Público,* June 30, p. 55.
Cachão, F. 2016. Crónica da pequena ilha. *Correio da Manhã,* June 21, p. 2.
Coelho, A. 2016. Londres é nossa. *Público,* July 3, p. 44.
Correio da Manhã. 2016a. Fiquem connosco, pedem Tusk e Costa, June 21, p. 36.
Correio da Manhã. 2016b. Cameron pede voto na UE, June 22, p. 28.
Correio da Manhã. 2016c. Se correr mal peço desculpa, June 23, p. 29.
Correio da Manhã. 2016d. José Mourinho perde 700 mil euros, June 25, p. 30.
Expresso. 2016a. O futuro da Europa começa daqui a cinco dias, June 18, p. 1.
Expresso. 2016b. Estados desunidos na Europa, June 25, p. 1.
F., I. 2016. Boris Johnson pede 'dia da independência. *Correio da Manhã,* June 22, p. 29.
Ferreira, L. 2016. Abre-Olhos. *Correio da Manhã,* June 23, p. 2.
Gonçalves, P. 2016. Terramoto. *Correio da Manhã,* June 25, p. 27.
Guerreiro, P. 2016. Keep calm? Mas como? *Expresso,* June 25, p. 2.
Mexia, P. 2016. Vontade soberana. *Expresso,* June 25, p. 106.
Oliveira, D. 2016. Candeia que vai à frente. *Expresso,* June 18, p. 33.
Pereira, A. 2016a. Eles são o povo de Boris e querem 'salvar a democracia' britânica. *Público,* June 20, pp. 18–19.
Pereira, A. 2016b. Um sismo de grande intensidade que a Europa há muito temia. *Público,* June 25, pp. 2–3.
Pinto, J. 2016. A vontade de Shakespeare. *Expresso,* June 18, p. 33.
Pisco, P. 2016. Brexit e egoísmo nacional. *Público,* June 21, p. 47.
Público. 2016a. A equação Farage *versus* Cox, June 19, p. 64.
Público. 2016b. Cameron apela aos Britânicos para não desistirem da Europa, June 22, p. 1.
Público. 2016c. Um dia triste, June 25, p. 3.
Público. 2016d. Yes or no? In or out? Cameron or Johnson?, June 4, p. 2.
Rangel, P. 2016a. A falsa *pax britannica. Público,* June 21, p. 46.

Rangel, P. 2016b. Brexit: Shakespeare em Londres e em Lisboa. *Público*, June 22, p. 44.

Ribeiro, D. et.al. 2016. E agora UE? *Expresso*, July 2, p. 28.

Ribeiro, F. 2016. Europa dividida entre castigar os britânicos e acalmar as águas. *Público*, June 26, p. 8.

Sá, H. 2016. A geringonça europeia. *Público*, July 2, p. 53.

Sousa, T. 2016a. É o destino da própria Europa que se joga no referendo britânico. *Público*, June 4, pp. 4–5.

Sousa, T. 2016b. O que é ser pro-europeu? É discutir a Europa. *Público*, June 12, p. 62.

Sousa, T. 2016c. Please, don't go. *Público*, June 18, pp. 6, 8.

Sousa, T. 2016d. David Cameron, o europeu. *Público*, June 23, p. 4.

Tavares, J. 2016. O bode está cansado de expiar. *Público*, June 30, p. 56.

CHAPTER 14

'Little England Beats Great Britain': Italian Media Coverage of the EU Referendum 2016

Rinella Cere

INTRODUCTION

Italy is one of the core founding members countries of the European Economic Community (EEC), along with Belgium, France, Luxembourg, the Netherlands and the then West Germany; and, for most of its post-Second World War history, has been a strong supporter of the European unification project. In the last two decades, however, with the rise of new political formations such as the Lega Nord, the entrance into the political arena of Silvio Berlusconi, and more recently with the establishment of the Movimento 5 Stelle (Five Stars Movement), henceforth M5S, there has been a marked change and anti-European sentiments have become more widespread in the political culture as a whole. This in turn has affected media coverage of European Union (EU) affairs and has steered the views of the Italian public towards a more negative reading of the European unification project. Other factors have also played a

R. Cere (✉)
Sheffield Hallam University, Sheffield, UK
e-mail: r.cere@shu.ac.uk

© The Author(s) 2018
A. Ridge-Newman et al. (eds.), *Reporting the Road to Brexit*,
https://doi.org/10.1007/978-3-319-73682-2_14

role in the change, especially monetary union, introduced in 2002, and the 'uncontrolled' exchange rate that resulted in twofold increases in the prices of goods and services (of course this was a national problem rather than a European one, as the same problem did not arise in quite the same way in the other countries which introduced the euro).

The EU referendum 2016 followed hard on the heels of the December 2016 Italian referendum on constitutional reform promoted by the then Prime Minister Matteo Renzi of the centre-left Partito Democratico (Democratic Party). That referendum had been called to introduce a reform of the Italian constitution and, while it was a complex process which cannot be described in detail here, suffice it to say that it was opposed both by the right and some of the left-wing political forces in Italy. In one of its prime aims, which was to abolish the second house (The Senate), it was generally perceived by constitutionalists, as well as the more informed general public, as a move to concentrate powers in the first house (La Camera, or Chamber of Deputies) and the Prime Minister's hands. In the event, Renzi lost (it was a simple yes/no referendum), but this referendum was also largely reported as a verdict on the EU and its future by social media (the favoured medium of communication of M5S) as well as by much of the centre-right press; these media capitalized on the 'No' to the reform and somewhat arbitrarily circulated the idea that Italy was now on course to call a referendum on membership of the EU in the same way as the United Kingdom (UK) has done. Alongside this, on the left of the political spectrum, there was also a call to reform the democratic process within the EU in order to make it more accountable to the people of the individual countries and to combat policies of austerity, along the lines of movements such as European Alternatives (https://ea10.eu/it/) or DiEM25 (https://diem25.org/).

The following chapter examining Italian media coverage of the British EU referendum in 2016 confirms that Italy is still a stronger supporter of the EU than a country like the UK, albeit with some qualifications about the nature of its democratic processes and neoliberal economic policies, but not quite in the same measure as when I analysed media coverage of the Maastricht summit (Cere 2001).

FROM MAASTRICHT TO 'BREXIT'

Since its establishment with the Maastricht Treaty signed in February 1992 (the summit took place on 9–10 December 1991), the EU has forged ahead with many of its commitments, from the establishment of the Schengen

Agreement, which abolished internal borders between the signatory countries (currently 26), to the introduction of the eurozone in 1999, followed by the currency itself on 1 January 2002 (currently 19 countries) and the gradual enlargement to include countries of the former Eastern Bloc. The EU currently has 28 members, soon to be 27 with the departure of the UK.

The UK, ever since it joined in 1973, has been a 'reluctant partner'; this was probably most visible during the Thatcher Government, with its endless demands for rebates to the UK's economic contribution, still a key factor in 2016 during the Brexit (Britain's exit from the EU) campaign. In 1991, I compared the UK and Italian media coverage of the Maastricht summit. In doing so, it not only confirmed the hypothesis that anti-European feelings were circulated and reinforced regularly in news broadcasts across all the main UK terrestrial channels (then BBC, ITV and Channel 4), but also that these were pitted against a 'mythical' national unity, which was again debunked in the 2016 EU referendum results with Scotland and Northern Ireland voting for remaining in Europe. This theme of internal division, which I will discuss below, was definitely taken up in Italian media coverage.

As against this, Italian broadcast news coverage of the Maastricht summit (then provided by the three main public service channels, Rai1, Rai2 and Rai3) revealed total support for the Treaty and its outcome. In that study I had argued that the reasons behind this strong pro-European stance were based on the fact that Italy was a relatively young nation state and that, as argued by Paul Ginsborg (1994: 643–644), it had undergone a process of 'nazionalizzazione debole' (weak national identity formation) and hence looked to Europe for its identity. Another argument was tied to the fact that Italy could only function properly as a state if it looked to a supra-national body like the EU (this is still the case today). Fast forward 25 years, and 28 countries later: the unquestioning Europeanism long embedded in Italian political culture and media institutions alike has undergone some important transformations without, however, entirely changing the generally pro-European stance. This will become evident in the analysis below, which examines the media coverage of the UK's 2016 EU referendum and the Brexit result.

The Rise of Populism: 'Anti-Politics' Made in Italy

Right-wing populism is on the rise and the Brexit campaign was a good example of this with its insistence on immigration, tightening of borders, national control and presumed anti-politics, normally dressed up as criticism of the ruling elite (the paradox of course is that the leaders of anti-politics themselves emerge from those same elites). This is a phenomenon that has not been exclusive to European countries, as we have seen with the election of Trump in 2016, the ongoing rule in Russia of Putin and more recently the referendum victory of Erdoğan in Turkey, three leaders who undoubtedly make a perfect ideological fit with political populism. In Italy, in recent years we have seen this phenomenon fully characterized by figures and parties like Umberto Bossi and his Northern League, and Silvio Berlusconi and his party, formerly Forza Italia (also a national football slogan loosely translatable as 'Go on Italy') and now II Popolo della libertà (The People of Freedom) (Ruzza and Balbo 2013). The 'anti-politics' of the Italian populist parties has always had an anti-European core which, however, only properly found support after the financial crisis and the dire economic effects of this on all European nations, but especially the Mediterranean countries, Italy included.

In 2013, in the same vein of anti-politics, the organization led by the political satirist/comedian Beppe Grillo and his M5S movement ran in the national elections and won an unprecedented share of the vote, over 25% and nine million votes. This new political formation is the latest development in a political culture which has seen enormous transformations in political support for traditional centre and centre-left parties caused by the upheaval of the corruption scandals of the 1980s and early 1990s. These have resulted either in the parties' restructuring or in their complete demise, as was the case for the Christian Democratic Party which ruled Italy for most of the post-war years right up to the 1980s, and the smaller but influential Socialist Party which governed in coalition, alongside many other parties, right up to the *Tangentopoli* (kickbacks) trials of the early 1990s. These parties and many others of the centre and centre-left were significant players in Italy's relationship with the European unification project as they were largely supportive as well as promoters of a federalist idea of Europe.

Many studies have recently concentrated on the phenomenon of populism, although none has dealt in particular with its relationship to the EU. What has become evident, however, from the media post-Brexit, is that most countries have now substantial political populist elements, which have made their core objective the withdrawal of their countries from the EU. These have also sought reinforcement from one another in the run-up to their national elections and referendums, including Brexit. Photo opportunities have been relayed across the media involving

Nigel Farage, Beppe Grillo, Marine Le Pen, Matteo Salvini (the current Northern League leader) and Geert Wilders, in an unprecedented show of anti-European 'solidarity' (France's presidential elections in May 2017 were the latest of such tests with Marine Le Pen of the Front National running as a candidate).

Since the introduction of the neologism made up of the initial letters of 'Britain' and the word 'exit', many countries have followed suit and much European media coverage has adopted this linguistic shorthand to indicate the trend fuelled by right-wing populist parties to call for referendums to decide about membership of the EU. Italy is no exception and the word 'Italexit' has appeared in many articles covering the implications of Brexit for Italian anti-European parties, but the political picture is far more complicated in Italy as contradictory messages about Europe have circulated especially since the more recent emergence of the political formation M5S.

THE ITALIAN PRESS AND THE EU REFERENDUM 2016

Italy does not have a tabloid press and celebrity, entertainment and lifestyle news remain largely consigned to weeklies and monthlies. The only available dailies which are exclusively leisure-oriented are the sport papers which, on Mondays (following the weekend sports fixtures), exceed the readership of most of the national newspapers. It is also the case that newspaper readership is low compared to other European countries; 2017 figures from the Federazione Italiana Editori Giornali (FIEG) of 58 papers, most of them regional (reflecting the continuing regional character of Italian political culture), reveal a readership of over 4 million from a total population of just over 60 million, with the paper copies still having a much larger readership than the digital versions, in spite of the increased digitization of Italian society and with nearly 40 million active Internet users (Soluzione Group 2017). It is, however, important to consider that the main national titles, which have a combined readership of nearly half of the above figure, are information-heavy papers with politics, national and international, heading the selection of news, a trend that can be traced back to the origins of the press in Italy following national unification in 1861 (Sorrentino 1995: 27).

The two national papers with the largest readership are *Il Corriere della Sera* and *La Repubblica*, respectively of the centre and centre-left of the political spectrum. The third largest is *La Stampa*, a Turin-based paper with a national distribution, still majority-owned by the Agnelli family (founder of the FIAT car manufacturing company), also aligned to the political centre. There are several other papers, with a much smaller readership, across the entire political spectrum from left to right; and only one newspaper still aligned to a political party, *L'Unità*, formerly the organ of the Italian Communist Party founded by Antonio Gramsci in1924, now known as the Partito Democratico (Democratic Party).

The British referendum received wide coverage across all the daily press in Italy, as well as being the main news item on the front page of all of them the day after the result was announced. The main frame for all the centre, centre-left and left-wing papers was one of support for the Remain camp; however, within these there were some important differences in the argumentation and reasons for their support. The right-wing press frame was predictably supportive of the Brexit camp, but again with some distinctions among different titles.

Similarly, a content analysis of three major newspapers in 13 European countries, along with Russia and the USA, undertaken by the European Journalism Observatory in the week that followed the referendum, found that the majority of the press analysed was critical of the UK's vote to leave the EU, with the exception of Russia. In the particular case of Italy, a substantive sample of 249 articles was considered from the two major papers mentioned above (*Il Corriere della Sera* and *La Repubblica*) and also from the right-wing paper *Il Giornale* (owned by Berlusconi's media and publishing companies, respectively Fininvest and Mondadori). As in my qualitative analysis of Italian coverage of Brexit (see immediately below), Italy was found to be in line with most of the European press in its pro-Remain trend, with the exception of Berlusconi's paper, which the study described as having some of 'the most enthusiastic pro-Brexit coverage' (European Journalism Observatory 2017). This is not surprising given the ownership of the paper and the anti-European stance taken by the various coalition governments formed by Berlusconi's party with either the Lega Nord and/or the former Alleanza Nazionale (National Alliance) in the last twenty years, right up to his Government which ended in 2011.

In my own analysis of the press coverage of the EU referendum 2016, I picked out three dominant themes: the economic fallout, with related articles about the role of the European Central Bank (ECB); immigration and the openly racist campaign of the Leave camp, including extensive coverage of the killing of MP Jo Cox; and populism and its electoral base in the UK and the division in the vote.

THE ECONOMIC IMPACT OF 'BREXIT'

Many articles in the Italian papers concentrated on the economic impact of the referendum in relation to the UK, Italy the EU and even international relations. On 24 June, the day immediately after the referendum and the victory of the Brexit campaign, the markets' negative response was covered in all the papers, left and right, albeit with different concerns. In the same vein, sterling's immediate loss of 10% of its value against the euro was also mentioned across all the papers. Metaphors of doom abounded in the coverage of the economic implications of Brexit as well as in other areas of analysis, especially on the political and economic future of the EU as a whole.

La Repubblica dedicated many articles to the economic fallout of the UK referendum, concentrating on the effects of the fall in value of sterling against the euro but also how the latter was itself under pressure as a result of this outcome, and how the ECB was dealing with this crisis. Alongside its national editions, this newspaper has ten local sections dependent on regional distribution in Bari, Bologna, Firenze, Genova, Milano, Napoli, Palermo, Parma, Roma and Torino. These concentrated on questions relating to the effects on the local economy, one example being an article from the Emilia Romagna section titled 'Brexit, Emilia, all the fears regarding exports' (Anon, *La Repubblica*, 26 June 2016a); London is one of the region's biggest markets, with product sales there worth about €3.5 billion. This type of coverage was replicated, however, in all the various regions covered, from Sicily to Piedmont.

Il Corriere della Sera and *La Stampa* in particular also carried many articles on the financial markets post-referendum with discussions about its effect on the Milan Stock Exchange; similar language was used across the two papers, with the word 'panic' in all the titles and subtitles. Right-wing papers like *Libero* and *Il Giornale* adopted similar titles (for example, 'Stock Exchanges slump' [Editorial, Il Giornale, 24 June 2016a]), but the analysis of the economic outcome in both papers, especially in *Libero*, veered towards a connection with and a prediction about potential future developments, namely requests for similar referendums on the part of many countries in Europe, the total suggested in the title was 32, though this clearly includes some of the candidates in line to join (Editorial, *Libero*, 24 June 2016b).

L'Unità, two days after the referendum, dedicated its first 15 pages to the British referendum with extensive coverage of many related issues. Its front page on 25 June (see figure), with its 'Italianate' English title 'Disintegration Day', also carried a subtitle about the collapse of

l'Unità

Catherine Meurisse, sopravvissuta alla strage di Charlie Hebdo, racconta la sua ricerca di leggerezza P. 18

Fondata da
Antonio Gramsci
nel 1924

Questo giornale
ha rinunciato
al finanziamento
pubblico

€1,40

Anno 93 n. 173
Sabato, 25 Giugno 2016

unita.tv

L'isola
che non c'è

Perché ora
si volta pagina

Matteo Renzi

Il popolo britannico ha scelto. Noi rispettiamo questa decisione, e ora si volta pagina. È un giorno senza precedenti. È un giorno non facile.

Segue a pag. 8

Disintegration Day

● Brexit è la tempesta perfetta. Europa nel panico. Populisti in festa. Cameron si dimette
● Crolli storici dei mercati e venti di secessioni. Renzi: l'unica via d'uscita è rifare l'Unione **P. 2-13**

Adesso apriamo
il cantiere Europa

Sandro Gozi

Il 23 giugno diventerà un giorno storico nella storia dell'Europa. Purtroppo, non come avremmo voluto. La Brexit apre scenari inediti seguiranno dei passi formali e dei negoziati, che dovremo condurre con trasparenza e chiarezza, e con dei tempi rapidi. Ma è in momenti come questi che la politica deve rialzare la testa e dimostrare che la storia europea è più forte di chi vuole distruggerla.

Perché l'Europa è casa nostra: l'abbiamo fondata, fatta crescere, e continueremo a difenderla. In Europa viviamo in pace da 70 anni. Sono troppo vaste le sfide transnazionali che si attendono per poter pensare di fare a meno della Ue: le migrazioni, la sicurezza, la giustizia sociale e la creazione di nuovi posti di lavoro, l'ambiente. Dovremo, ad esempio, occuparci molto di più di tutela dello Stato di diritto una priorità che il governo italiano sostiene da tempo, e che è sempre più attuale nell'Europa complessa e difficile di oggi. Vinceremo queste battaglie solo se sapremo essere uniti, non se ci chiuderemo nei nostri sterili egoismi.

L'Italia continuerà a difendere l'Unione Europea dal nazionalismo, ma continuerà a battersi, come ha fatto in questi ultimi due anni, affinché la Ue cambi.

Segue a pag 15

Mercati, visti,
Erasmus
Cosa cambia
con l'addio

Sarà un processo lungo di almeno due anni, ma già alcune conseguenze **P. 7-9**

È lo scenario
peggiore

Umberto De Giovannangeli

Non è la trama di un film dell'orrore di un sogno che si è trasformato in un incubo: è una prospettiva inquietante che da oggi può diventare realtà. **P. 4**

Ma adesso
serve misura

Angelo De Mattia

Il presidente del Consiglio europeo, Donald Tusk, commentando ieri l'esito del referendum britannico, ha rievocato l'antico adagio che dice «Ciò che non uccide, ti rafforza». **P. 10**

Staino

LA GRAN BRETA-
GNA SE N'È ANDATA
DALL'EUROPA

COME NOSTRO FIGLIO
DI CASA. TANTO L'AFFITTO
GLIELO PAGHIAMO NOI.

Trump, Le Pen, Salvini
Estremisti scatenati

● I nazionalisti continentali sperano nell'effetto domino. Il magnate americano esulta in Scozia: non sa che lì i cittadini erano contro la Brexit... **P. 5-9**

L'INTERVISTA A FITOUSSI
«È stato
uno schiaffo
all'austerity»

P. 4

L'INTERVISTA A CASINI
«Ascoltiamo
il disagio
dei cittadini»

P. 8

L'INTERVISTA A VACCA
«Solo il Pd
può arginare
una Italexit»

P. 10

POPULISMI
Il bisogno di
un partito vero

Franco Marini

Sul voto amministrativo non c'è da minimizzare ma nemmeno da drammatizzare. **P. 15**

Questa crisi è
una opportunità

Filippo Taddei

L'uscita della Gran Bretagna dalla Unione Europea segna un giorno di crisi per il progetto europeo. È un giorno triste per noi e per i nostri figli ma non è un funerale. Non è quindi lo sconforto che dovrebbe prevalere in queste ore, quanto piuttosto l'insoddisfazione. L'insoddisfazione per l'incapacità della politica britannica di convincere il proprio popolo di quanto poco senso abbia una Gran Bretagna che si estranea dai più grandi e ambizioso progetto democratico di pace e prosperità del mondo: l'Unione Europea.

Che le crisi siano opportunità è ormai il luogo comune per politica e di provincia e cultori dell'etimologia. La realtà è che le crisi sono un'occasione per rompere l'inerzia del processo politico e superare la pigrizia di classi dirigenti stanche e incapaci. Siccome si tratta di un'occasione e non di una certezza, è facile comprendere lo scetticismo di molti tra noi. Quello scetticismo è lo stesso che ha portato da sconfiggere in tutte le forze dei rinviati.

Non dobbiamo però commentare l'errore di criticare i risultati del referendum su Brexit, specie quando si sono messo a votare molto più persone della norma (72%). Il invece nostro dovere comprendere quel risultato offrendo risposte alle domande poste da quel voto.

Segue a pag 15

I saggi maestri Jedi dietro la comunicazione del Pci. Pietro Folena presenta il libro di Graziella Falconi **P. 21** the markets, with indexes down in all the financial centres of Europe, coupled with a political comment about 'secessionist winds', including an interview with David Martin, the leader of the Scottish Labour MEPs in the European Parliament, on page five. The contextualization of the economic impact of Brexit received further in-depth coverage in an interview with the French economist Jean-Paul Fitoussi: 'It's a no to austerity. If the EU does not change, soon other Brexits' (De Giovannangeli, *L'Unità*, 25 June 2016). In another economics-related article in *L'Unità*, there was also a mention of the worst collapse in the value of sterling since Black Wednesday in 1992. This kind of economic contextualization is typical of the left-wing press in Italy.

'Brexit' and Immigration

Immigration was the dominant theme of the Leave campaign in Britain and the openly xenophobic campaign of the conservative press, both tabloids and broadsheets, was the target of many critical articles in the centre-left and left-wing press in Italy in the run-up to the referendum. With the results in, and the victory of the Brexit vote confirmed, discussion in the press changed to the theme of the status of immigrants in the UK and, conversely, many articles also mentioned the status of UK nationals in the EU and in Italy. Significantly, I saw more articles on the implications for UK nationals post-referendum in the Italian press than in the British press (from a sample of all the British and Italian papers on 25 June 2016, two days after the referendum). On this day *La Stampa*, besides carrying more than one article with apocalyptic titles and subtitles ('Brexit, in 24 hours the world has changed'; 'Brexit, now facing the risk of a shock' [Molinari, *La Stampa*, 24 June 2016]), ran articles about immigrants' fear of having to leave London (the metropolitan-centred view of immigration is obvious here as if all immigrants resided in London) and conversely UK citizens having to leave the EU, and topics relating to pensions and work and visa status for both groups: 'Many foreigners fear having to leave London and many British people having to leave the EU' (Anon, *La Stampa*, 24 June 2016b).

A large part of the coverage in the press, but also a theme within the talk show and broadcast news analysed below, concentrated on the effects of Brexit on Italian immigrants in the UK. The Italian Iniziative e studi sulla multietnicità (ISMU Foundation) has traced migration flows into Italy over the last two decades, its most recent report showing that the immigrant population has grown from 750,000 to 5 million, meaning that Italy has gone from being an emigration to an immigration country (Cesareo 2014). Despite this, there still remains a substantial population drain, especially among the younger generation. A report from the Migrantes Foundation for 2015 tells us that there is still a constant trickle, if not a flow as in previous emigration waves (Italy, at least right up to the late 1960s, was still exporting manual labour migrants to mainly European countries, principally Belgium, Germany and France): 107,000 Italians, with the largest proportion in the 18–34 year range, many of them professionals, have left the country for European destinations, the highest number going to Germany, followed by the UK, Switzerland and France (Huffington Post 2016). Another important element of this report is a change in the provenance of the Italian emigrants: although the majority still originate from the South of Italy, increasingly there are also substantial numbers from the industrialized North.

Il Giornale, which, as mentioned in the study above, was predominantly pro-Brexit, paradoxically relayed a news item carried on social media about an Italian waiter being told to go home and give up his job to a British person: 'Now, Italian, you can go home so that a British person can take your place' (Nenzi, *Il Giornale*, 24 June 2016). He was emphatically described as the 'first victim of Brexit' (24 June 2016). Very little is verifiable about this story, which was taken from a Facebook site. This is one of the few examples which follow a more 'tabloid' logic in reporting the consequences of Brexit on Italian immigrants. *La Repubblica*, in a more serious discussion in its Palermo edition, also covered the immigration question, specifically in relation to Sicily, alluding to 'Those twenty thousand Sicilians "prisoners" of Brexit' who, the article argues, 'feel somewhat disoriented' as to what the future holds (Giorgianni, *La Repubblica*, 25 June 2016).

POPULISM, ANTI-POLITICS' AND THE BREXIT VOTER

The left-wing press concentrated many articles on the reasons why Brexit won in the Labour heartlands. The three left-leaning newspapers, *La Repubblica*, *Il Manifesto* and *L'Unità*, dedicated a number of articles to a more serious analysis of the reasons for the working-class vote for Brexit. The themes ranged across the rise of the right, populist politics and the economic consequences of neoliberal ideology. These were also linked to a shared trajectory in Italy where the working-class vote has partially moved away from left-wing parties towards populist organizations already discussed above such as the Northern League and M5S.

Il Manifesto published articles in translation by various English commentators. One by Karel Williams, 'Why the working class has voted leave' (1 July 2016), delves in-depth into the socio-economic reasons for the working-class vote for Brexit; Williams insists on the paradoxical case of the Brexit slogan of taking back control, when in reality working-class people have already lost control of their lives. This kind of in-depth class analysis is rarely available in the press in the UK; granted, *Il Manifesto* is not a large circulation newspaper but it is not minuscule either at nearly 40,000 copies (by way of comparison, such a circulation is four times larger than the British Communist Party paper, the *Morning Star*). Many other articles in *Il Manifesto* were serious pieces of journalism, where connections were made between populist politics and the vote for Brexit. In particular, it gave a great deal of space to the different positions within the different countries of the UK. Two examples, one before the referendum and one after, underline this: 'Belfast for Remain, nearly' (Terrinoi, *Il Manifesto*, 21 June 2016); 'Brexit divides the UK' (Clausi, *Il Manifesto*, 26 June 2016). The second article included an in-depth discussion about the meeting that took place between Theresa May and the leaders of Wales, Northern Ireland and Scotland, especially about their joint opposition to a hard Brexit.

This discussion was also taken up in articles about the death of the MP Jo Cox, which again received extensive coverage in the Italian press as well as on television. In the article 'Where are you going, England?' (Beasdale, *Il Manifesto*, 25 June 2016), consideration was given to the rise of extreme right-wing ideologies and how they are appropriated by disturbed individuals. However, as I have seen in other such coverage, the Italian press tends to favour political explanations over psychological ones (Cere et al. 2016).

In a similar vein, many articles in *L'Unità* discussed the new 'anti-politics' of populism, concentrating particularly on its grass-roots support in Italy with a rather extravagant title on 25 June, 'Our home-grown euro jackals led by Grillo's somersaults', although the article itself offers a serious analysis of the impossibility under present Italian constitutional rules of calling a referendum of the kind called in the UK. M5S was discussed, along with its many contradictory messages about staying in or leaving Europe, as well as the Lega Nord and yet another new right-wing formation, Polo Sovranista (Pro-sovereignty Bloc), which incorporates La Destra (The Right) and Azione Nazionale (all remnants of fascist parties), which are openly anti-European. *La Repubblica* and *Il Fatto Quotidiano* also published a number of articles before and after Brexit about the populist trajectory of contemporary politics, especially in relation to home-grown movements like the Northern League and M5S. (*Il Fatto Quotidiano* is a relatively new left-leaning daily established in 2009, whose current editor, Marco Travaglio, has written extensively on corruption scandals in Italy, especially in relation to Berlusconi.)

PORTA A PORTA POLITICAL TALK SHOW: THE 'ENGLISH' MYTH EXTENDED

On 24 June, all television news broadcasts on the Rai (Radiotelevisione italiana) public-service channels had as their first item the results of the Brexit referendum. Similarly, the commercial channels (Berlusconi's three channels and LA7) had extensive news coverage of the Brexit result and its implications. In terms of 'election specials', Rai1 offered *Porta a Porta* (Door to Door), a weekly fixture in its schedule, on the night of the referendum (I will discuss this in more detail below), while Rai3 broadcast a *TG 3 speciale Brexit* on the following night (24 June 2016). Also, on the 24 June, the independent commercial channel LA7 dedicated a special programme to coverage of the results of the referendum. There is no space in this chapter to discuss all these 'specials' in detail, but they were very much in line with the rest of the press in Italy, favouring the Remain argument. The third channel of the Italian public-service broadcaster, Rai3, which produces the TG 3 newscasts, has a left-leaning political allegiance, unlike Rai1.

Nearly 2 million Italian viewers watched the political talk show *Porta a Porta* on the evening of the UK's EU referendum with the title *La lunga notte di Brexit* (The long night of Brexit). This programme is a long-standing feature of Rai1's schedule, led by its equally long-standing conservative host Bruno Vespa. It was an extended programme that, as the title suggests, broadcast well into the night, lasting over three hours and ending just before the final result, which proved wrong the ongoing evening predictions of a victory for the Remain vote (blown up in percentages as part of the visual background to the show). One of the main characteristics of the programme was its usually long list of guests consisting of politicians and various social actors from across the political spectrum. On this occasion, guests also came from the economic and media worlds.

I have chosen to discuss *Porta a Porta* here as it runs 'against the grain' of Italian coverage of the UK's EU referendum and is a perfect illustration of 'performing talk' (Haarman 1999: 1), a mix of politics and entertainment, and the nearest thing to 'tabloidization' of politics in Italy. The other reason for looking at this political talk show in particular is that it typifies a peculiarly Italian cultural conception of the UK, based on the myth that the UK (read England) is a superior country (and friendly to Italy). Micossi and Perissich (2016) have recently argued that Italy has always been a supporter of UK membership of the European project (unlike the French). They also added that this support is motivated by two factors: first, 'a long tradition of friendship that, with the exception of the Second World War, goes back to the UK's support for the *Risorgimento*'; and second, somewhat more instrumentally, 'that Italy hoped that the UK could provide a welcome balance to the dominance of the Franco-German partnership' (2016: 2). Needless to say, successive British governments have not paid much attention to Italy's sympathy and support: 'Despite several attempts on the Italian side, this strategy has always led to disappointment; Britain, despite some polite noises, never really took any notice' (ibid.: 2).

This show is very distant from the journalistic culture which produced the Brexit coverage discussed above in the press; nonetheless, sections of the show followed some of the same themes: for example, on the topic of immigration, the economic impact, the death of the MP Jo Cox, the 'reluctant' European partner, and somewhat surprisingly, a heated discussion about the internal conflict within the Conservative Party. The treatment, however, was very different, partly due to the nature of the interaction between political guests from opposing parties (ranging from members of the leading party in the present Coalition Government [Partito Democratico] to a number of representatives from the opposition), as well as leading figures from the world of business, finance and academia. Also different was the organisation of disagreements, or rather the lack of it: the disregard of turn taking and 'extended disagreement sequences' (Diani 1999: 149) which often strayed from the 2016 EU referendum itself and into the ongoing problems of Italian governance (with a particularly excruciating sycophantic comment about the health of Berlusconi by a panel member from his party, Renato Brunetta, with no action by the host to stop it).

The myth-making exercise which circulates in Italian culture about the UK and England in particular alluded to above (in Italy as elsewhere, these two terms often stand as one and the same, without distinction, much to the chagrin of Scotland, Wales and Northern Ireland) was interspersed with sections of talk and external report items: for example, one of the reporters was stationed in an East London pizzeria. These various light 'breaks' incorporated performances by a pipe band in tartan uniforms (it was in actual fact a Roman pipe band); a lookalike Beatles band (whose music was rather good even if the wigs weren't) followed by the 'Beatles story', a visual item 'studded' with archival material from the 1960s; a dubious account of the role of Shakespeare in British culture and the celebration of the fourth centenary of his death falling precisely in the year of the referendum, albeit with a humorous comment about the indecisiveness of one the famous lines in *Hamlet*: 'to be or not to be […] in Europe'. It all came across as rather stereotypical and incongruous and with a slightly self-demeaning and nostalgic note of Italy 'losing' this special, original and superior friend as well as a partner member of the EU. *Porta a Porta* fits rather neatly into the categories that Dahlgren introduced as 'Newer [TV] formats' and especially the third category, that of 'infotainment' (1995: 54–55); ultimately it fell short of communicating an informed message about the political and economic implications of Brexit for the UK, Europe or Italy.

CONCLUSION

The Italian title of this chapter 'Little England Beats Great Britain' (Severgnini, *Il Corriere della Sera*, 24 June 2016) is a reference to the way people of the different nations within the UK voted, but also, less openly, it is suggestive of some 'inward-looking' stances evident in parts of England and Wales (England and Wales voted to leave the EU, whereas Scotland and Northern Ireland voted to remain). It was penned by *Il Corriere della Sera*'s London correspondent, Beppe Severgnini, inside the Reform Club, (named after the Great Reform Act of 1832 which modified the electoral system to grant the vote to small landowners, tenant farmers, shopkeepers and all male property owners, while still of course excluding working men [women were to wait far longer for the vote]) where he was based along with other foreign correspondents on the ground. The article, unequivocally pro-Remain, was couched in a discussion about an institution (the Club) and its building, which purports to represent the best of Britain: democracy, progressive liberal values and tolerance. Counter to that was what Severgnini described as the *perfida* (perfidious, perhaps better translated as vicious) campaign of the Leave side about immigrants. He went on to argue that the UK is no longer a superpower, but rather a middle-sized power that knows how to do some things well, but clearly not others, such as calling this referendum: a very different tone to the one described above in the talk show.

Alongside the lesson in history and architecture about the Reform Club, which did not appear directly relevant, the overall message was that the UK was not so much leaving, as 'running away [...] slamming the door behind it' (Severgnini, *Il Corriere della Sera*, 24 June 2016). A similar title, 'La Piccola Inghilterra' (Little England), also appeared on the front page of *L'Unità* a couple of days later on 26 June 2016, and in the following article references were made to the isolationism and xenophobic tendencies of Little England (Boldrini, *l'Unità*, 26 June 2016).

Two days after the UK's EU referendum an opinion poll asked Italians whether they still trusted the EU and the figure was below 40% compared to the earlier one in 2010 of 55%. Nonetheless, in a poll which asked the more specific question of whether to stay in or withdraw from the EU, the results were somewhat different: 53% were in favour of staying in and 39% wanted to leave, the rest being don't knows. The results perhaps reflected the Machiavellian character of the opinion poll: the 55% total was reached with two qualifications to the question: one, which stated that is better to stay in as Italy is weaker in comparison to the UK (24%); and two, it is more helpful to stay in for Italy (29%) (Risso, *L'Unità*, 26 June 2016). The majority of the press coverage seems not to reflect the first figure above of 40% in its predominant support for Remain, perhaps underlining the fact that the press is only read by a small section of the population. Overall the coverage was serious, although somewhat apocalyptic in tone. On the other hand, the political talk show resorted to a form of political and cultural populism, which left unclear many issues regarding how and why the British people voted against what many see as their own interests.

Bibliography

Academic Sources

Baldini, G. 2016a. *Ancora in Europa?* Bologna: Il Mulino.

Baldini, G. 2016b. *La Gran Bretagna dopo la Brexit.* Bologna: Il Mulino.

Baldini, G., and A. Cento Bull. 2009. *Italian Politics.* New York: Berghahn Books.

Barbati, J. 2014. Italy Turns from One of the Most Pro-Eu Countries, to the Most Eurosceptic. *Open Democracy,* February 21.

Caracciolo, L. 2016. Saluti dall'isola dei cinque occhi, Editoriale. *Limes, Rivista Italiana di geopolitica.* No. 6.

Cere, R. 2001. *European and National Identities in Britain and Italy: Maastricht on Television.* Lampeter: Edwin Mellen Press.

Cere, R., Y. Jewkes, and T. Ugelvik. 2016. Media and Crime: A Comparative Analysis of Crime News in the UK, Norway and Italy. In *Routledge Handbook of European Criminology.* London: Routledge.

Dahlgren, P. 1995. *Television and the Public Sphere: Citizenship, Democracy and the Media.* London: Sage.

Diani, G. 1999. The Management of Disagreement Between Interviewees in Italian TV Multi-Interviewee Interview Shows. In *Talk About Shows. La parola e lo spettacolo,* ed. L. Haarman. Bologna: CLUEB.

European Journalism Observatory. 2017. http://www.digitalpr.mobi/digital-in-2017-tutti-i-numeri-del-digitale-in-italia/ (Accessed 22 February 2017).

Federazione Italiana Editori Giornali. 2017. http://www.fieg.it/ (Accessed 13 March 2017).

Ginsborg, P. (ed.). 1994. *Stato dell'Italia. Il bilancio politico, economico, sociale e culturale di un paese che cambia.* Milano: Il Saggiatore.

Ginsborg, P. 2015. *L'Italia del tempo presente.* Torino: Einaudi.

Haarman, L. (ed.). 1999. *Talk About Shows. La parola e lo spettacolo.* Bologna: CLUEB.

Huffington Post. 2016. http://www.huffingtonpost.it/2016/10/06/rapporto-migrantes-emigrati_n_12370826.html (Accessed 15 March 2017).

Inglehart R. F., and P. Norris. 2016. Trump, Brexit, and the Rise of Populism: Economic Have-Nots and Cultural Backlash. Faculty Research Working Paper Series, RWP16–026, Harvard Kennedy School.

Limes, Rivista Italiana di Geopolitica. 2016. *Brexit e il patto delle Anglospie.* No. 6.

McGuigan, J. 1992. *Cultural Populism.* London: Routledge.

Micossi, S., and Perissich, R. 2016. The Brexit Negotiations: An Italian Perspective. *CEPS Policy Paper* (Centre for European Policy Studies), 25 October 2016, Brussels.

Moffit, B. 2016. *The Global Rise of Populism. Performance, Political Style, and Representation*. Redwood: Stanford University Press.

Murialdi, P. 2003. *La stampa Italiana dalla Liberazione alla crisi di fine secolo*. Bari: Laterza.

Pellizzetti, P. 2017. *Italia invertebrata. Personaggi e argomenti della decadenza del dibattito pubblico*. Milano: Mimesis.

Ruzza, C., and L. Balbo. 2013. Italian Populism and the Trajectories of Two Leaders: Silvio Berlusconi and Umberto Bossi. In *Right-Wing Populism in Europe: Politics and Discourse*, ed. R. Wodak, B. Mral, and M. KhosraviNik. London: Bloomsbury.

Soldani, S., and Turi, G. 1993. *Fare gli Italiani*. Two Volumes, Bologna: Il Mulino.

Soluzione Group. 2017. http://www.digitalpr.mobi/digital-in-2017-tutti-i-numeri-del-digitale-in-italia/ (Accessed 22 February 2017).

Sorrentino, C. 1995. *I percorsi della notizia. La stampa quotidiana italiana tra politica e mercato*. Bologna: Baskerville.

Tronconi, F. 2016. *Beppe Grillo's Five Star Movement: Organisation, Communication and Ideology*. London: Routledge.

Wodak, R., B. Mral, and M. KhosraviNik (eds.). 2013. *Right-Wing Populism in Europe: Politics and Discourse*. London: Bloomsbury.

NEWSPAPER SOURCES

Anon. 2016a. Brexit, Emilia, All the Fears Regarding Exports. *La Repubblica*, June 26, p. v.

Anon. 2016b. Visas, Work, Pensions: The Practical Consequences for British and Italian People After Brexit, June 24. http://www.lastampa.it/ (Accessed 25 June 2016).

Beasdale, John. 2016. Where Are You Going, England? June 25. https://ilmanifesto.it/ (Accessed 25 June 2016).

Boldrini, Maurizio. 2016. The Spirit of "Little Britain" Has Won. *L'unità*, June 26, p. 7.

Clausi, Leonardo. 2016. Brexit Divides the United Kingdom. https://ilmanifesto.it/ (Accessed 26 October 2016).

De Giovannangeli, Umberto. 2016. It's a No to Austerity. If the EU Does Not Change, Soon Other Brexits. *L'Unità*, June 25, p. 4.

Editorial. 2016a. The UK Votes for Brexit. Cameron Resign. Stock Exchanges Slump, June 24. http://www.ilgiornale.it/ (Accessed 24 June 2016).

Editorial. 2016b. Domino Effect, Europe is Done for. The 32 Bombs That Will Wipe It Out, June 24. http://www.liberoquotidiano.it/ (Accessed, 24 June 2016).

Giorgianni, Cesare. 2016. Those Twenty Thousand Sicilians "Prisoners" of Brexit. *La Repubblica*, June 25, p. ii.

Molinari, Maurizio. 2016. Brexit, in 24 hours the World Has Changed; Brexit, Now Facing the Risk of a Shock, June 24. http://www.lastampa.it/ (Accessed 2 June 2016).

Nenzi, Rachele. 2016. Brexit, Shocking Story from an Italian: Go Home So that a British Person Can Take Your Place, June 24. http://www.ilgiornale.it/ (Accessed 25 June 2016).

Risso, Enzo. 2016. We Either Renew Europe or Europe Will Die. *L'Unità*, June 26, p. 6.

Severgnini, Beppe. 2016. Little England Beats Great Britain, June 24. http://www.corriere.it/ (Accessed 25 June 2016).

Terrinoi, Enrico. 2016. Belfast for Remain, Nearly, June 21. https://ilmanifesto.it/ (Accessed 22 June 2016).

Williams, Karel. 2016. Why the Working Class has Voted Leave, July 1. https://ilmanifesto.it/ (Accessed 1 July 2016).

CHAPTER 15

EU Referendum 2016 in the Greek Press

Giorgos Katsambekis and George Souvlis

INTRODUCTION

This chapter addresses the media coverage of the so-called 'Brexit' (Britain's exit from the EU via a 2016 vote) referendum in the Greek press. More specifically, we look into the websites of four major newspapers with national circulations that are located at different points of the political spectrum: *Dimocratia* (right-wing, radical right), *Kathimerini* (conservative/centre-right), *To Vima* (progressive/centre-left) and *Efimerida ton Syntakton* (left-wing/radical left). Our main objective is to bring out the varying representations and constructions in Greece of the 2016 EU referendum in the United Kingdom (UK), in a bid to highlight their different meanings of popular sovereignty and democratic legitimacy.

Our methodology draws inspiration from the tradition of the 'Essex-school' of discourse analysis, which focuses on the social production of meaning, emphasizing the discursive construction of antagonisms

G. Katsambekis (✉)
Loughborough University, Loughborough, UK
e-mail: G.Katsambekis@lboro.ac.uk

G. Souvlis
European University Institute, Florence, Italy
e-mail: george.souvlis@eui.eu

© The Author(s) 2018
A. Ridge-Newman et al. (eds.), *Reporting the Road to Brexit*,
https://doi.org/10.1007/978-3-319-73682-2_15

257

and frontiers as well as collective identities (see Howarth et al. 2000; Howarth 2000). Covering the period of twenty days before and ten days after the referendum day, we present some preliminary findings and conclusions based on an analysis of the articles that were directly related to the 2016 EU referendum and the Brexit outcome. More particularly, we were interested in tracing central references (or nodal signifiers), key polarities and ideological frames that were privileged in each case. Through this investigation, we expected to find different constructions of the referendum as a tool for decision making and/or consultation; as well as varying conceptions of popular sovereignty and of the notion of 'the people' and hence democratic legitimacy itself. Lastly, we expected to find associations between the significance attributed to the UK's EU referendum and the stance that each newspaper adopted during the Greek referendum in 2015, but also vis-à-vis political antagonisms that are found specifically in the Greek context.

Recalling the Greek Referendum

Let us briefly recall what had happened in the Greek referendum of 5 July 2015. The result delivered a clear win to the 'No Camp' (61.3% vs 38.7%) in rejecting the bailout conditions offered to Greece by its European partners in yet another adjustment programme. The result of the vote demonstrated a deep political, age and class polarization that has been a conspicuous characteristic of electoral contests in the austerity era. In addition to the political and party dimension of the polarization, sharp polarization was also evident between age groups, which had existed previously but not to that extent. Indeed, the anti-austerity stance of young people had already been recorded in the 2012 election and was maintained in the European and national elections of 2014–2015. According to Yannis Mavris, the generation gap in voting behaviour reached new heights in the Greek referendum due to the clear-cut 'yes' or 'no' choice for voters. In the 18–24 age group, 85% voted 'No' and in the next highest age group (25–34), 72%. The vast majority of young people, whose lives are seriously affected by austerity, overwhelmingly opposed the continuation of this mixture of policies. This pattern of social polarization of voting confirms a Eurosceptic social divide, as well as the class nature of the 'No' vote, which has been observed historically in similar referendums on EU issues (Mavris 2016). Hence, we find it particularly interesting to reflect on the ways in which the connection between the Greek and British referendums was established, as well as the underlying objectives behind it. In other words, we are interested in enquiring into how the emphases and constructions which were put on the debate around Brexit within the Greek press could also illuminate Greece's own responses to issues arising from its ambivalent and often turbulent relationship with the EU during the years of crisis and austerity and in particular during its own referendum. (For a similar approach on the occasion of Scotland's 2014 independence referendum, see Blain et al. 2016.)

Proliferating Referendums in Crisis-Hit Europe

Studying the various aspects of referendums in Europe means that we are immediately involved in the long debate around the 'democratic deficit' and indeed the ongoing crisis of representation (and orientation) that the EU has been facing in recent decades (Habermas 2013; Mair 2013). After all, these referendums would not acquire such prominence in public debates throughout the Continent if they were not directly connected with crucial stakes regarding the prospects, but also the very existence, of the EU, as well as with significant issues regarding the quality of representation, participation and citizen engagement in most European societies. Such issues are related to the responsiveness of national and European institutions, and more crucially to the ways in which people see themselves as members/citizens of the national and European community. The last couple of years has offered plenty of occasions for such reflection, with a significant number of referendums taking place in EU countries: Greeks went to the polls in July 2015 as Greece was standing on the verge of bankruptcy and decided to reject yet another bailout programme; the British decided to leave the EU in June 2016; the Hungarians rejected EU migrant quotas in October 2016 with a stunning 98.3% (although turnout was very low, rendering the referendum invalid); and the Italians rejected the Constitutional reforms proposed by the Government of Matteo Renzi in December 2016.

Although these referendums seem connected to rather context-specific developments within each country, after a closer look, one might trace common characteristics and shared stakes. Most importantly, those stakes seem to be closely related to what is perceived as 'mainstream' politics in today's Europe; at least, as represented by the European elites and by the public discourse of the EU's top officials. Even in the case of Italy, where the referendum focused on a domestic issue, the campaign soon centred around issues that had to do with the eurozone, the EU and the country's place within it. In other words, the 'official' EU, during the years of crisis and austerity, seems to have been on the losing side whenever the citizens of a given member state are called to the polls; whenever the people are given the chance to directly get involved in decision making. Indeed, this is not the first time that the European elites have been confronted with 'unruly' popular masses who tend to vote against their plans. We can recall, for example, what happened with the referendums on the Maastricht Treaty in 1992 and 1993 in Denmark as well as for the European Constitution and the Lisbon Treaty in France, the Netherlands and also Ireland in 2005 and 2008 (Hooghe and Marks 2006; de Vreese 2007; Binzer et al. 2010; FitzGibbon 2010). We saw in these cases that whenever a national citizenry voted against a proposal/treaty that came from the top of the EU, the latter, in collaboration with national political elites, would seek ways to undo or bypass that vote (see also Katsambekis 2017: 207).

In this sense, it is not an exaggeration to say that political elites across Europe are increasingly being confronted with social uprisings and popular mandates that they do not like and probably do not understand: Greeks risking their place in the eurozone, defying the dogma of perpetual austerity; Italians risking a governmental crisis and the rise of an unpredictable 'populist' in Beppe Grillo; the British choosing their own solitary way out of the EU, again falling victim to what are widely presented as 'populists' and 'opportunists'; and the Hungarians being mesmerized by the xenophobic authoritarianism of a 'talented demagogue' in Viktor Orbán.

To be sure, this is not just a 'European story,' since the latest and probably most important such unexpected electoral outcome came from the other side of the Atlantic, with the election of Donald Trump as the 45th President of the United States in November 2016. In this context, the phenomenon of what we can call 'unruly electorates' is not something peculiar to Europe. It is a phenomenon closely related to the state of Western democracies today in general (see Cook et al. 2016); with the way that contemporary democratic and representational systems function; with the ways in which citizens experience politics and express aspirations and frustrations; and with the particular meaning and importance that modern societies attribute to the notion of popular sovereignty and democracy itself.

In this predicament, and as socio-political stakes rise and 'unexpected' electoral outcomes seem to pave the way towards a more fragmented world of newfound (national) sovereignties and isolationisms (from Trump to Marine Le Pen, and from Brexit to Viktor Orbán), the role of social scientists regarding critical interpretation, scientific reflection and radical imagination becomes crucial. Indeed, we need to thoroughly rethink the condition of democracy in today's Europe and the broader 'West'; we need to reflect on the quality and the limits of representation, on the meaning of popular sovereignty and the prospects of popular engagement and participation in times of crisis.

Within this context, the present chapter offers a very modest contribution. It critically analyses the ways in which the 2016 EU referendum was presented, represented and indeed constructed by the press in Greece. Our guiding hypothesis is that the EU referendum in the UK gave a chance to the Greek press not just to report on the relevant developments within another European country, but also to actively advance different visions of the democratic society, different meanings of democratic procedure and the meaning of popular sovereignty, and different understandings of the European project. Before moving on with our analysis, we need to stress that the Greek public sphere was already sharply polarized due to the new ideological divides and socio-political cleavages that were brought about by the 2008 financial crisis (Katsambekis 2016). In addition, Greek society and its political system had been further polarized between those supporting the bailout programmes and austerity policies and those opposing them since Greece's first bailout programme in 2010. This divide was simplified as a position in favour of or against the so-called 'memoranda'.

Moreover, the fact that Greece had already held its own referendum in July 2015, which brought it to the verge of breaking with the eurozone and the EU itself, made the related discussion in print and electronic media even more contentious and intense. In this sense, every commentary and analysis on the British case could easily be translated into a statement on the rights and wrongs of the Greek referendum, a chance to re-engage with the main dividing lines that pervade the Greek public sphere within the context of the ongoing crisis: austerity vs anti-austerity, pro-memorandum vs anti-memorandum, Europeanism vs Euroscepticism, populism vs anti-populism, and so on (Stavrakakis 2013; Katsambekis 2014; Kioupkiolis 2014; Mylonas 2014; Nikisianis et al. 2016).

GREECE'S PUBLIC SPHERE IN THE YEARS OF CRISIS AND AUSTERITY

Greece is not an 'average' European country. Admittedly, it has been at the forefront of the crisis that hit Europe after 2009, and it has suffered one of the most severe recessions historically witnessed in times of peace. Between 2008 and 2015 the country's gross domestic product contracted by approximately 26%, unemployment soared to 27% (with youth unemployment nearing 50%), salaries and pensions were brutally cut, social welfare deteriorated, and inequalities were further widened. After more than a decade of steady growth, Greece was faced with conditions resembling a total socio-economic collapse, something that rather naturally affected the political system itself, causing a deep crisis of legitimation, with traditional forces collapsing and new 'players' coming to the fore. Greek society and its political system were polarized between those supporting the bailout programmes and austerity policies and those opposing them. The traditional parties, New Democracy (ND) and Panhellenic Socialist Movement (PASOK), had to collaborate in government after the autumn of 2011, in order to move on with the implementation of the bailout programmes, first in coalition with the extreme-right and populist party Popular Orthodox Rally (LAOS) and then with the moderate and social-democratic party Democratic Left (DIMAR). Against the traditional forces, Coalition of the Radical Left (SYRIZA), a coalition of radical left parties and groups, soon rose to prominence with the promise of ending austerity and cancelling the memoranda. The rest of the story is more or less known. SYRIZA collaborated in government with the anti-austerity right-wing party Independent Greeks (ANEL), but the government they formed soon had to agree to a new memorandum, rendering the memorandum/anti-memorandum divide rather obsolete. Now the traditional parties (ND and PASOK, along with a new liberal-centrist party, POTAMI), in opposition, would vehemently fight the SYRIZA-led government as the incarnation of irrational populism, clientelism and corruption. Despite the fact that since 2015 SYRIZA has significantly moderated it discourse and policies, moving closer to social-democracy, the political scene in Greece remains sharply antagonistic and polarized, something which is also reflected in the print and online media (see, for example, the 'pro-populist'/'anti-populist' divide in the discourse of Greek newspapers as it has been thoroughly analysed in Nikisianis et al. 2016).

Scope, Theory and Method

To be sure, referendums are rather 'extraordinary' tools within the institutional arsenal of liberal democracies (see Mendelsohn and Parkin 2001). They introduce a direct-democratic process into the workings of systems defined by representation and mediation; a process whereby the 'sovereignty of the parliament' seems to be challenged by the directly expressed will and sovereignty of 'the people'. Referendums thus designate a paradoxical moment, in the sense that 'the people' might impose on their delegates a mandate that exceeds or even contradicts the one on which they were initially elected. As such, they highlight the tensions that pervade the ambiguous relation between representatives and the represented, elites and the people, direct engagement and delegation (see Pitkin 2004; Tormey 2015). Referendums are also distinctive in that they temporarily impose on society a binary logic ('yes or no'), dividing citizens around a key question with no more than two possible answers. Lastly, referendums can be seen as defining a confined and relatively autonomous space with its own peculiarities, as they disrupt 'politics as usual', imposing their stakes on all other issues present in the public sphere. Such tensions, polarities and disruptions inevitably manifest in the debates that unfold in the respective public spheres.

Following this general understanding of the referendum process, in what follows we aim to highlight and critically assess the narratives, interpretive schemas and frames that are present in the articles of four of the most popular newspapers in Greece. We will do so by adopting a discursive perspective, drawing on the basic principles of discourse analysis. 'Essex School' discourse analysis, in particular, offers an already tested toolkit for understanding the operation of public discourses and clarifying their role in shaping identities and motivating political action by ascribing meaning to subjects/objects, while also drawing lines of difference and division (Howarth and Stavrakakis 2000). Discourse, in other words, is understood as a set of meaningful practices that shape individual and collective identities, construct socio-political antagonisms and motivate certain kinds of actions. In this context, we treat the analyses and commentary pieces of newspapers as samples of public discourse that play a crucial role in shaping the attitudes, stances and identities of their subjects/readers. It is thus crucial to clarify the terms along which such discursive practices articulate their message and hegemonic appeal:

What signifiers appear to be privileged or acquire a nodal position? What are the key antagonisms and polarities that shape each discourse? What coherent narratives seem to take shape in each case?

Indeed, we are not interested in commenting on the quality of reporting in the newspapers and articles under examination: whether this or that reporter did a good job in terms of journalism ethics, communicating to the public the necessary information in a well-documented, unbiased and 'neutral' way. Our aim is rather to show how the UK referendum was represented and *actively* constructed through different interpretive and ideologico-political frameworks; how it was 'used' in order to articulate meaningful arguments that touched upon a series of issues, from contemporary Greek politics and the management of the crisis by the Greek government(s), to fundamental issues regarding popular sovereignty, representation, democratic institutions and the future of the EU.

In terms of primary material, we have collected and analysed all the accessible articles referring to 'Brexit' that were published twenty days before and ten days after referendum day on the official websites of four leading Greek newspapers with national circulations (see Table 15.1 for circulation data).

In a bid to capture the ideologico-political diversity of the Greek press, we chose four newspapers that cover the whole political spectrum, starting from the right and radical right, moving to the centre-right and centre-left, and finally reaching the left and radical-left. Those newspapers are: (1) *Dimocratia* (Δημοκρατία/Democracy); (2) *I Kathimerini* (Η Καθημερινή/*The Daily*); (3) *To Vima* (Το Βήμα/*The Tribune*); and (4) *Efimerida ton Syntakton* (Εφημερίδα των Συντακτών/The Editors'

Table 15.1   Circulation data/website readership for June 2016. *Source* Data from europenet.gr, argoscom.gr and direct contact with newspapers

Newspaper	Website	Circulation of print edition	Website readership/ unique users
Dimocratia	www.dimokratianews.gr	297,770	700,000 (approx.)
Kathimerini	www.kathimerini.gr	612,650	1,656,703
Vima	www.tovima.gr	224,870	n/a
Efimerida ton Syntakton	www.efsyn.gr	227,880	565,440

Newspaper). All of them are daily newspapers, except *Vima* which is weekly, but renews its online content on a daily basis. We collected our material from the official websites of the newspapers, including articles that were in their print editions. Among our main criteria for choosing these newspapers were to cover the most significant ideologico-political orientations, and also the fact that their material is free to read (other newspapers with national circulations retain a significant portion of their content for subscribers only). More specifically, we gathered a total of 870 articles from the websites of these four newspapers that were tagged under 'Brexit' (see Table 15.2 for details). Needless to say, we do not claim that this sample suffices to draw conclusions that are representative of the Greek media sphere as a whole. That is why we understand this more as a 'pilot study'.

In what follows, we present the main findings that came out of an in-depth qualitative assessment of these articles. The basic axes around which we structured our inquiry can be formulated as follows:

- Key signifiers
- Key polarities: representation and 'construction' of socio-political antagonisms
- Key solutions suggested or implied regarding democracy in the UK, the EU and Greece's predicament
- Stances vis-à-vis 'the people', popular sovereignty, majority rule, direct-democratic processes.

Three crucial additional questions that we take into account throughout our analysis can be formulated as follows: What is at stake for each newspaper? What could Brexit mean for Europe? Is the referendum a suitable tool for such decisions or not?

Table 15.2 Articles on 'Brexit' per newspaper/website

Newspaper/website	Articles on 'Brexit'
Dimocratia	65
Kathimerini	311
Vima	272
Efimerida ton Syntakton	222
TOTAL	870

EU REFERENDUM 2016 IN THE GREEK PRESS

In this section, which is divided into four subsections, we aim to reconstruct the basic elements and narratives privileged in each newspaper/website. In all cases we maintain that despite the divergences and variation, a common narrative and corresponding ideological/political positioning can be traced and critically assessed.

DIMOCRATIA: A RIGHT-WING DEFENCE OF 'BREXIT', A NATIONALIST DEFENCE OF 'THE PEOPLE'

Dimocratia was launched in 2010 and presents a peculiar yet particularly interesting case in the Greek press. Ultra-conservative, at times close to radical right views, but with a robust circulation and links (until recently) to the right-wing of ND, which is currently the main opposition party and has been the traditional force of the right/centre-right in Greece since 1974. In fact, *Dimocratia* was fairly open in its support of ND when Antonis Samaras was the party's leader (2009–2015). The newspaper adopted a vocal, right-wing, nationalist critique of the EU, interpreting Brexit as an opportunity for the UK to regain its national sovereignty against the cosmopolitan and pro-globalization forces that have dominated Europe since the 1990s. At the same time, the prevailing (rather Islamophobic) view in *Dimocratia* was that Brexit would hopefully reduce the inflows of immigrants or even push towards the implementation of deportation policies or policies of closed/hard borders, especially against Muslims, who are portrayed as undermining both the UK's and Europe's values and civilization (Kranidiotis 2016). The *nation*, is thus one of the key references (perhaps *the* central reference) in the newspaper's articles on Brexit, arguing that we need to 'return to the nations', which are the 'treasures of civilizations, the arks of memories, aspirations, collective struggles and agonies, of faith, pain, and of the very meaning of life' (*Dimocratia* 2016a).

The voters in favour of Brexit were portrayed as comprising mainly working-class strata, people who have suffered from the economic crisis and were pitted against the rich cosmopolitans of London who supported 'Bremain'. Moreover, Brexit voters were described as utterly alienated from and frustrated with Brussels. In this context, the EU's bureaucracy was castigated as an ensemble of incompetent and self-interested individuals who are completely detached from the harsh social realities of the member states, ignoring the fact that their policies are the root of suffering for societies around Europe. The British and their political personnel were described as 'great men' in contrast to Greece's Prime Minister and SYRIZA leader Alexis Tsipras, who was portrayed as a coward who betrayed the 2015 referendum decision in Greece for fear of triggering a process leading to Grexit. The British, on the contrary, were expected to move on with Brexit proudly and courageously (Charvalias 2016; Kranidiotis 2016).

There was also a strong geopolitical emphasis on the analysis of the referendum and Brexit, which was presented as a chance to undermine Germany's interests and hegemony in Europe, with Germany being described as the 'Fourth Reich', having destroyed the rest of Europe with the imposition of austerity politics (Charvalias 2016). In this sense, any political move that could seriously challenge Germany's hegemonic position was understood as being in the interest of the rest of the European peoples; in the interest of each people-as-nation. Following this line of argumentation, commentators stressed that Greece should have opted for 'Grexit' after the referendum of July 2015, in a bid to undermine Germany's position. Hence, taking into account the major geopolitical shifts that Brexit would bring forth, it was argued that Greece should align itself with Britain and the 'Anglo-Saxon world' and reduce its relations with Germany (Kefalas 2016). Interestingly, in arguing for such a position, the newspaper's editors used the Greek dictator Ioannis Metaxas as an example, saying that while Metaxas ('the Prime Minister of victory' from 1936 to 1941) was closer to Germany, he chose to align with Britain since this was the best way to serve the national interest of Greece (*Dimocratia* 2016b). The prime example in terms of geopolitics for Greece and the rest of the European states in the post-Brexit era seems to be that of Victor Orbán, one of closed borders, one that defends national identity and culture against immigrants and refugees, but also against the 'supranational construct' of the EU. The very title of a *Dimocratia* editorial during the period under scrutiny was quite revealing in itself: 'The emancipation of homelands' (*Dimocratia* 2016c).

Lastly, referendums as an institution and process were considered to be the most genuine expression of democracy, where the citizens can express themselves in an unmediated and direct way. Crucially, the notion of democracy defended by the newspaper seems inextricably linked to that of national sovereignty. In this sense, Brexit was seen as a moment of democratic renewal, as it (supposedly) reinforced national sovereignty in times of globalization and withering-away of the nation state. The EU itself was considered undemocratic because it undermines the power of nations. Not surprisingly, then, Greek politicians were urged to follow the example of the British, working towards the creation of an alliance between nations ('homelands') against today's cosmopolitan and undemocratic EU.

KATHIMERINI: AN ANTI-POPULIST CRITIQUE OF BREXIT, A TECHNOCRATIC DEFENCE OF EUROPE

Kathimerini is perhaps the most historic newspaper of the broader conservative camp in Greece. Founded in 1919, it has gradually adopted a more moderate position, embracing a centre-right orientation, (mildly) liberal on cultural issues and firmly market-oriented on economic ones. During the period of the British referendum, the newspaper dealt extensively with the institution of the referendum as such; it did so more than any other among the newspapers that we have investigated. In particular, it juxtaposed the institution, role and significance of the referendum with that of Parliament. The former was described as a tool that is utterly undemocratic, used, in the words of Margaret Thatcher, by 'dictators and demagogues' (MacShane 2016), while the latter was seen as a genuine representation of the interests of the people. Referendums, in this rationale, are used by opportunist and populist leaders, in conditions of crisis, while they are actually pursuing their own aims. The people are easily deceived by such leaders, because of their ignorance and inability to understand the political stakes and potential consequences in all their depth and complexity. In this way, referendums are not so much a tool for the expression of the people's will and sovereignty, but rather a means for opportunist and irresponsible leaders to serve their own interests and perpetuate their hold on power. As such, they pose a major threat to countries in conditions of crisis, since they undermine the much needed social and economic stability (Pagoulatos 2016).

Former British Prime Minister David Cameron was presented as a typical example of an opportunist and irresponsible leader in calling for a referendum. He did so in a bid to reinforce his own position within his party, taking a gamble without any 'real need' to open such an important issue to popular contestation. The outcome of his decision created the conditions for the rise of rather marginal figures of the far-right, like Nigel Farage, initiating a chain-reaction that has undermined the stability of the EU as a whole. These populist far-right leaders took the chance to spread 'fake news', disorientating and deceiving the British electorate (Athinakis 2016). The British thus voted in a deeply emotional and irrational way; the only ones thinking rationally being the 'Bremainers' (Mandravelis 2016).

Not surprisingly, commentators in *Kathimerini* suggested that referendums should not be conducted, since they are essentially undemocratic and easily manipulated by populist actors, leading to the 'wrong' results. Political leaders may hold referendums only if they are absolutely sure about the final result and only if this is in favour of the interests of their countries (Zoulas 2016). Politics itself seems to be understood as a field made for experts and technocrats, where everything should be rationally calculated and predetermined. The popular masses (often ignorant and uneducated, emotional and irrational) are thus better confined to their role as an electorate in national/regional elections and should not be able to directly determine the policies of a given state on issues that are too complicated for them to understand. Moreover, referendums were presented as putting in danger the global economy itself as well as the global equilibrium, giving democratic legitimacy to policies determined by the opportunism and self-interested behaviour of populist leaders (Papadimitriou 2016).

Lastly, there was a clear comparison between Tsipras and Cameron as PMs in *Kathimerini*. Both were described as incompetent leaders who had undermined and endangered the process of European integration and stability by calling for unnecessary referendums (Maglinis 2016; Zoulas 2016). The British people were compared to the Greeks, concluding that they did not learn from Greece's mistakes and were similarly deceived into voting for a catastrophic decision. Brexit thus seems devoid of any emancipatory or democratic content. Moreover, for *Kathimerini* there were clear indications that racist motives played a crucial role in shaping the people's vote, with Farage and Boris Johnson's anti-immigrant rhetoric striking a chord with a significant segment of British society (Athinakis 2016). Jeremy Corbyn was held equally responsible for not running a successful campaign in favour of Remain. In a rather grim mood, Brexit was presented as a dangerous development that is bound to empower more populist, nationalist and anti-EU politicians across Europe (like Marine Le Pen in France). The biggest danger here would be more referendums that might challenge the EU as we know it. A key polarity thus arises for the newspaper: that between moderate, Europeanist and anti-populist forces around Europe, on the one side, and extreme populists of the left and right who are posing a serious threat to Europe and liberal democracy. Indeed, *populism* is the most often mentioned danger for the EU and democracy as such, putting forth a key polarity between the forces of 'irrational populism' and those of 'liberal rationality', a view that confirms the relevant study of Zinovia Lialiouti and Giorgos Bithymitris (2013) who suggest that 'anti-populism' is one of the defining characteristics of this newspaper.

VIMA: BREXIT AND THE FEAR OF POPULISM

Vima is one of the historic newspapers of the broader progressive camp in Greece. Founded in 1922, it has, diachronically, probably been the most influential newspaper in political issues and has been closely linked to the centre and centre-left in the country's democratic history. It was published daily in print until 2011, but since then it only publishes its Sunday edition in print, but updates its online content on a daily basis. The newspaper's position seems quite similar to that of *Kathimerini* on several issues. Brexit in most of its opinion articles was regarded as putting in danger the whole project of the EU, while referendums were primarily seen as useful tools in the hands of populists and demagogues who aim to serve their own interests. Some commentators went as far as to characterize referendums as an 'epidemic that threatens to destroy the EU' (Kapsilis 2016). The popular masses and mainly the working classes were seen as prone to adopting racist and anti-immigrant attitudes that are advocated by populist and nationalist politicians who are consciously and constantly lying to the people. The vote for Brexit was thus primarily described as *a result of populism*, as an outcome that poses a serious threat to the stability of the European economy (Makris 2016); a view that coincides perfectly with that expressed in *Kathimerini*. Populism, in this context, seems to be conflated with demagoguery, with the lies that politicians are supposed to tell in their efforts to manipulate the people/citizens as they try to maintain their position in power. Tsipras was seen as the archetype of the 'populist' politician who risked Greece's place in the EU in the summer of 2015 just to keep his hold on power (Makris 2016). However, the crucial difference with the views expressed in *Kathimerini* is that for *Vima* referendums could still be useful as a process of decision making or consultation under certain circumstances. The problem diagnosed by the newspaper is that at moments of crisis and instability, they seem to serve only populist politicians, so for now they should be avoided (Exadaktylos 2016).

The newspaper insisted to the same degree and maybe even more than *Kathimerini* on the issue of 'populism' and the threat that it poses for democracy and Europe. It seems that any views or attitudes that are in any sense challenging to the structure and workings of today's EU are immediately qualified by the newspaper as 'Eurosceptic', 'populist' and surely dangerous. Hence, Tsipras was seen as the Chávez of Europe and Greece is supposed to be experiencing a political project similar to *chavismo* (Papadopoulos 2016). SYRIZA, along with Podemos in Spain, are for the newspaper the parties of the new radical/populist left that are putting the process of European integration in danger. Corbyn, accordingly, was also held responsible for Brexit, for not carrying out a more effective campaign in favour of the remain vote, organizing a rather half-hearted campaign (Exadaktylos 2016).

Lastly, *Vima* seems to reject austerity as the basic explanatory factor behind Brexit. Connecting the relevant discussion again to Greece, the main argument here was that rhetoric regarding austerity is in essence a tool to legitimize the policies of self-interested politicians, like Tsipras (Athanasopoulos 2016a, b). The remedy to populist and Eurosceptic politics then is the adoption of an outright Europeanist position that would not undermine in any way the European project, economic stability and further integration. Thus, a key polarity similar to *Kathimerini* emerged in most articles of *Vima*: that between responsible and rational management of political matters on the one side, and irresponsible irrational populism on the other (quite crucially, populists of the left and the right seem to pose an equal danger to liberal democracy).

EFIMERIDA TON SYNTAKTON (EFSYN): IN DEFENCE OF POPULAR SOVEREIGNTY, AGAINST NEOLIBERALISM

While *Dimocratia* is distinct in its outright nationalist position, and the two centrist newspapers *Kathimerini* and *Vima* express slightly different orientations of the same liberal-centrist and anti-populist position, *Efsyn* presents a less clear case in terms of positioning vis-à-vis Brexit. Established in 2012, this newspaper operates as a co-operative and comprises mainly people who used to work in *Eleftherotypia*, a historic, independent left-leaning newspaper that was first published in 1975 and was shut down in 2014. *Efsyn* today expresses views that cover the spectrum from the parliamentarian centre-left to the extra-parliamentarian radical left.

In contrast to the three newspapers examined above, *Efsyn* does not express a clear-cut position vis-à-vis Brexit. In particular, we were able to discern two broad lines of argumentation; both positioned to the left of the political spectrum, but differentiated in terms of commitment to the European project. Both lines recognized that the EU as it stands has several significant problems in terms of its structure, policies and democratic legitimacy. Those expressing rather Eurosceptic views saw Brexit as an emancipatory moment, one that could pave the way for the reinvigoration of democracy and popular sovereignty (Patelis 2016). This positioning was linked to an anti-capitalist and anti-imperialist tradition that has been diachronically strong within the broader left in Greece. The EU was thus seen as an imperialist capitalist mechanism that needs to be decisively undermined and fought. The referendum, in this perspective, opened up potentialities for emancipatory and egalitarian politics, creating opportunities for regaining democratic control of the state and economy, by taking back the power to implement social and economic policies that have been rendered unthinkable within the European constraints and limitations (Makrodimopoulos 2016; Stamatopoulos 2016).

Those adopting a more Europeanist position feared that Brexit would intensify nationalist tendencies, considering it more or less impossible for it to take on a progressive content. The main argument here was that Brexit would reinforce the dynamic of the far right within other EU countries (more crucially in France) so it is something that the progressive forces should try to avoid (Stathoulia 2016). Such views were partly similar to arguments also expressed in *Vima*. What was also stressed here was that Brexit would not pose a meaningful threat to the neoliberal status quo in any sense; it would rather reproduce it. This strand of left-wing Europeanism opposes the Eurosceptic arguments (expressed in the same newspaper) that Brexit could take on an anti-capitalist orientation. The counter-argument is that Brexit would neither undermine austerity nor re-invigorate social policies in Britain, as such policies are expected to be further pursued by the British Conservatives outside the EU constraints (Stathoulia 2016).

So in reality the British people seem to have voted for Brexit not because of the austerity imposed by the EU, but rather due to the effects of Thatcherism dating back to the 1980s. In this sense, Brexit occurs as a reply to the structural changes caused in Britain by the hegemony of neoliberalism. Hence, the popular frustrations that fuelled the vote for Brexit are rooted in the very neoliberal policies that were implemented throughout the 1980s and 1990s (Giannoulopoulos 2016). However, the right-wingers campaigning for Brexit have managed to channel and represent those frustrations within a nationalist narrative that pitted the British people against Brussels, but also (and crucially) against immigrants, Muslims and minorities (Giannoulopoulos 2016). From this interpretation it follows that the Greek and British referendums are of a different nature. In the former, the question was one that called upon the people to vote in favour of or against the European elites (who were supposedly responsible for what happened in Greece during the crisis); in the latter, the referendum was turned into a vote on those who were not British, against EU elites, against immigrants, etc. (Giannoulopoulos 2016). Crucially, it is in this line of argumentation that 'populism' made its appearance in *Efsyn* as a driving force behind Brexit. Apart from such comments, most of the articles in *Efsyn* did not insist on comparisons of Britain's EU referendum with the Greek referendum and the way Tsipras dealt with it, nor did it stress the 'danger of populism,' something which contrasts with what we have seen earlier in *Dimocratia, Vima*, and *Kathimerini*.

Lastly, and despite the differentiations already mentioned, referendums as processes and institutions were praised by most commentators, being described as significantly enriching and deepening democracy; and not undermining it. Crucially, *Efsyn* was not concerned with the 'danger of populism' as is the case with *Kathimerini* and *Vima*; there are only a very few exceptions here, like the article of Giannoulopoulos mentioned above, who seems to conflate populism with nationalism and demagoguery. For this newspaper, the divide between the popular masses and the political/economic elites is a real issue with tangible effects and not a construct of populist demagogues. Indeed, this seems to be the main explanatory factor of the very result of the referendum: an anti-establishment vote against the elites both in Britain and in Brussels. Hence, far from adopting an anti-populist position (like *Kathimerini* and *Vima*), *Efsyn* seems rather to adopt elements of a quasi-populist understanding of the referendum and the stakes for Europe, a view which seems to confirm the study of Nikos Nikisianis et al. (2016) that places *Kathimerini* and *Vima* clearly on the 'anti-populist' side of the spectrum and *Efsyn* at the so-called 'pro-populist' side.

CONCLUSION

In this chapter we have presented some of the main narratives adopted in the Greek press vis-à-vis the 2016 EU referendum. Due to space limitations, our research is of limited scope, as it does not cover the whole Greek press. Nevertheless, we examined a sample that we consider representative and that covers the most relevant ideologico-political positions. A first observation is that in all cases a rather polarizing logic seems to prevail. In the case of *Dimocratia*, polarities follow a classic nationalist schema, pitting the nations and 'homelands' against the cosmopolitan elites of Brussels, the forces of globalization and multiculturalism, as well as a hegemonic Germany. In the case of the centrist/mainstream newspapers *Kathimerini* and *Vima*, we see two slightly different versions of the populism/anti-populism divide, which has already been registered and thoroughly examined in the Greek press (Nikisianis et al. 2016; see also Stavrakakis et al. 2017). In this sense, we were able to confirm the endurance and salience of this divide during the days of the UK's EU referendum. In the case of *Efsyn*, and despite the differentiations among commentators and journalists within this newspaper, we saw a critique of neoliberalism which was expressed both in Eurosceptic and in Europeanist terms (although the official line of the newspaper is clearly one in favour of European integration, while advocating radical reforms to deepen democracy and social cohesion in Europe).

A more general conclusion here is that centrist/moderate newspapers and commentators (in *Kathimerini* and *Vima*) seem to present a rather sceptical or even elitist approach to the process of referendums (what might be called an 'anti-populist' or even 'demophobic' position), while newspapers that adopt more radical even anti-establishment positions (be they of different ideological persuasions) present a stance more in favour of the direct expression of the 'popular will' (which might also be understood as a 'populist' position); it is crucial to stress, though, that in the case of *Dimocratia* democracy and popular sovereignty are inextricably linked to the nation and national sovereignty, while in *Efsyn* democracy and popular sovereignty are envisioned in more inclusive and pluralist terms.

Brexit and the 2016 EU referendum was also a chance for the Greek press to re-engage with the result and significance of the Greek referendum of 2015. For *Dimocratia* the Greek referendum was a sign of resistance by the Greek people-as-nation against a German-dominated EU, but this was not respected by the 'spineless' administration of Tsipras. For *Kathimerini* and *Vima*, the UK and Greek referendums present cases of the same phenomenon: they were called by irresponsible and opportunist leaders and they were then hegemonized by irrational populists who channelled the people's grievances and passion towards catastrophic results. *Efsyn*, as we saw, presents a less clear-cut case. Nevertheless, it is clear that for this newspaper referendums constitute democratic processes through which the people are given a chance to voice their grievances and aspirations, and they should thus be taken seriously into account in the context of an EU that is becoming increasingly technocratic and detached from the problems and agonies of the popular strata.

References

Academic Sources

Blain, Neil, David Hutchison, and Gerry Hassan (eds.). 2016. *Scotland's Referendum and the Media. National and International Perspectives.* Edinburgh: Edinburgh University Press.

Binzer Hobolt, Sara, and Sylvain Brouard. 2010. Contesting the European Union? Why the Dutch and the French Rejected the European Constitution. *Political Research Quarterly* 64 (2): 309–322.

Cook, Joanna, Nicholas Long, and Henrietta L. Moore. (eds.). 2016. *The State We're In: Reflecting On Democracy's Troubles.* Oxford: Berghahn Books.

de Vreese, Claes H. (ed.). 2007. *The Dynamics of Referendum Campaigns: An International Perspective.* Basingstoke: Palgrave.

FitzGibbon, John. 2010. Referendum Briefing. The Second Referendum on the Treaty of Lisbon in Ireland, 2 October 2009. *Representation* 46 (2): 227–239.

Habermas, Jürgen. 2013. *The Crisis of the European Union: A Response.* Cambridge: Polity.

Hooghe, Liesbet, and Gary Marks. 2006. Europe's Blues: Theoretical Soul-Searching After the Rejection of the European Constitution. *Political Science and Politics* 39 (2): 247–250.

Howarth, David. 2000. *Discourse.* Buckingham: Open University Press.

Howarth, David, Aletta Norval, and Yannis Stavrakakis (eds.). 2000. *Discourse Theory and Political Analysis: Identities, Hegemonies and Social Change*. Manchester and New York: Manchester University Press and St. Martin's Press.

Howarth, David, and Yannis Stavrakakis. 2000. Introducing Discourse Theory and Political Analysis. In *Discourse Theory and Political Analysis: Identities, Hegemonies and Social Change*, ed. David Howarth, Aletta Norval, and Yannis Stavrakakis, 1–23. Manchester: Manchester University Press.

Katsambekis, Giorgos. 2014. The Place of the People in Post-Democracy. Researching "Antipopulism" and Post-Democracy in Crisis-Ridden Greece. *POSTData* 19 (2): 555–582.

Katsambekis, Giorgos. 2016. "The People" and Political Opposition in Post-Democracy: Reflections on the Hollowing of Democracy in Greece and Europe. In *The State We're In: Reflecting on Democracy's Troubles*, ed. Joanna Cook, Nicholas Long, and Henrietta L. Moore, 144–166. Oxford: Berghahn Books.

Katsambekis, Giorgos. 2017. The Populist Surge in Post-Democratic Times: Theoretical and Political Challenges. *The Political Quarterly* 88 (2): 202–210.

Kioupkiolis, Alexandros. 2014. Towards a Regime of Post-Political Biopower? Dispatches from Greece. *Theory, Culture and Society* 31 (1): 143–158.

Lialiouti, Zinovia, and Giorgos Bithymitris. 2013. Crisis, Hegemony and the Media. The Case of SKAI/Kathimerini. *Greek Political Science Review* 40: 139–173 [in Greek].

Mair, Peter. 2013. *Ruling the Void: The Hollowing of Western Democracy*. London: Verso.

Mavris, Yiannis. 2016. Rise and Fall. Voter Support for Syriza Before and After the Referendum of 5 July 2015 [in Greek]. http://www.mavris.gr/en/693/rise-and-fall/print/.

Mendelsohn, Matthew, and Andrew Parkin. 2001. *Referendum Democracy: Citizens, Elites and Deliberation in Referendum Campaigns*. Basingstoke: Palgrave.

Mylonas, Yannis. 2014. Crisis, Austerity and Opposition in Mainstream Media Discourses of Greece. *Critical Discourse Studies* 11 (3): 305–321.

Nikisianis, Nikos, Thomas Siomos, Yannis Stavrakakis, and Titika Dimitroulia. 2016. Populism vs. Anti-Populism in the Greek Press, 2014–2015. *Synchrona Themata*, 132 (3): 52–70 [in Greek].

Pitkin, Hanna Fenichel. 2004. Representation and Democracy: Uneasy Alliance. *Scandinavian Political Studies* 27 (3): 335–342.

Stavrakakis, Yannis. 2013. Dispatches from the Greek Lab: Metaphors, Strategies and Debt in the European Crisis. *Psychoanalysis, Culture and Society* 18 (3): 313–324.

Stavrakakis, Yannis, Giorgos Katsambekis, Alexandros Kioupkiolis, Nikos Nikisianis, and Thomas Siomos. 2017. Populism, Anti-Populism and Crisis. *Contemporary Political Theory*, online first. https://doi.org/10.1057/s41296-017-0142-y.

Tormey, Simon. 2015. *The End of Representative Politics*. Cambridge: Polity.

NEWS SOURCES

Athanasopoulos, Angelos. 2016a. Brexit and Greece: The Merciless Questions. *To Vima*, June 27. http://www.tovima.gr/opinions/article/?aid=810890.

Athanasopoulos, Angelos. 2016b. Europe in Front of the Abyss After the "British Accident". *To Vima*, June 26. http://www.tovima.gr/politics/article/?aid=810657.

Athinakis, Dimitris. 2016. When Lives Are Played in Dice. *Kathimerini*, June 30. http://www.kathimerini.gr/865576/article/epikairothta/kosmos/otan-oi-zwes-paizontai-sta-zaria.

Charvalias, Giorgos. 2016. "Cutter" to the Fourth Reich. *Dimocratia*, June 25. http://www.dimokratianews.gr/content/63923/koftis-sto-4o-raih.

Dimocratia. 2016a. Editorial, 'The Return of the Nations'. *Dimocratia*, June 25. www.dimokratianews.gr/content/63912/i-epistrofi-ton-ethnon.

Dimocratia. 2016b. Editorial, 'The Scent of Brexit'. *Dimocratia*, June 18. www.dimokratianews.gr/content/63653/aroma-toy-brexit.

Dimocratia. 2016c. Editorial, 'The Emancipation of Homelands'. *Dimocratia*, July 6. http://www.dimokratianews.gr/content/64280/i-heirafetisi-ton-patridon.

Exadaktylos, Theofanis. 2016. "Little England" Does Not Care for the Bigger Picture. *To Vima*, June 26. http://www.tovima.gr/opinions/article/?aid=810650.

Giannoulopoulos, Giorgos. 2016. Brexit's Message. *Efsyn*, July 3. http://www.efsyn.gr/arthro/minyma-toy-brexit.

Maglinis, Ilias. 2016. Bullets and Stabbings. *Kathimerini*, June 25. http://www.kathimerini.gr/865035/opinion/epikairothta/politikh/kai-sfaires-kai-maxairies.

Kapsilis, Alexandros. 2016. Europe in Times of Referendums. *To Vima*, June 11. http://www.tovima.gr/finance/article/?aid=807061.

Kefalas, Alkiviades Konstantinos. 2016. Euroexit and "Dirty Greeks" *Dimocratia*, July 3. http://www.dimokratianews.gr/content/64181/euroexit-kai-vromoellines.

Kranidiotis, Failos. 2016. If the "Pourquois" Prevail. *Dimocratia*, June 26. http://www.dimokratianews.gr/content/63941/epikratisoyn-oi-poyrkoyades.

MacShane, Denis. 2016. If Brexit Happens, It Won't Be Long Until Grexit Comea Along. *Kathimerini*, June 12. http://www.kathimerini.gr/863410/article/oikonomia/die8nhs-oikonomia/an-symveito-brexit-den-8a-arghsei-na-emfanistei-kai-to-grexit.

Makris, Petros. 2016. Playing at the Ballots with Marked Cards. *To Vima*, June 28. http://www.tovima.gr/opinions/article/?aid=811056.

Makrodimopoulos, Dimitris. 2016. Why Brexit? *Efsyn*, June 23. http://www.efsyn.gr/arthro/giati-brexit.

Mandravelis, Paschos. 2016. The Advantage of "No". *Kathimerini*, June 28. http://www.kathimerini.gr/865356/opinion/epikairothta/politikh/to-pleonekthma-toy-oxi.

Pagoulatos, George. 2016. The Anatomy of Brexit. *Kathimerini*, June 26. http://www.kathimerini.gr/865096/opinion/epikairothta/politikh/anatomia-enos-brexit.

Papadimitriou, Babis. 2016. Populism Pushed the Domino in the EU, 2. *Kathimerini*, June 28. http://www.kathimerini.gr/865354/opinion/epikairothta/politikh/o-laikismos-esprw3e-to-ntomino-sthn-ee.

Papadopoulos, Pavlos. 2016. Alexis Tsipras: The "Little Guy" That Wants to Become Emperor. *To Vima*, June 26. http://www.tovima.gr/politics/article/?aid=810626.

Patelis, Dimitris. 2016. Referendum Now: Out of the EU-Prison of Peoples. *Efsyn*, June 28. http://www.efsyn.gr/arthro/dimopsifisma-tora-exo-ap-tin-ee-fylaki-laon.

Stamatopoulos, Giorgos. 2016. No Tears for the British. *Efsyn*, June 27. http://www.efsyn.gr/arthro/ohi-dakrya-gia-toys-vretanoys.

Stathoulia, Theodora. 2016. Britain, the EEC and History. *Efsyn*, June 13. http://www.efsyn.gr/arthro/i-vretania-i-eok-kai-i-istoria.

Zoulas, Konstantinos. 2016. For Those in Favour of Holding Referendums. *Kathimerini*, June 25. http://www.kathimerini.gr/865032/opinion/epikairothta/politikh/gia-toys-8iaswtes-toy-dhmoyhfizein.

PART IV

Beyond European Single Market Countries

CHAPTER 16

Turkish Newspapers: How They Use 'Brexit' for Domestic Political Gain

Lyndon C. S. Way

INTRODUCTION

Liberal accounts of the role of the press acknowledge that objectivity is a Western ideal rather than a universal reality (Chalaby 1998). Turkish news is a far cry from what we expect in the West in terms of objectivity and balanced coverage (Way and Kaya 2015; Way and Akan 2017). In fact, news media have a history of being closely aligned to political interests (Özgüneş and Terzis 2000: 414), their emergence in the nineteenth century being part of the state's modernization projects (Kocabaşoğlu 1993: 1). The role of news as a state organ rather than a source of information 'set the trend in the Turkish press in the coming years, a trend which is characterised by "opinion" articles rather than news and information' (ibid.: 96). Turkey's press coverage of foreign news is given low priority, reflected in terms of space and dominance on websites and in physical newspapers. Furthermore, these are almost exclusively externally sourced. In the case of the UK's referendum, stories were sourced almost exclusively from Reuters and Agence France-Presse and then cut

L. C. S. Way (✉)
Liverpool Hope University, Liverpool, UK
e-mail: wayl@hope.ac.uk

© The Author(s) 2018
A. Ridge-Newman et al. (eds.), *Reporting the Road to Brexit*,
https://doi.org/10.1007/978-3-319-73682-2_16

and pasted into the website. Alternatively, opinion pieces are sourced from mostly Turkish writers who include 'home grown' elements such as opinions on foreign events as well as domestic politics. So in opinion pieces about Brexit, concerns expressed include President Recep Tayyip Erdoğan's authoritarian tendencies and the 18 March EU-Turkey refugee agreement which led to hopes over visa-free travel for Turkish citizens, a revival of negotiations for Turkey's accession to the EU, and billions of euros in financial assistance. Here, I analyse how opinion pieces about the 23 June 2016 EU referendum do little to inform readers about its consequences on their lives, but instead are used as a springboard to criticize the government from a viewpoint which advantages those closely associated with the newspaper.

Turkish-British Relations

Turkey and the UK have a long and (mostly) mutually supportive past. Diplomatic relations between Turkey and the UK go back as far as the sixteenth century, when the UK appointed its first ambassador William Harborne to the Ottoman Empire in 1583 ('Relations between' 2017). The past has seen the two nations at times on the same side of conflicts and at others on opposite sides, though the 2000s saw 'a golden era in Turkey-UK bilateral relations'. This era of good relations included reciprocal head-of-state visits (including Queen Elizabeth in 2008, David Cameron in 2010, Turkish President Gül in 2010 and Erdoğan in 2011 and 2012), co-operation in NATO, Cyprus and the UK's endorsement of Turkey's bid to be an EU member state ('Relations between' 2017). Indeed, commercial and economic ties have benefited from good relations and continued into 2016, with bilateral trade amounting to $17 billion dollars and the UK ranked second in Turkish exports and 11th in imports ('Commercial and Economic' 2017).

However, by the time of the UK's referendum, the golden age had passed. Turkish government reactions to Gezi Park protests of 2013 caused international condemnation. The government's consistent attacks on the free press and media resulted in European governments and organizations deeming Turkey's media 'not free' ('Freedom of the Press' 2016) and President Recep Tayyip Erdoğan 'an enemy of democracy' ('Turkey: in latest' 2016). With international concern over Turkey's deterioration in human rights, freedom of speech and democracy, UK Prime Minister David Cameron's close relations with Turkey were under strain.

Turkish Domestic Politics

This deterioration in democracy and corresponding Turkish-UK relations can be partly explained through the rise in power of Erdoğan and the Justice and Development Party (AKP). AKP is an economically liberal and socially conservative political party founded in 2001 by members of existing Islamic and conservative parties, winning its first national election a year later. With the exception of its 7 June 2015, short-lived, minority victory, AKP has won a majority in each national election. Unlike administrations before it, AKP brands itself as an alternative to 'Kemalism'. 'The Kemalist modernization process' or 'Kemalism' has been the dominant ideology throughout Turkish political history up until AKP swept to power. It has its roots in the Turkish national independence war from 1919 to 1922, when Turks and Kurds fought against the occupying forces who had carved up the remnants of the Ottoman Empire after the First World War. Spearheaded by Mustafa Kemal Atatürk (the founder of the modern Turkish Republic), Kemalism aimed to modernize Turkey by creating a homogeneous, secular and Western society (Mango 1999). Today the main opposition parties adhere to Kemalism in one form or another, as do most mainstream oppositional newspapers. For example, the Republican People's Party (CHP) embraces a Western outlook and secularism whilst the Nationalist Movement Party (MHP) emphasizes the Turkish nation and state. In contrast, AKP's approach is less Western-looking, representing itself as a bridge between Islam, democracy, and neoliberalism (Uzgel and Duru 2010). AKP's turn away from the West has accelerated since 2007, where there has been 'the gradual Islamization of the AKP's discourse and policies' (Boratav 2016: 6).

Turkish News Media

Along with this political turn has come a clampdown on the media. Relations between the media and politics can be characterized in terms of Hallin and Mancini's (2004) 'Mediterranean or Polarized Pluralist Model'. Turkey has a politically oriented press, high political parallelism in journalism; the state plays a significant role as owner, regulator, and funder of media as it oversees a high degree of ideological diversity and conflict in society. Turkey's media are dominated by the Turkish Radio and Television Corporation (TRT) and five private media conglomerates.

This near monopoly is a result of Turkish media policies since 1993 which introduced private broadcasting and actively pursued a private conglomerates policy 'to promote the formation of media conglomerates with a secure capital-holding base and to minimize the number of dominant media players in the public arena' (Özgüneş and Terzis 2000: 10). A smaller number of players means it is easier to control. According to the European Journalists Association, Turkish media are heavily dominated by large multi-sector groups controlling newspapers, radio, and television channels.

Turkey's media experience heavy censorship and state control (Christensen 2005: 182). In 2016, Turkey was ranked 151st out of 180 countries in Reporters Without Borders' world press freedom index. These very low marks reflect an ongoing trend since AKP gained control of power. The number of jailed journalists is one of the highest for any country in the world. As of March 2016, more than 70 people, most of them journalists, have been prosecuted for 'insulting' Erdoğan since his election to President in August 2014. The *Cumhuriyet* newspaper's Editor-in-Chief, Can Dundar, who described the process of arrests as a 'kind of deterrence policy,' was arrested and is now in exile for crossing swords with Erdoğan. In the run-up to the June 2015 elections, the World Association of Newspapers and News Publishers (WAN-IFRA) called on the Turkish government 'to urgently recognize the importance of plural voices within the media and to provide the conditions for independent sources of information' ('WAN-IFRA calls' 2015). Due to this repressive atmosphere, 'opposition' is stifled in its output, it subtly articulating discourses critical of the government whilst promoting political perspectives advantageous to its owners and associates (Way and Akan 2017; Way et al. 2018). It is in this political and media context that I examine how Turkish news media represented the UK's referendum in opinion pieces.

SAMPLE OF NEWS SELECTED FOR ANALYSIS

Unlike the Western press, Turkish newspapers and websites feature both news and opinion pieces in almost equal measure. Due to a lack of resources, foreign news stories are almost exclusively externally sourced, cut-and-paste offerings from the major news agencies such as Reuters, Associated Press and Agence France-Presse. Though which stories news producers chose to publish is significant, I opted not to concentrate on these as there is little in the way of a Turkish perspective. Instead, I decided to concentrate on opinion pieces, as they are an integral part of what readers consume as news. These more 'home-grown' offerings are well read, where many writers hold celebrity status for their writing and perspectives on events. Nevertheless, writers work within an environment where most mainstream media are either directly or indirectly under the control of the government (Jenkins 2012; Way and Kaya 2015; Way and Akan 2017). If there is any opposition, this is subtle and carries the risk of repercussions (Way and Akan 2017).

Opinions in the spectrum of Turkish news range from those that give unquestioning praise for AKP and their actions to those which subtly interrogate (Way et al. 2018). Here, I examine the *Hurriyet Daily News* English-language newspaper website. I chose this site because its news stories can be seen as occupying the middle of this spectrum, a position which on first reading represents the government and its policies with very little in the way of criticism or praise (Way and Akan 2017). It also gives access to a position many Turks read, with *Hurriyet Daily News* boasting of being 'the leading news source for Turkey and the Region'.

In fact, *Hurriyet Daily News* is the English-language website of the larger Turkish-language *Hürriyet* website and newspaper. *Hürriyet*, with a circulation of approximately 350,000, is owned by the Doğan Media Group (DMG), which was the largest media group in Turkey before 2011. It used to be outspoken in its criticism of AKP, from a staunch Kemalist position. However, a quarrel between Erdoğan and the owner of the group, Aydın Doğan, resulted in Erdoğan publicly threatening Doğan for his critical and 'irresponsible journalism'. Erdoğan subsequently excluded Doğan from any government contracts and dispatched tax inspectors to DMG. The government found DMG guilty of 'tax evasion' and imposed a fine reported to be between ₺3.7 and ₺4.9 billion (well over £1 billion). After secret negotiations, DMG paid a small percentage of the fine, had to sell off some of its media assets to Erdoğan-friendly owners, and has since turned a blind eye to AKP, though I argue here that opinion pieces still criticize from a Kemalist position. Despite these setbacks, its website was the tenth most visited in Turkey and the second most visited newspaper website ('Top sites' 2017).

To acquire my sample, I typed in 'Brexit' into *Hurriyet Daily News's* search engine. I chose to examine news coverage in the three-month build-up to the referendum (starting 23 March) to one month after (23

July), this time being where Brexit was newsworthy in Turkey, producing 105 written digital pieces. Of these, there are 63 news stories and 42 opinion pieces. Although all opinion pieces in the wider sample are examined and considered, in the spirit of critical discourse analysis (CDA), I examine in-depth 12 opinion pieces that seem to represent the wider sample and illustrate how the UK's referendum was covered in Turkish opinion pieces.

Approach to Analysis: Critical Discourse Analysis

I examine opinion pieces in depth using CDA. My approach to CDA assumes that linguistic choices reveal broader discourses articulated in texts (Kress and van Leeuwen 2001). These discourses can be thought of as models of the world, giving a clear sense of 'what view of the world is being communicated through semiotic resources' (Abousnnouga and Machin 2010: 139). The aim of analysis is to reveal what kinds of social relations of power, inequalities and interests are perpetuated, generated or legitimated in texts both explicitly and implicitly (Van Dijk 1993). This chapter examines how opinion pieces recontextualize events around the referendum. By recontextualization, I mean how social actions are represented which 'always involve transformation, and what exactly gets transformed depends on the interests, goals, and values of the context into which the practice is recontextualised' (van Leeuwen and Wodak 1999: 96).

Transformations involve deletions, rearrangements, substitutions and additions (van Leeuwen and Wodak 1999: 98). I also examine the role of presuppositions. Presuppositions are 'a taken-for-granted, implicit claim embedded within the explicit meaning of a text or utterance' (Richardson 2007: 63). These are powerful ideological tools, where '[t]he unsaid, the already said, the presupposed, is of particular importance in ideological analysis, in that ideologies are generally embedded within the implicit meaning of a text rather than being explicit' (Fairclough 1995: 108). These implicit 'taken for granted' claims enforce ideologies without questioning them (Richardson 2007: 187). Though CDA demands a close reading of texts, social and historical contexts are essential in determining the meaning potential of choices made in texts. For this reason, I have included a political and media contextualization to help understand what is being communicated.

ANALYSIS OF NEWS

Throughout the wider sample, there are a number of discourses that articulate positivity surrounding Britain whilst negatively representing Brexit. 'Britain' is collocated throughout the sample with positive lexica such as 'an advanced democracy', 'historically a strong friend [of Turkey]', and 'a good example for Turkey to follow'. Alongside this, Brexit is collocated with a 'risky decision', 'the persistent demand of the right-wing [UK]' and 'falsely based assumptions', while headlines include 'The Brexit Challenge', and 'Brexit: The apocalypse'. A positive view of the UK is part of a Kemalist discourse that sees Turkey and its future closely aligned to a strong healthy Europe while the idea of Brexit indicates the possibility of a crumbling political entity.

Praise towards the UK and criticisms of Brexit are often linked to criticisms of AKP and Erdoğan. Consider this extract that comes from a piece written around Cameron's resignation after the referendum: 'The UK is not the only example, but one of the features of advanced democracies is that there is a functioning in-party democracy and there is no domination by the leader.'

Here, Britain is named as an 'advanced democracy', one which Turks should strive to achieve. Though one may debate whether indeed resigning after a political loss is an indicator of an advanced democracy, this is presupposed. The piece includes Cameron saying the UK needs 'fresh leadership and [...] a new prime minister'. Here, the piece recontextualizes his actions in terms of putting one's party before one's career. This takes on great significance in Turkey at the time. It was at this point, while Erdoğan was clearing the political path for his long-coveted presidential system, that he forced Turkey's Prime Minister Ahmet Davutoğlu to resign because of his lack of enthusiasm for a presidential system. As such, the story rearranges recent events in such a way as to put Erdoğan's actions in stark contrast to Cameron's. This contrasting is further elaborated upon where politicians from advanced democracies do 'not regard their party as their property, their child, or their army; when necessary the leader withdraws'. The result is an articulation of negativity towards AKP and Erdoğan, whilst the West is praised, in line with Kemalist discourses.

In fact, opinion pieces are used almost inevitably as a platform to criticize Erdoğan and AKP. One common discourse is Erdoğan's authoritarian tendencies. However, on many occasions, who enunciates such criticism is unclear, making accountability difficult; for example, in 'EU criticism of Turkey concerning press freedom' the 'EU' is named as an actor who criticizes, though such impersonal attribution muddies the water as to actually *who* is criticizing. At other times, agency is even more abstract with actions being agentless, which not only excludes representations of power to those performing the acts, but also makes such statements difficult to defend and verify. Consider:

> There is growing concern both in the international community and within Turkey's civil society that human rights and freedoms are seriously challenged by creeping authoritarianism, a danger which intends to demolish the democratic pluralistic thread of society.

Here, agency for 'growing concern' is not identified; however, lexical choices emphasize the validity and magnitude of this concern with it being 'international' and 'within Turkey'. Furthermore, human rights and freedoms are 'seriously challenged' with a 'danger' that aims to 'demolish' democracy. These lexical choices make clear negativity is given to 'creeping authoritarianism', though again this authoritarianism is not identified. Constructions such as these allow the newspaper to make accusations aimed at the government without having to give specifics or identify their sources, whilst articulating discourses that criticize the government.

In other opinion pieces, we see a more direct attack on Erdoğan and AKP. Sometimes they are named as 'increasingly authoritarian president and his supporters'. Even in these more direct attacks, clear agency is still missing, possibly as a defence against joining the hundreds of others in Turkish jails who criticize Erdoğan. Consider:

> Given the manner in which Turkey is regressing democratically under the rule of Recep Tayyip Erdoğan, though, Sarkozy needn't have tweeted this at all. If Turkey's EU membership is 'unthinkable' today, Turkey is as much to blame as anyone else.

Though Erdoğan is implicated in the act of 'Turkey is regressing democratically', he is not given agency. Instead, he is represented in a prepositional phrase beginning with 'under', a grammatical strategy used to de-emphasize and represent with less power (Van Dijk 1993). In the second sentence, Erdoğan is excluded from the sentence, again disempowering, though to 'blame' for EU membership being 'unthinkable'. These types of sentence structures disempower and de-emphasize Erdoğan whilst surrounding him in negativity. Events recontextualized in this way are in the interests of Kemalists who would like to see Erdoğan out and replaced with politicians closer to their political position.

van Leeuwen and Wodak (1999: 104–105) note how claims and views can be legitimized through a number of strategies. One is personal authorization that involves attributing a statement to a person with institutional authority. Here, criticism aimed at AKP from 'other' authoritative sources is used to legitimize Kemalist critiques. In the following extract, a UK politician describes why Cameron claimed Turkey would not be joining the EU any time soon, a well-publicized statement he made as part of his Remain campaign. Consider:

> UK Chancellor of the Exchequer George Osborne explained what happened: 'Turkey has gone backwards. There are concerns about democracy and human rights there. British government policy is that it should not join the European Union today.'

Here, a UK politician is named formally with honorifics, representing him with power and authority (van Leeuwen 1996). He is active, emphasized at the beginning of the sentence in a low modality, connoting power and certainty (van Leeuwen 1995). His reported speech recontextualizes recent events in Turkey as going 'backwards'. Again we find 'concerns about democracy and human rights' are agentless, though context dictates this is the result of AKP.

Another discourse throughout the sample is one that negatively represents AKP's affiliations with Islam. Namings play a role: AKP and its supporters are named as 'our Islamists', 'rising religious extremism' and those who are 'running after establishing an Islamist regime based on one man'. Also in these representations of AKP, both AKP and Islam are represented as backward. Consider:

> [...] they want this [EU] membership to be on their subjective terms, not on the basis of the EU's objective rules. They consider these rules, especially with regards to pluralistic democracy, to be unsuitable for the Turkey they hope to create based on their Islamist outlook.

Here, and seen throughout the sample, we see AKP named as 'they'. Van Dijk (1993) demonstrates how pronouns are used to articulate 'us' and 'them' ideological groupings. Here, 'they' is used to distinguish between 'us' Kemalists and 'those' AKP supporters. What is also articulated here is that although the EU (and Kemalists who want to be associated with the West) are 'objective', AKP are associated with being 'subjective', find democracy 'unsuitable' and 'hope to create a society with an Islamist outlook'. Here we find AKP and Kemalist desires polarized, one represented negatively as 'subjective' and the other 'objective'. The subjective position is represented negatively by not wanting a secular democracy and being associated with Islam. Here again we see a recontextualization which, through additions such as creating a secular objective and Islamist subjective polarity, articulates criticism of AKP through a Kemalist perspective.

Opinion pieces about the referendum also represent Erdoğan and AKP as manipulative, Brexit playing into AKP's un-liberal ideals. AKP statements which claim they want to join the EU are 'simply dishonest' because 'the EU link is thought to weaken their political power'. Here, AKP actions are recontextualized in ways which make them seem dishonest in order to retain power. This is a theme throughout the sample. Consider:

> In fact, the truth is that as the anti-EU mood rises in governing party circles, the president and his party are glad that the EU is facing dissolution itself. The EU has been a liberal project of supra-national politics and founded on the idea of the compatibility of universal values like human rights and multicultural richness.

Here, it is presupposed that there is an anti-EU mood in AKP that is rising. This extract also recontextualizes AKP's reactions to Brexit abstractly by being 'glad', a mental process, again difficult to substantiate (Fairclough 1995). EU policies are contrasted with those of AKP, the EU's values recontextualized as 'a liberal project' compatible with 'universal values like human rights and multicultural richness'. These are lofty ideals, though many in the EU such as the United Kingdom Independence Party (UKIP), Geert Wilders's Party for Freedom in Holland, Germany's Alternative for Germany Party and Hungarian government actions all seem to disprove this representation. However, recontextualized as such, this opinion piece suggests Erdoğan is against such actions and values. In fact, elsewhere in this same story, 'Erdoğan and his Islamist/nationalist followers' who 'are enjoying Brexit' 'feel powerful' because they 'think' the 'EU is facing dissolution'. This means

AKP 'feels powerful enough that they don't need to pretend to be democrats who believe in universal values'. Not only do namings link Erdoğan with religious non-thinkers ('followers'), these actions such as 'enjoying', 'feel' and 'think' are abstract, a mental process and difficult to substantiate. However, writing as such recontextualizes AKP's reactions to Brexit as manipulative, AKP using Brexit as an excuse to become more authoritarian, Islamic and non-European, reflecting Kemalist criticisms of AKP.

Part of the criticism expressed in these opinion pieces criticizes both foreign and domestic policies. At the time, Turkey was embroiling itself more and more in Syria and Iraq in the fight against the Islamic State of Iraq and the Levant (ISIL), was at odds with Russia over Turkey's downing of a Russian jet, and was experiencing strained relations with Israel over a number of issues and with the EU and the USA over its infringements of human rights and press freedoms. These relations run counter to Kemalism, which emphasizes the importance of being a good neighbour and non-interference in external affairs (Mango 1999). However, AKP's foreign affairs here are recontextualized as 'Turkey's foreign policy is ailing', with Turkey 'now considered to be a country with a significant lack of impartiality in its foreign policy conduct'. The addition of 'now' emphasizes the idea that this was not always the case, that a failing foreign policy is something that has come about due to AKP.

Throughout the sample, AKP domestic policies are also criticized, as in 'Turkey's domestic politics is shattering'. Here, shattering is abstract, though later in the piece, the author identifies the shattering as Turkey's ongoing fight with its Kurdish population which has 'devastated the country but also increased the polarization' within Turkey. There is also criticism aimed at the recent (at the time) migrant policy AKP had agreed with the EU. Under the deal, in return for Turkey receiving 'irregular migrants' crossing from Turkey into Greece, the EU would resettle a Syrian migrant from Turkey, ease visa restrictions for Turks wanting to access the Schengen passport-free zone, offer €3 bn of financial aid to Turkey to help migrants and 're-energize' Turkey's EU membership bid. However, the deal was linked to 72 conditions, some of which AKP was unwilling to concede, such as its anti-terrorist laws which do not live up to EU standards. For this reason, the much coveted easing of visa restrictions had not come into effect. Here, the opinion pieces claim the deal is 'stumbling'. Elsewhere, 'the migrant agreement appears to have done more harm than good', though no details are forthcoming as to why. However, in all mentions of the migrant deal, it is AKP which is represented as at fault, it being 'an increasingly undemocratic Turkish government' that 'refuses to address the issue' of amending its laws.

CONCLUSIONS

Foreign news sourced from Turkish news outlets is for the most part not prioritized. It is domestic affairs that dominate in terms of volume and position on websites or in physical newspapers. Foreign news stories, almost always, are cut-and-paste affairs from news services, though indeed what is cut and what is pasted, and how it is shaped, is also of significance. However, in this chapter, I have examined opinion pieces, which are both plentiful and 'home-grown' for the most part. These allow newspaper writers to express their opinions on events that have an impact on their readers.

The chapter has examined how *Hurriyet Daily News*, with a tradition of Kemalist support, has recontextualized the UK's EU referendum. What emerges is that events before and after the referendum have been recontextualized not so much to inform the reader about the referendum, but to criticize the AKP Government. This is done through the prism of Kemalism. Though, indeed, in a country where such voices are becoming more and more rare and criticism more and more subtle, it is also not without fault. By not informing Turkish readers about the referendum and its implications for Turkey, readers have been left ill informed. By using such events to articulate Kemalist discourses, readers, who are largely Kemalists themselves, are the already-converted being preached at. This does little to better inform the public on international matters that deeply affect Turkish life and the world around them.

REFERENCES

ACADEMIC

Abousnnouga, G., and D. Machin. 2010. Analysing the Language of War Monuments. *Visual Communication* 9 (2): 131–149.

Boratav, K. 2016. The Turkish Bourgeoisie Under Neoliberalism. *Research and Policy on Turkey* 1 (1): 1–10.

Chalaby, J.K. 1998. *The Invention of Journalism*. London: Macmillan.

Christensen, C. 2005. Breaking the News Concentration of Ownership, the Fall of Unions and Government Legislation in Turkey. *Global Media and Communication* 3 (2): 179–199.

Fairclough, N. 1995. *Critical Discourse Analysis: The Critical Study of Language*. London: Longman.

Hallin, D., and P. Mancini. 2004. *Comparing Media Systems: Three Models of Media and Politics*. Cambridge: Cambridge University Press.

Jenkins, G. 2012. *A House Divided Against Itself: The Deteriorating State of Media Freedom in Turkey*. Central Asia-Caucasus Institute Silk Road Studies Program. http://www.genocidewatch.org/images/Turkey_12_Feb_6_A_house_divided_against_itself_.pdf (Accessed 5 August 2013).

Kocabaşoğlu, U. 1993. *The Press Reform, 1919–1938* (Unpublished manuscript).

Kress, G., and T. van Leeuwen. 2001. *Multimodal Discourse: The Modes and Media of Contemporary Communication*. London: Hodder Education.

Mango, A. 1999. *Atatürk: The Biography of the Founder of Modern Turkey*. London: John Murray.

Özguneş, N., and G. Terzis. 2000. Constraints and Remedies for Journalists Reporting National Conflict: The Case of Greece and Turkey. *Journalism Studies* 1 (3): 405–426.

Richardson, J.E. 2007. *Analysing Newspapers: An Approach from Critical Discourse Analysis*. London: Palgrave Macmillan.

Uzgel, İ., and B. Duru. 2010. *AKP Kitabı Bir Dönüşümün Bilançosu*. Ankara: Pheoenix Yayınevi.

Van Dijk, T.A. 1993. Principles of Critical Discourse Analysis. *Discourse & Society* 4 (2): 249–283.

van Leeuwen, T. 1995. Representing Social Action. *Discourse & Society* 6 (1): 81–106.

van Leeuwen, T. 1996. The Representation of Social Actors. In *Texts and Practices—Readings in Critical Discourse Analysis*, ed. C.R. Caldas-Coulthard, and M. Coulthard, 32–70. London: Routledge.

van Leeuwen, T., and R. Wodak. 1999. Legitimizing Immigration Control: A Discourse-Historical Analysis. *Discourse Studies* 1 (1): 83–118.

Way, L., and A. Akan. 2017. Coverage of Bombings for Political Advantage: Turkish On-Line News Reporting of the 2016 Ankara Attacks. *Social Semiotics* 27 (5): 545–566.

Way, L., and E. Kaya. 2015. Turkish Newspapers' Role in Winning Votes and Exasperating Turkish-Kurdish Relations: The Ağrı Shootings. *Discourse & Communication* 10 (1): 82–100.

Way, L., G. Karanfil, and A. Ercifci. 2018. "See No Evil, Read No Evil": The Failing Role of Turkish Newspapers in Coverage of Turkey's 2016 Coup Attempt. *Critical Discourse Studies*.

PRIMARY SOURCES

Commercial and Economic Relations Between Turkey and the UK. 2017. http://www.mfa.gov.tr/commercial-and-economic-relations-between-turkey-and-england.en.mfa (Accessed 11 November 2017).

Freedom of the press. 2016. Freedom House. https://freedomhouse.org/report/freedom-press/freedom-press-2016 (Accessed 5 September 2016).

Relations Between Turkey and the United Kingdom. 2017. http://www.mfa.gov.tr/relations-between-turkey-and-the-united-kingdom.en.mfa   (Accessed 22 November 2017).

Top Sites in Turkey. 2017. https://www.alexa.com/topsites/countries;0/TR (Accessed on 23 November 2017).

Turkey: In Latest Escalation, 102 Media Outlets Closed by Decree. 2016. Reporters Without Borders. https://rsf.org/en/news/turkey-latest-escalation-102-media-outlets-closed-decree (Accessed 28 July 2016).

WAN-IFRA Calls on Turkish Gov't to Respect Pluralism in Media. 2015. *Hurriyet*, June 1. http://www.hurriyetdailynews.com/wan-ifra-calls-on-turkish-govt-to-respect-pluralism-in-media.aspx?pageID=238&nID=83262&NewsCatID=339 (Accessed 21 February 2016).

CHAPTER 17

Israeli Media and the EU Referendum 2016: Political or Economic Story?

Tal Samuel-Azran and Yair Galily

INTRODUCTION

The British people's decision to leave the European Union (EU) can be attributed to a variety of motives ranging from economics to politics, and to internal UK conflicts such as age, social and class gaps (Friedman 2016). The nature of the media, as well as the ensuing online discussions and interpretations of Brexit (Britain's exit from the EU) in different countries, can illuminate the nature and extent of globalization; specifically, whether the media and public portrayed Brexit as an event that concerns them, or whether it remains within specific spheres. Therefore, the notion that Brexit is a significant global event that concerns wide circles of the so-called global-village media and public is contestable. Israel is a country that could potentially be affected by the British people's decision to leave the EU on various levels. This chapter focuses on the predominant interpretations of the 2016 EU referendum and Brexit in

T. Samuel-Azran (✉) · Y. Galily
Interdisciplinary Center Herzliya, Herzliya, Israel
e-mail: tazran@idc.ac.il

Y. Galily
e-mail: ygalily@idc.ac.il

© The Author(s) 2018
A. Ridge-Newman et al. (eds.), *Reporting the Road to Brexit*,
https://doi.org/10.1007/978-3-319-73682-2_17

the Israeli media. The analysis aims to illuminate whether the referendum and its result were discussed and interpreted mostly from a narrow local perspective (for example, its implications on the Israeli-Palestinian conflict) or from a wider angle (for example, its implications for the UK, Europe and the world).

The study maps the discourses on the referendum disseminated in Israeli online media using Buzzilla (http://www.buzzilla.com), an online trend-tracking software tool, by first tracking which media sources (for example, financial versus mainstream versus entertainment online newspapers) discussed the referendum and to what extent. Subsequently, it examines which forums (for example, social networks, blogs, online newspapers) discussed the referendum and the interest generated in terms of number of participants. Finally, to add another dimension to the study of the Israeli interpretation of the Brexit on media platforms, we examine the contents and themes of user comments to an article concerning Brexit that appeared in *Ynet*, Israel's most popular online newspaper. The structure of the chapter is as follows: we begin with a description of the methods used and then move on to the results. Then, after identifying the main themes and the nature of discussion on the Brexit result in Israel's online public sphere, we discuss the findings' implications for globalization studies.

MENTIONS OF BREXIT IN ISRAEL'S MEDIA

The analysis examines the online media that covered the Brexit result and social discourse trends using Buzzilla, a trend-tracking software tool. Its technology is specifically designed for scalable web crawling of all the popular social platforms: social networks (public accounts only), forums, blogs, articles and user comments. We searched for mentions of the term 'Brexit' in Hebrew between 20 February 2016 and 20 February 2017 in order to include the mentions of the term over a one-year period, including around four months in the run-up to the 2016 EU referendum and around eight months afterwards.

Based on the search for the term 'Brexit' on Buzzilla, we found a total of 3343 mentions in the Israeli online public sphere, which reflects relatively little public interest in the referendum in comparison to other global events. For example, a search for Donald Trump using Buzzilla during the same period yielded 241,000 mentions in the Israeli online sphere, representing dramatically greater interest than the events in Britain. Of the 3343 mentions, 1506 were mentions in online newspaper articles (45%), 867 were mentions in Twitter feeds (26%), 458 were mentions on Facebook (14%), 379 were mentions of the term in online forums (11%) and 133 were mentions in blogs (4%). Nearly one-third, (1109 mentions) appeared in the course of one month, between 19 June and 19 July, a period that begins several days before Brexit and ends approximately four weeks thereafter.

Of the 1506 articles identified in the online newspaper-article category, 209 articles appeared in *Calcalist* (http://www.calcalist.co.il), Israel's most popular financial newspaper, and an identical number were published in *Globes* (http://www.globes.co.il), another popular and established financial newspaper. The third platform with the highest number of mentions was the online newspaper *NRG* (http://nrg.co.il), with 149 articles mentioning the term 'Brexit'. Next, in fourth place, is *TheMarker* (http://www.themarker.co.il), another financial newspaper with 118 articles, followed by the elite newspaper *Haaretz* in fifth place with 113 articles. Other news sources, such as *Ynet*, Israel's most popular online newspaper (http://www.ynet.co.il) and Walla! (http://www.walla.co.il), Israel's most popular portal, published significantly fewer articles than the above financial newspapers on the referendum, thus illustrating that it was a main concern mostly in financial and elite newspapers.

Following these findings, which gave us an indication that the referendum was of interest for Israeli media primarily as an economic event, we searched for the main terms associated with Brexit in all the financial newspapers, revealing that the most common terms were 'disaster' (231 occurrences), followed by 'crisis' (175 occurrences) and in third place 'opportunity' (124 occurrences). The analysis also revealed that most of the articles in the financial press containing mentions of Brexit dealt with its technical and intangible effects on the stock markets (for example, 'Credit Suisse: S&P will gain 2000 in the case Brexit will take place', *Calcalist*, 22 June 2016, http://www.calcalist.co.il/articles/0,7340,L-3691298,00.html).

Twitter is the second platform on which Brexit was most widely discussed after online news, according to our search using Buzzilla. This is in itself interesting as Twitter is a dramatically smaller and less popular platform in Israel when compared to Facebook. In fact, according to a recent estimate, Twitter has only 20,000 active accounts in Israel, in comparison to more than 1 million Facebook users. Nonetheless, despite its small scope, Twitter is known as a platform where leading Israeli journalists offer their current affairs analyses and intellectuals discuss current events; thus, the result is not entirely surprising.

While an analysis of all the Tweets concerning Brexit was beyond the resources of this chapter, we would like to note that, according to the output from Buzzilla, the tweet with the highest number of discussions (174 responses) was written by a Twitter account identified as Eyal, 26 June 2016, several days after the Brexit vote, who tweeted, 'a few unorganized thoughts about Brexit: there are three subjects that everyone mentioned, the class gap, the inter-generation gap, and xenophobia […]'. Most of the discussions responding to this tweet debated which of the three reasons was the most relevant, with Twitter users offering statistics and links to their analyses to support their arguments. Thus, arguably, there is some indication that the Twitter platform was characterized by an open rational debate where users contemplated the motives behind the Brexit vote.

The platform in third place in terms of the volume of discussions on Brexit was Facebook. Interestingly, Buzzilla indicated that 96% of Facebook accounts that mentioned Brexit attracted fewer than five comments, implying that the great majority of posts on Brexit garnered little or no participation. The Buzzilla results also showed that the majority of public Facebook accounts that mentioned Brexit (79%) were news sources, including the above-mentioned financial newspapers *Globes* and *TheMarker*, and portals such as Walla!.

Little mention of Brexit was found on other social networks. YouTube had six videos in Hebrew on Brexit, mostly from financial television shows, each with several hundred, and sometimes only several dozen views. The fourth online sphere in Israel in which Brexit was discussed was online forums, composed mostly of independent news websites such as *Rotter* (http://rotter.net), which attracted significantly less interest than the former realms. The fifth and final platform on which Brexit was mentioned is the Israeli blogs arena with only 28 posts, 18 of which appeared on the online financial blog *TheMarker Café* by Haaretz. This is perhaps unsurprising in light of Israel's limited blog scene, which typically engages in soft entertainment and gossip issues (Vaisman 2014).

THEMES IN USER COMMENTS IN ONLINE MAINSTREAM MEDIA

While Buzzilla revealed that Brexit was mostly discussed in online financial newspapers and Twitter, we complemented these findings with an additional analysis, specifically focusing on the discourse and themes concerning Brexit in the online mainstream media platforms. Israel is unique in the sense that its user comments scene is extremely active. Importantly, analyses of the user comments on Brexit in Israeli media are essential as studies illustrate strong effects of user comments on readers. A 2008 study using manipulated article content and associated comments found that readers were more strongly influenced by the comments than by the main article (Yang 2008). Other studies show that readers interpret user comments in online newspapers as a good gauge of public opinion despite their non-representativeness (Park and Lee 2007; Lee and Jae Jang 2010). A more recent study confirmed that comments can significantly influence readers' opinions on the news issues discussed, with positive comments resulting in more positive attitudes towards the issue and negative comments weakening readers' positive attitudes (Ahn 2011). Furthermore, studies show that in some countries, the great majority of Internet news readers read other readers' postings at least once a week (Na and Jun 2008) and an international poll conducted by Kantar Media research group (2012), comparing user comment readership, found that between 26% and 47% of readers worldwide read user comments regularly, although the figures vary from country to country. In Israel, between 32% (Shalev 2007) and 50% (Pereg 2008; Steinfeld et al. 2016) of online news readers report reading user comments.

Our content analysis aimed to identify the main themes that emerged in the 173 user comments discussing Brexit on *Ynet*, Israel's most popular online newspaper, in its most commented-upon article on Brexit. We examined user comments on an article reporting on the referendum result from 24 June 2016, entitled 'A drama in the UK: Chose to leave the EU' (http://www.ynet.co.il/articles/0,7340,L-4819743,00.html), which was the single most commented-upon news article on Brexit in Israel. After reading the user comments, we identified seven main themes and two coders coded the comments according to these themes. A reliability test based on a random sample of 60 posts showed a high level of inter-coder agreement (Krippendorf's Alpha coefficient no lower than .82). The user comments system on *Ynet* also displays the number of readers who supported or opposed the article in general (thumbs up or down). We contrasted the number of supporters and opponents by theme, and found that the main view appearing in the user comments was that Brexit was motivated by the UK's anti-Islam sentiment, with 57 comments along these lines and 570 thumbs-up supporting them. The second most common opinion was that Brexit marked the end of the EU, with 44 such comments and 361 thumbs-up supporting these comments. Next, 23 comments noted that Brexit meant the death of liberalism and 'political correctness', with 242 thumb-ups for these comments. The fourth most commonly mentioned reaction was that the stock exchanges were collapsing in light of the Brexit vote, with 19 comments mentioning this issue and 204 thumb-ups supporting these user comments. Next, 10 comments noted that the UK decision to leave the EU was an indication of a strong democracy, with 198 thumbs-up supporting these comments. Next, 5 comments noted that Brexit was a disaster for the UK and the world; these comments actually attracted negative sentiment from other readers, with an overall 98 thumbs-down in response to these comments. Finally, 5 comments pointed out that the results of the Brexit vote illustrated that preliminary polls are inaccurate (and portray pollsters' pro-liberal slant), with 243 thumbs-up for these comments. Some 13 user comments addressed other issues.

Therefore, the most prominent theme in the user comments was the argument that anti-Islamic sentiment triggered the Brexit decision, and, specifically, that the decision indicated the British people's realization that Muslims are trying to take over the UK through Muslim immigration that has, in turn, led to terrorism and to jihadists' efforts to recruit people to the so-called Islamic State. Many commentators compared the Muslim takeover scenario to the manner in which Muslims claim that Israel belongs to them, and compared what they believed Britain's response should be to the ways in which Israel needs to behave in order to deal with Muslim terrorism in light of these claims. Thus, for example, Comment Number 31 reads 'It's all because of the Muslims', gaining 49 thumbs ups. One of the comments that attracted the greatest support was 'The Brits opposed Eurabia', using the portmanteau word of Europe and Arabia to describe the conspiracy theory that states that Arabs are aiming to take over Europe by flooding the continent with Muslims and infiltrating it from within. Similarly, Comment Number 63, which read 'This is good news for the free world in its struggle against Islam', attracted 69 thumbs up.

The second most popular theme is the notion that Brexit marks the end of the EU, mostly expressed as a fortunate outcome. Notable examples that attracted the support of other users in the form of thumbs up include Comment Number 36 by a reader called Vic entitled 'excellent',# which reads 'I'll be happy if the anti-Israeli European Union is dismantled' with 27 thumbs ups, and a similar comment entitled 'Very good! Congratulations!' by a reader identifying themself as Itamar from Jerusalem, who points out that this will reduce traditional criticism toward Israel as both the UK and the EU will become less influential. In a similar manner, Comment Number 17, entitled 'The European Union is being dismantled' read: 'The British people are being smart and leaving before the EU ship sinks', and attracted 111 thumbs up.

The third most common theme in user comments (the death of liberalism and political correctness) discussed how the British public unmasked the liberals and put an end to the politically correct era that characterized the UK and liberals worldwide, marking the beginning of a new era dominated by a conservative, realistic right-wing political orientation. Thus, for example, Comment Number 78 read 'Another blow to the left-wing lies; apparently they are living in a dream but now no one believes them anymore', and attracted 15 thumbs up.

The economic implications of Brexit, which formed the overall main topic in the media, as mentioned above, was only the fourth most popular theme, represented by comments such as 'A huge collapse in the stock exchange markets around the world', with 44 thumbs up, and comments advising that it was optimum time to buy British pounds. The remaining themes were mentioned in comments with relatively similar frequency. These included the democratic value of a public referendum (commenters expressed their desire for a similar procedure on important decisions in Israel), and the inaccurate predictions on of the referendum results. Importantly and interestingly, the few comments that expressed sadness at the decision proved to be unpopular. For example, a user identified as Daria wrote in Comment Number 80 that Brexit was a disaster and not only for the UK, as illiterate right-wing voters determine the future of the world and destroy it; it attracted 16 (negative) thumb downs. Combining this with the above support for Brexit, we obtain a picture of commenters' general support for Brexit and the more conservative agenda in general.

CONCLUSIONS AND THEORETICAL IMPLICATIONS

This chapter has examined the Israeli media and public discourse regarding Brexit. Buzzilla, the trend-tracking analysis software tool used, revealed that most of the articles on Brexit appeared in the financial press, which implies that the referendum and the final Brexit result were of concern for Israeli online media mostly as an economic (rather than as a political or global) event, which may be the result of Brexit's potential direct impact on Israel's trade with the UK and on foreign currency markets. Like other foreign news topics, these are topics that are less extensively covered by mainstream media. On Twitter, the discussions were on economic, financial and political aspects as well. Put together, nearly one-half of all mentions were in online newspapers and another quarter on Twitter, indicating that Brexit was mainly a topic of the elite intellectual debate.

Overall, then, the indication is that in Israel, Brexit, which constituted a major foreign news event, remained mainly within the elite discourse, thus strengthening Sparks's (1998) argument that in the age of globalization, global news is primarily interesting and relevant for a small group of the global elite, and less interesting and relevant for the general public, indicating that the global-village idea has not quite yet materialized.

The analysis of the user comments written in response to articles in the general media revealed that many reactions to the Brexit vote were written from an Israeli domestic angle, considering the referendum result as a demonstration of UK, public anti-Muslim sentiment and a rejection of Muslim immigration to the UK. The second part of the study, then, strengthens the argument of the growing strength of the anti-liberal discourse in general and its growing presence in the online user-comments realm in particular, where the analysis was conducted (Wodak 2015).

Put together, then, our findings reveal that the Brexit vote was not interpreted in Israel as a global event but rather as a development of interest exclusively to the country's financial elite, who followed its implications for their own investments. Commentators outside this financial elite responded to articles about Brexit from a much more domestic perspective, whereby the UK's EU referendum result became associated with the Israeli-Palestinian conflict and was interpreted as an indication that the rest of the world has begun to see the Muslim spread as a threat. These findings support audience reception studies that show that the 'national' plays a central role in the understanding and interpretation of international news. Specifically, the findings of this study mirror Jensen's (2003) study of the reception of international news by audiences in seven countries, which found that interpretations of foreign news are influenced by how each country views its own global position and status.

These findings strongly contradict the globalist paradigm and notion of the emergent global culture, which builds on the argument

(Featherstone 1990; Fluorney 1992; Fluorney and Stewart 1997; Hannertz 1997; Volkmer 1999) that the current global news environment is rapidly transforming political communications within nations. According to Volkmer (1999), in the globalization era, international political communications reach beyond traditional, national public spheres and construct a global public sphere in which the public and the media are placing news events in a larger, regional, continental, multinational or global context (Volkmer 1999). As a result, Volkmer (2002) called for a 'paradigm change' in the presumed 'global/local' debate and suggested the global public-sphere notion as a better alternative.

In stark contrast to the optimistic globalist idea, this study strongly contradicts the global public-sphere notion. Instead, the findings of this analysis illustrate that in Israel, Brexit effectively remained primarily an issue discussed by elite groups rather than the mainstream public. In other words, Brexit did not trigger a mainstream, Israeli media debate but remained mostly within the confines of a limited elite debate. When it spilled over to the general public, the domestic perspective dominated the debate (and even a nationalistic sentiment erupted), further illustrating the myth of the global-village notion.

References

Academic Sources

Ahn, H. 2011. The Effect of Online News Story Comments on Other Readers' Attitudes: Focusing on the Case of Incongruence Between News Tone and Comments. PhD thesis, University of Alabama, Tuscaloosa.

Featherstone, M. (ed.). 1990. *Global Culture. Nationalism, Globalisation and Modernity*. London: Sage.

Fluorney, D.M. 1992. *CNN World Report. Ted Turner's International News Group*. London: John Libbey (Academia Research Monograph 9).

Fluorney, D.M., and R.K. Stewart. 1997. *CNN. Making News in the Global News Market*. London: University of Luton Press.

Hannertz, U. 1997. *Transnational Connections: Culture, People, Places*. New York: Routledge.

Jensen, K.B. (ed.). 2003. *News of the World: World Cultures Look at Television News*. New York: Routledge.

Kantar Media. 2012. Citizen Journalism: Latin America Takes the Lead. www.globaltgi.com/news/citizen-journalism-latin-america-takes-the-lead1/.

Lee, E.J., and Y. Jae Jang. 2010. What Do Others' Reactions to News on Internet Portal Sites Tell Us? Effects of Presentation Format and Readers' Need for Cognition on Reality Perception. *Communication Research* 37 (6): 825–846.

Na, E.K., and W.R. Jun. 2008. *A Study on Readers' Comments: Changes in the Online News Usage Pattern and the Implications for Discursive Public*. Seoul: Korea Press Foundation.

Park, N., and K.M. Lee. 2007. Effects of Online News Forum on Corporate Reputation. *Public Relations Review* 33 (3): 346–348.

Sparks, C. 1998. Is There a Global Public Sphere? In *Electronic Empires. Global Media and Local Resistance*, ed. D.K. Thussu, 108–124. London: Arnold.

Steinfeld, N., T. Samuel-Azran, and A. Lev-On. 2016. User Comments and Public Opinion: Findings from an Eye-Tracking Experiment. *Computers in Human Behavior* 61: 63–72.

Vaisman, C.L. 2014. Beautiful Script, Cute Spelling and Glamorous Words: Doing Girlhood Through Language Playfulness on Israeli Blogs. *Language & Communication* 34: 69–80.

Volkmer, I. 1999. *News in the Global Sphere: A Study of CNN and its Impact on Global Communication*. Luton: University of Luton Press.

Volkmer, I. 2002. Journalism and Political Crises in the Global Network Society. In *Journalism After September 11*, ed. B. Zelizer and S. Allan, 235–246. London and New York: Routledge.

Wodak, R. 2015. *The Politics of Fear: What Right-Wing Populist Discourses Mean*. New York, NY: Sage.

Yang, H.S. 2008. The Effects of the Opinion and Quality of User Postings on Internet News Readers' Attitude Toward the News Issue. *Korean Journal of Journalism & Communication Studies* 52 (2): 254–281.

NEWSPAPER SOURCES

Friedman, G. 2016. 3 Reasons Brits Voted for Brexit. *Forbes*, July 5. https://www.forbes.com/sites/johnmauldin/2016/07/05/3-reasons-brits-voted-for-brexit/#462948881f9d.

Pereg, N. 2008. Active surfing: 75% of Online Users Read Forums, Some 50% Read Users' Comments. *Globes*, August 18. www.globes.co.il/news/article.aspx?did=1000373048 [Hebrew].

Shalev, A. 2007. A New Survey Finds: Most Internet Users Do Not Read Users' Comments. *Ynet*, November 7. www.ynet.co.il/articles/0,7340,L-3468737,00.html [Hebrew].

CHAPTER 18

Whose News? How the Canadian Media Covered Britain's EU Referendum

Christopher Waddell

INTRODUCTION: CANADA'S DOMESTIC POLITICAL LANDSCAPE

Coverage in Canada's media of Britain's 2016 European Union (EU) referendum campaign, the vote outcome and the immediate aftermath were inevitably coloured by the Canadian political climate and the increasingly precarious financial state of the country's media. Many of the issues around the relationship of the United Kingdom (UK) with the EU that emerged during the campaign (the economy, trade and immigration) were at play in Canada as well in the first half of 2016, but without the same degree of polarization visible in the EU referendum campaign.

The previous October, Canada's Liberal Party, led by Justin Trudeau, defeated the Conservative Government of Stephen Harper after a decade in office. Trudeau successfully campaigned on an activist agenda, pledging to run deficits to support infrastructure spending, and focusing his election pitch on improving the economic circumstances for the 'middle class' without ever defining that term. A key campaign difference

C. Waddell (✉)
Carleton University, Ottawa, ON, Canada
e-mail: chris.waddell@carleton.ca

© The Author(s) 2018
A. Ridge-Newman et al. (eds.), *Reporting the Road to Brexit*,
https://doi.org/10.1007/978-3-319-73682-2_18

between the Liberals and Conservatives was Trudeau's pledge that if elected, by the end of 2015 his Government would bring 25,000 Syrian refugees to Canada, sponsored by private individuals, community and religious groups as well as by the federal government. It was a minuscule number compared to the waves of migrants sweeping across Europe at the time, but it was a statement about open borders and the need to accommodate refugees and immigrants.

In contrast, Conservatives campaigned on fears about the security threats immigrants posed. They called for a ban on women wearing the niqab in citizenship ceremonies (which was already a very rare occurrence) and proposed setting up an informant line where the public could anonymously report 'barbaric cultural practices' to the authorities. The Liberals won a significant majority, cutting the number of Conservative seats in the Canadian Parliament almost by half and eliminating nearly all the gains the Conservatives had made in most of the country's urban areas in the preceding 10 years. The Conservatives were reduced to being primarily a rural party. The nativist appeal by the Conservatives failed miserably in Canada's ethnically diverse cities, so, not surprisingly, most Canadians could not relate to the anti-immigrant subtext of the following spring's Leave campaign in Britain's EU referendum, 2016.

Similarly foreign to Canadians was the antipathy of the Leave side to the EU. Canadians saw that issue primarily through the prism of trade. Both the Liberals and Conservatives had supported the Comprehensive Economic and Trade Agreement (CETA) which Canada had concluded with the EU in 2014 under Harper, after seven years of negotiations. CETA took advantage of the general consensus among Canadians that the country benefited from freer trade, open borders and labour mobility. That belief remained strong throughout 2016, as Canadians watched the presidential primary campaign in the USA where Republican candidate Donald Trump regularly decried the more than 20-year-old North American Free Trade Agreement (NAFTA) between Canada, Mexico and the USA as the worst deal the USA had ever signed. He also promised to reject the Trans Pacific Partnership (TPP) trade agreement that included Canada, negotiated by the Obama Administration, but also rejected by Democratic Party presidential candidate Hillary Clinton.

Trudeau won the election and the Liberals met their commitment on Syrian refugees, a move that generated widespread national pride. Overcoming initial Belgian resistance, Canada and the EU signed CETA at the end of October 2016, and the European Parliament ratified it in

February 2017. So on some of the most polarizing issues in the referendum campaign that formed the core of the Leave pitch to voters, there was significant consensus although not unanimity among Canadians in support of the positions the Remain side advocated. Canadians favoured immigration and were proud of their multicultural society. They saw the benefits of free trade both in their own NAFTA arrangement and in negotiating new deals successfully with Europe and the Pacific Rim countries. Included in that was broad support for labour mobility. Canadian media coverage tended to focus on those issues during the referendum campaign.

In the almost two years since Canadian news organizations had covered Scotland's 2014 referendum, consolidation, cutbacks and closures of media outlets underway at that time, had gathered steam. On that occasion, Canadian coverage focused little on issues in the campaign except for the last few days, concentrating on whether the result would be a Yes or No. The last-minute potential for a surprise result stoked interest in the campaign's final days. When the No side won relatively easily, the Canadian media moved on almost immediately with little coverage of the aftermath of the vote.

Canada's Fading Media

Across Canada from 2008 to 2016, 169 news outlets closed or merged into other outlets (Public Policy Forum 2017, p. 45). They were at the mercy of steep declines in advertising revenue at newspapers (which traditionally relied on advertising for about 80% of their revenue) and over-the-air television stations (with almost 100% of revenue coming from advertising). By 2016, newspaper advertising revenue was only 43% of what it had been in 2003 (Public Policy Forum 2017, p. 18). Canadian news organizations, with their highly concentrated ownership, responded in predictable ways as noted over the years by a range of scholars (Hardy 2017, pp. 10–11, 16). Cutbacks and layoffs of reporters and editors narrowed the range and quality of the content of publications, broadcasts and online media. Unions representing journalists estimate more than 12,000 jobs have been lost, most in the past decade (Public Policy Forum 2017, p. 28). It has meant the same content is increasingly shared across all members of a chain, regardless of their geographic location in a country that spans more than 5000 kilometres. Audiences noticed and they left, looking elsewhere for news. Declining audience numbers meant advertisers would pay less for commercials or would move their advertising online at a fraction of the price of newspaper display advertising. It resulted in even less revenue for news organizations. They responded by cutting more reporters and the cycle began to resemble a death spiral.

Postmedia, Canada's dominant publicly traded news organization, with more than 60 daily newspapers and related websites across the country, was caught in such a decline. Its properties included the *National Post* (the country's second national newspaper) and the major papers in a dozen of Canada's largest cities. Losing revenue, it responded across its media outlets by cost-cutting through consolidation. Editing and page assembly for all its major city dailies were centralized in one city. At the same time, all the papers in the chain were ordered to run the same material, again centrally edited to cut individual newsroom costs. For example, an EU referendum story or opinion column that appeared in the *Montreal Gazette* would on the same day also be in other Postmedia papers, such as the *Vancouver Sun*, the *Calgary Herald*, the *Ottawa Citizen* and often in the *National Post* as well. This narrowing in the range of viewpoints came as individual newspapers lost their ability to select news stories and opinion from independent sources.

The standardization of content across all the Canadian newspapers and websites in a chain was evident in coverage of Scotland's referendum, but it became more prevalent in the EU referendum campaign. Postmedia was not the only owner that responded this way. Torstar Inc., also publicly traded, which owns the *Toronto Star*, Canada's largest newspaper, and dailies in other Ontario urban centres, frequently used identical stories and columns across several publications in different communities, as did the privately owned Brunswick News with the three dailies in New Brunswick. Television had already gone through similar consolidation with fewer reporters and editors in newsrooms and centralized control rooms overseeing and operating newscasts in multiple communities.

The contractions in Canada's media could be seen in other ways, too. During the preceding decade, Canadian news organizations cut the number of their foreign correspondents, eliminating European and Asian bureaus and even cutting reporters based in the USA. Postmedia now had just one travelling correspondent outside of North America. Canada's only wire service, the Canadian Press, abandoned its London bureau in 2004. So most Canadian news organizations relied for international news on foreign journalists working for international wire services

(Associated Press, Bloomberg News, Thomson Reuters, Agence France-Presse) as well as the syndication services of newspapers such as the *Daily Telegraph*, the *Washington Post* and the *New York Times*. By 2016, international news and commentary produced for Canadian audiences by Canadian journalists based outside the country had become an increasingly rare commodity.

There were though a couple of exceptions. The Canadian Broadcasting Corporation (CBC), the public broadcaster, with its extensive television, radio and online presence and an all-news specialty channel, maintains a London bureau, although it too has had staff cuts over the years. RadioCanada, its French-language sister, also has a reporter in London, as does the CTV Television Network (CTV), the country's major private-sector television broadcaster and Global, the other privately owned national television network. The *Globe and Mail*, Canada's self-proclaimed national newspaper, printed and distributed across the country, has two full-time journalists in London; one focusing on international news and the other reporting primarily to the newspaper's business section, Canada's major source of business and economic news.

Others such as Postmedia and the *Toronto Star* sent reporters and columnists to Britain to cover the final days of the campaign. The Leave victory on 23 June meant some of them stayed a few extra days to follow the immediate aftermath, but within a week they were gone. It goes without saying that sort of parachute and episodic coverage can't match the sophistication, depth and context provided by journalists who live on a daily basis in the countries they cover. Many of these elements shaped the news Canadians received about Britain's EU referendum and how they perceived the Leave and Remain campaigns, the result and the aftermath.

METHODOLOGY

This study collected all the EU referendum stories found in the Canadian Newsstand Complete database between 3 June and 3 July 2016 (Canadian Newsstand Complete). This includes English-language newspaper and online stories and television-broadcast scripts plus television-broadcast scripts in French from RadioCanada's nightly main television newscast *Le Téléjournal*. These stories were assembled in a multifield searchable database that identified the date and name of the publication or broadcast, the place line, the headline and reporter, categorizing each entry as news, columns, single opinion pieces from outside contributors, editorial or letter to the Editor. Each story was also labelled according to the story's main subject or issue, with many coded as covering multiple issues.

COVERAGE OF THE CAMPAIGN AND THE VOTE

Had the referendum gone the way most Canadians and the Canadian media anticipated, it likely would not have generated much beyond passing coverage. While the database search produced 667 references during the almost three weeks before the vote and ten days after, slightly more than three-quarters of them were published or broadcast on referendum day (23 June 2016) or later.

Media coverage during the campaign was largely reactive. Those news organizations with London-based reporters seemed to have a campaign coverage strategy, dealing with issues and trying to tap public sentiment in various ways. For the rest of the Canadian media, coverage was episodic, with no sense of an overall plan, perhaps as they perceived the result to be a foregone conclusion. After voting to remain, the media consensus seemed to conclude, things would quickly return to normal and the story would fade away. Many news organizations relied on syndication or wire services for stories based on major news developments such as the murder of British MP Jo Cox (*CBC The National, RadioCanada Téléjournal,* 16 June 2016; *Calgary Herald, Ottawa Citizen, Regina Leader-Post, Saint John Telegraph Journal, Edmonton Journal, Moncton Times Transcript, National Post,* 17 June 2016), or the Leave side's attacks on Bank of England Governor Mark Carney, a Canadian and former Governor of the Bank of Canada, for his predictions about the economic problems that would follow a leave vote (*National Post, Globe and Mail, Calgary Herald, Montreal Gazette, Regina Leader-Post, Ottawa Citizen,* 18 June 2016). Columns and opinion pieces written from Canada often accompanied wire-service news stories from Britain. The columnists often had broad mandates to write about almost anything, yet limited knowledge of the referendum campaign's details.

After 23 June 2016, there was a dramatic increase in the volume of coverage of the referendum. The unexpected and, in Canadian eyes, inexplicable result, David Cameron's resignation, the brutal jockeying to replace him, the Labour revolt against Jeremy Corbyn, the prospect of months and maybe years of economic uncertainly while exit negotiations took place, and public demonstrations and demands that the referendum result be ignored by the British Parliament, were newsworthy and relatively simple and easy to understand and explain to audiences.

Limited coverage prior to 23 June 2016 also reflected the diminished resources of news organizations in Canada. It may also have been the result of past Canadian media experience with referendums. The two on Quebec separation from Canada in 1980 and 1995 were both won by the No side, despite the Yes side at times leading in opinion polls during the 1995 campaign. That year the result was very close, with a 50.5% victory for No and a turnout of 93.5% of eligible voters.

The relatively easy victory of the No camp in the September 2014 referendum on Scotland's independence from the UK may also have led to complacency in Canadian coverage in the days before the EU vote. In Scotland, as in Quebec in 1980, polling suggested the result might be closer than in fact it was. The general sense in the Canadian media was based on its domestic referendum experience that the status quo is often under-represented in pre-vote polling. In some circumstances, it may be less socially acceptable for voters to say they like things the way they are, so respondents tell pollsters they want change then vote for continuity. That certainly has been evident in past gaps between support for Quebec sovereignty found in polls and the actual results from elections. All that might have reinforced the view of Canadian media managers that the referendum result was a foregone conclusion. In fact there were only three editorials written by newspapers prior to the vote, none of which supported the Leave side (*National Post, Globe and Mail, Toronto Star*, 18 June 2016a, c). Interest grew with the result on both editorial and news pages, with 16 editorials published in the 10 days after 23 June 2016. Post-vote coverage in Canada initially concentrated on surprise and confusion about the Leave victory, expressed on editorial pages, in published letters to the Editor in newspapers, and a jump in the number of EU referendum stories in the media.

Over the month from 3 June to 3 July 2016, news stories were almost half of the total collected in this sample, but 65% of those news stories were about events after the vote. Opinion, whether in columns written by employees of news organizations or one-off analyses by academics and others, amounted to 35% of the sample. Again, here, post-vote commentary dominated with four-fifths of opinion pieces published after 23 June 2016. Letters to the Editor accounted for almost 10% of published material but 90% of those letters from the public were responding to the results of the vote; another sign that before 23 June 2016 most Canadians saw the result as a foregone conclusion.

Further emphasizing that point, the volume of print and online EU referendum coverage really began on 18 June 2016, the Saturday before the vote. (In Canada, Saturday, not Sunday, papers are the largest of the week.) Almost 40% of the 97 news stories published prior to 23 June 2016 came in those last five days. In that way, print and online coverage mimicked television, which concentrated its pre-vote newscast coverage in that same final week.

News stories did not mean reporting was done from Britain. In many cases the news stories focused on reaction, whether it was economic concerns on Canadian stock and commodity markets or political responses in Canada to the turns in the campaign. Throughout the period under study, only 30% of referendum coverage in the Canadian media emanated from the UK. Of that, the overwhelming preponderance was from journalists writing from London. That could also have reinforced Canadian complacency in the week leading up to the vote, as London was the centre of Remain strength. While there were occasional stories from outside London, they were certainly the exception.

Slightly more than 40% of the coverage in Canadian media from London-based journalists came from wire and syndication services: Associated Press, Bloomberg News, *Daily Telegraph* and the *Washington Post*. So almost half the news Canadians received from on-the-scene journalists about the 2016 EU referendum campaign and the post-vote political confusion about Britain's future in the EU came not from Canadians overseas and reporting home using examples and context familiar to a domestic audience. It came from wire-service reporters writing for US or global audiences.

It was different with Canadian news outlets that had London-based correspondents, some of whom had covered the 2014 Scottish independence referendum as well. The *Globe and Mail*'s two reporters in London accounted for almost a quarter of the London-based stories carried in the Canadian media during the period. While television networks in Canada paid only limited attention to the 2016 EU referendum, half the coverage provided by the two major English-language broadcasters (CBC and CTV) came from Canadian reporters based in their London bureaus. The CBC also sent a London-based reporter to Brussels to do several stories on European reaction, beginning on the night of 23 June 2016 as votes were counted. RadioCanada had almost as many stories from London as did the CBC.

With just less than one-third of the coverage during the whole period coming from Britain, slightly more than a third came from Toronto, the country's media centre. About 12% of the referendum coverage came from journalists based in Ottawa, Canada's capital. That reflected both futile attempts to get the Trudeau Liberal Government to take a stand on the referendum issue during the campaign, the fate of CETA and the fact that the outcome (Brexit) was in the spotlight as Trudeau, met US President Barack Obama and Mexican President Enrique Peña Nieto in Ottawa on 29 June 2016. They discussed North American issues including highlighting their support for NAFTA as a counterbalance to the referendum vote's rejection of the EU.

The coverage from journalists in Canada consisted mostly of columns and commentary playing off the news rather than reporting it. The only exception was the degree to which financial pages covered daily stock-market fluctuations and offered investment advice both in the period just before the vote and in the confusion about Britain's future in the EU in the days after 23 June 2016. That news-column split was true even at the *Globe and Mail*. While about 40% of its coverage was news, almost as much came in columns written in Toronto. It also had more letters to the Editor on the EU referendum and its immediate aftermath than any other publication in Canada, and wrote four editorials during the course of the campaign, advocating forcefully for the Remain side. Less than a week before the vote, it offered this advice:

Dear Britain, We're sitting here on the other side of the pond, and we're scratching our heads. We hadn't been paying much attention to the Brexit debate until now, because we figured you'd never go through with it. Everyone knows what happens to Humpty Dumpty when he falls off the wall, so we weren't betting on you giving him a shove. Only now it looks like you might.

Which leaves us with one question: Why? [...] You've got a good deal going with the EU. This is a club that every country in the region wants to join. Not only are you a member, but all sorts of unique arrangements have been made so that your membership is like no one else's [...] We know Britain's heart really isn't in the EU, but it doesn't have to be. On 23 June 2016, look to your interests, and to the stability of your own country. From where we sit, they appear to be better protected inside a Europe where Britain has already carved out a unique arrangement. (*Globe and Mail*, 18 June 2016b)

After the vote, describing the outcome as 'pure folly', the *Globe* put Britain's decision in a Canadian context:

> The whole bloody mess would never have happened were it not for Prime Minister David Cameron's promise to hold a referendum as a means of securing his re-election. His misjudgement will go down in British history as one of Neville Chamberlain proportions. It is especially galling for Canadians to see this result after going through two referendums on the breakup of the country and coming out the other side as a united, stronger nation. We are evidence that moving forward and settling disputes in a respectful fashion are the surest ways of bringing prosperity, and now the country from which we were spawned has turned its back on that lesson. (*Globe and Mail*, 25 June 2016)

It recommended Britain and the EU:

> [...] try to come to a mutual arrangement that would allow the status quo to remain with only modest changes [...] If a deal were reached, the UK could hold another referendum, this one based on substance, not on emotion. Don't rush to leave, Britain. You've made one horrible mistake. Don't make another. (*Globe and Mail*, 25 June 2016)

By contrast, Postmedia's flagship newspaper and the *Globe's* national competitor, the conservative *National Post*, walked a fine line in a measured 23 June editorial noting the xenophobia in the Leave campaign but not endorsing either side:

> Whichever way the vote goes, the campaign has made clear that while open borders create many winners, there has been a stark failure to mitigate the impact on those who feel left behind. It is not a small community, and it shares the same sense of abandonment that has spurred the surprising success of Donald Trump's US presidential quest, despite the offensiveness of the candidate and the ugliness of his message. Open borders bring greater prosperity, but they do not erase inequity, and Western powers have done a demonstrably poor job of preparing people to deal with the challenges they bring. In or out of Europe, Britain reflects the failure of governments on both the right and left to successfully integrate economic advances with the needs of populations to adjust. The anger will only grow if that underlying failure is not addressed. (*National Post*, 23 June 2016d)

Perhaps a better sign of where Postmedia stood was its decision to run Boris Johnson's weekly *Daily Telegraph* column, in which one of the leaders of the Leave campaign proclaimed:

> There will still be intense and intensifying European co-operation and partnership in a huge number of fields: the arts, the sciences, the universities and on improving the environment. [...] British people will still be able to go and work in the EU; to live; to travel; to study; to buy homes and to settle down. [...] The only change—and it will not come in any great rush—is that the UK will extricate itself from the EU's extraordinary and opaque system of legislation [...] This will bring not threats, but golden opportunities for Great Britain—to pass laws and set taxes according to the needs of the UK. (*National Post*, 28 June 2016)

The *Globe's* editorial stance reflected the general context within which the referendum debate and result were reported in Canada. The issue was covered as primarily a debate about economics. The economy, trade, stock markets, investments and the value of the pound were themes in more than a third of coverage. Before the vote, stories were frequently framed around the economic cost of leaving the EU. What was characterized by Leave supporters as the Remain side's scare campaign suggesting economic ruin following a split had echoes of the same dire economic predictions by the federal side in Canada in the 1995 Quebec referendum. That almost cost the federalists the victory.

The ephemeral questions posed in stories before 23 June 2016 became more focused in the greater volume of coverage that speculated about the meaning of the Leave victory and what would happen next. Is it a sign of anti-immigrant nativism sweeping Western democracies? Are the Leave vote and rise of Donald Trump in the USA expressions of the same anti-elitism from those feeling dispossessed by globalization and the digital economy? Could Britain be better off economically outside the EU? Could it develop trading relationships and what would a British split from the EU mean for CETA? While the Leave side pointed to CETA as a model of what an independent Britain could achieve in trade agreements, there was little enthusiasm for such a separate deal expressed in the Canadian media, perhaps because of the knowledge that it took so long to negotiate and the deal was not yet ratified.

Canadians also had a special interest in the role of Mark Carney. His interventions (particularly those in the campaign's final days that noted the possibility of a recession, slower growth and higher inflation if Britain left the EU) were covered by both Canada's national newspapers and other Postmedia outlets (*Globe and Mail*, 17 June 2016a; *National Post, Montreal Gazette, Calgary Herald, Vancouver Sun, Ottawa Citizen, Saskatoon Star-Phoenix*, 18 June 2016a). Stories also noted the post-vote possibility that Carney would be pressed to resign based on what Leave campaigners vociferously argued was the Bank's failure to remain neutral throughout the campaign (*Globe and Mail*, 25, 27, 30 June 2016, 1 July 2016c; *National Post*, 27 June 2016a; *Ottawa Citizen*, 28 June 2016b; *Saint John Telegraph-Journal*, 30 June 2016).

Next to the economy, the most common theme of EU referendum coverage was politics, politicians and political manoeuvring. Most of that came in the days after the vote as the Leave side revealed it had no idea how to implement its exit from the EU and the Conservative and Labour parties were consumed by leadership politics and parliamentary caucus revolts.

Immigration and labour mobility was raised in about 10% of the stories, but generally as a secondary issue behind the economic implications of leaving. Other campaign concerns, such as European rules and regulations threatening British sovereignty, were barely mentioned in Canadian media. Post-vote, there was also attention paid to Scotland's circumstances and the prospect of the Leave victory leading to a second Scottish independence referendum to leave the UK to remain in the EU (*Toronto Star*, 24, 25 June 2016a, b; *RadioCanada Téléjournal*, 26 June 2016b; *Fredericton Daily Gleaner*, 25 June 2016; *Globe and Mail*, 29 June 2016a; *Montreal Gazette, Calgary Herald, National Post*, 27 June 2016; *National Post*, 28 June 2016b; *Globe and Mail*, 2 July 2016b).

Television Coverage

Television coverage differed from that in print and online. The CBC introduced the referendum campaign in its coverage of the Queen's 90th birthday on 12 June 2016, and did not resist brief video highlights of the comic Leave versus Remain referendum flotilla battle on the Thames between United Kingdom Independence Party (UKIP) leader Nigel Farage and Irish musician Bob Geldof three days later. That day, the CBC also ran a longer story sending its reporter to Boston, Lincolnshire to examine the immigration debate. Two days later it turned to the aftermath of the Jo Cox murder, the temporary suspension of the campaign and the divisions in British society created by the referendum campaign (*RadioCanada Le Téléjournal*, 16 June 2016).

The CBC was the only Canadian news outlet with a reporter in Brussels on 23–24 June 2016 (*CBC The National*, 23 June 2016, 24 June 2016). It continued to focus on the story over the weekend with an EU referendum and Brexit panel discussion on its Sunday evening newscast trying to look ahead as well as recapping the tumultuous first days after the vote. In video clips that week, it also covered Farage's post-vote appearance at the European Parliament, Barack Obama's suggestion in Ottawa that Brexit hysteria was overblown, and an increase in racist attacks in Britain. Other news organizations used wire-service stories to follow post-vote developments at the European Parliament (*Saskatoon Star-Phoenix, Montreal Gazette*, 29 June 2016; *Moncton Times-Transcript, Saint John Telegraph-Journal*, 29 June 2016).

CTV's coverage began on 10 June, noting *Der Spiegel* urging Britain to stay in the EU and featuring a story explaining support for the Leave campaign through interviews with voters in the Romford market, east of London. It also covered the referendum Thames flotilla with voice-over of video from the confrontation. Post-vote coverage centred on the political fallout focusing on party leadership, an apparent rise in racist attacks and public demonstrations in support of staying in the EU.

By 3 July 2016, the volume of coverage had started to fall significantly from the post-vote peak. But that week from 26 June to 2 July 2016 produced 25% of all the news stories collected in the database search and two-third of all the referendum coverage over the month. That post-vote period also saw a significant switch in coverage from news to opinion. Leading up to the vote, just over 60% of the coverage was news while columns and opinion made up a quarter of the total coverage. After the vote, news dropped to under 40% of total coverage, despite the post-vote political chaos, while columns and opinion accounted for about one-third of everything published and broadcast. Facts and quotes were being replaced by opinion.

Conclusion

Canadian media coverage of the EU referendum campaign, the vote and aftermath was largely reactive, heavily concentrated in the post-vote period with limited campaign coverage or serious examination of the issues as enunciated by the Leave and Remain campaigns. To the extent there was a coverage strategy by most news organizations, it seemed based on the assumption the Remain side would win and Britain would still be in the EU on 24 June 2016. The Canadian media reinforced that perception by covering the campaign primarily through an economic lens, coloured by Canada's own positive experiences and support for trade agreements and the globalization of trade and manufacturing supply chains. A similarly positive view of the benefits of immigration may also explain why the xenophobic elements of the Leave campaign and the 'oppressive' nature of EU regulations received relatively little attention prior to 23 June 2016.

The campaign coverage also laid bare the shrinking horizons of Canadian news organizations as they faced growing financial pressures. For most Canadians, much of their foreign news now comes from wire or syndication services, reporting for global audiences. This is a worldwide trend noted in a 2013 European Commission study of media freedom and pluralism (Hardy 2017, p. 16). Canadian media with London bureaus and journalists (the *Globe and Mail* and the television networks) provided coverage with greater breadth and depth because they were there, immersed in the campaign on a daily basis and able to put the aftermath into a context Canadian audiences might better understand. Some Canadian media sent journalists to Britain to cover the final few days before the vote, staying for a few days after 23 June 2016. It was better than wire-service reporting but their coverage inevitably lacked the range and depth of that provided by those based in Britain.

Canadian coverage of the referendum campaign also highlighted another trend: the shift away from reporting to commentary, as after 23 June 2016 there was an almost equal share of news stories and opinion in Canada's media, virtually all of the latter written by those sitting in Canada, far from where the news happened. Finally, the superior quality and breadth of EU referendum coverage provided by Canadian news organizations with their own Canadian journalists based in London clearly demonstrated what Canadian audiences lose when the majority of their media hand over responsibility for covering the world to others.

REFERENCES

Belanger, J.-F. 2016a. Maintien de la Grande-Bretagne au sein de l'EU: une députée militante est tuée, la campagne référendaire est suspendue. *RadioCanada Téléjournal*, June 16.

Belanger, J.-F. 2016b. Maintien de la Grande-Bretagne au sein de l'EU: une députée militante est tuée, la campagne référendaire est suspendue. *RadioCanada Téléjournal*, June 26.

Carmichael, K. 2016a. Brexit Puts Spotlight on Carney; Widening Political Crisis Adds to Challenge Facing Central Banker. *National Post*, June 27.

Carmichael, K. 2016b. Carney at Centre of Storm. *Ottawa Citizen*, June 28.

Cook, L. 2016. EU Leaders Plot a Future Without Britain, Demand Answers (Associated Press). *Moncton Times-Transcript, Saint John Telegraph-Journal*, June 29.

Daigle, T. 2016. British MP Jo Cox Dies After Being Shot. *CBC The National*, June 16.

Deacon, M. 2016. Brexit Leader Laughs While Brussels Boos; Farage Jeered at Emergency Session (Associated Press). *Montreal Gazette, Saskatoon Star-Phoenix*, June 29.

DiManno, R. 2016a. Scotland Will Decide Future of Britain. *Toronto Star*, June 24.

DiManno, R. 2016b. 'Leave' Adds Fuel to Scots' Fire. *Toronto Star*, June 25.

Editorial. 2016a. The End of Civilized Discourse. *National Post*, June 18.

Editorial. 2016b. The U.K. Is Better in than out. *Globe and Mail*, June 18.

Editorial. 2016c. British Should Stay in EU and Fix It. *Toronto Star*, June 18.

Editorial. 2016d. Will They Stay or Will They Go? *National Post*, June 23.

Evans, M. 2016. Reactions in Brussels Tonight to the Referendum Results in the UK. *CBC The National*, June 23.

Hardy, Jonathan. 2017. Money, (Co)Production and Power. *Digital Journalism* 5 (1): 1–25. https://doi.org/10.1080/21670811.2016.1152162.

Harley, N., R. Mendick, and G. Rayner. 2017. We Have Lost a Great Star'; British PM Pays Tribute to Pro-EU Politician Shot to Death After Meeting with Her Constituents. (*Daily Telegraph*) *Calgary Herald, National Post, Ottawa Citizen, Regina Leader-Post, Edmonton Journal*, June 17.

Ivison, J. 2016a. Carney Steps into the Brexit Firing Line. *National Post, Montreal Gazette, Ottawa Citizen, Vancouver Sun, Saskatoon Star-Phoenix*, June 18.

Ivison, J. 2016b. Britain Drifts Rudderless, in Risk of Breakup; Scots and Northern Irish Mull. *National Post*, June 28.

Johnson, B. 2016. The State of the Kingdom is Strong. *National Post*, June 28.

Katz, G. 2016. Turmoil Deepens as Scotland Threatens to Block Brexit; Labour's Corbyn Faces Revolt in Shadow Cabinet (Associated Press). *Montreal Gazette, Calgary Herald, National Post*, June 27.

Kelbie, P., and S. Pogatchnik. 2016. Scots, Irish Eye U.K. Escape After Brexit (Associated Press). *Fredericton Daily Gleaner*, June 25.

Lawless, J., and G. Katz. 2016. British Lawmaker Dies After Shooting Attack (Associated Press). *Saint John Telegraph-Journal, Moncton Times-Transcript*, June 17.

MacKinnon, M. 2016a. Scotland to Lobby EU on Staying in Bloc. *Globe and Mail*, June 29.

MacKinnon, M. 2016b. Scotland Prepares for a New Life After Brexit. *Globe and Mail*, July 2.

Meakin, L. 2016. Carney in Brexit Crisis Confronts Own Future at Three-Year Mark (Bloomberg). *Saint John Telegraph-Journal*, June 30.

Parkinson, D. 2016. Best Man to Guide Britain's Economy? He's Already on the Case. *Globe and Mail*, June 30.

Public Policy Forum. 2017. Shattered Mirror: News, Democracy and Trust in the Digital Age [pdf] Ottawa. https://shatteredmirror.ca/wp-content/uploads/theShatteredMirror.pdf (Accessed 8 March 2017).

Waldie, P. 2016a. Carney Fights Back over Brexit. *Globe and Mail*, June 17.

Waldie, P. 2016b. UKIP Leader Who Led the 'Leave' Charge Has Harsh Words for Trudeau, Carney. *Globe and Mail*, June 27.

Waldie, P. 2016c. Carney Signals Interest Rate Cut in Store. *Globe and Mail*, July 1.

CHAPTER 19

Russian Media and the EU Referendum 2016

Helena Bassil-Morozow

INTRODUCTION

The Russian media's attitude towards the 2016 EU referendum and 'Brexit' (Britain's exit from the EU) can be summed up in the headline which the Latvia-based online Russian-language outlet *Meduza* ran on 25 June 2016c: 'United Kingdom leaves EU. Why should we care?' The article goes on to list the main issues associated with Brexit: Why Britain does not want to be part of a prestigious union; the effect of Brexit on European Union (EU) citizens currently living in the UK; Whether the 2016 EU referendum vote offers a binding and final exit; Whether the UK economy is likely to suffer as a result of uncertainty. However, in the last paragraph, it returns to the issue of the relevance of Brexit for Russia:

> *How will this affect Russian citizens? This is not our business.*
>
> There is no direct threat (or obvious benefits) from Brexit for us: we have always had to apply for visas to travel to the UK, and London will remain the financial centre of Europe where many wealthy Russian citizens live. The only downside is that property prices may fall.

H. Bassil-Morozow (✉)
Glasgow Caledonian University, Glasgow, Scotland
e-mail: Helena.Bassil-Morozow@gcu.ac.uk

© The Author(s) 2018
A. Ridge-Newman et al. (eds.), *Reporting the Road to Brexit*,
https://doi.org/10.1007/978-3-319-73682-2_19

There are also indirect threats, though. If Brexit triggers a 'domino effect', and causes the fall of the European Union, the economic recession will be back (not to mention more short-term economic effects). This, in turn, will result in the fall of oil and gas prices—and a decrease in consumption of Russia's key exports.

The headline reflects the overall attitude of Russian media towards the outcome of the 2016 EU referendum in the form of Brexit: it is a geographically distant and politically confusing process. It is happening far from 'our' country. We cannot grasp its causes, follow its trajectory or predict its outcome. Besides, we have enough problems with our own crazy politicians and nationalists. Our economy is suffering from a combination of the 'Dutch disease' (a sudden increase in the country's wealth caused by the discovery of raw materials such as oil and gas) and the effect of Western economic sanctions. Why should we care indeed?

THE PRO-GOVERNMENT PRESS ON BREXIT

Inward-looking and defensive, the 'official' government-controlled Russian media have traditionally showed relatively little interest in foreign news unless it directly concerns Russian interests or politics. This tendency has been evidently inherited from the Soviet times when the deeply insular, ideologically biased media reflected the country's political isolation. As a result, Brexit, which in the UK looks like a major event which will define the economic and political life of the country for generations, is seen by Russian commentators as a vague phenomenon of dubious importance. Most of the material about Brexit is reactive: translations and summaries rather than original pieces. These often incorporate what Russian journalists probably see as 'commentary', usually in the form of clumsy jokes or sarcastic statements.

The openly pro-Putin outlet *Komsomolskaya Pravda* published a number of sarcastic articles about Brexit. The newspaper's name literally means 'The Komsomol truth'. The Komsomol (the All-Union Leninist Young Communist League) was the top tier of the Soviet system of peer groups, and the entry tier of the Communist Party, right above the 'Young Pioneers'. It accepted older teenagers (normally 15–19 years old) who, upon joining the organization, could proudly call themselves 'Komsomolets'.

Komsomolskaya Pravda was established in 1925 as the official outlet of the Komsomol organization. After the collapse of the Soviet Union in 1990, the outlet became a very successful low-quality tabloid, very much like *The Daily Mail* in the UK. Now it has close links with Gazprom (a Russian oil and gas giant), which bought it in 2006, ensuring close monitoring of content by the government. In fact, Gazprom's choice of the outlet to transform into the government's mouthpiece reflects the newspaper's legacy as the tightly controlled mouthpiece of the Party.

One of the first in the series of articles about Brexit in *Komsomolskaya Pravda* is titled 'Referendum Results: the UK voted to leave the EU', and contains the ramblings of a journalist interviewing random people on the streets on the day of the referendum. The author is convinced that 'there is no country in the world more indifferent towards the 2016 EU referendum than Russia. This is regardless of the joint joke by the Prime Minister David Cameron and Foreign Minister Philip Hammond that '"the only parties interested in the UK leaving the EU are Russia and Putin"' (Sapozhnikova 2016). The article is full of schadenfreude and openly shows the author's hope for the swift demise of the EU. Another article, also dated 24 June, describes the currency fluctuations in Europe in doomsday terms, and prophesies that things will get worse both for the UK and Europe (Belyakov 2016).

A more interesting piece in the same newspaper, however, contains an interview with Putin himself. Firstly, he denies that Russia is in any way happy about the referendum result. Such insinuations, Putin says, are manifestations of 'a low-quality political culture'. He also commented, quite confidently, on reasons for the 'leave' vote:

> No one wants to feed other countries and subsidize weaker economic systems. It also looks like mass migration to the EU made people in the UK concerned about safety and security. People want to be more independent. The EU has too much power. People are different: some individuals approve of the erosion of national boundaries; others don't. However, which path to choose it entirely up to the British people. We have never interfered with this choice, and will not interfere with it in future. (Smirnov 2016)

The same interview is repeated in another pro-government medium, *Moscovsky Komsomolets* (translated as 'the Komsomolets of Moscow'), with the added subtitle 'Putin Accuses Cameron of Low Political

Culture'. Like *Komsomolskaya Pravda, Moscovsky Komsomolets* (MK) was a party-line newspaper in the Soviet time and became a seedy tabloid during Perestroika. It is still supporting the official party line, albeit the agenda has changed.

Another *MK* article, 'Brexit: New Reality, or the British Thaw', discusses the reaction to Brexit of other Russian politicians, including Russian Foreign Minister Sergey Lavrov and Vladimir Putin's Press Secretary Dmitry Peskov. Their views betray a mixture of hope, bitterness and resentment. For instance, Peskov says: 'We hope that in these new circumstances there will emerge an awareness of the importance of good relations with Russia' (*Moscovsky Komskomolets*, 24 June 2016d). Meanwhile, Lavrov's view is deliberately insulting: 'I can't comment on clinical cases. This is the UK's own business' (*Moscovsky Komskomolets*, 24 June 2016d). The combination of the two attitudes, 'Brexit is a clinical case', with its connotations of insanity, and 'it's their internal business', which feigns indifference, shows the interviewees' barely disguised and anxious interest in the dynamics of political power in the West.

Yet, the title of the article is full of hope for a positive change in attitudes towards Russia: 'The Thaw' is a popular metaphor in Russian politics, originally referring to the post-Stalin era characterized by a relaxation of censorship and media control, increased creativity in the Soviet entertainment industry and a more open relationship with the West. In 2014, after the annexation of Crimea by Russia, the USA and the EU responded with a list of sanctions as a means of putting pressure on Russia 'to behave in a civilized manner', and to return the peninsula to Ukraine. The sanctions, which included a travel ban for a number of high-profile politicians, the freezing of assets of a number of companies and individuals, an import ban on goods and a ban on investment, have crippled the Russian economy. The rouble has also dipped sharply against the dollar. Applied to the context in which Brexit happened, the term 'thaw' implies hope for the lifting of economic and political sanctions, thus directly contradicting the tough stance expressed by the Russian politicians in the interviews.

THE CASE OF *MEDUZA*

Fighting against this backward attitude in the Russian-language media and in the country in general is a handful of dissident media organizations, mostly amateur or semi-professional, and social-media based.

One of them is an established online news outlet evocatively called *Meduza*. Originally a Russian-language outlet (its English version was launched in 2015), *Meduza* is one of the few Russia-focused media daring to speak 'the truth'; that is, offering alternatives to 'official truths'. *Meduza* is one of the few available media outlets in Russian that are not state-controlled. Its headquarters are in the capital of Latvia, Riga, away from Moscow's controlling hand.

The outlet's Editor-in-Chief, Galina Timchenko, used to occupy a similar position at the online news outlet Lenta.ru, but was removed from it, along with a number of other journalists, following a shake-up by the pro-Putin oligarch Alexander Leonidovich Mamut. The name *Meduza* has obvious references to the snake-haired, terrifying mythological character Medusa the Gorgon, whose look could turn people to stone. Such a name carries connotations of vengeance, wrath as well as references to exile (she ended up in Africa where she shed her snakes).

The English part of the website was launched to connect Russia with the West and vice versa: to allow English-reading Russians to obtain alternative views on the political and economic situation in the country. In this way, *Meduza* links the West and the East as it translates Russian realities into English. This is how its creators describe their mission:

> *Meduza* is based in Riga, Latvia. Most of the people in our newsroom moved here after resigning from Lenta.ru, when Chief Editor Galina Timchenko was fired in what we believe was an act of censorship. Our team includes some of Russia's top professionals in news and reporting.
>
> *Meduza* produces a wide variety of news stories, and here, on its English-language version, you'll find the stories most vital to understanding what's really going on in Russia. We translate and tailor these stories, making them accessible to a global audience. We do it fast and we get our facts straight. We also translate original reports by *Meduza*'s news staff and special correspondents, as well as contributing our own original material.
>
> Serving as Russia's free press in-exile is a role forced on us, and it's still new to us. But we value our independence and strive to be a reliable, trusted outlet for objective, verified, and unbiased information about Russia and the former Soviet Union, as well as a source for sharp insights about one of the world's most enigmatic regions. (*Meduza*, 2 February 2015)

Unlike the pro-government news outlets, *Meduza*'s reporting on Brexit has been fairly impartial. For instance, an article titled 'UK against the EU: What was Happening in the Country Before and During the Referendum' is a series of sketches of political events on the streets of London on 23 June 2016. For this report, *Meduza*'s correspondent in London asked locals from both Leave and Remain camps about their reasons for voting in a particular way. Whereas the pro-Putin newspapers and media outlets are full of derogatory terms for British politicians, any famous names in *Meduza*'s article are mentioned in an unbiased manner. Even British newspapers do not treat David Cameron and George Osborne in such dispassionate terms.

The outlet's reporting of Russian politicians' reactions to Brexit is also neutral. Most of the articles on the subject combine careful assessment of the situation with statements by Russian politicians. A good example of this kind of journalism is the article published in *Meduza* the day after the referendum:

> Since Moscow has close ties with European nationalists, all news from the EU is primarily regarded from the point of view of the future of economic sanctions. Many Russian politicians saw the decision of the British people to leave the European Union as a positive sign [...] 'We hope that the new political realities will bring about an understanding that the UK needs to build good relations with Russia', said the president's press-secretary Dmitry Peskov

> At the same time, Peskov warned against drawing any direct correlations between the referendum and sanctions against Russia: 'Even within the EU itself there are different view on the sanctions against Russia. I don't think Brexit will change much.'

> Later on Putin himself weighed in on the debate: 'Regarding the economic and political sanctions against Russia, I don't think Brexit will change anything in our relations with the EU', said the Russian president. He also added that 'the number of binding decisions by the European parliament which the EU countries have to implement is very high. Even in the former USSR the constituent republics were more devolved. It is not surprising that most UK citizens do not like this dependence on the EU', Putin said. (*Meduza*, 24 June 2016b)

WHAT IS A WHOEXIT?

It is interesting that, while Putin accused Cameron of 'low-quality political culture', virtually every Russian official of note communicated their view of Brexit using offensive or denigrating expressions. One of these officials was Maria Zakharova, whose full title is 'Director of the Information and Press Department of the Ministry of Foreign Affairs of the Russian Federation'. Shortly after the referendum, another ex-Soviet newspaper (and now an outlet toeing the official party line), *Izvestija* ('The News'), published an overview of Zakharova's Facebook statement in which she suggested that the terms 'Brexit' and 'Grexit' should be replaced with the word 'Whoexit'. Here is the full statement which was published on Zakharova's official Facebook account under public access:

> It looks like Victoria Nuland's famous remark ['Fuck the EU!'] which she made in a telephone conversation with the US ambassador in Ukraine in 2014 has become reality. What can I say [...] if the EU keeps denying its countries the right to make independent decisions concerning international affairs and imposition of sanctions, there will be referendums even worse than this one. Russia has already been congratulated by the busybody Mikhail [sic] McFaul & Co who sincerely believe that the Dead Sea was also destroyed by Russia. Yet, I would like to remind those who have retained the ability to think independently that for the past couple of years both London and Brussels have been controlled by US politics.

> By the way, each time Europe actually listened to Russia and followed its advice (for instance, on the issues of the invasion of Iraq or the need for political intervention in the Iranian Nuclear Programme), it actually got positive results, and did not lose face unlike those who blindly followed Washington.

> I find the UK Government's initial reactions to the referendum daunting. We keep insisting that Brexit is your own business, and not in any way ours. I think we have expressed ourselves clearly regarding this matter. Yet, the British Foreign Secretary Philip Hammond spits in the face of his own nation by announcing that 'he hopes that Brexit will not result in the weakening of sanctions against Russia'. How smart! [sic] This is becoming more and more interesting. Here I am just following Hammond's train of thought—it was his idea to link the sanctions to Brexit. Having always put pressure on the EU to introduce and maintain the anti-Russian measures, the UK's political establishment has led EU citizens into a dead end, and then sort of announced: 'Thank you very much for the nice dinner. We had a great time, please pay our bill. Bye!'

> They will never leave us alone, it has always been like this. For God's sake, stop shifting the blame for all your mistakes onto Russia! My advice to the British political elites would therefore be: learn to respect the decision of your own people to leave the EU the way Russia respects their decision.

We don't meddle in your political affairs. Meanwhile, I won't be surprised if soon, instead of words denoting different countries' exits from the EU, such as 'Brexit and 'Grexit', there will emerge a more universal word: 'Whoexit' [©].

'Whoexit' sounds like an insult in Russian. While the word looks like a bad pun in English, and can be interpreted as 'we don't care who exits the European Union and who does not', in Russian it is actually very close to the word 'hui', a profane version of 'penis'. Its closest match in English would probably be 'dick'. To a Russian ear, 'Whoexit' has a vaguely profane meaning, something between 'We don't give a f**k' and 'You are a d**k'.

Being Scared and Towing the Party Line

Russian media appear to be well trained to deal with the politicians' dubious and sometimes openly abusive statements, which are duly reported by both neutral and pro-government media, but there are no opinions whatsoever expressed in the reports. These totally impartial news articles are the result of two decades of political 'cleansing' of the profession. Media outlets convey the information with a sort of quiet desperation, ideologically fuelled aggression, or alternatively with false and perceivably weak enthusiasm.

For instance, the rather neutral *Vedomosti* did its best to present Zakharova's Facebook entry without any emotional colouring or even a shade of opinion. The title states: 'The Press Secretary of the Foreign Ministry Maria Zakharova Copyrighted the Term "Whoexit"'. It goes on to report, in a rather official-sounding and cumbersome way (in which one can also sense irony) that 'the Press Secretary of the Foreign Ministry of Russia placed the © sign after the word "Whoexit" which she thinks will be useful as the European Union gets weaker, and all the other terms describing exit from it will be depleted'.

The author of the article also cautiously juxtaposes the Facebook diatribe with the official statement on Brexit of the Russian Foreign Ministry, thus emphasizing (with a degree of cautious and delicate humour) the discrepancy between the artificiality and pretence of the mask presented by Kremlin officials to the outside world, and the barely controlled gleeful rage going on underneath the surface: 'In the Foreign Ministry's official statement concerning the 2016 EU referendum,

Zakharova pointed out that "the results of the referendum have clearly shown serious problems within the EU" and that "much will now depend on how the British Government interprets the vote"'.

Whereas any such statements quickly become memes on Russian social media, readers in Europe and the UK are mostly unaware of them. *Meduza*'s publication in English on the subject is an attempt to expose the bullying behaviour of Russian politicians in the West. Published on 27 June 2016, it is titled 'Let's all pause and ponder this incredibly awkward suggestion by the spokesperson of Russia's Foreign Ministry':

> The spokesperson for Russia's Foreign Ministry, Maria Zakharova, coined the term 'Whoexit' last week in response to the result of the British referendum on leaving the European Union [...]

> Zakharova's joke, posted on Facebook, is a play on the Russian swear word that rhymes loosely with the English word 'who'—the language's most ubiquitous obscenity (which generally translates as 'dick,' though its applications in Russian are far wider and more terrifying) [...]

> Zakharova is not the only Russian politician or public personality to have expressed her views on Brexit on social media. Politician and businessman Boris Titov wrote: 'It seems that it has happened: UK out!!! In my opinion, the most important long-term consequence of this development is that Europe will be ripped away from the Anglo-Saxons and that means from the United States. This is not the freedom of Great Britain from Europe, but the freedom of Europe from Britain. [Which means that] we are not too far from a united Eurasia—perhaps within 10 years.' (*Meduza*, 27 June 2016e)

Anti-Western Ideology and Brexit Schadenfreude

Careful not to overstep the line, news outlets manage to report the most ridiculous and scandalous statements by Russian politicians in a bland and unexciting manner. Yet, Zakharova's words are not far removed from the Russian political realities and do, in fact, reflect the spirit of the brainwashed segment of the Russian public. Regarding Brexit reporting, this tendency has been exacerbated by the fact that the EU referendum does not top the list of breaking news for an average citizen in Russia. Sarcastic jokes aside, both the public and the media treat Brexit as a remote issue.

This is not so unusual if one regards this lack of interest in the context of Galtung and Rouge's News Values framework (initially published in 1965). A quick reminder of the twelve values constituting the framework:

1. Frequency
2. Threshold
3. Unambiguity
4. Meaningfulness
5. Consonance
6. Unexpectedness
7. Continuity
8. Composition
9. Reference to elite nations
10. Reference to elite people
11. Reference to persons
12. Reference to something negative (Cohen and Young 1981: 60)

Thanks to the geographical distance and cultural gap, the fate of the Brexit story in Russia is shaped by several news values: by (F4) Meaningfulness on the one hand and by (F12) Negativity, (F10) Reference to Elite Nations and (F6) Unexpectedness on the other. Interestingly enough, Meaningfulness has outweighed the other three news values in terms of sustaining the Russian public's interest in the result of the referendum.

According to Galtung and Rouge, the category of meaningfulness can be further subdivided into (F4.1) Cultural Proximity and (F4.2) Relevance. As a political phenomenon, Brexit is both culturally and geographically distant from Russia and therefore is not seen there as a particularly newsworthy piece. On the other hand, it is a piece of negative information about two of Russia's arch-enemies: the UK and Europe. That these two parties are not getting on well is, on the one hand, a manifestation of (F12) Reference to Something Negative and, on the other, good news for Putin's anti-Western propaganda machine. This negativity (at least, in theory) should increase the importance of Brexit in the eyes of the Russian public.

Brexit news also appeals to (F9) the Elite Nations value. All the countries directly or indirectly affected by Brexit can be seen as 'elite', particularly compared to the way Russian people see themselves. Russian self-perception is characterized by a feeling of inferiority in relation to the more enlightened West. This feeling often forms a toxic combination with patriotism and defensive behaviour, the two traits encouraged and promoted by the pro-Putin media. When bad things happen to 'elite nations', this is good news indeed for those who control the Russian masses' attitude towards the West.

Pro-Putin media generate examples of this every day. For instance, on 28 July 2017 *Moskovsky Komsomoletz* published an article discussing an incident with a sanctioned Russian politician, Dmitry Rogozin, whose plane had to turn back as it reached Romania on the way to the Republic of Moldova. Romanian authorities barred him from the country's airspace as a persona non grata. The plane had to land in Minsk instead. Rogozin's reaction to the decision was a threat to 'show the bastards what we can do to them'.

The *Moskovsky Komsomoletz* article consisted of an interview with an expert(a pilot with forty-three years' experience) who was asked to comment on the possible dangers of such a situation (*Moskovsky Komsomoletz*, 28 July 2017). Predictably, the pilot mentioned in his assessment that Russia 'does not have friends except for the army, navy and military aviation'. He also suggested that Romania could not possibly have acted differently because 'European countries are dependent on US credit. Countries like Romania are only alive because America gives them financial aid.' The West, the interviewee insisted without specifying what this collective term exactly entails, enforce sanctions because they simply hate Russia for no apparent reason.

Ironically, in the middle of the interview, he was asked whether he had ever been in an emergency situation. He replied: yes, many times, the most dangerous incident being when he had to fly Vladimir Zhirinovsky (an infamous Russian politician) to Saddam Hussain's birthday party. The airport where they were supposed to land was a secret one, and the pilots weren't given any information about its whereabouts. Eventually, the pilot continued, the Mother of God and the Almighty helped them find the right place.

This incident, as well as the way it was recalled by the interviewee, shows the essence of Russia's perception of individual responsibility as opposed to the West: irrational and superstitious, people with such an attitude look for a scapegoat to blame for their own mistakes and backwardness. A pilot, the interviewee still believes in being saved by the Mother of God (which in Russian sounds suspiciously like a swear word since Mother has many connotations, from Mother Russia and Mother Earth to 'I fucked your mother'). It also does not occur to him to blame the receiving party (Saddam Hussain in this case) for failing to provide them with the correct information in order to land safely.

An individual is a person who takes responsibility for his or her actions. Uploading this responsibility to an Almighty, any kind of mother or looking for someone to blame for one's own failings means the person can't separate him or herself from the outside world. Russia's response to Brexit reflects this attitude perfectly: 'The hateful West is (hopefully) falling apart, and we have told you it's going to happen. Not that we are bothered at all, though. Let them rot. We don't need Western rationality because planes are flown by God's grace anyway.'

So, Does Russia Care About Brexit?

Russian-speaking media can be roughly divided into two groups: the official pro-Government outlets and the smaller group of websites (such as *Meduza*), radio stations (Dozhd) and social media pages keen to reveal the truth about the Russian political realities. Yet, regardless of the emotional colouring and ideological content of Russian media's reporting of Brexit, they are all united by the subject of sanctions against Russia. Russia only cares about referendum results if it means progress in terms of its relations with the West. The pro-Putin outlets also display barely disguised *s*chadenfreude regarding the future of the EU. However, the details of the complex phenomenon of Brexit are lost on both Russian media and Russian people. As the famous Russian saying goes, 'the shirt you are wearing is always closer to your body than the one worn by another'. In other words, Russia has too many problems of its own to think about Brexit, and is mostly interested in how the new political situation will affect its status and welfare.

Bibliography

Academic Sources

Cohen, Stanley, and Jock Young. 1981. *The Manufacture of News: Deviance, Social Problems and the Mass Media*. London: Constable.

News Sources

Anon. 2015. Welcome to *Meduza*. *Meduza*, February 2. https://meduza.io/en/feature/2015/02/02/welcome-to-meduza.

Anon. 2016a. *Meduza*, June 25. https://meduza.io/feature/2016/06/25/velikobritaniya-vyhodit-iz-es-a-nam-to-chto.

Anon. 2016b. The EU Needs to Change, or it Will Fall Apart. *Meduza*, June 24. https://meduza.io/feature/2016/06/24/neobhodimo-pereizobresti-evropu-inache-ey-grozit-raspad.

Anon. 2016c. The UK Has Voted to Leave the EU, But Why Should We Care? *Meduza*, June 25. https://meduza.io/feature/2016/06/25/velikobritaniya-vyhodit-iz-es-a-nam-to-chto.

Anon. 2016d. Peskov on Brexit: New Realities, or the British Thaw, *Moscovsky Komskomolets*, June 24. http://www.mk.ru/politics/2016/06/24/lavrov-i-peskov-o-brexit-novye-realii-ili-britanskaya-ottepel.html.

Anon. 2016e. Let's all Pause and Ponder this Incredibly Awkward Suggestion by the Spokesperson of Russia's Foreign Ministry. *Meduza*, June 27. https://meduza.io/en/lion/2016/06/27/let-s-all-pause-and-ponder-this-incredibly-awkward-suggestion-by-the-spokesperson-of-russia-s-foreign-ministry.

Anon. 2017. Could Dmitry Rogozin's Plane Have Crashed? *Moskovsky Komsomoletz*, July 27. http://www.mk.ru/politics/2017/07/28/mog-li-rukhnut-samolet-dmitriya-rogozina.html?utm_source=push&utm_term=push_290717.

Belyakov, Evgeny. 2016. Black Friday for Europe. *Komsomolskaya Pravda*, June 24. http://www.kp.ru/daily/26546/3563164/.

Sapozhnikova, Galina. 2016. Referendum Result: British People Have Voted to Leave the EU. *Komsomolskaya Pravda*, June 24. http://www.kp.ru/daily/26546.4/3562629/.

Smirnov, Dmitry. 2016. Putin on Brexit: Nobody Wants to Subsidize Other Countries. *Komsomolskaya Pravda*, June 24. https://www.kp.ru/daily/26547.7/3563180/.

PART V

Conclusion

CHAPTER 20

Constructing Brexit: Crisis and International Political Communication

Anthony Ridge-Newman, Fernando León-Solís
and Hugh O'Donnell

Introduction

The lexical content of the chapters of this book demonstrates that to some extent the neologism 'Brexit' (Britain's exit of the European Union [EU]) is a term that has become synonymous with the campaign and the event of the 2016 EU referendum. The omnipotence of Brexit in the United Kingdom (UK) has been to such an extent that the referendum has since earned the nickname the 'Brexit referendum' across public and scholarly discourses (for example, Vasilopoulou 2016). The phrase implies that the referendum itself is characterized by the 'Leave'

A. Ridge-Newman (✉)
Liverpool Hope University, Liverpool, UK
e-mail: ridgena@hope.ac.uk

F. León-Solís
University of the West of Scotland, Paisley, UK
e-mail: Fernando.leon-solis@uws.ac.uk

H. O'Donnell
Glasgow Caledonian University, Glasgow, Scotland
e-mail: H.ODonnell@gcu.ac.uk

© The Author(s) 2018
A. Ridge-Newman et al. (eds.), *Reporting the Road to Brexit*,
https://doi.org/10.1007/978-3-319-73682-2_20

outcome and thus places the 'Remain' contingent of the debate out of the foreground. It is a reminder of the quote attributed to George Orwell that supposedly 'history is written by the winners' (1944). However, although closely related, Brexit and the EU referendum do not foster the same meaning and these evolutions of language can be misleading.

Lexical frames can be loaded with meaning, and potentially influence the construction of narratives in the public sphere (Higgins 2017). The term 'Brexit' has become analogous with associated neologisms like 'Brexiter(s)' and 'Brexiteer(s)', which refer to the individual(s) supporting the Leave campaign and thus advocating Britain's withdrawal from the EU. The antonym 'Remainer' denotes supporters of the Remain side. Volatility is a common characteristic of referendums (LeDuc 2002; Schuck and de Vreese 2009). It seems the term 'Brexit', during the EU referendum debate, became laced with pejorative connotations. The term came to resemble a synonym for EU 'crisis' and 'disaster', shown to be consistent themes across this book. Similarly, post-Brexit, the term 'Remainer' morphed into 'Remoaner', denoting the vocalized dismay of the Remain side following the Brexit outcome of the referendum. For some on the Remain side, the word Brexit has become loaded with unpalatable connotations that embody their antithetical position. As this chapter discusses, it is not only the UK that is fraught with tensions vis-à-vis the EU. The EU and the media of its member states are engaged in powerful debates that drive wider impacts across Europe.

Brexit is one of a number of EU events that has revealed underlying tensions across the Continent. Yet, for much of the national and international media, Brexit has come to symbolize something negative: a disastrous outcome and catastrophic crisis for the UK and EU. It is likened to the EU's Eurozone and migrant 'crises' and some have begun to group the three events together as Europe's 'triple crisis' (for example, Caporaso 2017). Colin Hay offers a useful unpacking of the definition of 'crisis' and provides a relevant (re-)conceptualization of the word:

> [...] as a moment of decisive intervention and not merely a moment of fragmentation, dislocation or destruction. This reformulation suggests the need to give far greater emphasis to the essential narrativity of crisis, and the relationship between discourses of crisis and the contradictions that they narrate. The result is an analysis of crisis as a moment of transformation—a moment in which it is recognised that a decisive intervention can,

and indeed must, be made. It is argued that during such moments of crisis a new trajectory is imposed upon the state. The intense and condensed temporality of crisis thus emerges as a strategic moment in the structural transformation of the state. (1999: 317)

In this sense, Brexit could be framed, in positive terms, as the voters' intervention in a crisis in the EU from which the British state appears to be on course to take a different direction. However, as a number of the analyses of EU referendum narratives in this book suggest, much of the global news media positioned Brexit as a focal point in a wider EU crisis (for example, *BBC News* 2016). The EU referendum was a British democratic exercise in the wake of successive EU events; for example, earlier issues related to Syrian diaspora (Bauböck 2017) and financial pressures on the Eurozone (Matthijs and McNamara 2015). Arguably, from the Eurosceptic perspective in Britain, it seems logical to vote for Brexit as a solution to what is considered to be a growing crisis at the core of the EU (Caiani and Guerra 2017). Therefore, in contrast, it suggests that in many of the locales featured in this book, there was an inherent bias in the reporting of Brexit issues that resulted in the construction of crisis narratives for which the EU referendum and Brexit bore the brunt in global public discourse. Moreover, it demonstrates contradictions in the European media. According to a range of studies, the European news media are yet to embrace a collective promotion of Europeanization (de Vreese 2007; Valentini and Nesti 2010; Papathanassopoulos and Negrine 2011; Lloyd and Marconi 2014). Further studies examining to what extent specific news media are both anti-Brexit and Eurosceptic would be of significant value to the literature. The heterogeneity exhibited across the UK media cases, and the nature of divergent voting outcomes in different UK regions, suggests that the UK itself could be viewed as a contradiction of countries within one state insofar as contradictory outcomes are symptomatic of crisis (Hay 1999).

The chapters of the book offer a number of cases that strongly suggest public discourse in the run-up to the EU referendum, both nationally and internationally, was constructed around ideological biases that generated narratives which ultimately and consistently placed the potential of a Brexit outcome in the foreground of the debate, as if it were an inevitability. Rather than a public sphere rooted in a sober neutrality (Castells 2008) in which both cases could be rationalized, it seems public discourse was constructed with distinct themes around crisis and fear that inadvertently emphasized Brexit as a predetermined destination and, thus, a threat to continuity and the existential fabric of the EU (Patel and Reh 2016).

The evidence across this book shows many examples in which the news media across a range of international locales appear to have constructed narratives in the run-up to the 2016 EU referendum and shortly following the Brexit vote. Therefore, this concluding chapter is oriented on the basis that the media did construct narratives around Brexit. It allows the attention to turn to the central question of this project (see Chapter 1), aimed at assessing how the media went about constructing Brexit in relation to international political communication theories that address the domestication/heterogeneity and globalization/homogeneity of news content (Clausen 2004). This chapter aims to do this by comparing how the national and international media cases reported the road to Brexit in 2016.

CONSTRUCTING BREXIT

A significant body of research, much of which explores topics related to international threats, such as terrorism, war and conflict, revolution and environmental risk (for example, Liebes 1992; Lee and Yang 1996; Lee et al. 2001; Clausen 2004; Nossek 2004; Höijer et al. 2006; Ruigrok and van Atteveldt 2007; Handley and Ismail 2010; Ismail 2010; Jia and Kideuk 2010; Trevino et al. 2010; Eide and Ytterstad 2011), has tested the hypothesis that localized news media construct foreign news through a 'domestication' process (Gurevitch et al. 1991), demonstrating heterogeneity across contexts. In ardent support of this tradition, Alasuutari et al. argue that in local contexts the 'national character' (2013: 693) of international news content is not eroded by trends in the reporting of globalized news stories.

Domestication (heterogeneity) of international news, as a phenomenon, is evident in locales across all parts of this book. In the UK cases of Scotland (Chapter 4) and Gibraltar (Chapter 8), and to some extent in Northern Ireland (Chapter 6), rather than the term 'domestication', given that, for the purposes of this book, such locales fall within the national context of the UK, the term localization (heterogeneity) of domestic news, a closely related phenomenon, is perhaps more appropriate. Five of the seven European Single Market cases exhibit domestication of foreign news, including France (Chapter 9),

Spain (Chapter 12), Portugal (Chapter 13), Italy (Chapter 14) and Greece (Chapter 15). Turkey (Chapter 16), Israel (Chapter 17), Canada (Chapter 18) and Russia (Chapter 19) are the four locales beyond the Single Market cases, all of which show strong evidence of domesticated news content. Therefore, the majority of case studies presented in Parts III and IV of this book point towards Brexit issues undergoing a domestication in international contexts. Interestingly, the localized heterogeneity (akin to domestication) evident in some UK local contexts appears to also be flavoured by nuanced local character (Alasuutari et al. 2013).

In contrast, the globalist paradigm (Volkmer 1999, 2003) suggests that the reporting of the EU referendum and Brexit in international contexts should result in the construction of homogenized narratives across global content vis-à-vis the EU referendum and Brexit. As outlined in subsequent sections, homogeneity is much less evident beyond the UK and Single Market locales. However, there is a significant observable trend across seven of the UK and Single Market cases (see below) in which a single Brexit metanarrative was constructed around crisis frames. It suggests that in the run-up to the EU referendum, and shortly after the result, media content across Europe exhibited a degree of European homogeneity that contributed to wider public discourse with a metanarrative that constructed Brexit as a crisis. This finding demonstrates evidence for the globalist paradigm (Volkmer 1999) in UK and Single Market contexts, but less so in the wider international context. Therefore, overall, trends in both homogenization and heterogeneity (Clausen 2004) appear evident in the international and national reporting of Brexit and the EU referendum 2016.

Crisis, Disaster and Fear

Chapter 1 of this book begins with a *BBC News* (2016) story which illustrates global media reaction to the Brexit outcome of the 2016 EU referendum. Like many of the chapters in this book, the BBC article gives examples of international media that contribute to a metanarrative of Brexit as an international crisis akin to a natural disaster. Crisis frames and periods of significant political change have a long-standing relationship (Hay 1999). Key crisis frames found across the lexical examples in this book include: 'fear', 'threats', 'conflict', 'danger', 'catastrophe', 'panic', 'existential crisis'; and lexical choices related to natural disasters like: 'tsunamis' and 'earthquakes'. Brexit was even framed as a 'Shakespearean tragedy'. Crisis frames are featured most frequently in the UK and European Single Market (Chapters 2, 3, 6, 8, 11, 12, and 13).

Beyond the Single Market, Chapter 17 identifies a high frequency of references to the framing of Brexit as a 'crisis' in the Israeli media.

It is apparent that the use of crisis frames constructing narratives around 'fear' and 'disaster' are most evident in the British and European cases. Therefore, in general, a key finding of this project is that the news media serving locales with closer cultural, political and economic proximities (Straubhaar 1991) to, first, Britain and, second, the EU, exhibit higher discursive tendencies in constructing Brexit as a crisis. This trend represents a degree of European homogeneity and thus the finding supports the globalist paradigm (Volkmer 1999) in the Single Market context, but less so in the wider international context.

PART II: THE UK AND COMPETING NARRATIVES

The complex blend of heterogeneity and homogeneity across the UK cases highlights the need for nuanced research that comparatively examines contemporary media relationships, media flows and media cultures between England, Northern Ireland, Scotland, Wales and, to some extent, the UK's overseas territories and dependencies. Academic debates on media systems have largely focused on the UK as one unit (Hallin and Mancini 2012; Brüggemann et al. 2014). Existing system models have value for wider comparative studies, but, perhaps, overlook some important intrasystemic idiosyncrasies that could assist a more useful elucidation of media dynamics in the UK.

In Part II of this book, the wider UK context demonstrates how British media conflated issues (for example, migration and Brexit), which resulted in the use of crisis frames and the construction of discourses of conflict (Chapter 2). Similarly, in the Scottish and Welsh contexts, discourses of danger and fear are evident (Chapter 3). The potential for contradictions in 'crisis' narratives (Hay 1999) perhaps explains some of the potentially paradoxical outcomes of the UK cases. For example, some cases, like Chapter 3, show likenesses in the construction of narratives in Scottish and Welsh media. However, Chapters 4 and 5 suggest key structural variances between the two locales that led to distinct differences in outcomes.

Comparisons between the 2014 Scottish independence referendum and the 2016 EU referendum in Chapter 4 support the thesis that discourse can be dependent on 'cultural proximity' (Straubhaar 1991). Discourses in the 2016 EU referendum in Scotland were shown to be more convivial compared to the independence referendum in 2014, which is likely to be the more emotive referendum campaign issue for many Scots. Scotland's and England's (London) television discourses appear to have been divergent during the EU referendum campaign, which suggests that heterogenous (akin to domestication) patterns are not purely restricted to global contexts. Chapter 5 argues that Wales' media is English media, thus diminishing the role of the Welsh newspapers examined in Chapter 3. It therefore begs the question: To what extent does this phenomenon impact on correlations in English and Welsh votes? That said, the Northern Irish voted more akin to Scotland in the EU referendum, and yet there is evidence suggesting that, like Wales, English media narratives hold prominence in Northern Ireland, while being integrated with the nationalist and unionist dynamics specific to Northern Irish politics (Chapter 6). As such, the Northern Ireland case appears to exhibit a combination of characteristics observable in the Scottish and Welsh cases.

Chapter 7 argues a co-construction of referendum narratives in public discourses between politicians and journalists. It speaks to a potential balancing of mediatized politics, which is the logic that asserts developments in media power impact on political processes (Strömbäck 2008). A related factor and consistent theme observable across a number of the UK chapters is that English news appeared to be policy-light and campaign-heavy in its reporting of the referendum, meaning there was a focus on the 'strategy' or 'game' frame (Esser and D'Angelo 2006; Aalberg et al. 2012) rather than issue politics. It is somewhat akin, although not to the same extent, to media obsession with the dynamics of contemporary US presidential campaigns (Wells et al. 2016). However, the Scotland TV case (Chapter 4) suggests news at regional levels in the UK not only holds the potential to be more culturally specific to the locale, but also more policy-focused, thus promoting a more richly informed democracy. It suggests there is potential for divisions in the quality of reporting in the UK and, therefore, unequal exposure and access to quality information and debate during elections and referendum campaigns.

The Gibraltar case shows a clear construction of patriotic discourse that overtly boasts of the territory's ties to Britain. It also appears to have driven discourses of fear about the UK leaving the EU and resultant implications related to the territory's relations with neighbouring Spain (Chapter 8). The overseas territory Gibraltar exhibits similar news localization (akin to domestication) trends as Scotland, a mainland contingent of the UK. However, the extent to which Gibraltar's discourse differs from Britain's means it resembles more closely the international cases in Parts III and IV.

Therefore, perhaps unsurprisingly, it appears more foreign when compared to the other British locales, especially because British patriotism, as a dominant discourse, is unique to the Gibraltar case. Overall, the UK cases exhibit mixed discourses of constructed heterogeneity in some news contexts that competed with wider, more homogenous, British metanarratives primarily constructed centrally in London (Clausen 2004).

Part III: Media Euroscepticism and Heterogeneity

In Part III, themes from the findings suggest the construction of distinct and heterogeneous Brexit narratives across the different European Single Market (excluding the UK) locales. It is particularly evident in Southern European cases, which is in contrast to more homogenous Europhile metanarratives present in certain Northern European contexts. Chapter 9 suggests that French discourses were ideologically loaded with critiques of the English, rather than the British as a whole, which potentially indicates a 'subtle prejudice' (Pettigrew and Meertens 1995) against the English within the French media. In contrast, the central Spanish media in Madrid is thought to have placed the emphasis on Europe, rather than Britain, in constructing Brexit as Europe's 'existential crisis' (Chapter 12).

Growing media Euroscepticism across Europe is highlighted in the stark divisions in the Italian press (Chapter 14). Perhaps the most distinctly Eurosceptic case is Greece, which is shown to be embedded in ideological critiques of distaste for German hegemony while positively framing Brexit as an assertion of democracy (Chapter 15). This is juxtaposed against the negative framing of a dis-United Kingdom within a narrative constructed around Brexit being a failure of democracy in much of the German, Austrian and Swiss media (Chapter 10); and other negative framing in the Norwegian media (Chapter 11). These two opposing positions fit with Simões-Ferreira's argument that the news media are a discursive agent, with incumbent responsibilities, which play a role in both constructing and deconstructing European identity (Chapter 13).

Divisions between Northern and Southern EU states have not escaped scholarly analysis (Matthijs and McNamara 2015), nor has German power in Europe avoided academic critique (Matthijs 2016). It is interesting how these pre-existing narratives in their respective locales were evident and used in the construction of ideologically rooted news content. Brexit as an international event, which was repeatedly framed as an existential crisis in Europe, became integrated with dominant local domestic frames. It seems evident that the news output in European Single Market locales was strongly associated with their own historical relationships with the EU and the accompanying power dynamics. It has been argued that German hegemony itself contributes to 'crisis' in the EU (Matthijs 2016; Currie and Teague 2017). The heterogeneous and domesticated approach to constructing EU crisis narratives in Single Market locales suggests that German hegemonic forces are yet to dominate news media flows. Perhaps a driving factor is the historic divergence between the EU's 'Big 3' (France, Germany and the UK), resulting in 'polyphonic' (Bain et al. 2017) public discourse and split (heterogeneous) media narratives across the continent.

Part IV: The Domestication of Brexit

The theme of heterogeneity in media content continues in Part IV in the domestication of Brexit in the Turkey case (Chapter 16). The use of Brexit events as a proxy for critique of the Turkish government demonstrates how the domestication of foreign news can act as a 'lever' in the politics of geographical locales with limited connection to the original storyline (Alasuutari et al. 2013). Like the Spanish case, the authors of Chapter 17 about Israel are explicit in suggesting there is evidence of the domestication of Brexit in Israeli media. In Chapter 18, the domestication theme is thought to continue in the Canadian case in which the Brexit debate is argued to have been constructed through the prism of Canada's trade relationship with the EU. Interestingly, Canada's economic interests appear to take precedence over any cultural connections the country has with the UK through the Commonwealth, which holds potential to inspire positive narratives about future opportunities in British-Canadian trading partnerships. It supports the argument that, particularly in relation to economic discourse, the news media tend to emphasize negative narratives (Hester and Gibson 2003).

Russia (Chapter 18) is perhaps at the extreme end of domestication with its state-controlled media and relatively dismissive approach to Brexit as a peripheral foreign event. Russia's unique historical and cultural characteristics, as a somewhat reluctant democracy with authoritarian traditions, its focus on intrastate affairs, and blurred relations between the media and politicians, culminate in a contemporary statist media system with a hybrid blend of Western and Eastern influences (Vartanova 2012). It is therefore no surprise that the extent of heterogeneity in the Russian case, when compared to others in this book, means it sits apart in terms of thematic output. Furthermore, the chapter speaks to wider debates about the Russian state's approach to counteracting the 'transatlantic democracy' associated with the EU and USA (Babayan 2015).

CONTEXTUALIZING THE DOMESTICATION OF BREXIT

In the international media cases, the concept of 'domestication' was visible beyond wider debates about the suitability of referendums as political instruments. The Israel case (Chapter 17) revealed the widespread idea that Brexit had been motivated by the UK's anti-Muslim sentiment and the fear of the 'Islamization' of Britain, a notion that should be understood in the context of the Israel-Palestine conflict and Israel's wider relations with the Arab world. In Europe, the Norway case (Chapter 11), which reminds readers the Norwegians rejected EU membership through referendums in 1972 and 1994, the 2016 EU referendum opened a space for Norwegian-centric debates about Norway-EU relations. The mainly anti-Brexit Canadian media stance was likewise related to the internal dynamics of the country. The liberal majority, led by Canadian Prime Minister Justin Trudeau, struggled to identify with the alleged 'anti-immigration' contingents of the Leave campaign and denunciations of open borders and labour mobility. Moreover, the EU-Canada Comprehensive Economic Trade Agreement (CETA), supported by Canadian Liberals and Conservatives alike, contributed to the EU being viewed through a positive lens in Canadian public discourse. Perhaps similar to reaction in Scotland, Canadian shock vis-à-vis the result should also be seen from the domestic view in the context of the two independence referendums held in Quebec. In all cases, it was a vote for the status quo, which was also the widely held expectation for the outcome of the 2016 EU referendum.

REPORTING BREXIT: REFLECTIONS, RELEVANCE AND IMPACT

The following sections assess the relevance of this book in relation to growing Eurosceptic tendencies in European media; and the book's potential for research impact beyond the academic context, before offering some final conclusions. In the interests of sobering the Brexit debate, it begins some reflection and a reality check.

Brexit Reality Check: 'Crisis' and 'Disaster'?

Through the use of crisis frames, it seems that some news media in the UK and beyond all too readily liken significant democratic events, like Brexit and Trump, to danger and natural disasters. It amounts to talking up impacts and generating a discourse of fear, which is a tactic more readily associated with right-wing populism (Wodak 2015). Using lexical choices otherwise selected to frame war, terrorism and natural disasters in order to sensationalize a democratic event like the EU referendum has negative impacts on debate and discourse; and undermines democracy overall, because it distorts the context and nature of the topic (Street 2010). Constructing a narrative of Brexit as a threat and disaster indicates a 'dissemination of fear' (Smith 1985). At most, Brexit is a challenge for the EU to overcome and a period of uncertainty/transition for the British people. Likening Brexit to the devastation of natural disasters, the atrocities of war, or the injustice of terrorism, only serves to undermine the prominence of much more terrifying global events when they occur. Media overreactions to a democratic vote suggest a sensationalism and/or lack of media balance that construct a skewed reality. It can only lead to further accusations of 'fake news' and exacerbate erosions of the public's trust in the media.

Euroscepticism in the News Media

Eurosceptic trends in news media (Daddow 2012) seem to reach beyond the UK. Chapters in this book suggest that four locales (France [Chapter 9], Portugal [Chapter 13], Italy [Chapter 14] and Greece [Chapter 15]) demonstrate notable Eurosceptic tendencies in media content. These are all Eurozone-EU member states of the Southern European region, three of which, excluding the bigger EU power France (Bain et al. 2017), have experienced economic challenges since joining the Euro currency. The findings suggests that political and economic forces and regional commonalities can impact on ideological factors in news content across the EU. Such findings also feed into the wider debates that indicate a growing crisis for the EU (Caiani and Guerra 2017). It highlights the need for clarification on the suspected impacts of German hegemonic forces on smaller EU states (Matthijs 2016; Currie and Teague 2017).

It appears that events leading up to the Brexit outcome of the 2016 EU referendum catalysed deeper self-reflection on the question of Europe in the increasingly Eurosceptic Southern European states. When compared to the less Eurosceptic news coverage in the Austrian, German, Norwegian and Swiss media, it seems there was a higher tendency towards a significant domestication of Brexit in Southern Europe, where Eurosceptic forces are more evident. The referendum and Brexit events appear to have acted as a discursive catalyst for internal self-reflection in much of the Southern European media cases. Therefore, the Europhile ideal in which the European public sphere would embody a transnational citizenry with equal access and ability to understand and interpret communications in relation to EU policies and initiatives (Schlesinger 1999) seems a distant prospect.

Impact: Brexit Beyond the UK

Chapter 1 sets out three of Adler-Nissen et al.'s (2017) potential impact considerations for analysing perceptions of Brexit beyond the UK. Therefore, it seems relevant to reflect on how this project speaks to those considerations. Firstly, this book serves as a marker for how Brexit debates in British media compare to those in international contexts, which now contributes to the debate about where British identity sits in the context of wider European integration. Secondly, the book provides British policymakers and Brexit negotiators with a broad understanding of how Brexit is viewed and reported in international media contexts. This project, therefore, has the potential to enhance strategies related to EU-UK negotiations. Thirdly, as this and other related projects contend, Brexit might not be an isolated case. Euroscepticism is a growing trend across the EU. This book could help inform the policymakers and communications professionals at the centre of the Europeanization project, especially if the EU aims to survive potential future eruptions in Eurosceptic news discourse across Southern Europe and, perhaps, beyond.

Conclusions

In the run-up to and shortly after the UK's 2016 EU referendum, national and international media exhibited both homogenization and heterogeneity in certain geographical contexts. Construction of a met-anarrative that framed Brexit as a crisis is evident across a number of chapters, particularly those representing the UK and European Single Market locales. It suggests that, at the European level of reporting, the EU referendum campaign and Brexit were represented by a more homogenous discourse than is evident in the cases beyond the Single Market. These wider and more international examples had greater distance from the issues and the greater inclinations to domesticate the Brexit narrative. The next subgroup demonstrating evidence of significant domestication of foreign news content is the more Eurosceptic Southern European countries. These are followed by the more politically distinct, yet more Europhile, UK locales, like Scotland and Gibraltar. The homogenized European metanarratives of crisis and disaster were integrated with the domestication of news content in a number of locales, thus demonstrating the presence of 'national character' (Alasuutari et al. 2013) when reporting the road to Brexit in the international contexts. Therefore, it suggests that national and international media representations of Brexit were mixed; and that the international political communication of Brexit included competing flows of globalized and domesticated news content.

BIBLIOGRAPHY

PRIMARY SOURCES

BBC News. 2016. Brexit: What the World's Papers Say. *BBC News,* June 24. http://www.bbc.co.uk/news/world-europe-36619254 (Accessed 22 January 2018).

Caporaso, J.A. 2017. Europe's Three Crises. *EuVisions,* June 19. http://www.euvisions.eu/europes-three-crises/ (Accessed 24 January 2018).

Orwell, G. 1944. 'As I Please' Newspaper Column, *Tribune,* February 4.

ACADEMIC LITERATURE

Aalberg, T., J. Strömbäck, and C.H. De Vreese. 2012. The Framing of Politics as Strategy and Game: A Review of Concepts, Operationalizations and Key Findings. *Journalism* 13 (2): 162–178.

Adler-Nissen, R., C. Galpin, and B. Rosamond. 2017. Performing Brexit: How a Post-Brexit World is Imagined Outside the United Kingdom. *The British Journal of Politics and International Relations* 19 (3): 573–591.

Alasuutari, P., A. Qadir, and K. Creutz. 2013. The Domestication of Foreign News: News Stories Related to the 2011 Egyptian Revolution in British, Finnish and Pakistani Newspapers. *Media, Culture and Society* 35 (6): 692–707.

Babayan, N. 2015. The Return of the Empire? Russia's Counteraction to Transatlantic Democracy Promotion in Its Near Abroad. *Democratization* 22 (3): 438–458.

Bain, J., B. Greenland, M. Knodt, and L. Nielsen. 2017. A Polyphonic Marketplace: Images of EU External Energy Relations in British, French and German Media Discourses. *Comparative European Politics* 15 (1): 115–134.

Bauböck, R. 2017. Europe's Commitments and Failures in the Refugee Crisis. *European Political Science* 17 (1): 140–150.

Brüggemann, M., S. Engesser, F. Büchel, E. Humprecht, and L. Castro. 2014. Hallin and Mancini Revisited: Four Empirical Types of Western Media Systems. *Journal of Communication* 64 (6): 1037–1065.

Caiani, M., and S. Guerra. 2017. *Euroscepticism, Democracy and the Media: Communicating Europe, Contesting Europe*. London: Palgrave Macmillan.

Castells, M. 2008. The New Public Sphere: Global Civil Society, Communication Networks, and Global Governance. *The ANNALS of the American Academy of Political and Social Science* 616 (1): 78–93.

Clausen, L. 2004. Localizing the Global: "Domestication" Processes in International News Production. *Media, Culture and Society* 26 (1): 25–44.

Currie, D., and P. Teague. 2017. The Eurozone Crisis, German Hegemony and Labour Market Reform in the GIPS Countries. *Industrial Relations Journal* 48 (2): 154–173.

Daddow, O. 2012. The UK Media and 'Europe': From Permissive Consensus to Destructive Dissent. *International Affairs* 88 (6): 1219–1236.

de Vreese, C. 2007. A Spiral of Euroscepticism: The Media's Fault? *Acta Politica* 42 (2/3): 271–286.

Eide, E., and A. Ytterstad. 2011. The Tainted Hero: Frames of Domestication in Norwegian Press Representation of the Bali Climate Summit. *International Journal of Press/Politics* 16 (1): 50–74.

Esser, F., and P. D'Angelo. 2006. Framing the Press and Publicity Process in US, British, and German Election Campaigns: A Comparative Study of Metacoverage. *The Harvard International Journal of Press/Politics* 11 (3): 44–66.

Gurevitch, M., M.R. Levy, and I. Roeh. 1991. The Global Newsroom: Convergences and Diversities in the Globalization of Television News. In *Communication and Citizenship: Journalism and the Public Sphere in the New Media Age*, ed. P. Dahlgren and C. Sparks, 195–216. London: Routledge.

Hallin, D.C., and P. Mancini. 2012. Comparing Media Systems: A Response to Critics. In *Handbook of Comparative Communication Research*, ed. T. Hanitzsch and F. Esser, 207–220. New York: Routledge.

Handley, R.L., and A. Ismail. 2010. Territory Under Siege: "Their" News, "Our" News and "Ours Both" News of the 2008 Gaza Crisis. *Media, War and Conflict* 3 (3): 279–297.

Hay, C. 1999. Crisis and the Structural Transformation of the State: Interrogating the Process of Change. *British Journal of Politics and International Relations* 1 (3): 317–344.

Hester, J.B., and R. Gibson. 2003. The Economy and Second-Level Agenda Setting: A Time-Series Analysis of Economic News and Public Opinion About the Economy. *Journalism and Mass Communication Quarterly* 80 (1): 73–90.

Higgins, M. 2017. Impending Crisis in Scotland: Political Discourse in Interesting Times. In *Crisis and the Media*, ed. Marianna Patrona. Amsterdam: John Benjamins.

Höijer, B., R. Lidskog, and L. Thornberg. 2006. News Media and Food Scares: The Case of Contaminated Salmon. *Environmental Sciences* 3 (4): 273–288.

Ismail, A. 2010. Making Sense of a Barrier: US News Discourses on Israel's Dividing Wall. *Journal of Communication Inquiry* 34 (1): 85–108.

Jia, D., and H. Kideuk. 2010. Global Risk, Domestic Framing: Coverage of the North Korean Nuclear Test by US, Chinese, and South Korean News Agencies. *Asian Journal of Communication* 20 (3): 299–317.

LeDuc, L. 2002. Referendums and Elections: How Do Campaigns Differ? In *Do Political Campaigns Matter? Campaign Effects in Elections and Referendums*, ed. D. Farrell and R. Schmitt-Beck, 145–162. London: Routledge.

Lee, C.-C., and J. Yang. 1996. Foreign News and National Interest: Comparing US and Japanese Coverage of a Chinese Student Movement. *International Communication Gazette* 56 (1): 1–18.

Lee, C.-C., Z. Pan, J.M. Chan, and C.Y.K. So. 2001. Through the Eyes of US Media: Banging the Democracy Drum in Hong Kong. *Journal of Communication* 51 (2): 345–365.

Liebes, T. 1992. Our War/Their War: Comparing the Intifadeh and the Gulf War on US and Israeli Television. *Critical Studies in Mass Communication* 9 (1): 44–55.

Lloyd, J., and C. Marconi. 2014. *Reporting the EU*. London: IB Tauris.

Matthijs, M. 2016. Powerful Rules Governing the Euro: The Perverse Logic of German Ideas. *Journal of European Public Policy* 23 (3): 375–391.

Matthijs, M., and K. McNamara. 2015. The Euro Crisis' Theory Effect: Northern Saints, Southern Sinners, and the Demise of the Eurobond. *Journal of European Integration* 37 (2): 229–245.

Nossek, H. 2004. Our News and Their News. *Journalism* 5 (3): 343–368.

Papathanassopoulos, S., and R. Negrine. 2011. *European Media*. Cambridge: Polity Press.

Patel, O., and C. Reh. 2016. Brexit: The Consequences for the EU's Political System. UCL Constitution Unit Briefing Paper, pp. 1–5.

Pettigrew, T.F., and R.W. Meertens. 1995. Subtle and Blatant Prejudice in Western Europe. *European Journal of Social Psychology* 25 (1): 57–75.

Ruigrok, N., and W. van Atteveldt. 2007. Global Angling with a Local Angle: How US, British, and Dutch Newspapers Frame Global and Local Terrorist Attacks. *Harvard International Journal of Press/Politics* 12 (1): 68–90.

Schlesinger, P. 1999. Changing Spaces of Political Communication. *Political Communication* 16 (3): 263–279.

Schuck, A.R., and C.H. de Vreese. 2009. Reversed Mobilization in Referendum Campaigns: How Positive News Framing Can Mobilize the Skeptics. *The International Journal of Press/Politics* 14 (1): 40–66.

Smith, S.J. 1985. News and the Dissemination of Fear. In *Geography, the Media and Popular Culture*, ed. J. Burgess and J. Gold, 229–253. London: Croom Helm.

Straubhaar, J.D. 1991. Beyond Media Imperialism: Assymetrical Interdependence and Cultural Proximity. *Critical Studies in Media Communication* 8 (1): 39–59.

Street, J. 2010. *Mass Media, Politics and Democracy*. Basingstoke: Palgrave Macmillan.

Strömbäck, J. 2008. Four Phases of Mediatization: An Analysis of the MEDIATIZATION of Politics. *The International Journal of Press/Politics* 13 (3): 228–246.

Trevino, M., A.M. Kanso, and R.A. Nelson. 2010. Islam Through Editorial Lenses: How American Elite Newspapers Portrayed Muslims Before and After September 11, 2001. *Journal of Arab and Muslim Media Research* 3 (1/2): 3–17.

Valentini, C., and G. Nesti. 2010. *Public Communication in the European Union*. Newcastle upon Tyne: Cambridge Scholars Publishing.

Vartanova, E. 2012. The Russian Media Model in the Context of Post-Soviet Dynamics. In *Comparing Media Systems Beyond the Western World*, ed. D.C. Hallin and P. Mancini, 119–142. New York: Cambridge University Press.

Vasilopoulou, S. 2016. UK Euroscepticism and the Brexit Referendum. *The Political Quarterly* 87 (2): 219–227.

Volkmer, I. 1999. *News in the Global Sphere: A Study of CNN and Its Impact on Global Communication*. Luton: University of Luton Press.

Volkmer, I. 2003. The Global Network Society and the Global Public Sphere. *Development* 46 (1): 9–16.

Wells, C., D.V. Shah, J.C. Pevehouse, J. Yang, A. Pelled, F. Boehm, J. Lukito, S. Ghosh, and J.L. Schmidt. 2016. How Trump Drove Coverage to the Nomination: Hybrid Media Campaigning. *Political Communication* 33 (4): 669–676.

Wodak, R. 2015. *The Politics of Fear: What Right-Wing Populist Discourses Mean*. London: Sage.

INDEX

© The Editor(s) (if applicable) and The Author(s) 2018

A. Ridge-Newman et al. (eds.), *Reporting the Road to Brexit*,

https://doi.org/10.1007/978-3-319-73682-2

CPSIA information can be obtained
at www.ICGtesting.com
Printed in the USA
LVOW13*1534100518
576718LV00002B/3/P